The Chicago School of Sociology

THE HERITAGE OF SOCIOLOGY
A Series Edited by Morris Janowitz

Martin Bulmer

The Chicago School of Sociology

Institutionalization, Diversity, and the Rise of Sociological Research

The University of Chicago Press
Chicago and London

Martin Bulmer is senior lecturer at the London School of Economics and Political Science, the University of London.

The University of Chicago Press, Chicago 60637
The University of Chicago Press, Ltd., London

Printed in the United States of America

93 92 91 90 89 88 87 86 85 84 54321

Library of Congress Cataloging in Publication Data

Bulmer, Martin.
The Chicago school of sociology.

(The Heritage of sociology)
Includes bibliographical references and index.
1. Chicago school of sociology. I. Title. II. Series.
HM47.U62C43 1984 301'.07'1177311 84-8494
ISBN 0-226-08004-8

To the memory of my father,
Charles Trevelyan

Contents

Illustrations

Figures

Tables

Preface

To attempt to write the biography of part of an academic institution, even one as well documented as the University of Chicago, is more challenging and problematical than to write the biography of an individual. This book seeks to provide a reinterpretation of the "Chicago school" of sociology in the early twentieth century, together with some discussion of developments in neighboring social science departments in the university. Its theme is the rise of empirical social research in a university setting and the institutional conditions, within and outside the university, that fostered its growth. The University of Chicago, established as a new foundation in 1892, has exercised a quite disproportionate influence upon the course of empirical social science. Between about 1915 and 1940 it dominated sociology and political science in the United States. The Chicago "schools" in both disciplines became the leaders of a movement away from general theory, social philosophy, or purely historical work toward the firsthand empirical investigation of society by means of personal documents, observations, and interviewing, conducted within an implicit general theoretical framework. Programs of collaborative research were conducted by members of quite highly integrated, local networks of teachers and graduate students concerned with common scientific problems. In sociology, such communities of scholars are rare.

The history of the social sciences at the University of Chicago is unusual in the extent of published material on the subject (though not in the survival of archival material about all the major figures, for whom documentation is very uneven; see Note on Documentary Sources). A comprehensive coverage of the major figures is provided by other titles in this series, the uniqueness of which is a tribute not only to the perspicacity of Morris Janowitz but to the underlying strength of the historical tradition of the social sciences at the university. This study does not, therefore, aim to cover ground already gone over. For example, excellent biographies are available of Robert E. Park (by Fred H. Matthews) and of Charles E. Merriam (by Barry D. Karl). A good general overview of the Chicago achievement is provided by Robert Faris's *Chicago Sociology, 1920–1932*, a work based on the author's personal knowledge and recollections, plus extensive secondary sources. This is complemented by Winifred Raushenbush's memoir of Park and James Carey's study of the background and orientation of members of the Chicago school in the

1920s, both of which make use of the recollections of students studying at the period. All of these studies have been drawn upon where appropriate, but the argument of this book is different.

Its focus is upon the institutionalization of empirical sociological research within one American university, rather than upon the biography of an individual or the development of a strand of social thought. It is centrally concerned with the development of methods of empirical research, an area which crosscuts several disciplines including sociology, political science, psychology, anthropology, statistics, and economics and also leads outside the academic world to consider, for example, the social survey movement, the Bureau of the Census, and independent research organizations. Within the university, more attention is deliberately paid to crosscutting, interdisciplinary links. These are essential to understanding the creativity of Chicago social science, yet have been somewhat neglected (apart from the case of George Herbert Mead) in studies of the history of sociology or political science.

The alternative interpretation offered seeks to counter a certain particularity and single-mindedness in the recent literature on Chicago sociology and a tendency to reinterpret Chicago sociology in the light of present concerns. Such reinterpretation tends to result in misunderstanding of the conditions of creativity which fostered the growth of the social sciences in the 1920s. Interest in social psychology, symbolic interactionism, and the influence of George Herbert Mead has resulted in a large number of books and articles in recent years, most recently Paul Rock's *The Making of Symbolic Interactionism* and David Lewis and Richard Smith's *American Sociology and Pragmatism: Mead, Chicago Sociology, and Symbolic Interaction*. Though I do not wish to diminish the importance of these studies, they do give a certain slant to writing about the Chicago department and fail signally to represent the diversity, which was one of its hallmarks. There is far more to Chicago sociology in the 1920s than, for example, the mini-industry of Mead studies would suggest. This book seeks to some extent to redress the balance. It can be criticized for its neglect of Mead. This is quite deliberate, in view of the inordinate amount of scholarly attention he has already received.

The reasons for the tendency to treat Chicago in the 1920s as a precursor of contemporary symbolic interactionism and qualitative sociology are to be found in the intellectual character of qualitative and quantitative traditions. Qualitative sociologists are explicitly self-conscious about the origins of their style of work. Ethnographic field research and an interpersonal theory of social behavior were indeed very important stands in the Chicago school. It is impossible not to associate Mead or Blumer or Hughes, or Howard S. Becker, with a style of qualitative work coming out of Chicago. Yet this can easily lead to exaggeration. There was also a strain of quantitative research—done by such important figures as Burgess, Ogburn, Thurstone, and Stouffer—but this is virtually forgotten. It is forgotten because of lack of traditions in this area. Progress in quantitative methods over a long period of time is regarded by their practitioners as more cumulative and scientific than in the case of qualitative research. There is less desire to examine the roots of the subject and a marked tendency to dismiss the relevance of the history of such methods for present practice. The antihistorical orientation of quantitative methodologists, coupled with the fragmentation of the history of methodology between different disciplines, results in major lacunae.

The history of research methods is significant because it enables one to trace the rise of empirical sociology. The Chicago school represented the first successful American program of collective sociological research. As such it had a very significant impact. The program was supported by foundation grants, raising interesting questions about the determination of scholarly concerns by outside funding agencies. And the period saw the creation of quite an elaborate research organization within the university, which prefigured the modern, research-oriented, heavily funded graduate department. Institution builders such as Burgess and Merriam naturally receive less attention in the history of the social sciences than great theorists; yet they made an important contribution.

It is probably impossible to write the history of one's own discipline without preconceptions, and I am no exception to this generalization. Three of these preconceptions should therefore be made clear. One is that disputes about the rival merits of quantitative and qualitative methods of social research are about as fruitful as asking whether the arm or the leg is a more important part of the human body. Each is useful for different purposes—one can be a one-armed footballer or a one-legged typist—but in general both are necessary for a full and active life. Second, it is my view that the legacy of the Chicago empirical sociology of W. I. Thomas, Robert Park, and Ernest Burgess has, with good reason, been both stronger and more fruitful than the residue from the writings of the first generation of American sociologists, Ward, Ross, Giddings, Sumner, and Small. With the exception of Cooley, their theories are today rightly largely forgotten. Charles Merriam is a more enigmatic and perhaps less admirable figure than Thomas or Park; yet he, too, despite the lack of a solid core to his thought, was most influential in turning American political science in a more empirical direction. What characterized above all the achievement of the Chicago school of sociology was the ability to bring theory and research together in a fruitful way. The rarity of this achievement in the context of a collaborative research program that changed the character of American sociology makes it a phenomenon worthy of detailed study.

Third, the special character of the city of Chicago is of preeminent importance. Max Weber, visiting the city in 1904 on his way to the Saint Louis Exhibition, found it incredible and compared it to a man whose skin had been peeled off and whose intestines were seen at work.[1] Chicago, wrote Lincoln Steffens, was "first in violence, deepest in dirt; loud, lawless, unlovely, ill-smelling, new; an overgrown gawk of a village; a teeming tough among cities."[2] My father, an English visitor to the city in 1898, compared it with "Liverpool placed on the shore of a sweet watered tideless sea." He met Jane Addams, Florence Kelly, and Graham Taylor and stayed at the university with Charles Zueblin. He saw Chicago through a politician's eyes, its faults and its strengths, its growing public spirit and the pride in the city among its leading citizens.[3] The paradoxes these observers at the turn of the century saw so vividly were caught above all in Carl Sandburg's poem "Chicago," which spoke of the city "Laughing the stormy, husky, brawling laughter of youth." Life was raw, often harsh and brutal for its inhabitants, and yet there was pride and self-confidence—important components in the growth of the Chicago schools of sociology and political science.

> Come and show me another city with lifted head
> singing so proud to be alive and coarse and
> strong and cunning.
> Flinging magnetic curses amid the toil of piling job
> on job, here is a tall bold slugger set vivid
> against the little soft cities.[4]

Acknowledgments

The debts incurred in the course of working on this study over a number of years are considerable. Among those who were students at the University of Chicago before 1930, Herbert Blumer, Ruth Shonle Cavan, Leonard S. Cottrell, Jr., Manuel C. Elmer, Robert E. L. Faris, Philip M. Hauser, Helen McGill Hughes, Harold F. Gosnell, Una M. Hayner, William Rutherford ("Pat") Ireland, and Ernest R. Mowrer were most helpful in answering questions about their early years at the university. Everett C. Hughes, over a long period, provided a great deal of information, and I still recall with pleasure a conversation in a hotel in Bloomsbury Square in London one December in the early 1970s which first gave me a real sense of the academic strengths of the University of Chicago.

From fellow academics, colleagues, and friends working on, or with an interest in, the history of the social sciences, I have received many suggestions and pointers along the route to the appearance of this book. I would like to acknowledge the contribution made in one way or another by the late Christopher Bernert, Marc Blaug, Mogens Blegvad, Donald J. Bogue, Robert Burgess, A. W. Coats, James S. Coleman, Jean M. Converse, Lewis A. Coser, Michael Featherstone, Donald Fleming, Rudolf K. Haerle, Jr., Valerie Hall, Lee Harvey, Paul M. Hirsch, Stanley N. Katz, Ellen Lagemann, Barbara Lal, Barbara Laslett, Catherine Marsh, Peter J. Mills, Louis Moss, G. Duncan Mitchell, Anthony Oberschall, Harold L. Orbach, Robert Parke, Jennifer Platt, Michael Powell, Patrick Reagan, John Rex, Peter H. Rossi, Guenther Roth, John Smith, Evan A. Thomas, Jim Thomas, Asher Tropp, Michael Useem, and Louise C. Wade. Such far-flung networks play an indispensable role in sustaining one's interest and enthusiasm.

At the University of Chicago my research was facilitated particularly by William J. Wilson (then chairman of the Department of Sociology) and Dean of Social Sciences Robert McC. Adams, while I was a visiting scholar in the Department of Sociology. It benefitted from discussion and advice from Leo A. Goodman, Barry D. Karl, William H. Kruskal, Donald N. Levine, Michael Schudson, George J. Stigler, George W. Stocking, Jr., and Fred L. Strodtbeck. Margaret Fallers talked to me about the life and work of her father, E. J. Chave, and his collaboration with L. L. Thurstone. Susan Green, Dennis Wheaton, and Sally Kilgore provided intellectual companionship and an opportunity to talk about the project to videotape distinguished contemporary sociologists upon which they were engaged. Elsewhere in the city, Albert Hunter and Robert F. Boruch, at Northwestern University, provided helpful information. James Bennett, of the University of Illinois at Chicago Circle, not only shared with me his extensive knowledge of life-history methods in the social sciences, but helped in tracking the history of the Institute of Juvenile Research.

It is a moot point whether the history of the social sciences is better written by social scientists or by historians. The two outstanding works, the biographies by Matthews and Karl, are both by historians. Certainly some sociologists have not made sufficient use of the available documentary materials. I have attempted to do so and am indebted above all in exploring the available sources to Robert Rosenthal, curator, and Michael Ryan, former assistant curator of the Special Collections Department, Joseph Regenstein Library, University of Chicago. Mr. Rosenthal has built up a very strong collection of material on the history of the social sciences at Chicago and continues to expand that collection, which is an indispensable source for work on the subject of this book. They and their staff (including Albert Tannler and Daniel Meyer) provided a great deal of assistance in the course of this research. The photographs that appear on pages 81–88 are drawn from University of Chicago Archives and the Office of News and Information. I should also like to thank Assistant Dean Ruth Vogeler, who helped in gaining access to records at the time in the custody of the Division of Social Sciences, University of Chicago. Dr. J. William Hess and his staff at the Rockefeller Archive Center, Pocantico Hills, North Tarrytown, New York, provided guidance and help in working on the records of the Laura Spelman Rockefeller Memorial.

The research reported in this monograph has received financial support from three sources. At an early stage, there were small grants from the University of Durham Research Fund. Between 1980 and 1982, three grants from the Social Research Division of the London School of Economics enabled me to make three short research visits to the University of Chicago. And the tenure of a (British) Social Science Research Council Personal Research Grant from January to March 1980 made possible an extended research visit of six weeks to the University of Chicago, which greatly advanced the course of this work. Della Nevitt supported my request for leave from LSE to take up this award.

My study of the Chicago school was begun originally under the supervision of Ronald P. Dore, while holding a University of London Postgraduate Studentship in Sociology. If the final product is rather different from what was originally envisaged, I am nevertheless glad to acknowledge his support and interest over the years since it was begun. More recently, over a period of three years, Donald G. MacRae provided knowledgeable, sympathetic, but pointed advice in just the right quantities, though he is not to be held responsible for all my views about social science at the University of Chicago in the 1920s.

The encouragement and critical questioning of Edward Shils over a number of years has helped materially in the completion of this work. His unrivalled personal acquaintance with the University of Chicago since the early 1930s provided background in depth. Even if Thomas Kuhn errs slightly in saying that Professor Shils has read everything, his encyclopaedic knowledge of the history of the social sciences, reflected in his brilliant essays on the subject, are a constant source of inspiration. This work was considerably improved as a result of his comments on an earlier draft. Morris Janowitz, the editor of the Heritage of Sociology series, suggested that this book be written, and his guidance and support are much appreciated. His comments on an earlier draft led to beneficial changes in the arrangement of the material presented here.

Valerie Campling typed this manuscript with meticulous care and accuracy. Gay Grant has provided admirable general secretarial support over the last eight years. My wife Joan put up with my absences from London on research visits which, in the words of the song, were a case of

> Going to Chicago, going to Chicago,
> Sorry that I can't take you.

More important, over a number of years she sustained a belief, which I did not always share, that this work would one day be completed. Now that it is, I am happy to acknowledge how much it owes to her.

1 The Significance of the Chicago School of Sociology

Different sociologists read different significance into different phases of the discipline's history. Some dwell on the earliest precursors in social thought such as Montesquieu, Hegel, or Saint-Simon. Some focus on eminent nineteenth-century thinkers such as Alexis de Tocqueville, Auguste Comte, Karl Marx, and Herbert Spencer. Others put Emile Durkheim and Max Weber at the center of the pantheon. Yet others are more interested in early academic sociologists such as Georg Simmel, Ferdinand Toennies, L. T. Hobhouse, Roberto Michels, W. I. Thomas, Robert Park, or Karl Mannheim. Alongside these names can be put those who made a significant contribution to empirical social research, including in the nineteenth century Adolph Quételet, Frederic Le Play, Charles Booth, and Seebohm Rowntree among others. These figures all had varied interests, varied conceptions of the sociological task, and varied institutional locations. Until the late nineteenth century, most worked outside the orbit of universities, often depending on private wealth to pursue their interest in the subject. Yet with the exception of Durkheim and Robert Park, they shared a common characteristic. All were individual scholars working on their own in relative isolation from others who pursued similar intellectual concerns. Of course, they were in touch, through correspondence and face-to-face encounters, with scholars who had cognate interests, but their typical mode of working was solitary. It is true that Weber's circle in Heidelberg provided a degree of regular intellectual exchange. Only the Durkheim school centered on Paris and the Chicago school[1] with Park at the center were collective intellectual enterprises of an integrated kind. As such, they are unusual in the history of the social sciences.

Why, during the 1920s, was the University of Chicago such a creative center for the growth of the Chicago school of sociology? This study seeks to examine how and why, between 1915 and 1935, sociology flourished so notably on the Midway at a university which since its foundation in 1892 had exercised a quite disproportionate influence upon the development of the social sciences in the United States. The dense, highly integrated, local network of teachers and graduate students carrying out a program of research in one city centered around common problems, which was characteristic of Chicago sociology in the 1920s, has few parallels at the time or since. Not only was Chicago the leading center of sociology in the world at this period, but the hallmark of the department's approach was one of broad, collective intellectual endeavor. Nor was sociology unique. The Chicago school of philosophy, founded by John Dewey, was at the height of its influence. The Chicago school of political science was gaining in influence and reputation. The Chicago school of economics was over the horizon. These parallels will be pursued later in the book.

A "school" in the social sciences may be thought of as akin to the term used in art history to designate a group of contemporaries sharing a certain style, technique, or set of symbolic expressions and having at some point or other in time or space a high degree of interaction (e.g., the impressionists, the Bauhaus, etc.).[2] A local example would be the Chicago school of architecture, centered on Louis Sullivan and Frank Lloyd Wright.[3]

Several ideal-typical characteristics may be seen to distinguish a school of social science. It has a founder-leader and a group of his or her followers, usually ranging in number from one to three dozen members. This leader has a relatively dominating personality. The group is usually drawn together by a set of ideas, beliefs, and normative dispositions, articulated by the founder-leader, which are somewhat at odds with those prevailing in the discipline at the time. A school typically seeks to modernize or renovate the discipline. It consists of

> a scientific community integrated around a central figure, an intellectual charismatic leader, and a paradigm of empirical reality which is subject to investigation. The paradigm's core formulations are those of the founder-leader, but the full-blown paradigm is typically a collective enterprise, fashioned by the founder-leader and his immediate entourage.[4]

Schools flourish in settings with an institutional affiliation, typically an academic site of general excellence in a great metropolitan area. A journal, review, or other means of regularly publishing research is required to communicate with a wider scholarly public, as well as to integrate the activities of dispersed members of the school. A school is thus considerably more than a collection of distinguished individual scholars working in a leading department. It implies the existence of collaborative scholarly activity integrated through the work of one or more leading figures in the school.

In Chicago sociology, the two leading figures were W. I. Thomas and Robert E. Park. Both were men of broad intellectual culture whose work advanced the discipline theoretically. They shared a commitment to empirical research and to grounding broader and more general insights in the results of inquiries made into the contemporary world. The hallmark of the Chicago school of sociology was this blending of firsthand inquiry with general ideas, the integration of research and theory as part of an organized program. The Chicago school was not, as it has occasionally been portrayed, committed to unbridled empiricism, though the impulse toward empirical inquiry was very strong. From *The Polish Peasant* to the study of the local urban community, the Chicago school of sociology teems with efforts at generalization and what has come to be called the Chicago approach to theory.[5] Though the emphasis in the chapters that follow is upon the development of empirical sociological research in the Chicago department, this theoretical tendency was a salient part of the Chicago conception of sociology.

Equally important was the fact that the department was a community of scholars committed to the "best" of contemporary sociological and methodological perspectives. Although there were differences of emphasis there was no one dominant approach. It is an error of historical interpretation to identify the Chicago school too closely with the sociology of social problems, or sociological social psychology, or the work of George Herbert Mead, or an embryo symbolic interactionism. The department's orientation to sociology was varied and eclectic, and its strength lay in this diversity. "In the 1920s there was at Chicago no doctrine with a name ending in 'ism'; rather there was a deliberate effort to avoid creating such a thing. Knowledge was being created, but was far from ready to be forced into a doctrine or to be given any short label."[6] A major aim of this study is to portray and explain this diversity and its relationship to the creative intellectual flowering which took place under the inspiration of Thomas and Park.

More than any other work, *The Polish Peasant in Europe and America*,[7] published in 1918–20, marks the ascent of Chicago sociology to a position of national and international leadership. A classic work blending empirical data and generalization, it exemplified the Chicago approach and had a major impact upon subsequent developments. It was the first of a series of empirical studies carried out in Chicago which appeared at this time. The next major piece of empirical research to appear, the massive report of the Chicago Commission on Race Relations, *The Negro in Chicago* (1922),[8] was largely the work of Charles S. Johnson with the inspiration of continuous guidance from Robert Park. The following year, the University of Chicago Press's *Sociologial Series* was inaugurated with Nels Anderson's *The Hobo* (1923). Later works in this series extended the study of the city in many directions. They included Ernest R. Mowrer's *Family Disorganization* (1927), Frederic Thrasher's *The Gang* (1927), Ruth Shonle Cavan's *Suicide* (1928), Louis Wirth's *The Ghetto* (1928), Harvey Zorbaugh's *The Gold Coast and the Slum* (1929), E. Franklin Frazier's *The Negro Family in Chicago* (1931),

Paul G. Cressy's *The Taxi-Dance Hall* (1932), and Walter Reckless's *Vice in Chicago* (1933). Norman Hayner's *Hotel Life* appeared in 1936 from the University of North Carolina Press.

In addition, a number of important monographs in criminology reporting results of work at the Institute for Juvenile Research, of which Ernest Burgess was the guiding spirit, appeared at the end of the 1920s. These included an ecological study by Clifford Shaw, Henry D. McKay, Frederick Zorbaugh, and Leonard S. Cottrell, Jr., *Delinquency Areas* (1929), John Landesco's *Organized Crime in Chicago* (1929), two life histories edited by Shaw, *The Jack-Roller* (1930) and *The Natural History of a Delinquent Career* (1931), as well as Shaw and McKay's seminal and classic work on the causes of delinquency, *Social Factors in Juvenile Delinquency* (1931), carried out for the Wickersham Crime Commission.[9]

This does not exhaust the range of empirical studies; the Sociological Series included a number of monographs on subjects other than those related to the city of Chicago, including Lyford Edwards's *The Natural History of Revolution* (1927), E. T. Hiller's *The Strike* (1928), and Pauline Young's *The Pilgrims of Russian-Town* (1932). The urban sociological research was supervised by Robert E. Park and Ernest W. Burgess, who provided a conceptual and theoretical framework. Park had first adumbrated his conception of the city as an object of study in 1915.[10] He and Burgess together edited *The City* (1925) and Burgess edited the collections *The Urban Community* (1927) and *Personality and the Social Group* (1929). Their best-known general work was their major text, popularly known as the "green bible," *Introduction to the Science of Sociology* (1921). Almost all the monographs, whether about Chicago or not, contained an introduction by either Park or Burgess which set out the general significance of the results which were presented.

William F. Ogburn had published his major theoretical work on *Social Change*[11] before he came to Chicago in 1927. His major research at Chicago in the late 1920s had two aspects. First, his work for President Hoover's Committee on Recent Social Trends culminated in the publication of *Recent Social Trends*[12] in 1933, but also encompassed an annual issue of the *American Journal of Sociology*[13] presenting a statistical picture of social developments during the year. Second, he and his associates pursued various ecological statistical studies of phenomena such as voting, birth rates, marriage, and the family. In other but related departments at the same time, Charles Merriam, Harold F. Gosnell, Harold Lasswell, and Leonard D. White were carrying out pioneering studies in political science, L. L. Thrustone in psychology was designing scientific methods of attitude measurement, while the economist Henry Schultz was laying the foundations of econometrics.

The impressive body of theoretically informed empirical social research conducted by members of the Chicago school of sociology stimulates reflection about the contribution empirical research has made to the development of the social sciences. Many of the figures in the pantheon, such as Tocqueville, Karl Marx, Le Play, Durkheim, made use of empirical data in their work and (in the case of Tocqueville and Le Play) themselves made firsthand observations or collected material by a primitive kind of interviewing. Yet before the beginning of the twentieth century sociology was predominantly a pursuit of scholars working in libraries, whose interests were philosophical, theoretical, or historical. First- or even secondhand acquaintance with the contemporary world was not seen as a necessary requirement for fruitful sociological generalization. Much empirical social research—whether political arithmetic, census-taking, or early social survey work—was carried on, but its connection to sociology was at best tenuous and more often negligible. To be sure there were good reasons for this, notably the factual character of research of this kind, the routine nature of much of the work involved, and the complex division of labor required. All the more significant, therefore, are the relatively rare periods, as at Chicago between 1915 and 1935, when strong and influential "schools" of empirical social science have arisen in a university setting.

Empirical social research does not always wear well with time. Its content may seem dated or even antiquated with the passage of years, becoming of relatively minor interest when set against more lasting ideas and generalizations. Who, for example, nowadays pays much attention to the extensive sociographic researches of Ferdinand Toennies, by comparison with his concepts of gemeinschaft and gesellschaft?[14] A good deal of empirical research that is uninformed by general ideas can rapidly appear unimportant and trivial. And yet sociological work which blends empirical data with theory, or sets the data within a more general framework, has a lasting quality, whether it is *Le Suicide, The Polish Peasant in Europe and America,* or *The Gold Coast and the Slum*. Such work is of major and lasting significance. This study reflects upon the conditions that brought about this change at Chicago.

Robert Park was originally a journalist, a fact that has been made much of. This diverts attention away from the extent to which he and his associates saw the work they were engaged upon as scientific. The title of the famous textbook was *Introduction to the Science of Sociology*. Firsthand empirical research became more significant in the early twentieth century because it was a way in which the propositions of the developing social sciences could be tested more rigorously and scientifically. The social sciences were also influenced by trends toward more systematic empirical inquiry in the biological sciences and in psychology.[15] One aim of this monograph is to understand the intellectual significance of the rise of empirical sociological research in the early twentieth century and the role played in that rise by the Chicago school.

One major contribution that Chicago sociologists made was to the development of specific research methods in sociology. In the history of empirical research, Chicago comes between the early twentieth-century social survey movement, aimed at social reform, and the later scientific social survey, which developed from the late 1930s on. Yet the distinctive methods of research associated with the Chicago school—the use of personal documents, intensive field work, documentary sources, social mapping, and ecological analysis—were discontinuous with the two forms of the social survey. Nor was the emphasis exclusively upon qualitative research methods. To identify Chicago too closely with intensive field research, or to pose antitheses between the "soft" ethnographic research of the Chicago of Park and Burgess and the "hard" survey research of the Columbia of Lazarsfeld and Merton, is to perpetuate an error. Quantitative methods were also important from an early date in sociology and in other related disciplines, an aspect of the Chicago school often overlooked in the literature. The department's commitment to excellence of all kinds, not a preference for particular types of methodology, was the overriding feature of the period. There were many strains and controversies, but it was a community of scholars committed to a common goal. The development of research methods between 1915 and 1930 proceeded on a broad front, limited only by the stage reached in the development of the social sciences.

Able scholars and good ideas are necessary conditions for productive scholarship, but the successful establishment of an enduring academic tradition also requires the creation of the appropriate institutional structure. This book focuses upon the institutional establishment of the social sciences, particularly sociology, at the University of Chicago up to the early 1930s. Institutional establishment denotes the relatively dense interaction of persons who conduct an intellectual activity

> within a social arrangement which has boundaries, endurance, and a name. The interaction has a structure. The more intense the interaction, the more its structure makes place for authority which makes decisions regarding assessment, admission, promotion, allocation; the authority also sets the criteria for the selection of those particular traditions which are to be cultivated in teaching and inquiry. . . . The high degree of institutionalization of an intellectual activity entails its teaching and investigation within the regulated, scheduled, and systematically administered organization. The organization regulates access through a scrutiny of qualification, and it provides for the organized assessment of performance; it allocates facilities, opportunities, and

> rewards for performance, e.g., study, teaching, investigation, publication, appointment, etc. It also entails the acquisition of the resources—monetary or material—needed to support the activity from outside the particular institutions. It entails too, provision for the diffusion of the results of the activity beyond the boundaries of the institution through publication in the most general sense of making the results available to the public, lay or specialized.[16]

The dominant themes in previous work on Chicago social sciences have been the biography of individuals (such as Robert Park and Charles Merriam), the delineation of intellectual currents (such as pragmatist philosophy or symbolic interactionism), or the history of particular disciplines.[17] This study adopts the different strategy of looking at the university itself as an institution that fostered the growth of the social sciences over a forty-year period. During the 1920s, moreover, a transformation took place in the character of American academic sociology and political science.

At this time many of the features of the modern social science department—large-scale research grants, the use of ancillary staff and purchase of equipment, graduate work linked to research programs, intensive graduate seminars, attention to methodology teaching, emphasis on publication—first began to take shape. The foundation of Johns Hopkins, Clark, and Chicago universities at the end of the nineteenth century had introduced research to center stage and made the Ph.D. a requirement for the would-be academic scholar. The early professionalization of social science went hand-in-hand with these developments.[18] In the early years of the twentieth century, however, the model remained that of the lone scholar working with a few graduate students and one or two assistants, mainly upon library and documentary materials. Between 1915 and 1930 a significant shift occurred toward larger-scale research, more often of a collaborative kind, and on occasion also interdisciplinary. Methods of firsthand empirical research were increasingly used, and within a short time several social sciences became much more empirical in character.

Sociological research at the University of Chicago between 1915 and 1930 was the first successful example of the integration of extensive research into a university department of sociology. At first this consisted principally of university teachers' own small-scale investigations coupled with similar pieces of work by the graduate students whom they supervised individually. At Chicago in the 1920s not only was there an integrated pattern of research, but an infrastructure and simple research organization to support it were created, coupled with outside financial support for the work which was being done. This new pattern represented a major departure for academic social science.

One facilitating factor was the availability of financial support for social science from newly established philanthropic foundations such as the Carnegie Corporation and the Laura Spelman Rockefeller Memorial. To what extent this support shaped and influenced the direction taken by sociology and political science in the 1920s is debatable. It was certainly allied to a belief in the potential usefulness of social science and its value in the shaping of public policy. The earlier marriage of fact-finding with moralism—characteristic of the social survey movement—was replaced by a more mature view of the relation between social science and social action. There was a greater readiness in the 1920s to see academic social science as providing knowledge useful to society.[19] The view of usefulness taken by scholars such as Park and Merriam was a rather olympian one, but it represented an important change in orientation.

Viewed in historical perspective, the Chicago school was the first great flowering of sociology in the United States. The founding fathers of American sociology—Lester F. Ward, William Graham Sumner, Franklin H. Giddings, Edward A. Ross, Charles Horton Cooley, and Albion W. Small—did not develop ideas or systems that in their entirety have had a lasting influence upon sociology. Cooley's intellectual influence has probably been greatest. Sumner and Ross wrote monographs that are still read. The principal legacy of this first generation was the institutional establishment of sociology in American universities, with varying degrees of success.[20] Albion Small (1854–1926) played a key role, succeeding in building up the University of Chicago as a strong center whereas the other five, with the partial exception of Giddings, left no institutional legacy. Small founded the Department of Sociology at the University of Chicago in 1892, the first such department in any university in the world giving undergraduate and graduate degrees. The lack of decisive influence of the ideas or institutional effectiveness of the other five is of some importance in understanding Chicago's subsequent success.

Lester F. Ward (1841–1913), the first president of the American Sociological Society, was best known for his *Dynamic Sociology* (1883). His career was as a government paleobotanist, and Ward introduced biological terms into his sociological writings, which emphasized the role of psychological factors in social change. Ward set the tone of evolutionary naturalism characteristic of the first generation of leading American sociologists[21] but modified it to allow for human agency. His writings had a considerable influence in the period up to 1910, but, lacking a university position, Ward was not able to influence graduate teaching significantly or to train followers who would carry on his ideas.[22]

This was not true of William Graham Sumner (1840–1910), the second president of the society, who taught sociology at Yale. Sumner was not only a major theorist but a dynamic and popular teacher who brought sociology to the attention of thousands of students. Sumner was a thoroughgoing exponent of Darwinian and Spencerian evolutionism, which he incorporated into his social theory to produce a kind of "social darwinism." The processes of social selection and the survival of the fittest were consonant with individualist and laissez-faire philosophical and political premises. His most important work was *Folkways* (1907), which made extensive use of the printed comparative literature of anthropology and ethnography to analyze the origin of moral codes and social customs. His influence was limited by three factors. Yale at the time was an undergraduate college, and Sumner did not attempt to develop graduate studies or attract a significant number of graduate students. His extreme laissez-faire orientation aroused considerable criticism from other social scientists including Small.[23] And the very strong commitments of Sumner's few followers tended to isolate them from other social scientists.[24] "No sociologist save Comte has ever been blessed or cursed by such reverent discipleship as has Sumner."[25]

Franklin H. Giddings (1855–1931), the third president of the society, was in a stronger position to influence the sociological community from Columbia, and to some extent did so, but he too expected overfervent discipleship among his students, a weakness from which Small was almost entirely free. Giddings, who had a background in editorial journalism, began teaching sociology at Columbia University in 1893, and remained there until his retirement in the late 1920s. Unlike Ward or Sumner, Giddings taught several students who subsequently became leading sociologists of the next generation, including William F. Ogburn, Howard Odum, and Stuart F. Chapin. Giddings was unusual among early sociologists in being interested in quantitative methods as a means of making sociology more scientific. Although his own work in this area did not amount to much, it influenced a number of his students in quite important ways.[26] His theoretical system was centered on the concept of "consciousness of kind." The virtues of Giddings's methodological and theoretical ideas were severely marred by his personality and prejudices, which prevented Columbia's becoming a first-rate sociology department.[27]

Edward Alsworth Ross (1866–1951), a friend of Small's, contributed extensively to the *American Journal of Sociology* in its early years, wrote an important work entitled *Social Control* (1901), and for many years headed the sociology department at the University of Wisconsin, though by training he was an economist. No other American sociologist had so interesting and colorful a life, and therein lies the explanation of Ross's lack of lasting influence. Though a brilliant teacher and voluminous writer, "Ross was as much a publicist and social reformer as he was a professional sociologist."[28] His early academic career culminated in his dismissal from Stanford University in 1900 for criticizing the labor policies of the founder of the university.[29] A few years later, he moved to Wisconsin, where he remained until his retirement in 1937, but he did not build up the department as a strong center of graduate study. Wisconsin was not a national university in the manner of Chicago, but drew its students from and returned them to Wisconsin. Ross had no patience in supervising students, as Park had, and no interest in field research. Indeed, many of his activities as populist, muckraker, and social reformer took him outside the university and in later years on frequent trips overseas, which he valued more highly than sociology. He was opposed to the professionalization of sociology and its narrowing down to the activities of academic scholars. Nevertheless, he himself was no mean scholar and *Social Control* is a work of lasting importance. In it he attempted to develop a social-psychologically based general sociological theory of the foundations of social order.[30]

Charles Horton Cooley (1864–1929), like Ross, began his academic career as an economist but soon moved into sociology. He spent almost all his life at the University of Michigan. He was a withdrawn, almost reclusive man, who suffered from ill health and disliked administration, large-scale research, and departmental grandeur. During his time at Michigan sociology did not flourish there, but he himself was scholarly and widely read, and his writings had a considerable influence on sociologists at the time, including those of the Chicago school in the 1920s. Cooley's social psychological theory emphasized the extent to which the individual and society were complementary. Society was an organic process, in which the development of the individual was socially influenced to a considerable extent. Cooley's concept of the "looking-glass self" fitted with some of G. H. Mead's ideas and brought into social theory the idea of human personality as being influenced by social pressures. Cooley's work was also important for introducing the distinction between primary and secondary groups.[31]

All these early sociologists, including Small, were concerned to develop general theory as a foundation for the discipline. Though their positions varied in terms of materialism versus idealism, determinism or voluntarism, and society and the individual, all sought to establish the social realm as an independent and autonomous field of study. With the partial exceptions of Sumner and Giddings (who did library research), none made significant empirical studies, though Small urged that sociology should move in a more empirical direction, emphasizing the necessity of field work and direct observation. The six men differed significantly in terms of personality and political and professional orientation. Cooley and Giddings were severely handicapped by personality characteristics, which prevented their assuming effective academic leadership. Ross and Sumner's political and philosophical orientations hindered their becoming influential sociologists, though in different ways. Ward's academically marginal position prevented his exercising significant influence on the future institutional development of American sociology. Only Small, despite the fact that his general theory was less powerful than that of Sumner, was able to influence future developments through his position at Chicago.

This first phase of American sociology ended with the publication of *The Polish Peasant in Europe and America* in 1918–20,[32] which although it coincided with Thomas's departure from the university, signalled the advent of the Chicago school. To understand these developments, however, one must look considerably further back at the history of the city, the University of Chicago, and the place of the social sciences within them.

2 Chicago: The City and Its University

A "school" of social science typically displays a shared approach to a common set of problems which have been specified by the leader(s) of the school. The Chicago school was characterized by a commitment to empirical research on the city of Chicago, focusing upon its ethnic and racial intermixture, its social problems, its urban form and its local communities. These studies were set in the context of a theory of social change (in the case of W. I. Thomas) and a careful conceptual framework and theory of social process (in the case of Robert Park). They were markedly different from the scholarship of the first generation of American sociologists, both in their focus on the city of Chicago and in their empirical nature. This distinctive emphasis may be explained in part by the character of the city and of the new University of Chicago, established in 1892.

Youth provides one key to understanding. In the early and middle nineteenth century, Chicago was an outpost of American civilization on the western frontier of the country. It did not have the long history of cities on the Eastern Seaboard and was the chief metropolitan center in a region where book learning was not a common trait. Men such as Abraham Lincoln, Mark Twain, or Louis Sullivan, in different walks of life, lived through action rather than the written word. The dominant culture of the Middle West was not bookish at this period, though the influence of clergymen and schoolteachers was not negligible. Tradition was primarily an oral tradition.[1] This was not surprising in an area which only recently had been settled in large numbers. In 1800, there were only a few thousand Americans in what is now Illinois. The state of Illinois was only created in 1818. The first settlers were families in search of their own land, which had to be won from the forest. Urban growth followed rural settlement, to provide centers of public and commercial life.[2]

Chicago was a new city in a relatively newly settled region. This newness was reflected in the openness, excitement, flux, and verve of the city of Chicago. Simply in terms of demographic change, the picture was a striking one (see table 1). In 1840, Chicago was insignificant. By 1850 it was a fair-sized town. Between 1850 and 1890 Chicago grew from a small town into a great city of more than one million people, outstripping twenty-three older cities in the process to become the second largest American city after New York. In the forty years from 1890 the rate of

TABLE 1
The Population of Chicago, 1840–1930

Year	Number	Percent increase
1840	4,470	—
1850	29,963	570.3
1860	109,260	264.6
1870	298,977	173.6
1880	503,185	68.3
1890	1,099,850	118.6
1900	1,698,575	54.4
1910	2,185,283	28.7
1920	2,701,705	23.6
1930	3,375,329	24.9

SOURCE: Ernest W. Burgess and Charles Newcomb, eds., *Census Data of the City of Chicago, 1920* (Chicago: University of Chicago Press, 1931), p. 5.

growth slowed, but the population of the city increased over three times to 3.375 million people.[3]

In the four decades before the establishment of the University of Chicago in 1892, the city had thus altered out of all recognition, a process hastened physically by the Great Fire of 1871, when the old city of wooden buildings was largely destroyed to be replaced by buildings of stone and steel. The growth of the city owed a great deal to the coming of the railways. By 1860, Chicago was at the center of a web of lines, the jumping off point for the western part of the country, and the commercial and business center of the Middle West. Its exchanges, stockyards, and industries grew apace. Migrants came from the rural areas of the Middle West, some bringing with them respect for learning, particularly religious learning. From these circles, the business and professional classes were drawn. As the century advanced, foreign immigrants met the growing demand for labor. Chicago became an ethnic melting pot of Germans, Scandinavians, Irish, Italians, Poles, Jews, Czechs, Lithuanians, and Croats. In 1900, half of the population of 1.7 million had been born outside the United States. Black migration was slower. Blacks comprised only 2 percent of the city's population in 1910, though the proportion had risen to 7 percent by 1930.[4]

In 1890 Chicago was a relatively new city, a boiling, turbulent, industrial metropolis that knew what it meant to be great, but had hardly had time to absorb the knowledge. It was a city of paradoxes, caught brilliantly in Carl Sandburg's poem "Chicago."[5] It had its dark side, a city of exploitation and human degradation. Industrialization led to industrial conflict, most dramatically in the Haymarket Riot of 1886 and the Pullman Strike of 1894. It was, wrote Lincoln Steffens, "first in violence, deepest in dirt; loud, lawless, unlovely, ill-smelling, new; an overgrown gawk of a village, the teeming tough among cities. Criminally it was wide open; commercially it was brazen; and socially it was thoughtless and raw."[6]

Chicago was also, however, a city of learning and culture. The influence of Protestant religion upon Midwesterners mainly of German and Scandinavian origin had fostered respect for book learning. Part of the matrix of the seriousness of the University of Chicago lay in this tradition. From an early date, Chicago's business elite prided itself on support for Theodore Thomas and the musical tradition of the Chicago Symphony Orchestra founded in 1891. The Art Institute, set up in 1879, had occupied an Italian Renaissance style building since 1893. The core of its fine collection of classical and impressionist paintings was formed before the end of the nineteenth century.[7] A considerable number of Chicago businessmen were book collectors. The Chicago school of architecture not only contributed the skyscraper to American urban civilization, but created the first coherent urban architectural style indigenous to the continent.[8] The city's literary reputation was solidly established by poets such as Carl Sandburg, who worked as a local journalist, and novelists such as Theodore Dreiser,[9] Sherwood Anderson, Frank Norris, and Robert Herrick.

The cultural confidence of the city was symbolized by its successful bid to be the home of the World's Columbian Exposition of 1893 (also known as the World's Fair or the Chicago Fair), celebrating the four hundredth anniversary of the discovery of America.[10] Though some Easterners wondered whether the fair would be much more than a "cattle show on the shore of Lake Michigan," thoughtful observers such as Bostonians William James, Henry Adams, and Charles Eliot Norton recognized that the creative center of cultural forces in America was moving from Boston and New York to Chicago. The university, once established, was thus not an isolated cultural beacon in a sea of commercial darkness. H. L. Mencken described Chicago as "the most civilized city in America . . . and the most thoroughly American."[11] For Robert Park, a quarter of a century later, the city—above all, Chicago—was

> something more than a congeries of individual men and of social conveniences . . . something more than a mere constellation of institutions and administrative devices. The city is, rather, a state of mind, a body of customs and traditions . . . a product of nature and particularly of human nature.[12]

It was in this urban milieu that the University of Chicago was established in 1890, admitting its first students in 1892. Though a Baptist foundation supported by the philanthropy of John D. Rockefeller, Sr., the university was only established after substantial promises of financial support were obtained from the local community.[13] Its first president, William Rainey Harper, set out to found a university devoted to basic research and graduate training.[14] Within a short time, and with the support of leading members of the Chicago elite, he made it one of the foremost universities in the country. Harper's conception of the university as a center for research and inquiry was distinctly different from the undergraduate college and even from Johns Hopkins, established with a strong research orientation in 1879.[15] At Chicago, senior professors were appointed to teach exclusively in the graduate schools. The main purpose of graduate education, Harper maintained, was "not to stock the student's mind with knowledge of what has already been accomplished in a given field, but rather so to train him that he himself may be able to push out along new lines of investigation."[16]

Harper, who was endowed with enormous energy, enthusiasm, and vision, was determined that the conditions would be created in the university to foster such an orientation. First-class academic staff, "the best available men in the country,"[17] were of primary importance. Many of those he approached were suspicious of a new university in a rough Midwestern location, but enough accepted his offers for the university to open with a strong teaching faculty. The appeal of the new foundation lay less in large salaries than in the freedom for research and educational innovation that it offered.[18] The academic climate in which Park and Burgess in sociology and Merriam and Gosnell in political science worked in the 1920s was one formed in the 1890s, when the university was new. This aspect has not been emphasized enough in studies of Chicago sociology.

Harper was determined that research should be fostered, something which the contemporary American college did not do.

> It is only the man who has made investigation who may teach others to investigate. Without this spirit in the instructor and without his example, students will never be led to undertake the work. Moreover, if the instructor is loaded down with lectures he will have neither time nor strength to pursue his investigations. Freedom from care, time for work and liberty of thought are prime requisites in all such work. . . . It is expected that Professors and other instructors will, at intervals, be excused entirely for a period from lecture work, in order that they may thus be able to give their entire time to the work of investigation. Promotion of younger men in the departments will depend more largely upon the results of their work as investigators than upon the efficiency of their teaching, although the latter will by no means be overlooked. In other words, it is proposed in this institution to make the work of investigation primary, the work of giving instruction secondary.[19]

Harper not only encouraged his staff at all levels to concentrate upon research and to publish, but he sought to provide the means of publication. Even before the university had admitted its first students, the university press was established, "not as an incident, as an attachment, but . . . as an organic part of the institution."[20] Through the press, the influence of the university would be greatly enlarged and carried around the world. Each department was encouraged to establish its own academic journal or departmental series, in which the results of the research of their staff would be published.

The University of Chicago was not the first university to pioneer such an emphasis upon research, but Harper was the most effective and enduring institution-builder among the triumvirate of himself, Daniel Coit Gilman at Johns Hopkins University, and G. Stanley Hall at Clark University. The foundation of Johns Hopkins in 1876, "perhaps the single most decisive event in the history of learning in the Western hemisphere,"[21] marked the beginning of the end of American migration to Germany for higher education[22] and the establishment of an indigenous research tradition in American higher education. The primary commitment at Hopkins to laboratory and seminar work was unfamiliar on American soil, though many on the staff had had experience in Germany, whose institutions of higher learning had such a formative influence on the modern American university. Two qualities marked out the Hopkins atmosphere, a sense of freedom and commitment to achievement.[23] There was little ritual or ceremony. The pressure toward hard work was intense, enforced by a constant, close-range comparison with one's peers.[24] The influence of Johns Hopkins was present at Chicago through Albion Small and John Dewey. Small earned his Ph.D. in history at Johns Hopkins in 1888–89, Dewey his Ph.D. there in 1883–85 studying philosophy and psychology.[25] The atmosphere of graduate study at the period was summed up by Josiah Royce: "One longed to be a doer of the word, and not a hearer only."[26]

The pioneering role of Johns Hopkins was next followed by Clark University at Worcester, Massachusetts; its first president, G. Stanley Hall, had been professor of psychology at Johns Hopkins.[27] When the university opened in 1889, its aim was to create an all-graduate setting, devoted to pure scientific research. A distinguished staff was recruited, and the promise of scientific achievement was good. It foundered almost immediately because of the university's benefactor, Jonas Clark, who, unlike the benefactor of Hopkins, was still alive and living in the town. John D. Rockefeller, Sr., at Chicago refused either to lend his name to the university or involve himself in its running, despite being milked by Harper for gigantic endowments. He maintained an aloof distance. Jonas Clark insisted on almost day-to-day involvement in the running of "his" university and rapidly came into conflict with Hall. Local hostility to the university was one factor, but the main bone of contention was the conflict between graduate research and undergraduate teaching. When the trustees refused to establish an undergraduate college, Clark withdrew his support at the end of 1892. This crisis hastened the departure of many of the faculty and aided Harper in his recruiting drive for the University of Chicago. Hall later complained that Harper had "raided" his institution and added insult to injury by offering Hall himself a chair, but the decline of Clark University was already underway when that event occurred in April 1892, and thereafter was complete.[28]

The University of Chicago was the third of the new universities devoted primarily to research to be established at the end of the nineteenth century, and the most lasting. The initial success of Johns Hopkins was not maintained into the early twentieth century, because of budgetary crises and uninspired leadership, coupled with competition from older eastern universities.[29] For the idea that universities were primarily the inheritors and purveyors of the store of existing knowledge, and only secondarily in the business of discovering new knowledge, was changing gradually. By 1890, Harvard had established a Graduate School of Arts and Sciences.[30] At Columbia, John W. Burgess was instrumental in setting up the Graduate Faculty of Political Science in 1880.[31] The obligation to teach was not greatly diminished, but these developments showed a determination to foster research among both teachers and the growing body of graduate students.[32]

The experiment at Clark foundered in part because it was too exclusively committed to graduate training and research. A broader-based institution, like Chicago, with an undergraduate college and a vigorous university extension branch, was better placed to encourage a thriving graduate school. Harper's original plan for the university integrated graduate education and the research orientation of staff with other functions, while giving them pride of place. The "delicately poised equilibrium" between teaching and research was maintained, not thrown overboard, but the emphasis was altered in favor of research.[33]

This was a lasting innovation of profound importance. Prior to this time, research had to be fitted in after a university teacher's other and primary responsibility, to teach, had been accomplished. Most American universities did not particularly encourage research, nor reward it by career advancement.[34] One solution to the fostering of research could have been the creation of independent research institutes separate from universities. In the United States, this did not occur, with rare exceptions. Instead research and teaching were combined within a single institution, following the model of the German universities at which many neophyte American scholars studied in the later years of the nineteenth century. It would be a mistake to emphasize too greatly the achievement of a single university in this process, but William Rainey Harper was one of the most effective agents in bringing about this transition.

The influence of the ideal of the nineteenth-century German university upon these American developments is well established.[35] The emphasis both in German and increasingly in certain American universities, such as Chicago, upon the advanced seminar and graduate instruction was part of this belief in the crucial position of research. If the seminar assumed central importance as a means of teaching,[36] the setting in which serious scientific investigation was conducted was the laboratory. At least, this was so in natural science; its equivalent in the study of human beings was Wundt's psychological laboratory in Leipzig, opened in 1879.[37] What, however, of the other social sciences whose methods were nonexperimental? Where did the political scientist, economist, or sociologist go to do research? The answer, for the most part, was to the library or to the study or to the archives, to work on printed materials and unpublished documents. Firsthand inquiries in the field were unusual, though not unknown.

The institution of the Ph.D. as the goal of the advanced student, to be gained by graduate study organized around the seminar, was central to this transformation. By the 1890s, graduate study and, increasingly, possession of the Ph.D., had become requirements for permanent appointments as university teachers, even for those who had studied in Germany without gaining the degree. Quite senior academics returned to university to attend graduate school, such as Albion Small at Johns Hopkins in 1888 at the age of thirty-four and W. I. Thomas at Chicago in 1893 at the age of thirty.

The content of the graduate seminar would vary. Students reported on the progress of their researches, reviewed the literature, discussed particular articles or monographs, read long papers, or the group might devote itself to the intensive study of documents. Much depended on the quality and character of the teacher. Particular individuals such as John W. Burgess at Columbia, W. G. Sumner at Yale, Frederick Jackson Turner, and G. Stanley Hall inspired great loyalty and dedication in their students. The close and fruitful work of Robert E. Park and Ernest Burgess with their students after 1917 was a later example of the successful graduate seminar in social science that had been instituted in several universities in the previous thirty years. In these early years, few were devoted to empirical research, but the creative atmosphere is well caught by Albion Small's description of his experiences at Johns Hopkins in 1888–89. A group of thirty students, from all the social sciences, met five mornings a week at a long table in a dingy old garrett:

> First a historian would have us, then an economist, then a political scientist, or a sociologist, or a lawyer. When a specialist in either of these fields, or in some division of practical social affairs, came from Washington or Philadelphia or New York, to

> talk to the seminar, faculty and students pooled their critical equipments, and in the interest of an all-round view of the subject attempted to test every man's theory from all the standpoints represented in the group.[38]

The advanced seminar in the American university was conceived of as training for the academic profession. In this respect it differed from the German system, where there was no conception of a career leading upwards. In the United States, graduate instruction depended upon the state of the subject and the energy of the professors, who shaped a system designed to train professional researchers.[39]

At the University of Chicago from 1892, this emphasis on graduate study for the Ph.D. and on research and publication by graduate students and teachers was fostered.[40] Pursuit of the ideals of research was an austere calling, inspiring its own kind of commitment. Albion Small's hyperbole in 1905, on assuming the deanship of the Chicago graduate school (which he held until retirement in 1924), caught the mood:

> There is more glory for a graduate school in stimulating one mind to a genuinely critical attitude toward conventional ideas than in graduating countless contented repeaters of commonplace formulas. The first commandment with promise for graduate schools is: Remember the research ideal, to keep it holy![41]

William G. Hale, foundation professor of Latin, believed that the graduate student must "be gifted by nature with a certain amount of celestial fire," while the teacher must possess highly specialized relevant knowledge, not just be an estimable gentleman. He must (the masculine pronoun was ubiquitous) have the power of creative scholarship, himself be a master who leads his students and is in the forefront of his field internationally.[42]

The competitive spirit helped to keep the University of Chicago in the forefront. Unlike the bureaucratized and hierarchical structure of German and, to a lesser extent, British universities of the time, the American university system between 1860 and 1920 lacked an "establishment" or central authority. There was a plurality of institutions of various types, which competed amongst themselves. This decentralized and competitive system fostered not only a growing hunger for knowledge based on research, but the expansion of the university system to supply that hunger.

The University of Chicago set out, from the beginning, to be a university of national and international stature. This was a necessary part of its research orientation. So long as universities confined themselves to teaching, they were visible only locally and to those whom they had taught. (Where this included, as at Harvard and Yale, major segments of elite groups, it also rendered their institutions more visible.) Achievements in research, however, were public property, and individuals, departments, and institutions could be assessed vis-à-vis competitors nationally and internationally. The desire to achieve "the best," to be "great," to rank in the same class as the leading German universities was arrived at through the visibility that research afforded. Universities and departments were stratified according to judgments about the worth of the research they were producing. Specialization meant that the individual investigator had to look beyond his immediate colleagues for stimulation to a national and international community with its own hierarchy of eminence.

> The names of institutions were never completely severed from the names of individuals and the deference accorded to individuals for their respective achievements was diffused into their institutions. In this way specialization in research supported the translocal elements of the scientific and scholarly community and its stratification.[43]

The University of Chicago came out of such comparisons well and established itself early as one of the great American universities. Although its research orientation helps to explain this, the fate of Clark and the decline of Johns Hopkins after 1890 suggest that more was involved, and this outcome was far from being a foregone conclusion. An explanation of this early ascendancy of the University of Chicago is complex but essential for understanding the later flowering there of social science.

Harper as president was a major contributing factor. One of the most effective university presidents of his age, he created the university, put it in the front rank, and ensured that it remained there.[44] His vision, energy, brilliance, and zeal, coupled with a strong religious belief and a continuing commitment to his own research, left a lasting mark. He imbued the University of Chicago with a sense of its own uniqueness, which is essential to understanding the later achievements of the social sciences at Chicago, which are the subject of this study. As the historian of the university observed:

> The plans Harper made could hardly have been more significant than the way in which he worked. Men make universities, Robert Herrick observed, as once they made great temples, blindly, not conceiving the ultimate ends to which they will be devoted, out of some inner necessity of their spirits. There is that quality in the history of the Harper administration.[45]

Harper's judgment was most apparent in the criteria he used to recruit his academic staff when the university opened. Gilman at Johns Hopkins had faced little opposition in seeking a research-oriented faculty of distinction, but competition by 1890 was stiffer. Harper was brilliantly persuasive and would never accept "no" for an answer. He did not succeed in attracting all those whom he sought. His blandishments were resisted at many eastern universities. For example, he could not come to terms with historian Herbert Baxter Adams and political economist Richard T. Ely at Johns Hopkins. Had either of them been appointed, Chicago sociology might have moved in a very different direction.[46] But he was largely successful, managing in a short space of time to recruit a very strong group of senior colleagues, including eight former presidents of universities and colleges. The most notable included William G. Hale in Latin and J. Lawrence Laughlin in economics (both from Cornell), Thomas C. Chamberlin in geology (president of the University of Wisconsin), Hermann von Holst in history (from the University of Freiburg), and Albion Small in sociology (president of Colby College). Fifteen of the leading scientists at Clark University, including Albert A. Michelson, the physicist,[47] were lured to Chicago as a result of Hall's difficulties. John Dewey moved to Chicago from the University of Michigan in 1894.[48] Of the first 77 instructors and professors in 1892, 14 had German Ph.D.'s (5 from Leipzig) and 21 had American Ph.D.'s (9 from Yale).[49]

A first-class academic staff could not be obtained without money to pay salaries at a level high enough to attract them from elsewhere. The success of the University of Chicago in early becoming a leading university owed a great deal to the personal beneficence (and faith in Harper) of John D. Rockefeller, Sr. Over a period of two decades, Rockefeller gave the university in total $35 million in endowment and to meet current expenses, before calling a halt in 1910 with a final gift of $10 million. The history of Harper's financial dealings with Rockefeller, mediated through Frederick Gates, showed Harper at his most persuasive and enterprising.[50] The university was skillfully led from deficit to deficit, with fresh infusions of Rockefeller help at frequent intervals to expand even further the horizons of the institution, until upon Harper's death in 1906 his successor Harry Pratt Judson began to exercise more financial caution.[51] Teachers, with the exception of some of the head professors, were not highly paid, but Harper's entrepreneurship helped to obtain funds for building and research facilities which they appreciated.[52]

The fact that Chicago was a private university, with funds from a philanthropic source, meant that it was much freer to emphasize research than state universities in the Midwest, its main local competitors, who were constrained by their legislatures to devote their main efforts to teaching. This freedom was always a somewhat uncertain and hand-to-mouth existence, but it gave Chicago an undoubted advantage. It also permitted the university a greater coherence as a private institution, developing graduate and professional schools and able to resist demands to expand undergraduate numbers. Quality and innovation could be fostered without interference from outside pressures.[53]

In 1892, a visitor entering Cobb Hall asked a cleaning lady where to find the president of the university. "I dunno," she replied, "I jes' scrub." When the visitor repeated the remark to the president, Harper replied, "We are beginning to specialize, you see."[54] Academic specialization provides a partial clue to the early success of the university.[55] Specialization meant seriousness of purpose and the intention of contributing to knowledge. It meant no self-indulgence, getting on with the job,[56] exposing one's work to the scrutiny of others and submitting to the judgment of one's peers. The specialist scorned the academic dilettante. Academic journals, which Chicago spawned, became the mode of communication of the specialist. Specialization did not only erode the position of the amateur, particularly in natural and social scientific research,[57] but it also gave research-oriented universities the edge against institutions in which the teachers were primarily generalists devoted to undergraduate teaching. Specialization coupled with serious attention to publication pushed the University of Chicago to the forefront.

The shift in American sociology and political science toward the firsthand empirical study of society and the tendency of the University of Chicago to produce "schools" have a good deal to do also with the close ties between the university and the city. Harper's experience of the Chautauqua movement for mass adult education in the 1880s[58] led him to create a strong university extension branch. He believed that knowledge must be communicated, that the university was in every sense an institution of public service. The localism that characterized and gave focus to the social science research of Robert Park and Charles Merriam in the 1920s had its roots in the origins of the university.

The democratic ethos of Chicago, by comparison with New York and Boston, challenged members of the staff of the new university to understand what was happening in the city around them.[59] The ending of the World's Fair in the winter of 1893/94 left the university in a desolated area of boarded-up houses and closed hotels, on a "rough sand-lot with a swamp marked by a few scrub oak trees, where frogs croaked us to sleep at night . . . all bleak and grim." The bustle and glamour of the fair was replaced by "the spectacle of poverty—men, women, and children marching to the garbage dumps and, in spite of unoccupied buildings galore, sleeping in jails or the City Hall. From our windows in Graduates Hall [recalled Robert Morss Lovett] we saw Coxey's army of unemployed straggle north to seek shelter and food in the city"[60] en route to Washington, D.C., in 1894. The concerns of more liberal teachers at the university matched those of liberal reformers among the urban elite, such as Jane Addams and Graham Taylor, who had established settlement houses and sought practical means to alleviate some of the effects of urbanization and mass immigration.

Harper's expectations of sociology were rather vague, but embodied the idea that it would contribute to the solution of social problems. Albion Small clearly believed that the discipline would contribute to social improvement. The Chicago social sciences from the outset, as Janowitz has pointed out, embodied "a tradition that asserts that effective sociological analysis per se is a relevant contribution to the efforts of collective problem-solving, because a clearer understanding of social reality serves to stir the visions of men and women."[61] The later fertility of the Chicago school under the influence of Thomas and Park owed a good deal to the reform interests of a number of academics, which created among social scientists a sense of intimacy with the city. Steven Diner has shown in detail how reformers inside and outside the University of Chicago cooperated in movements of urban reform. Members of the university combined scholarly research and teaching with public service and an interest in social betterment.[62]

Two other influences strengthened this interest in the city. The visibility of social conditions was probably greater than in the other large metropolises of America. Max Weber, when he visited Chicago in 1904, wrote that it was like looking at a man whose skin had been peeled off and whose intestines are seen at work.[63] Moral sentiment gave force to the concern to do something about these conditions. Liberal Protestantism was strong in the Middle West and looked increasingly to sociology to provide a "scientific" support to the social gospel. Thus Charles Henderson, who both taught sociology and acted as university chaplain, took a most active part in organizations concerned with the reform of social services in the city up to the time of his death in 1915.[64]

Early empirical social research was one of the principal consequences of these interests in urban social problems and their reform. Social conditions in late nineteenth-century American cities were exposed by muckraking journalism, of which the best known were studies by Jacob Riis in New York, *How the Other Half Lives* (1890) and *Battle with the Slums* (1892). In his earlier career in journalism, Robert Park had crossed Riis's path. In Chicago, Jane Addams was one of the leading activists for reform. Hull-House became not just an independent social agency but a center at which reformers, politicians, and academics discussed social problems in depth.[65] In Chicago, some of the earliest local surveys were carried out by members of the settlement house movement, many of whom were middle-class women college graduates, for whom social welfare was one of the few socially acceptable forms of work open. They included the *Hull House Maps and Papers* (1895), under the direction of Jane Addams, Robert A. Woods's *The City Wilderness* (1898), and Robert Hunter's *Tenement Conditions in Chicago* (1901).

Members of the university staff with reform interests were more actively involved than in almost any other large or medium-sized American city at the period:

> It was above all at Chicago that the active stratum of "reformers," businessmen, clergymen, journalists, lawyers, and social workers, reached out to the University of Chicago and sought its aid in any form in which members of the University could offer it. The University of Chicago was an organ of enlightenment—of scientific knowledge—when the reformers believe that the scientific knowledge of society and the wisdom and courage of those who proferred it were indispensable to them.[66]

Social scientists were active in organizations such as the Union League Club and the City Club, founded in 1903, whose membership also included leading Chicago professionals and businessmen. A number took part in early, reform-oriented, social surveys, including Ernst Freund in the Law School and James Hayden Tufts and George Herbert Mead in philosophy.[67] Mead, for example, whose scholarly work for four decades was purely philosophical, became involved in a number of social inquiries outside the university. Beginning with educational research associated with the Dewey laboratory school, Mead supervised a number of studies in the city. In the period 1910–16 he took part in a project that aimed to carry out in Chicago something like the famous Pittsburgh survey of 1906–9. A major study of the stockyards was carried out in 1910–12, with a staff of ten working on the project for two years. In 1912, Mead was proposing the establishment of a central statistical bureau to consolidate, coordinate, and gather data on local social conditions with a view to making it possible to plan social action and public policy on a scientific basis.[68]

The impact of these early reform initiatives was not as great as the reformers hoped. The magnitude of the urban problems faced was so great that philanthropy was inadequate to deal with many of them. In some areas the policies pursued were palliatives that proved ineffectual. Nevertheless, a considerable impact was made both upon the public consciousness and upon certain politicians and government officials. Some social legislation bore the influence of the municipal reform movement.

The standards of the empirical research conducted were not very rigorous and were frequently marked by inadequate conceptualization, absence of theory, and strong tinges of moralism. Henderson, Zueblin, and other early members of the Department of Sociology did not have the passion for scientific understanding that W. I. Thomas and later Robert Park brought to the study of urban society. But they were part of a milieu that created the conditions on which Thomas, Park and Merriam were to build. Had this milieu not been present, their work might have taken other forms; Thomas, for example, might have carried on with ethnographic work in the manner of Sumner. At this period, too, the connection between social science and public policy was first established, with a distinctly local focus. This tradition of local social involvement was the soil that nurtured the urban studies of the Chicago school of sociology and made the relationship between the university and city different from that in New York or Boston.

Involvement in public affairs led to certain tensions. Liberal and radical teachers at the university might find that complaints were made about them to the president, who generally defended his staff staunchly. The main blemish upon the body politic was the Bemis case,[69] but in general the university was self-confident and expansionist, certain of its own excellence while deeply serious and committed above all to the advancement of knowledge. As a new institution, it lacked the social pretensions of Harvard and Yale; indeed the University of Chicago, although a Baptist foundation, was remarkably free from denominational coloring. It was coeducational from the outset, and although leading American universities in the North discriminated overtly against blacks in admissions policy until far into the twentieth century, Chicago seems to have been more willing than some to admit black students.[70] Its early years molded its character, establishing the lines along which it would develop in future.

Many in the East were skeptical that a new foundation could succeed, or be anything other than an academic backwater. At Yale, Harper was chided for giving up a secure position in a great institution for a new and untried institution in the West.[71] Marion Talbot, the young professor of household science and later dean of women, who left Boston for Chicago in 1892, recalled that "Chicago seemed a very wild and woolly place to my friends." On her departure a friend pressed into her hand a little box. " 'It holds,' she said, 'a fragment of Plymouth Rock.' This was symbolic of the attitude of our Boston friends toward the new educational venture in Chicago. It was something built on the sands. The academic system with which Boston was familiar was founded upon a rock."[72]

Robert Herrick, himself an emigrant from Boston, caught the spirit of the new university in his novel *Chimes*, which describes a university (Eureka) closely modeled on the University of Chicago, with its president Dr. Harris. The exchange is between two young teachers, Clavercin and Miss Stowe (the latter bearing some resemblance to Marion Talbot).

"So you are in it too?" Clavercin inquired curiously.

"Experimentally, for the present", Miss Stowe replied with a priggish precision of speech, yet being agreeably modulated in tone as the speech of the East, he found it a relief. "I am assisting Mrs. Crandell in organizing the woman's side of the university and working in my subject, social science, at the same time."

She did not say that she was a doctor of philosophy, having passed a very brilliant examination for the degree at Johns Hopkins, and that her thesis, about to be published by Eureka's new Press department, upon *Primitive Marriage Forms* was likely to attract considerable attention.

"This growing industrial center is a rich field for social research", she explained condescendingly. "We are about to open a university settlement in connection with my department out in the steel works".

"Ah!"

There was an ironic tone to the young man's explanation: they did not consider the new science of "sociology" highly where he came from . . . By this time they had abandoned the stuffy anteroom and were standing on the entrance steps to "Founder's Hall", a little to one side of the throng of incoming students.

"It's all so queer", the young man confessed with a puzzled expression on his rather delicate, fair, face.

"Why so?" Miss Stowe demanded roundly. "It's new, of course—what did you expect? I find the newness stimulating".

(Along with "temporary" and "contact", Clavercin placed "stimulus" on his private index of words that must never be used.)

Miss Stowe's asperity indicated a suspicion that the young man, fresh from the old puritan tradition, was tainted with dilettantism, popularly supposed to be the secret vice of Harvard. She herself being more robustly nurtured did not find the bustle of the raw campus displeasing.[73]

Universities tend to be rather traditional institutions, being slow to change. As a new institution, the University of Chicago was relatively free from the constraints of older American academic tradition and was able to set out in a new direction. Once established, it held to this direction, so that when our story begins the main features of the university remained substantially the same. Harper died of cancer at the age of forty-nine. His successor, Judson, was still in office in the early 1920s, together with a number of foundation professors including the next president, Ernest Burton, and Albion Small in sociology. Above all, the value placed on graduate training, research, publication, academic leadership nationally and internationally, and excellence remained strong tenets of the university, allied to a continuing interest and involvement in the city. This involvement included some efforts at reform-oriented social research, opening a path that others could later follow. The flowering of the social sciences at the University of Chicago in the 1920s has to be understood as emerging from this background and history, as well as from the disciplinary and interdisciplinary climate of the time.

3 The Establishment of the Social Sciences

Chicago sociology developed slowly after the university opened in 1892, as part of the gradual institutionalization of the social sciences. Though it finally flowered under Thomas and Park after 1915, its roots were deeper, nourished by the invigorating scholarly climate in which it matured and the influence of currents of thought from other disciplines. Intellectual and personal ties also knit together a number of early members of the social science staff, as a result either of participation in Chautauqua, senior professors bringing younger protegés (such as Veblen and Mead), or family friendship (particularly strong among the philosophers.[1]) The intense intellectual community that Harper created was important for sociology in its formative years at the end of the nineteenth and beginning of the twentieth century.

Philosophy produced the first "school" at the university, John Dewey's pragmatism. Writing in 1903, William James paid tribute to what had been achieved in a remarkably short time.

> Chicago University has during the past six months given birth to the fruits of ten years of gestation under John Dewey. The result is wonderful—a *real school* and *real thought*. Important thought, too! Did you ever hear of such a city or such a University? Here [at Harvard] we have thought, but no school. At Yale a school but no thought. Chicago has both.[2]

The nucleus of pragmatist philosophers formed in the 1890s was not only influential in the first fertile decade under Dewey, but over the following quarter-century until the philosophy department was torn asunder by Robert Hutchins's attempts to reconstruct it in 1930.[3] Though John Dewey only spent ten years at Chicago, between 1894, when he came as head professor of philosophy from Michigan, and 1904, when he left for Columbia after a disagreement with Harper over his Laboratory Schools, his colleagues remained.[4] Mead came with him in 1894 from Michigan, being preceded by James Hayden Tufts. James Rowland Angell, who headed the department of psychology from 1904 to 1920, originally came to Dewey's department in 1895, the year in which Park's close friend Edward Scribner Ames received the Ph.D. Addison Webster Moore came in 1894 from Cornell to study with Dewey.[5] The influence of the Chicago school of pragmatist philosophy extended over a generation of Chicago social science, setting the tone and providing a general orientation to scientific inquiry. Mead, Tufts, Ames, and Moore were all still active in the university during the 1920s,[6] Tufts acting as vice-president of the university from 1923 to 1925, a particularly crucial period in the expansion of social science research. Sociologists in recent years have been interested in the impact at Chicago of George Herbert Mead,[7] but the importance of the Chicago school of pragmatist philosophy as a whole is considerably wider, particularly for its influence upon the history of empirical research.

The central orienting idea of Chicago pragmatism was that of activity, which was seen as having biological, psychological, and ethical dimensions. It linked to functional ideas of organic process, most explicit in Angell's psychology. The activity was undertaken by a conscious agent who had feelings and emotions. And the activity had a purpose or object toward which movement was directed. The three elements, moreover, were interconnected. Biological process was not merely mechanical, the agent was a human being, not just the bearer of ideas, and ends were provisional and subject to change in the light of circumstances.

The resulting world view had several important features. The biological foundations of human purpose were emphasized, as was the derivation of intelligence from these biological needs. Hence the importance of the study of psychology as part of philosophy. This influence can be traced, for instance, in W. I. Thomas's famous classification of motives—the "four wishes"—which attributed no cognitive content to any of the wishes. Then, activity entailed actions. The philosopher was concerned with a process of change that affects people and objects. Thus several of the leading philosophers, such as Tufts and Mead, were active in social reform movements discussed in the previous chapter. The social location of action was emphasized, above all in Mead's work. Consciousness was not self-generating but the outcome of social processes in which a number of individuals interacted. Ends were seen as relative to the circumstances in which action was undertaken. Goals were not fixed.[8]

Pragmatism involved rejection of the dualism between mind and matter, subject and object, knowledge and things known. Dewey had been influenced while a graduate student at Johns Hopkins by Hegelianism, in which the dualism between object and subject disappears, and subject and object become a single identity in a dynamic process. Man's thought about the social world is a form of disguised self-knowledge. But if Hegelian idealism provided the justification for a radical break with other schools of philosophy, its influence was transformed as Dewey's thought developed, particularly as he became more interested in modern science.[9]

At Johns Hopkins, Dewey was taught psychology by Stanley Hall, from whom he learnt about scientific method and the rigors of experimentalism. Never tempted to become an experimental psychologist, he was nevertheless strongly influenced.[10] Dewey's textbook *Psychology* was published in 1887.[11] His aim in it was to mediate between physiology and philosophy, and in doing so he laid the foundations for social psychology. The Hegelian doctrine of the individual reproducing universal consciousness helped to rid him of the assumption that man has a "ready-made mind set over against a physical world as an object" and helped convince him "that the only possible psychology, as distinct from a biological account of behavior, is a social psychology."[12]

The aim remained to clarify the nature of activity. The instrumental view of truth developed by Dewey saw a close parallelism between judgments of truth in science and such judgments about ideas and beliefs.

> The "instrumental" view of truth taught so successfully at Chicago [is] the view that truth in our ideas means the power to "work" . . . Messrs. Dewey, Schiller, and their allies in reaching this general conception of all truth, have only followed the example of geologists, biologists, and philologists.[13]

This linkage between the development of pragmatism and the development of natural science was important in stimulating practical activity, including empirical social inquiry.

These ideas found expression in Dewey's educational work, particularly in his "laboratory schools." Dewey was head of what in 1902 became the university's School of Education, in which he had set up in 1896 an elementary school as a pedagogical laboratory where the theories being developed in the philosophy department could be applied to learning.[14] Dewey (as well as Mead and Tufts, who were also involved) saw education as education for democracy, in which the potential of the individual should be realized to the fullest. The "laboratory school" gave the research orientation of the university a meaning in tune with the "instrumental" philosophy being advocated. A philosophy of action must be an active philosophy. The attitudes and habits of men and women were profoundly influenced in youth by education, so the effort devoted to education was justified as part of the philosophical movement.[15]

The instrumental pragmatism of the Chicago school of philosophy was influential upon the other social sciences at Chicago, even if not totally dominant. Possibly the most direct influence, though still the subject of controversy, was the role played by George Herbert Mead, who was greatly influenced by Dewey, in the graduate teaching of the sociology department. The origins of symbolic interactionism are to be found in Mead's teaching, and for many years he became "*the* social psychologist for sociologists."[16]

The impact of philosophy was also mediated through the psychology department under Angell. This was the department in which Ellsworth Faris, who took the place of W. I. Thomas in the sociology department when the latter left Chicago in 1918, gained his Ph.D. in 1914 under Dewey, Mead, and Angell.[17] Faris's later attacks on instinct theory reflected Dewey's critique of the innate possession of human capacities. In 1917, for example, Dewey insisted in an article in the *Psychological Review* upon a distinction between the physiological and cultural levels of human existence.[18]

W. I. Thomas drew his ideas from various sources, one of which was Dewey. He once described Dewey as the "medicine man" of modern America,[19] though elsewhere he claimed to have influenced Dewey more than Dewey influenced him.[20] This claim is doubtful, for the traces of Dewey's influence upon him are quite strong. In particular, Thomas's conception of a process of social organization, then disorganization, then reorganization has a very clear parallel in Dewey's (prior) conception of the frustration of impulse, the coming into play of imagination, and the reorganization of conduct following the disorganization consequent on frustration.[21]

Pragmatism's influence should not be exaggerated. In economics and political science, other strands from statistics and experimental psychology counterbalanced the influence of philosophy. In sociology it had little direct influence upon Albion Small or Charles Henderson. Nevertheless, there was a distinct and detectable influence, even upon Robert Park. The pragmatist philosopher Edward Scribner Ames taught divinity students and was pastor of the Hyde Park Church of the Disciples of Christ, where he put into practice his liberal religious ideas. Ames was also a close personal friend of Robert Park, who attended his church and even taught Sunday School for a while. Park often entertained members of the divinity school at his home. The combined influence of philosophy and sociology upon the teaching of divinity at Chicago was considerable. As a former student of William James, Park was sympathetic to Ames's philosophical outlook.[22]

At a general level, the influence of Chicago philosophy helped to develop an approach to social inquiry that marked a distinct break with the more abstract system-building characteristic of a previous generation. It encouraged the direct empirical study of society through firsthand inquiry. In contrast to the more bookish types of scholarship at the older universities, pragmatism fostered an interest in empirical investigation. In economics, for example, Dewey's influence was greatest upon Wesley Mitchell the institutionalist, whose career at Columbia was devoted to improving the tools of economic measurement.[23] The power of the philosophy of instrumentalism carried through several decades of social science work at the university. It was summed up in the 1930 festschrift to Tufts, Mead, Moore, and Ames. All the contributors, from a range of disciplines, were

> in some sense or other empiricists, keen upon the use of hypotheses and experimental verification . . . Axioms, postulates, rational deductions, ideas, and ideals are all deemed valuable when they can be made to function in actual experience, in the course of which they meet with constant modification and improvement . . . All display the attitude of enquirers rather than of expositors of absolute knowledge; their most confident affirmations are expressed in a tone that shows that they do not regard them as final.[24]

Pragmatism at Chicago was early recognized to constitute a school of philosophy. The same was not true of sociology or political science, whose schools only developed a generation later. The foundations for the school of sociology were laid at the earlier period, but in the form of necessary institutional conditions rather than high intellectual achievement. Harper's policy in appointing foundation professors was to seek outstanding scholars rather than fitting individuals to departmental specifications.

University presidents at this period had considerable power in making appointments and determining where new appointees should be located. This permitted organizational innovation of a type that hardening disciplinary boundaries in later years made increasingly difficult. When his approaches to Herbert Baxter Adams and Richard T. Ely at Johns Hopkins seemed unlikely to succeed,[25] Harper sounded out Albion W. Small, president of Colby College, a small Baptist institution in Maine. Small's response to Harper was to suggest that he create a new department of sociology:

> The academic work which I would do for the rest of my life, if perfectly free to select for myself, would be to organize such a department of sociology as does not exist to my knowledge.[26]

To this suggestion Harper was receptive. As president of a new university he had considerable power to create a new department if it seemed appropriate to do so. His concern with fundamental research and advanced training, combined with a desire that the new university should be socially useful, resulted in the appointment of Small as head professor of social science in 1892 at the age of thirty-eight. The other appointments to the department, made by Harper rather than by Small, reflected Harper's policy of shaping departmental activities to fit the individuals he had chosen. Keen that anthropology should be represented, he hired Frederick Starr, head of ethnology at the American Museum of Natural History and a Chautauqua associate. He joined Small's department, which became a joint one.

As a specialist in charity administration, Harper recruited Charles Henderson (1848–1915), a Baptist minister who had been active in social reform in the 1870s and 1880s. Henderson was keen to continue the ministry, and so combined the university chaplaincy with teaching and research. Finally, Harper had appointed Alice Freeman Palmer, former president of Wellesley College, as professor of history and dean of women students. Palmer insisted that her friend Marion Talbot be appointed assistant dean of women, but also secured her appointment as a teacher of home economics. Harper agreed, and Miss Talbot continued to teach "sanitary science" within the department of sociology until a separate department of household administration was set up in 1904.[27]

When the university opened, then, the department of social science and anthropology had four members, only one of whom, Albion Small, was committed to developing the field of sociology as an academic discipline. In some respects Small was an unlikely figure to establish the world's first department of sociology. Born in Maine in 1854 and brought up in the Puritan family of a Baptist minister, he seemed set to follow his father. As an undergraduate at Colby from 1872 to 1876, he studied Greek, Latin, mathematics, and moral philosophy. He then went to Newton Theological Seminary in Massachusetts, graduating as a Baptist minister in 1879. But he did not want to become a minister, one of the many liberal Protestants who moved from divinity to sociology at this period. In 1879, Small decided to go to Germany to study his other great interest, the social sciences, at the universities of Berlin and Leipzig. While in Germany, he married Valeria von Massow, the daughter of a Prussian general, and was influenced particularly by the social economists Adolph Wagner and Gustav Schmoller, founders of the Verein für Socialpolitik. From them he acquired an ethical view of social science embodying a promise of scientific social reform, which he was to retain to the end of his life.[28]

Returning to Colby in 1881, he taught history and political economy. A light teaching load, because his subjects were new and regarded with suspicion by older colleagues, permitted him time for extensive reading of history, political economy, and sociology. When in 1889 Small was appointed head of the college, he replaced a course in moral philosophy traditionally taught by the president with a new course in sociology and wrote and privately printed a small textbook for it, *Introduction to a Science of Society* because nothing suitable existed.[29] Small's year of graduate study at Johns Hopkins in 1888–89 was a seminal influence. He gained his Ph.D. in constitutional history on the beginnings of American nationality, but acquired also a favorable impression of the new pattern of advanced graduate work that Harper was seeking to foster.

Albion Small remained head of the Department of Sociology at the University of Chicago from 1892 until his retirement in 1924 at the age of seventy. In those thirty-two years he laid the foundations of the achievement of the department in the 1920s and established its national preeminence to a quite remarkable extent. How this preeminence was achieved may be accounted for by several factors. One was the result of a suggestion made to Small by President Harper in 1895. The University of Chicago Press had been established as part of the university at the outset. When the magazine *University Extension World* folded in 1895 Harper called in Small and suggested the establishment of a sociological journal, to be published by the press with the funds available.[30] The first issue of the *American Journal of Sociology (AJS)* appeared in the same year with Small as founder, editor, and major contributor. The location of *AJS* at Chicago was a means of exercising considerable influence over American sociology. No other sociological journal was founded until the setting up of *Sociology and Social Research* in 1921 and *Social Forces* in 1922.

Small's influence was not confined to editing the journal. He was an extremely able and energetic administrator, both within the university and in the growing sociological profession. He became dean of liberal arts at the university at an early date and was dean of the Graduate School from 1904 to 1924. He helped to found the American Sociological Society (ASS) in 1905 and took an extremely active part in running the organization. He also edited most of the papers published by the society in its early years. This connection between the ASS and Chicago, which continued during the 1920s, was one factor in its influence upon sociology nationally. Another administrative task of importance that Small undertook was as organizer and vice-president of the Saint Louis Congress of Arts and Sciences in 1904. He spent much of the previous year travelling in Europe to bring leading European social scientists to the event, among them Max Weber and Gustav von Ratzenhofer. Small's ability as an administrator and organizer thus helped to put Chicago into the position of leading department.[31]

Albion Small's own intellectual contributions to the development of sociology were less striking. These were not negligible, but "Small's own accomplishments as a sociologist are much less significant than his accomplishment as the creator of an institutional setting and atmosphere in which other scholars could investigate and teach."[32] He devoted considerable effort to defining the scope of sociology, and the textbook he wrote with George Vincent was an attempt to map out the field for teaching purposes.[33] Small believed that sociology was a science, that it was changing from a discursive to an objective discipline grounded in empirical study, and that it was a cumulative discipline with a nomothetic, theoretical character.[34] He was markedly sympathetic to empirical research, once remarking that the observation of children in the schoolyard was more valuable for sociology than the study of medieval town and borough charters.

At the same time, sociology was also an ethical discipline and the social scientist had a distinctive role to play in the improvement of society. His expertise and commitment enabled him to be involved in social reform without espousing the position of any class or interest group. Scientism and moralism were integrally connected. A consequence of this view was that though sociology framed causal explanations, these were not wholly mechanistic and deterministic. There was some place for human volition and will in social action. Small also considered that sociology was a holistic discipline, not seeking to study particular subfields, but taking a synoptic view of social processes and providing a general integrated account of the structure of society. He also favored interdisciplinary work,[35] an influence felt in the 1920s.

Small's own work did not include empirical research. By contrast, Charles Henderson taught and wrote on charity organization, labor problems, and social insurance, and "dependent, defective, and delinquent classes" and was involved in many local organizations and commissions. He took an empirical approach to social problems, but one grounded in a deep religious faith. He once wrote that "to assist us in the difficult task of adjustment to new situations God has providentially wrought for us the social sciences and placed them at our disposal."[36] His younger more secular students found this moralism distasteful. Nevertheless, Henderson was important in strengthening links between the university and the city in the field of social welfare and fostering curiosity about urban life among younger scholars such as W. I. Thomas and Ernest Burgess.[37]

Charles Zueblin, whom Harper appointed to the staff in 1894 and who stayed until 1907, taught mainly in the University Extension Department. His main interests lay in municipal reform, on which he was a very popular lecturer but he can hardly be called a sociologist. Nevertheless, his interest in contemporary urban problems was, like Henderson's to pave the way for the research orientation that later characterized the department.[38]

In addition to Small and Henderson, George E. Vincent and William I. Thomas, the third and fourth students to gain the Ph.D. in sociology (both in 1896), were rapidly added to the teaching staff, making up, with Small and Henderson, the Big Four of the early years of the department.[39] Vincent, the son of the founder and president of Chautauqua, taught in the department from 1896 and co-authored with Small an important early textbook *An Introduction to the Study of Society*. He moved progressively into academic administration, leaving Chicago to become president of the University of Minnesota in 1911.[40] In 1917 he became president of the Rockefeller Foundation, in which role he reappears in this story at a later stage.

William Isaac Thomas (1863–1947), the son of a minister from Virginia, had studied literature and classics at the University of Tennessee and was the first Ph.D. to graduate there in 1886.[41] He started to teach natural history and Greek, but in 1888–89 spent a year in Germany where he studied folk psychology and ethnology and decisively changed his intellectual orientation. He returned to teach English at Oberlin College, where he became interested in sociology through reading Herbert Spencer. In 1893, at the age of thirty, he enrolled to do graduate work at the University of Chicago. From 1895 to 1918 he taught there full-time in the Department of Sociology and Anthropology, becoming a full professor in 1910. He was also the first member of the sociology department to receive a large grant from outside sources for research.

Among the early members of the department, Thomas was the most outstanding scholar with the most fertile mind. If Small encouraged empirical research from above, Thomas led the movement on the ground, combining theory and research in his work in a way altogether unusual at the time. As Janowitz observes, he "epitomized the basic intellectual outlook of the Chicago school."[42] Thomas began work at Chicago as an ethnographer.[43] The "folk psychology" of Moritz Lazarus and Heymann Steinthal, which he had studied in Germany, was a major influence. He was impressed by their objective and meticulously scientific methods of gathering comparative data on the peasant societies of preindustrial Europe and on nonliterate societies. His dissertation "On a difference of the metabolism of the sexes" led to work on social aspects of sexual behavior and the publication in 1907 of *Sex and Society: Studies in the Social Psychology of Sex*,[44] which, although based on a speculative evolutionary scheme, was a break with customary biological determinist explanations of human behavior. His contribution, one historian of science has written, "was a new definition of attitude that cut to the heart of the matter more incisively than any previous formulation: attitude as a simultaneous mobilization of the cognitive and emotional faculties."[45]

Thomas's interest in race problems was apparent in a number of articles he published from 1904 onward, and in this field, too, he did much to separate sociology from crude biological ideas about race differences. His *Source Book for Social Origins* (1909) was a collection of ethnological materials, concerned even at this time with sociological explanations and the need to fuse theory and empirical materials.[46] Thomas's ideas changed considerably over time,[47] but he was one of the outstanding figures in the establishment of sociology as a discipline permitting the autonomous study of social influences upon human differences, free from biological or genetic assumptions.[48]

In 1908 Thomas began a major research program, with external funding, to study the European peasant in his own country and in the United States. This study was the first landmark in the history of the Chicago school. The outcome, Thomas's great work of empirical sociology (with Florian Znaniecki), *The Polish Peasant in Europe and America* was a classic monograph.[49]

Thomas did not share the social reform orientation of Charles Henderson. His approach was characteristically more detached and scientific, seeking to develop theories to explain different forms of social organization and different kinds of social personality. Thomas eschewed moralism and prescription and analyzed the most morally heated questions—such as sexual behavior and prostitution—in a quite dispassionate manner, seeking to understand behavior anthropologically rather than to judge it or change it. Robert Park in later years described Thomas as having the interests of a poet or literary man rather than a politician or practical man.[50] Thomas did have social reform interests, particularly in the position of women, but these did not obtrude in his scholarly work.[51]

W. I. Thomas was the most productive and original scholar in the department in its first two decades. Moreover, it was he who first met Robert Park and who was instrumental in persuading Park to accept, in 1913 at the age of forty-nine, a one-semester appointment at Chicago as professorial lecturer, which Park continued to hold until his appointment as a full professor in 1922. He retired in 1934. A graduate of the University of Michigan, where he had studied with John Dewey, Park had originally spent ten years as a newspaperman before returning to study with William James at Harvard. From Harvard he went to Germany, where he completed the Ph.D. Returning to America, he joined forces for a period with the Congo Reform Association, before working for seven years as Booker T. Washington's secretary. It was at a conference at Tuskegee that Thomas and Park first met in 1912.[52] Despite being paid to teach only one or two quarters of the year, from 1913 onward Park preferred to spend most of his time in Chicago and worked on a number of projects during his early years in the city, including the Carnegie "Americanization" studies and advising Charles Johnson on his research for the Chicago Commission on Race Relations. He also began to teach graduate seminars and to supervise graduate students. The partnership between Thomas and Park only lasted until 1918, when Thomas was dismissed from the university, but it marked the beginning of the great period of the Chicago achievement.[53]

Graduate work in the department during the early period also developed, though in no sense was it an integrated program. Between 1895 and 1915, thirty-six Ph.D.'s were awarded, to students drawn from a wide variety of backgrounds. The department was the first department offering graduate instruction in sociology in the world. In developing an indigenous American model of graduate study, the Germanic influence was very strong, exposing young scholars to an alternative to the American college.[54] In sociology, all the leading figures before 1915 except Vincent had spent a period of advanced work in Germany, though in addition Small, Thomas, and Vincent had American Ph.D.'s. Small studied at Berlin and Leipzig in 1879–81, Thomas at Gottingen and Berlin in 1888–89, Zueblin at Leipzig in 1889, Henderson at Leipzig (where he took the Ph.D.) in the later 1890s, and Park at Berlin, Strassburg, and Heidelberg (where he took the Ph.D.) between 1899 and 1903.[55] George Herbert Mead studied at Leipzig and Berlin in 1888–91. Few of them had studied any sociology, for it scarcely existed as a separate academic subject in Germany. Small had studied political economy, Thomas ethnology and the folk psychology, Zueblin had studied divinity (as a result of Harper's influence while at Yale), while Park's main work was in philosophy with Windelband, though he attended lectures by Georg Simmel in Berlin. In the case of Small, Park, and Thomas (and possibly Mead, though there is no evidence of whether he personally studied with Wundt in Leipzig), this experience was important for their subsequent intellectual development.[56] One important consequence of this experience, particularly for Small, Thomas, and Park, was the openness to European scholarship which it engendered. The Chicago school was characterized by an awareness of European social thought and social inquiry.

Another kind of openness was the absence of rigid boundaries between disciplines. Thomas, for example, drew variously from the work of the anthropologist Franz Boas, the physiologist Jacques Loeb, the psychologist Adolf Meyer, as well as from Lazarus, Steinthal, and the psychologist William Wundt. Albion Small, believing that the task of sociology was to synthesize the findings of the "special" social and natural sciences, placed great importance on having graduate students take courses in philosophy, psychology, history, political science, political economy, divinity, and household administration.

In two fields, sociology had close links which, though progressively more attenuated, were very important in influencing the Chicago outlook. Both owed a good deal to Charles Henderson; after his death in 1915 they withered rapidly. The divinity school in Chicago placed considerable emphasis upon the sociological interpretation of the Bible on account of the presence of Shailer Mathews, a former colleague of Small at Colby College, whom Small had originally planned to bring to the sociology department. As well as Mathews himself, Small, Henderson, and Zueblin were all clergymen; Vincent's father was a Methodist bishop and Thomas's a minister. While the divinity school acquired a sociological orientation, the sociology department in these early years had a marked Christian inclination. This was reflected in collaboration between the two departments in graduate teaching and in the creation of a section within the divinity school to teach "ecclesiastical sociology."[57] Many of the early graduate students in sociology were from clerical backgrounds or had themselves begun to study divinity. Some, like Thomas, moved sharply in a secular direction, but the residue from liberal Protestantism was an important formative influence.

It was also apparent in the links between sociology and social welfare. Over time, the relation between the two moved from an initial quite close connection to coolness and distance. This was partly a matter of intellectual maturation and the emergence of sociology as an independent discipline distinct from a concern with social improvement and reform. In this process, W. I. Thomas played a key role, although Albion Small also contributed. It was partly a matter of appointments to the department. Social welfare administration was taught in the sociology department by Charles Henderson until his death in 1915, by Marion Talbot until 1904, by Graham Taylor (who held a part-time professorial lectureship from 1902 to 1906), by Clarence Rainwater (from 1913 to 1916), and by Edith Abbott (who held a part-time appointment from 1913 to 1920). Whereas Henderson and Zueblin were reform-oriented, Robert Park was not. And it was partly a matter of the institutionalization of the teaching of social welfare. The main efforts in the early period were concentrated in Graham Taylor's independent School of Civics and Philanthropy. In 1920 this was brought into the university and renamed the School of Social Service Administration by Sophonisba P. Breckinridge and Edith Abbott, as an independent department quite separate from sociology.[58] This was then the arrangement which members of both departments preferred. Nevertheless, there was a certain legacy, specifically through the influence of Henderson and Zueblin, on Ernest Burgess, who gained his Ph.D. in 1913, and more generally through the urban research that was fostered. A sense of intimacy with the city was created. Even Thomas, whose early interests were in comparative ethnography in the manner of Sumner, was brought into contact with Chicago life. The coming of Park, with his great curiosity about urban life, fitted perfectly into this setting and gave it a more genuinely sociological accent than Henderson and others had given it.

During the 1920s, with Edward Sapir and Robert Redfield, anthropology was an important cross-fertilizing influence. The department remained a joint department of sociology and anthropology until 1929. Before 1923, however, the main anthropological contribution was provided by W. I. Thomas. This was despite the presence of Frederick Starr as a professor of anthropology. Starr was one of Harper's least successful appointments. Apparently chosen because he had been registrar of Chautauqua, he was poorly qualified in his subject. Though a popular lecturer, Starr was absent for long periods on field trips, took little interest in university affairs, and made more impact through his public pronouncements on issues of the day. Only when Starr retired in 1923, and Fay Cooper-Cole was appointed to replace him, did the anthropologists in the department begin to make a significant contribution.[59]

Interdisciplinary contact was encouraged by the small size of the teaching staff in each department and by the requirement that graduate students take courses outside their own discipline. The climate of study and research was one in which boundaries between disciplines were much more fluid and open than subsequently. The position of sociology at the University of Chicago around 1915 has to be seen in the context of its neighboring disciplines. Of these, philosophy, psychology, and economics were the leading departments with the strongest national reputations. Political science and anthropology were not yet established in academic strength or great reputation.

Philosophy has already been discussed. Under James Angell, psychology became firmly established as an empirical subject using experimental methods. Influenced by James and Dewey, Angell developed a functionalist theory of psychological processes and mind-body relationships. One of its main elements was the status accorded to the study of reflective consciousness as well as physiological states. Angell built a strong department, encouraging and supporting younger members. Among his graduate students were several of the new generation of scientific psychologists, notably John B. Watson the behaviorist, L. L. Thurstone, Walter van Dyke Bingham, and Beardsley Ruml, who reappears later in the book. Angell left Chicago to head the Carnegie Corporation in 1920 and shortly thereafter became president of Yale. In his autobiography, Angell paid tribute to the fertile interdisciplinary atmosphere in which he worked throughout his years in Chicago, including the influence of Small and Thomas in sociology.[60]

J. Laurence Laughlin, head of the department of political economy, was an extreme conservative, a dogmatic theorist, and a vigorous controversialist.[61] Until his retirement in 1916, however, Laughlin made Chicago a leading center of economic heterodoxy, for, like Angell, he genuinely respected the independence of his colleagues. At this period, there was nothing like a Chicago "school" of economics, rather the growth of a strong but diverse department.[62] Laughlin's most famous pupil was Thorstein Veblen, whom he brought to the university, promoted, and protected for as long as he could despite their radical difference of outlook. Another was Wesley Mitchell. Contacts between the sociology and political economy departments were less than in some other cases but were marked by controversy, particularly over intellectual jurisdiction in the teaching of statistics.[63]

Political science, like anthropology, bore the burden of uninspiring leadership. It was headed from the beginning by Harry Pratt Judson, who previously taught history at the University of Minnesota. Judson succeeded Harper as president of the university in 1906, but retained the headship of the department. This was disastrous. Judson was narrow-minded and restrictive and for the first twenty years of the century the department languished, with only three members, Judson, Freund, and Merriam.[64] The latter two had close and intimate contacts with the city. Ernst Freund, a German Jew, trained at Berlin and Heidelberg, taught jurisprudence and public law and played a major part in the establishment of the university's Law School in 1902. Believing that the state must intervene in the economy to protect the social welfare of citizens, he studied the actual processes of law enforcement and legislative drafting. He became the major legal expert on Chicago reform.[65] Manuel C. Elmer, who completed a Ph.D. in sociology in 1914 on social surveys of urban communities,[66] recalled that his most encouraging staff contact in the university was with Freund, who had close contacts with Hull-House and was more approving of Elmer's interests than his teachers in the sociology department.[67]

In the period before 1920, Charles Merriam's main energies were directed outside the university toward politics in the city. Only with the assumption of the chairmanship on Judson's death in 1923 did he begin to play a major role in the academic affairs of the social sciences and to strengthen the position of his department. Judson's impact was mainly negative, as in his dismissal of W. I. Thomas and the near-loss of Merriam to Columbia. However, his inadequacy as departmental head does show, by way of contrast, what Laughlin, Angell, and Small were able to achieve by effective departmental direction.

In sociology, Small's administrative and organizational abilities, the influences of Henderson and Thomas, together with the openness and flexibility of the graduate teaching program, paved the way for the achievements of the later years. The preeminence of the Department of Sociology at the University of Chicago within the discipline in America was already established in 1915. By then, Chicago was not the sole graduate department in the country. Other centers, however, such as Yale under Sumner, Wisconsin under E. A. Ross, and Michigan with Charles Cooley, were lesser centers. Only Columbia University under Franklin Giddings rivaled Chicago as a center of graduate teaching, particularly in the first decade and a half of the century.[68] By 1915 its influence was waning.

In the period 1895–1915 as many as 98 Ph.D.'s were awarded in sociology. Thirty-six were awarded by the University of Chicago; 24 by Columbia; 10 by Yale; 13 by Pennsylvania; 8 by New York University; 6 by Wisconsin; 1 by Michigan; and 1 by Ohio State.[69] Thus in 1915, Chicago was clearly the foremost graduate teaching department in the country, though the Columbia Department headed by Giddings ran it a close second.

While Chicago's quality and productivity after 1915 rose under Thomas and Park and then under Park and Burgess, Columbia's declined. In his later years before retirement in 1928, Giddings's influence on sociology at Columbia was mainly negative. The official history of the Columbia department records that

> Giddings did not succeed in building up a department that could compare either with that at the University of Chicago or with the other social science departments within the Columbia Faculty of Political Science. Until his retirement, he remained the only full professor whose primary field was academic sociology. Northcott reports that he "was a markedly dominating personality and very dogmatic in his views." Many of his colleagues in other departments resented what they considered to be his dogmatism, and resisted any efforts to increase the influence of sociology at Columbia.[70]

Even so, the Chicago sociology department in 1915 was rather small in size, uneven in quality, and not an enormously impressive intellectual enterprise. The contents of the *American Journal of Sociology* included a good deal of popular writing and work of mediocre academic worth. There were few distinguished research monographs. The Chicago department in the year of Henderson's death consisted of Small, W. I. Thomas, Scott Bedford (who taught urban sociology), Edith Abbott (part-time), and Robert Park (part-time). Despite Chicago's lead in the production of Ph.D.'s, it was by no means obvious at that date that Chicago would make a lasting contribution to sociology. Chicago's advantage lay in the institutional conditions created by Small, particularly before 1914, for the flowering of sociology, which took place under the influence of Thomas and Park. The institutional framework was erected before there was much content to put into it.[71]

The pace of growth after 1915 and the department's rise to total preeminence over Columbia by 1930 can be shown from two sets of data. Between 1900 and 1915, the department produced 24 Ph.D.'s, while between 1916 and 1930 it produced 59. The comparable figures for the M.A. were 53 and 101 degrees. In each quinquennium except one between 1900 and 1930 there was an increase in the number of Ph.D.'s awarded, from 7 in 1901–5 to 28 in 1926–30. A similar secular increase is observable in the number of M.A.'s awarded between 1900 and 1930, from 10 in 1901–5 to 46 in 1926–30.[72]

Quantity alone is no guarantee of excellence, but there is supporting evidence on quality. Of the first 40 presidents of the ASS, no less than 19 were either former graduate students or current or former staff of the University of Chicago, and in some cases two of these.[73] Up to 1923, only 3 out of 13 presidents of the society were associated with the University of Chicago. Between 1924 and 1950, 16 out of 27 presidents were Ph.D.'s or staff of the university (see table 2). This indicates the rise to eminence of the university in the post-1915 period, although it took some time for this to be reflected in elections to the presidency.

The only rival to Chicago was Columbia. Table 3 shows that 7 out of 30 presidents of the ASS between 1921 and 1950 were connected with Columbia University, all but one of them (MacIver) having been students of Giddings. A comparison of tables 2 and 3 also clearly shows that Columbia's challenge to Chicago was waning. Whereas in the first decade of the century Columbia was producing more future presidents, between 1912 and 1933 Columbia produced no Ph.D.'s who became president of the ASS, whereas Chicago produced 8.

In sociology, the period between 1915 and 1930 saw the height of the Chicago achievement. The influence of Chicago sociology declined considerably during the middle and late 1930s, a phenomenon considered further in the final chapter. The heyday of the Chicago school was between 1915 and 1930. The relative standing of different departments at

TABLE 2
Presidents of the American Sociological Society (1924–50)
Connected with the University of Chicago

Year	President
1924	Charles A. Ellwood, University of Missouri (Ph.D., Chicago, 1899)
1925	*Robert E. Park, University of Chicago* (staff, 1913-34)
1927	*William I. Thomas, New York* (Ph.D., Chicago, 1896)
1929	*William F. Ogburn, University of Chicago* (staff, 1927–51)
1931	Emory S. Bogardus, University of Southern California (Ph.D., Chicago, 1911)
1932	L. L. Bernard, Washington University (Ph.D., Chicago, 1910)
1933	E. B. Reuter, University of Iowa (Ph.D., Chicago, 1919)
1934	*Ernest W. Burgess, University of Chicago* (Ph.D., 1913)
1937	*Ellsworth Faris, University of Chicago* (Ph.D. in psychology, Chicago, 1914)
1939	*Edwin H. Sutherland, University of Indiana* (Ph.D., Chicago, 1913; staff 1930–35)
1941	Stuart A. Queen, Washington University (Ph.D., Chicago, 1919)
1942	Dwight Sanderson, Cornell University (Ph.D., Chicago, 1921)
1944	Kimball Young, Queens (graduate work at Chicago, 1917–19)
1947	*Louis Wirth, University of Chicago* (Ph.D., Chicago, 1926)
1948	E. Franklin Frazier, Howard University (Ph.D., Chicago, 1931)
1950	Leonard S. Cottrell, Jr., Cornell University (Ph.D., Chicago, 1933)

SOURCE: Compiled from H. W. Odum, *American Sociology* (New York: Longmans, 1951), pp. 7–9, and R. E. L. Faris, *Chicago Sociology 1920–1932* (Chicago: University of Chicago Press, 1970), pp. 135–40.
NOTE: Those in italics were past or present staff of the University of Chicago.

TABLE 3
Presidents of the American Sociological Society (1922–50)
Connected with Columbia University

Year	President
1922	James P. Lichtenberger, University of Pennsylvania (Ph.D., Columbia, 1909)
1926	John L. Gillin, University of Wisconsin (Ph.D., Columbia, 1906)
1929	*William F. Ogburn, University of Chicago* (Ph.D., Columbia, 1912; staff, 1919–27; staff at University of Chicago, 1927–51)
1930	Howard W. Odum, University of North Carolina (Ph.D., Columbia, 1910)
1935	F. Stuart Chapin, University of Minnesota (Ph.D., Columbia, 1911)
1938	Frank H. Hankins, Smith College (Ph.D., Columbia, 1908)
1940	*Robert M. MacIver, Columbia University* (staff)

SOURCE: H. W. Odum, *American Sociology* (New York: Longmans, 1951), pp. 7–9 and 122–97 *passim*.
NOTE: Those in italics were past or present staff of Columbia University.

Chicago also changed over time. The star of political science rose under Merriam's direction after 1923, aided also by the academic conservatism of Columbia. A national survey in 1925 ranked Chicago second after Harvard in the subject, recognizing its reputation for research and productivity of Ph.D.'s.[74] The department of political economy, after Laughlin's retirement in 1916, entered a fallow period. Although Jacob Viner joined the department in 1916 and Frank Knight in 1924, it was not until the late 1920s and the early 1930s, under Knight and Henry Simons, that the foundations of the modern Chicago school began to be laid.[75]

The Chicago school of sociology did not emerge out of the air. It arose in a particular intellectual and institutional context, where the academic developments of the preceding quarter of a century created the necessary conditions for W. I. Thomas, Robert Park, and Ernest Burgess to provide the intellectual content between 1915 and 1930. Despite an interest in the city, few notable empirical monographs had appeared. Indeed, this was true generally of American sociology. All the more remarkable, then, was the transformation that Thomas, Park, and Burgess were able to achieve.

4 *The Polish Peasant in Europe and America:* A Landmark of Empirical Sociology

The beginnings of the Chicago school are usually identified with the urban research of Robert Park and Ernest Burgess and their students, which began around 1920. The influence of W. I. Thomas, however, was of great significance, particularly through his massive study with Florian Znaniecki, *The Polish Peasant in Europe and America*,[1] published between 1918 and 1920. The significance of the publication of *The Polish Peasant* can hardly be exaggerated. Though it has been something of a neglected classic in the literature, referred to far more often than it has been read, it is a classic nevertheless. It was not the first American sociological monograph, but it was a landmark because it attempted to integrate theory and data in a way no American study had done before. It had, moreover, a major impact upon future developments. It is "the first great classic in American empirical sociology,"[2] "one of the half dozen most influential books in the history of social psychology."[3] Edward Shils has compared W. I. Thomas with his other great contemporaries, "Durkheim, Weber, and Pareto, in whose class he surely belongs."[4]

The Polish Peasant marked a shift in sociology away from abstract theory and library research toward a more intimate acquaintance with the empirical world, studied nevertheless in terms of a theoretical frame. Of the Big Four of the sociology department, it was only Thomas who became wholeheartedly committed to empirical research. At first, Thomas worked from documentary sources and did not do firsthand research. But in the first decade of the century his orientation changed, and as he later recalled:

> I explored the city. This last was also a matter of curiosity. I remember that Professor Henderson of sainted memory, once requested me to get him a bit of information from the saloons. He said that he himself had never entered a saloon or tasted beer.[5]

From the time of his earlier work on *Social Origins*,[6] Thomas had stressed the necessity of having concrete, objective detailed studies of social behavior and attitudes. The common element in the Chicago school of sociology, commitment to empirical research,[7] owed an enormous amount to the example set by Thomas.

The Polish Peasant had a triple importance as an empirical monograph. By using personal documents, it employed novel methods of empirical research and suggested directions in which empirical sociology could develop distinct from historical and comparative methods in the manner of Sumner or the social survey movement. By blending theory and data, it provided a basis for generalization and the forward movement both of sociology and social psychology. And by focusing upon the immigrant as the subject of study, it helped to strengthen sociology as an autonomous academic discipline. The subject became institutionalized in America in separate departments in part because no other social science dealt with the problems created by immigration.[8]

Thomas's interest in European immigration developed in the context described in the previous chapter. The reform orientation, the interest in the city, the concern in the sociology department with social problems, all had their effect on him, as did outside influences such as Upton Sinclair's muckraking novel about East European immigrants in the Chicago stockyards, *The Jungle*.[9] Thomas's approach, however, was detached, unemotional, and scientific,[10] marked by penetrating curiosity and the desire to understand human behavior rather than moral fervor and the desire to change society. In his theory of social disorganization, for example, Thomas attempted to interpret deviance from social norms or rules as culturally patterned behavior, not an adaptation to strain, in contrast to Durkheim's theory of anomie. This theoretical statement was an attempt to give a more scholarly form to concerns that had infused the beginnings of sociology in America and to make the study of social problems more scientific.

The decision to study an immigrant group reflected Thomas's Chicago location:

> Immigration was a burning question. About a million immigrants were coming here annually, and this was mainly the newer immigration, from southern and eastern Europe. The larger groups were Poles, Italians, and Jews. When I became a member of the faculty of Chicago, I gave, among other courses, one on immigration and one on social attitudes, and eventually I decided to study an immigrant group in Europe and America to determine as far as possible what relation their home mores and norms had to their adjustment and maladjustment in America.[11]

Immediately after gaining his Ph.D. in 1896, Thomas had visited Europe, on what he later described as a "sort of vagabonding trip."

> I reached the coronation of the czar the day after it was over, circulated among the peasants of several countries, and visited an exposition in Budapest where there were a lot of peasants. While looking at a group of these, I said to myself: "It would be very interesting to study a European group from which immigration is heavy and then study the representatives of the same group in America and see to what degree and in what respects their behavior in America is related to the habits of their home situation." That was the origin of *The Polish Peasant* but I did not get around to undertaking it until 1908.[12]

Thomas's work on *The Polish Peasant* was pathbreaking in another respect. To carry out the study, he received very substantial outside funding. In 1908 he obtained from Helen Culver, heiress of the Hull of Hull-House (who in all gave the university about one million dollars),[13] the then enormous sum of $50,000 with which to carry out research on immigrant problems.

> I was now in a rather alarming situation. I had made positive representations, I had got a lot of money, I had promised a great (also big) work, and what was I going to do about it? I first of all went over to Europe to locate a suitable group, where good materials were available. The choice was between the Italians, the Jews, and the Poles. The Poles are very repulsive people on the whole, but there had been a movement for "enlightenment" and freedom that had developed many documents and masses of material on the peasant, so I decided to bore in there.[14]

Between 1908 and 1913 Thomas spent a considerable time—about eight months a year—in Europe. The grant from Miss Culver paid for replacement teaching at the university in his absence, a policy Harper had encouraged to allow teachers time for their own research and another innovation for research in sociology. Thomas visited Warsaw, Cracow, and Poznan about six times each, and "travelled extensively among the peasants."[15] He learned enough Polish to make selections of materials and in these five years "accumulated materials equaling in volume the *Encyclopaedia Britannica*" from the three parts of the country.[16] During this time he also employed a Polish research assistant. "After about eight experiments with translators, I found a superior man, with university training, name Kulikowski."[17]

Thomas had plans for an even more ambitious study, most of which did not materialize, although he did later publish some of the comparative materials he had collected on other immigrant groups in *Old World Traits*

Transplanted.[18] In June 1912, for example, Thomas wrote from Berlin to Samuel Harper, son of the president and a Russian specialist at the university, about enlisting his help in a study of Russian peasants. He expected to remain in Berlin until August, then visit Posnan and Cracow for six weeks, then go to Hungary "where I have some work underway" and on to Italy until December or January. He would then travel to Liverpool (where Harper was spending a year) to discuss the Russian research, taking a month to do so if necessary. He would return via Ireland to the United States, where he was due on 1 April.[19] This extensive itinerary was in aid of a projected comparative study of the "mental and social life of the European peasant." Thomas planned to edit a number of "source books"—one each devoted to the Poles, Russians, Magyars, Slovaks, Rumanians, Italians, Irish, and East European Jews. (He was attempting to enlist Harper's assistance with the Russian volume). The aim of the volumes would be to describe the life of each group, to provide the basis for a comparative study of the Negro in America, and "to furnish a body of facts which will be of general service in the interpretation of racial and sociological problems."[20] Thomas's work on the European peasantry was conceived on a large scale. In this, in the funding of the project, and in the time he was able to devote to it, he was the prototype of the modern sociologist with large-scale external support.

In 1913, on his last visit to Warsaw, Thomas called on the Bureau for the Protection of Immigrants, where he met "a very charming and superior man who was in charge,"[21] Florian Znaniecki. This was his introduction to his future collaborator. Florian Znaniecki (1882–1958) was the son of a Polish landed family, a philosopher by training who had studied at Geneva, Zurich, and Paris, where he came under the influence of Henri Bergson. He also spent a brief period in the French Foreign Legion. He published in Polish *The Problem of Values in Philosophy* (1910), *Humanism and Knowledge* (1912), and an annotated translation of Bergson's *Creative Evolution* (1913).[22] Though he had on his return received the Ph.D. degree from the University of Cracow in 1909, Znaniecki was barred for political reasons from holding an appointment at a Polish university, then under Russian control. He therefore took the post as head of the Polish Emigrants' Protective Association.[23]

There is some uncertainty about whether Thomas did or did not invite Znaniecki to come to the United States to work with him.[24] When Thomas met him in 1913

> the function of this bureau, as I appreciated it at least, was to facilitate the emigration of undesirable citizens and to hinder the emigration of the desirable. At any rate the bureau had important records . . . Znaniecki agreed to copy some of his records

> for me, and I left $200 or $300 for that purpose. During this conversation Znaniecki said that he might possibly visit America to promote the publication of translations of certain Polish scientific works and that a learned society was promoting the undertaking, but might not be able to finance the trip completely. I said that if he came to America at any time I would give him as much work as he wanted to do, if that would help any.[25]

In 1914, Znaniecki came to the United States just before war broke out and called on Thomas in Chicago. As he could not return to Poland because of the war, Thomas employed him to work on his project—at first hourly and then on a salary—and a most fruitful collaboration ensued.[26] Their relative contributions to the work over the next four years, which culminated in the publication of *The Polish Peasant* in 1918, is a matter of some controversy. Some consider that Znaniecki was "the junior partner" and that Thomas had formulated the plan of the research and his main ideas before Znaniecki arrived in Chicago.[27] Others point out that although Znaniecki was relatively unschooled in empirical sociology on arriving in Chicago in 1914 and learned the tools of the trade from Thomas, he was well-read in the works of European sociologists and his theoretical knowledge was at least as extensive as that of Thomas.[28] He had also done some research on the sociology of emigration. It is quite clear that to regard Znaniecki as merely Thomas's assistant is incorrect, although Thomas was the more experienced researcher and it was he who provided the strong commitment to empirical inquiry.

Indeed, at the outset, according to Thomas in 1935, Znaniecki "was opposed to the documentation" by means of empirical materials and "did not hesitate to say so. He strongly urged a 'treatise,'"[29] but adapted to Thomas's conception of how the work would be shaped. Once he did so, he took a most active part. Paradoxically, while Thomas and a Polish research assistant had collected all the materials used on the peasant in Poland, Znaniecki collected all the materials on the Poles in America—from the records of Polish-American societies, juvenile court and social work records, and the like. Znaniecki collated the letters of Polish families in America and dealt with Wladek while he was writing his life history. He took a major part in drafting the book. "It would be true that he wrote more than I did, but also true that little stands as he wrote it,"[30] as Thomas revised, rejected, or rewrote.

Looking back, Thomas thought that "it would be quite impossible to establish who wrote what."[31] The two were true collaborators, for Znaniecki's interest in philosophy and methodology and his intimate knowledge of Polish society complemented Thomas's interest in sociology and social psychology and his detailed knowledge of the Chicago of the day. Moreover, it was Znaniecki who suggested that the authors add the

"Methodological Note." On the other hand, it was Thomas who persuaded Znaniecki to become a sociologist, so that at the time of their collaboration Znaniecki's contribution was more in the spheres of concrete knowledge about Polish society and of general methodology. In the last analysis, Thomas's was the preeminent part, for he pioneered empirical sociological research in a way that Znaniecki by himself would have been unlikely to do.[32] Znaniecki's book *Cultural Reality*, written in Chicago and published in 1919,[33] was primarily philosophical. *The Polish Peasant*, nonetheless, was their joint work, a work greater for being so than had either man produced the work alone.

The Polish Peasant, all 2,232 pages of it, is a work more revered or referred to than read. Its substance was the empirical study of Polish peasant life.

> Our object-matter is one class of a modern society in the whole concrete complexity of its life . . . . The Polish peasant finds himself now in a period of transition from the old forms of social organization that had been in force, with only insignificant changes for many centuries, to a modern form of life. He has preserved enough of the old attitudes to make their sociological reconstruction possible, and he is sufficiently advanced upon the new way to make a study of the development of modern attitudes particularly fruitful.[34]

The scale of Polish migration to the United States was very large. Between 1899 and 1910, Poles accounted for one-quarter of all immigrants to the United States, and they tended to settle in urban areas, particularly in large cities such as Chicago, Pittsburgh, Buffalo, Cleveland, and Detroit. Whereas immigration into America up to 1890 was very largely from northwestern Europe, between 1890 and 1914 immigrants were drawn largely from southern and eastern Europe.[35] At the late peak of immigration in 1907, for instance, 1.28 million people migrated to America, including 338,000 from Austria-Hungary and 258,000 from Russia. Chicago with its 360,000 Poles ranked after Warsaw and Lódz as the third largest Polish center in the world.[36]

There were several reasons for this changed pattern of migration. The replacement of sail by steam meant that as many people could come in one year at the turn of the century as came in one decade fifty years previous. Awareness of the possibility of migration spread slowly, too, as the process of movement was cumulative. There were significant relaxations in several southern and eastern European countries toward the end of the century in the laws relating to migration. Much immigration was due to political, religious, and cultural persecution in Eastern Europe. Anti-Semitism intensified after 1880, and Poles in particular were subject to political persecution. Though bound together by linguistic and cultural ties, Poland did not exist as a political entity between 1789 and 1918. Economic factors, however, were the principal reason for migration from Poland to America at this period. Emigration was not a once-for-all process. As *The Polish Peasant* demonstrated, it was part of wider social changes, and the decision to leave the country for America was only the last of a whole series of moves that Poles were making during this period. Return migration across the Atlantic was, moreover, not insignificant.

The Polish Peasant is a massive work that defies adequate treatment as a whole in a short space. Since excellent summaries and overviews are already available, the discussion here concentrates upon the research methods used to gather empirical data, the work's theoretical significance, and the work's wider impact.[37] It is necessarily selective, highlighting in particular its contribution to research methods. A summary of the substantive concerns and research techniques appears in figure 1.

Thomas's approach involved moving out of the library into the field, but he did not use the firsthand methods of the early social survey or participant observation. His main method of research was to gather what he called "documentary materials." As he wrote in 1912,

> I am especially interested in securing what I have called "undesigned records," that is, letters, data from newspapers, records of court trials, sermons, pamphlets issued by the clergy and by political parties, the records of peasant agricultural societies and any materials reflecting the mental, social, and economic life of the peasant and the Jew.[38]

One factor influencing Thomas to undertake the study originally had been the availability of certain types of document. He first looked at journals of folklore that discussed peasant life, but "they dealt with things such as the coloring of Easter eggs, figures in weaving, hedges, plows, outhouses, magical practices, etc."[39] He then discovered that in 1863 a weekly journal, published in Warsaw, the *Gazeta Swiateczna* had been established for the benefit of Polish peasants, as part of the general movement of enlightenment arising out of resistance to Russian rule. Peasants began to write to the newspaper on all sorts of topics. In 1909–10 Thomas purchased the files of the journal covering the last twenty years, which provided "the most important of all my sources"[40] gathered in Europe for the study. But this was only part of the material he gathered. In all, during eight periods of residence in Poland, Thomas collected about eight thousand documents or items.[41]

Thomas faced familiar methodological problems of gaining the trust and securing the cooperation of those whom he was studying and, more unusually, suffered from the impact of war.

> I was viewed with a great deal of suspicion by prominent Poles, because, while they claimed to be, and were, an oppressed minority, their oppression of the Ruthenians in Austrian Poland was more ferocious than their own oppression in Russian Poland. In this connection, a good many important documents, especially manuscripts, were withheld from me.[42]

The editor of the *Gazeta Swiateczna* refused to let Thomas copy eight thousand letters that the paper had received from Poles in America or to buy one of the only two complete sets of the *Gazeta* from 1863 in existence. After Thomas's last visit, the editor had a change of heart, and Thomas sent his research assistant to collect the material, which he did. At this point in 1914, however, war broke out, and Kulikowski, fleeing the country to avoid conscription, lost all this new material in Vilna.[43] The loss of about one-third of the materials gathered in Poland was a great grief to Thomas, but he treated it philosophically and thought it made little difference to the final result.[44]

The main sources used for the material published verbatim in *The Polish Peasant* were in fact Poles who had come to America. The use of series of letters in the analysis seems to have had a pragmatic origin. Thomas is supposed to have decided to use them when walking one day down the back alley behind his house, he had to leap aside to avoid rubbish being thrown from an upper window. Among the rubbish was a long letter, which he picked up, took home, and discovered was written in Polish by a girl taking a training course in a hospital, to her father discussing family matters. It then occurred to Thomas that such letters could be used as research material.[45] The letters used in the research were obtained by advertising in newspapers in Poland and in America. "We advertised in the Chicago Polish newspapers that we would pay ten cents each for every letter from a family member or friend submitted for us to read, and would return the letter. The idea was mainly to find here and there a big bunch of letters extending over a period of years from the same person, showing changes of attitudes over time. This turned out alright and it seemed we could have got a million letters. These persons brought the letters to Znaniecki in the office."[46] The series of letters were primarily to or from emigrants from Poland to America, drawn from different levels of society and parts of Poland, and representing all sections of peasant life.

The letters were published in family series with relatively little selection.[47] Each of the fifty series of letters had a theoretical introduction, there were numerous theoretical comments in the footnotes, and a two-hundred-page introduction characterizing Polish peasant society. The approach was inductive, and the materials were presented verbatim.

The use of letters as sociological data was original. So, too, was the second type of personal document in *The Polish Peasant*, the life history

Substantive Concern	Research Techniques
I. The organization of the peasant primary group (family and community) and the partial evolution of this system of organization under the influence of industrialization and migration.	By means of private letters (written entirely in the first person and without a view to publication) between immigrants in America and their families in Poland.
Subjects covered include the peasant family, marriage, the class system, the social and economic environment, religious and magical attitudes, and the theoretic and aesthetic interests of the peasant.	There are 762 letters in all, arranged into 50 series by family.
The letters are published more or less verbatim, and the authors make generalizations on the basis of their content.	
II. The life record of an immigrant. The autobiography of Wladek, an immigrant of peasant origins now in an occupation "of the lower city class" in Chicago, who "illustrates the tendency to disorganization of the individual under the conditions involved in a rapid transition from one type of social organization to another."	By means of a life history, a lengthy and detailed account by one individual of his life experience, given verbatim in 312 pages.
The authors claim that the document is representative of the experience of many individuals.	
The authors add interpretive notes.	
III. The strains and tensions within the primary group in Poland and its social and political reorganization on modern rather than traditional lines. Five problems are discussed: (1) leadership, (2) education of the peasants, (3) the press, (4) cooperative organizations, (5) role of the peasant class in the nation.	By means of third-person accounts of Polish life, from the files and archives of Polish newspapers, and from the Bureau for the Protection of Immigrants.
IV. The extent and kinds of social disorganization experienced by the peasant in America—demoralization, economic dependency, break-up of the conjugal relation, crime, etc.	By means of third-person reports from social work agency and court records, and records of Polish-American organizations.
The beginnings of self-help as a community, e.g., the formation of Polish-American organizations.	

Fig. 1. Summary of the substantive concerns and research techniques of *The Polish Peasant in Europe and America.*

of Wladek Wiszniewski. Its use may quite possibly have had a theoretical origin. Dilthey, for instance, thought highly of such material: "Autobiography is the highest and most instructive form in which the understanding of life comes before us."[48] Thomas and Znaniecki were originally in touch with Wladek through their advertisement for letter series. They were able to check the reliability of his account against the evidence in his series of family letters and found no major discrepancies. Although they paid the author to write the life history, from their own observations they thought that ambition, literary interest, and interest in his own life were his main motives in writing it. Thomas and Znaniecki reduced the original by half by summarizing events[49] described there and putting them in brackets in the account. The life history of Wladek occupied 312 pages, was extensively footnoted, and was followed by a short general analysis in which the authors characterized the personality of Wladek and traced its formation in different social settings.

The reliance on personal documents marked out *The Polish Peasant* as a new departure. The subsequent use in sociological research of personal documents, such as life histories, letters, diaries, and other first-person material, may in large measure be traced back to the influence of *The Polish Peasant*.[50] The life history of Wladek was the first systematically collected sociological life history. At the same time, Thomas and Znaniecki emphasized that the underlying aim was scientific generalization. The subjective point of view was being caught as part of a scientific enterprise. The use of personal documents aided the construction of social types. It was claimed, without clear support, that Wladek was a representative case.[51]

In addition to personal documents, Thomas and Znaniecki also used more conventional third-person documents including the Polish newspaper materials already mentioned, records from Polish-American organizations and churches, files of social agencies, and court records. The use made of these records and documents and their analysis was rather different from that made of personal documents. There was much more selection and a more analytical presentation.[52] Though less original, this was one of the earliest systematic uses of newspapers as a source of data.[53]

The contribution that Thomas and Znaniecki made to the development of methods of empirical social research did not extend to face-to-face observation and interviewing. Indeed, Thomas was pointedly critical of the interview, which he felt manipulated the respondent excessively. It was not a neutral instrument, but itself a social process. In 1912 he wrote: "interviews in the main may be treated as a body of error to be used for purposes of comparison in future observation."[54] On the other hand, he conceded that middle-class informants such as social workers, editors, teachers, and doctors could provide reliable information and were interested in doing so.

Such reliance on *Sachverständige* was also characteristic of the early stages of anthropological fieldwork. Informants who had firsthand contact with the subjects of research were used to provide reports on those subjects. Max Weber used such methods in his studies of Prussian agriculture.[55] Thomas did not take the step Park urged his students to take of going out to talk to and observe the subjects at firsthand. Thomas's approach, however, did not rely only upon secondhand reports. He attached such importance to the *Gazeta* materials because they included firsthand written communications from peasants to the newspaper. Indeed, the main methodological innovation of *The Polish Peasant* was in the use of firsthand documentary materials that Thomas and Znaniecki believed could constitute the basis of a generalizing social science.

> We are safe in saying that personal life records, as complete as possible, constitute the perfect type of sociological material, and if social science has to use other materials at all it is only because of the practical difficulty of obtaining at the moment a sufficient number of such records to cover the totality of sociological problems, and of the enormous amount of work demanded for an adequate analysis of all the personal materials necessary to characterize the life of a social group.[56]

This very strong claim was not borne out by subsequent developments, and within two decades the use of such methods had gone into a sharp decline, because of the greater efficiency of observational methods and the rise of the social survey. Nevertheless, at the time the claim was made, *The Polish Peasant* did change the direction of empirical methods of sociological research in the United States and influence some of the methods used by the students of Park and Burgess in the 1920s.

The importance of personal documents lay in the opportunity they provided to study the world from the point of view of the subject and this general methodological influence has been much more enduring. Indeed, for all the recent emphasis on the Meadian "I" and "me" in the history of Chicago sociology, Thomas and Znaniecki were more important antecedents of contemporary versions of social action theory through the example of their empirical research, than was Mead in the seminar room.

One of Thomas's original reasons for choosing the Poles as an immigrant group to study was their behavior in America, which often seemed incomprehensible. They vacillated between two extreme attitudes to authority, either passively accepting it, like peasants accepting their landlord, or behaving as if there were no limits to the boasted American "freedom," for instance, in what the American police called "Polish warfare."[57] Personal documents such as life histories and letters were used to try to understand why immigrants acted in the way they did. This involved studying their objective conditions, their preexisting attitudes, and their "definition of the situation."[58] Social change was to be understood as the product of continual interaction between individual consciousness and objective social reality.[59] Interpreting social behavior necessarily required knowledge of the subjective meaning that individuals attached to their action.[60]

> We must put yourselves in the position of the subject who tries to find his way in the world, and we must remember, first of all, that the environment by which he is influenced and to which he adapts himself is *his* world, not the objective world of science—is nature and society as he sees them, not as the scientist sees them.[61]

Their general methodological ideas were set out in an 86-page "Methodological Note" at the beginning of the book. This was written after the research was completed at the instance of Znaniecki.[62] Though similar in form to Durkheim's *Rules of Sociological Method*, which Znaniecki probably knew from his years studying in France, its content was different and, indeed, seemed designed to refute *The Rules*. Moreover, it bore distinct traces of pragmatism in the centrality given to activity.[63]

To be adequate, social theory must include both "the objective cultural elements of social life" or *social values*, and the subjective characteristics of the members of the social group or *attitudes*. A social value was defined as

> any datum having an empirical content accessible to the members of some social group and a meaning with regard to which it is or may be an object of activity. Thus a foodstuff, an instrument, a coin, a piece of poetry, a university, a myth, a scientific theory, are social values.[64]

An attitude was defined as

> a process of individual consciousness which determines real or possible activity of the individual in the social world. . . . The attitude is thus the individual counterpart of the social value; activity, in whatever form, is the bond between them. . . . By its reference to activity and thereby to the social world the attitude is distinguished from the psychical state."[65]

The authors stressed the combined social and individual components of social behavior, summed up in the principle that "The cause of a value or an attitude is never an attitude or a value alone, but always a combination of an attitude and a value." The authors specifically criticized Durkheim's formula that the cause of a social phenomenon must be sought, not at an individual level, but exclusively in another social phenomenon, for they argued that a fact in social theory must include both an attitude and a value, and "a succession of values alone cannot constitute a fact."[66]

External or objective factors played upon individuals, and through the subjective experiences of these individuals, led to certain forms of activity:

> Activity is the link between attitude and value: Indeed, every manifestation of conscious life . . . can be treated as an attitude, because everyone involves a tendency to action, whether this action is a process of mechanical activity producing physical changes in the material world, or an attempt to influence the attitudes of others by speech and gesture, or a mental activity which does not at the given moment find a social expression.[67]

It was in the relation between objective factors and subjective dispositions that causal explanations were to be sought.

The link between the individual and the social was found partly through their theory of social personality and Thomas's "four wishes." These were the wish for (*a*) new experience, (*b*) security, (*c*) response, and (*d*) recognition. The process by which the "temperamental attitudes" derived from the four wishes were transferred into character attitudes which formed the basis of the individual's social personality was through the interaction between the individual and the group. Such a process involved the individual "defining his situation."[68]

Social psychology was defined as the "science of attitudes," but was extended beyond individual psychology to be "the general science of the subjective side of social culture." Sociology, on the other hand, involved the study of social values, particularly those embodied in rules of behavior:

> The rules of behavior, and the actions viewed as conforming or not conforming with those rules, constitute with regard to their objective significance a certain number of more or less connected and harmonious systems which can be generally called *social institutions*, and the totality of institutions found in a concrete social group constitutes the *social organization* of the group.[69]

Sociology was the theory of social organization. *Social theory* embraced both sociology and social psychology, being concerned with the relationship between the individual and the social from the two different standpoints.

The Chicago school produced very few published statements of methodology in either its more general or more specific senses. The "Methodological Note" stood alone in this respect as a general statement, and its standpoint—particularly the emphasis upon the subjective dimension of social action—had considerable impact in the 1920s.[70] The influence of *The Polish Peasant* as an exemplary work of sociology lay not only in the "Methodological Note," however, for it was programmatic and contained only a set of general sociological orientations rather than a theory. The discussion bore little relation to the substantive analysis that followed.[71] The concept of values drew too heavily on idealism, while the most precisely specified concepts—Thomas's "four wishes"—lacked social anchoring. The authors were correct in saying that "*The Polish Peasant* claims to be, not mere sociography, but at least a fragmentary and tentative contribution to sociology, viewed as an inductive, analytic, classificatory, and nomothetic science,"[72] but this contribution was found in the introductions and footnotes to the empirical analysis rather than in the "Methodological Note."

For *The Polish Peasant* was a major macrosociological study of the interdependence of institutions, in the context of the social changes precipitated by urbanization and industrialization. Far from being mere description, though the data were woefully underanalyzed, a careful institutional analysis was made of the basic units of the primary group, then of the community, and then of certain larger entities such as the press, voluntary associations, and educational institutions. For each institution, the authors sought to define its formal properties. This analysis was linked to the theory of social disorganization. This was seen as originating precisely in the absence of mediating community institutions among Poles in the United States. At the societal level, the analysis of the role of the press was particularly incisive, though politics was entirely neglected and the role of tradition in Poland in explaining differences within the United States was underplayed.[73] This analysis was grounded in empirical materials to such an extent that the theory was understated and often implicit. But it provided a model for the Chicago tradition of research, blending empirical data and generalization as a contribution to theory-building.

The Polish Peasant was also one of the most important methodological contributions to the establishment through empirical research of *the social* as a distinct and legitimate area of inquiry. This was a particularly important point to establish in the study of immigration, where biological theories of ethnic and racial difference had a powerful influence. Thomas and Znaniecki rejected entirely any element of biological reductionism and sought to explain social behavior in terms of sociological and social psychological categories. The concept of "attitude" was the key to this change, which can be followed in the development of Thomas's ideas over time; some of his earliest writings still retained elements of instinct theory.[74] The concept of "attitude" embodied an intellectual revolution, referring to a mental state with no intrinsic physiological content. *The Polish Peasant* made the excision of reductionism stick.[75] In his ideas on race, Thomas was influenced by Franz Boas[76] and was hardly a highly original thinker. The synthesis and reformulation he and Znaniecki provided, however, was a notable step along the road to an autonomous empirical sociology of race and ethnic relations[77] and thereby to the secure establishment of an autonomous discipline.

Publication of the first two volumes of *The Polish Peasant* by the University of Chicago Press in 1918 was a landmark overshadowed for Thomas personally by his almost immediate departure from the university. The great tragedy that struck his career when he was fifty-five was not made public knowledge until Morris Janowitz published an account in 1966.[78] In recent years a good deal of attention has been focussed on cases of academic freedom in the late nineteenth and early twentieth centuries, whenever American university presidents treated political dissidents harshly.[79] Moral lapses were treated even more harshly, and without apparent controversy. Thomas was an outgoing man, enjoying company, good living, and a wide range of acquaintance. The subject-matter of some of his researches, for example, sexual behavior,[80] was daring for the time. Addressing the National American Woman Suffrage Association in Chicago in 1915, Thomas urged the granting of legitimate status to illegitimate children and better efforts for providing information about birth control. He was misquoted in the press,[81] which brought the wrath of President Judson down upon him, through his head of department, Small. Thomas was obliged to apologize in an abject manner.[82] The matter blew over, but it reinforced the view of Thomas as a controversial figure, a view clearly held by some members of the university. In October 1917, for example, Thomas clashed with Professor Shailer Mathews in the Divinity School, who had strenuously criticized Thomas's teaching in his course Social Origins.[83]

Thomas's connection with the University of Chicago ended in April 1918. In that month he was arrested at a Chicago hotel in company with a Mrs. Granger and charged with violation of the Mann Act and with false hotel registration. Mrs. Thomas was active in Henry Ford's peace movement, and it has been suggested that Thomas's arrest was a means of embarrassing and discrediting her. Though the charges were thrown out of court (where Thomas was represented by Clarence Darrow), there was extensive press coverage, partly because Mrs. Granger was the wife of an army officer serving in Europe. President Judson, supported by the trustees, moved directly to dismiss Thomas.[84]

Albion Small reportedly burst into tears upon hearing the news of Thomas's dismissal, but appeared to be convinced that he must depart. Robert Park attempted to defend him, but he then held only a marginal position in the university.[85] Charles Merriam brought Thomas from his home, where he had closeted himself away, to lunch in the faculty club, but it could only be a gesture.[86] There was no protest from the faculty, and at the time right to academic tenure did not exist. The matter might be dealt with in different ways, but universities of the period were wholly intolerant of what they judged moral laxity. Thorstein Veblen's career was blighted by the conflicts he provoked with university administrations through his sexual behavior. The psychologist Mark Baldwin was dismissed from Johns Hopkins in 1908 after being discovered in a Negro brothel.[87] John B. Watson ended his academic career in 1920 by announcing his intention to divorce (on leaving Johns Hopkins, Watson went to stay in New York with Thomas).[88] And in the 1920s, a president of the University of Chicago left office very suddenly for similar reasons. Thomas was thus not alone in his misfortune, for the moral climate of the period was chilly.

His dismissal was nonetheless a cruel and considered blow, which was pushed through with thoroughness. The University of Chicago Press, which had published the first two volumes of *The Polish Peasant*, was ordered by the president to terminate the contract and cease distribution of the volumes published. They and the plates were handed over to the author, who arranged for publication by Richard Badger of Boston.[89] Thomas's name was to be expunged from the university. On assuming the presidency over a decade later, it was suggested to Robert M. Hutchins in late 1929 by Edwin Wilson, president of the SSRC, that Chicago might make amends by reappointing W. I. Thomas. Hutchins replied sympathetically that "I have known and admired the gentleman for many years. I suppose he is still the leading sociologist in the United States."[90] Hutchins pressed the proposal with Harold Swift, chairman of the trustees of the university, who replied that he thought it neither feasible nor desirable to bring Thomas back to the university. "We deliberately chose as to whether we wanted him at the time and I, personally, see no reason to change the judgement."[91] When Hutchins pressed the point again, Swift replied that Thomas, at sixty-seven, was too old and that "the knowledge of his presence would do us more harm than his presence would do good."[92] He also implied that some members of the faculty—naming James Tufts and Shailer Mathews—would be implacably opposed. So there the matter rested, and the wrong was not undone.

Thomas's subsequent career was spent as a freelance research worker. He moved initially to New York, where he worked on the Carnegie Americanization study, then on *The Unadjusted Girl*, and later in the 1920s, with Dorothy Swaine Thomas, on *The Child in America*.[93] He did some teaching at the New School for Social Research and in the 1930s spent one year as a visiting lecturer at Harvard, at Sorokin's invitation. The most productive and fruitful years of his work as a sociologist ended with his departure from Chicago. The institutional base that Chicago provided was more steady than the uncertainties of freelancing and the intellectual milieu more nurturing. After he left Chicago, Thomas's psychological orientation grew stronger and the sociological and anthropological elements in his work weaker, probably because of this loss of an institutional anchor.

Like J. B. Watson, Thomas found research outside the university less productive, though he did not capitulate to commercialism as Watson did. Like Harold Lasswell[94] and Willard Waller,[95] in different ways, Thomas seemed to find less stimulus once he moved away from Chicago, and it is likely that there were particular features of the interdisciplinary atmosphere in the social sciences at Chicago that encouraged scholars like Thomas and Lasswell to produce of their best.

What the Chicago Department of Sociology might have achieved in the 1920s, had Thomas not been dismissed from the university, is one of the fascinating counterfactuals of academic intellectual history. As it was, the influence of Thomas was felt in part through the use of *The Polish Peasant* in teaching and the model it provided of an empirical monograph exemplifying the use of personal documents. The theory of social disorganization developed there was influential in several studies published in the 1920s. Social disorganization was defined as a decrease in the influence of existing social rules of behavior upon a group. The theory sought to explain how, in certain circumstances, social rules lose their effectiveness.[96] Harvey Zorbaugh, for example, wrote in *The Gold Coast and the Slum* that "the best analysis of the community and its control has been given us by W. I. Thomas in *The Polish Peasant* and in *The Unadjusted Girl*."[97] Ernest Mowrer in *Family Disorganization* drew directly upon both Thomas and Znaniecki's theory of social disorganization and their attitude-value distinction.[98] Frederic Thrasher in *The Gang* employed Thomas's concept of the "four wishes."[99] More diffusely, the repertoire of methods used by Park and Burgess's students was considerably influenced by the example of Thomas and Znaniecki. The collection of life histories, for instance, was used for studies such as Nels Anderson's *The Hobo*[100] and Paul G. Cressey's *The Taxi-Dance Hall*.[101]

Their influence was also felt more directly, through the close affinity between Thomas and Robert Park. In 1912, Park was still working as Booker T. Washington's secretary at Tuskegee and had organized the International Conference on the Negro, planned to bring together blacks from the United States, the West Indies, and Africa, in part in response to the Universal Races Conference in London the previous year.[102] W. I. Thomas was one of the invited speakers, and at this conference the two men first met. That a close intellectual relationship sprang up between them is apparent from correspondence between Thomas and Park in the following months. Thomas wrote to Park: "I am amazed to find how ignorant I was before I met you and how wise I seem to be now. Truly it was a great experience to meet you, greater than to meet all the other colored persons present."[103] Park reciprocated. "I found in Thomas, almost for the first time, a man who seemed to speak the same language as myself."[104] They immediately began comparing the situation of the Negro with that of the peasant and making plans for future joint publications and research visits together to the West Indies and possibly Africa. Thomas enthused: "Up to this point, golf has been my main interest, but I think I shall be pleased to work now in our vineyard."[105] They met in New York in June while Thomas was en route to Europe, and he wrote to Park from Berlin in July 1912: "I got a lot out of our visit and confirmed in my alliance with you."[106] Meanwhile, Thomas had raised with Small the possibility of appointing Park to a post teaching at Chicago. Small was very interested. Thomas suggested to Park the possibility of a part-time appointment for two quarters (as he himself currently had), so that they could go into the field together the other six months of the year.[107]

As a result, Park began teaching sociology at Chicago, initially in the fall quarter 1913, the next and subsequent years in the summer quarter, for a stipend of $500. The first course that he taught was "The Negro in America." From 1913 to 1918, Park and Thomas worked side by side in the department, and their collaboration continued after Thomas's dismissal, when he worked with Park on the Americanization studies for the Carnegie Corporation.[108] Later in the 1920s, Park organized a group of Chicago sociologists to nominate Thomas, successfully, for the presidency of the American Sociological Society and thus restore him to professional respectability.[109]

It is clear that Thomas exercised a powerful intellectual influence upon Robert Park and helped to shape his conception of empirical sociology. He helped him develop some of the theoretical insights he had derived from Simmel[110] and gave Park an appreciation of the relationship between sociological ideas and social research. Their five years together in the department coincided with Park's easing himself into the academic role.

When Thomas moved to New York, Park kept in close touch with him and stayed with him or visited when in the city. According to Park, Thomas's apartment smelled of Thomas—his pipe, his dusty books, and endless piles of papers—"as a lion's den smells of the lion."[111] Park was considerably influenced by Thomas in developing his conception of the sociological task, and this tie was not completely broken by Thomas's departure from the university, though contact became less frequent.

In later years, Park paid tribute to that influence. In 1939, he wrote an account in the *Bulletin of the Society for Social Research* of the origins of the society. The short article was in fact mainly a tribute to the influence W. I. Thomas had had on sociological research at Chicago:

> It is in the work of W. I. Thomas, I believe, that the present tradition of research at Chicago was established . . . . In [his] earlier writings . . . we . . . find the first positive expression of a

> point of view which has found a consistent expression in most, if not all, of the subsequent published studies of the students and instructors in sociology at Chicago.[112]

Starting with the *Source Book for Social Origins*, Thomas developed "the disinterested investigation of the origin and function of social institutions,"[113] emancipating sociology from its preoccupations with becoming a science of social reform or social welfare. Thomas helped sociologists to develop "that intellectual interest and natural curiosity which has been so largely responsible for the growth of science in other fields (social anthropology, for instance) which have not been dominated by practical and ethnocentric interests to the same extent that is true of sociology in the United States."[114] Thomas succeeded in imparting this interest and curiosity about human beings, particularly about their intimate thoughts and feelings, to his students.[115] Work like Thrasher's study of the gang or Shaw's life histories of delinquents enlarged our knowledge of the subjective aspects of life in the tradition of Thomas.

> Thomas's interest was always, it seems, that of a poet (although he never, so far as I know, wrote poetry) and of a literary man in the reportorial sense, and not that of a politician or of a practical man. He wanted to see, to know, and to report, disinterestedly and without respect to anyone's policies or program, the world of men and things as he experienced it.[116]

The influence of Thomas carried forward through the work of Park and Burgess by encouraging the empirical study of individual human beings rather than using informants or simply official data. The importance of the actor's "definition of the situation" was highlighted. And the potential for theoretically informed empirical work was classically demonstrated.

5 Sociology, the Social Survey Movement, and *The Negro in Chicago*

The Chicago school was the first sustained and effective group of academic sociologists to pursue an integrated research program in the United States. Giddings and his students at Columbia in the first decade of the century carried out a good deal of research, but they hardly amounted to a school and soon dispersed.[1] The explanation for Chicago's unusual fertility lies, as we have seen, in the particular character of the city and its main university and in the institutional and intellectual influence of Albion Small and W. I. Thomas. The movement toward a more empirical social science was, however, a national one, and it is important to consider the relationship between the style of research developed in the Chicago department and other types of social research current at the time.

Viewed in a larger perspective, developments at Chicago between 1915 and 1930 were part of a trend in the early twentieth century toward more rigorous methods and a more "scientific" self-conception on the part of American social scientists. This was most strongly evident in J. B. Watson's behaviorism in psychology and Wesley Mitchell's quantitative studies of economic behavior, but similar trends were evident in sociology by the end of the 1920s. Various influences have been adduced to explain these changes. One was the example of natural science, particularly biology, and of behaviorist psychology upon the other social sciences. Another was increasing defensiveness about overt ethical and political stances in scholarly work, associated with the decline of Progressive reform movements. In part, the trend to science was an attempt to resolve tensions between small-town and rural values and large-city, metropolitan styles of life, which posed fundamental choices at this period. Generational change was also important; men such as Watson, Mitchell, and in sociology Ernest Burgess were among the first generation of American social scientists to receive their Ph.D.'s in America, not in Germany.[2]

In sociology there was an additional complication. Academic sociology and empirical social inquiry have not been coterminous at any stage in their respective histories, yet the relationship between the two is particularly important in examining the history of social research methods. Prior to 1915, the main examples of empirical social research were to be found outside the university, particularly in the social survey movement. Yet herein lies a paradox.

In Britain, where the social survey originated in the late nineteenth century, there has been a high degree of continuity between the social surveys of Charles Booth and Seebohm Rowntree, the methods of investigation favored by the Webbs, the statistical surveys of A. L. Bowley, the interwar surveys such as the *New Survey of Life and Labour in London* and academic social survey research after World War Two.[3] In the United States there has been both much more marked discontinuity, but also much greater variety in the repertoire of research methods employed in sociology. Not only did the term "social survey" largely change its meaning between the early social survey movement and the later growth of social survey research (particularly under the influence of Paul Lazarsfeld) after 1940. But in between, from about 1915 to 1935–40, academic research in sociology at the University of Chicago relied on methods other than the social survey to gain knowledge about society. A central theme of this work is to try to understand how this discontinuity occurred and why Chicago sociologists developed the methods they did.

In order to do so adequately, the earlier discontinuity, between academic sociology before 1915 and the extraacademic survey movement, deserves attention. Chicago graduates were part of a tradition which was aware of the survey movement but distinguished their work from it. In her influential research methods textbook, *Scientific Social Surveys and Research*, for example, Pauline V. Young made clear that the social survey movement and social research were distinct, tracing the beginnings of the latter to the work of W. I. Thomas. The social survey was concerned primarily with social problems and social planning and even then did not analyze social problems in great depth. Social research was distinguished by its greater scope, its formulation of hypotheses or propositions about social action, and the attempt to formulate theories or laws to explain social phenomena.[4]

The American social survey movement had diverse origins, and contained within it different strands.[5] Its roots go back to the middle of the nineteenth century, when a number of small surveys on the "dangerous classes," orphans, and other groups were carried out. The increasing pace of urbanization and attendant social problems in the later nineteenth century stimulated social inquiry, particularly in association with the settlement house movement. The models for early surveys such as those done at Hull-House in Chicago were undoubtedly Charles Booth's studies of poverty in London.[6] Another contribution came from the muckraking journalism of Jacob Riis and others, very much part of the Progressive tradition. The connections between social reform and the growth of social surveys was even more direct than in Britain. Reform and investigation went hand in hand for the settlement house workers, who often had an exaggerated idea of the influence of statistics, and an idealistic belief that if people were told the truth, reform would follow naturally.[7]

That there was no necessary connection between the method of the survey and moral and political impulses was shown by one of the earliest sociological surveys, that of the black sociologist W. E. B. Du Bois. *The Philadelphia Negro* (1899) was strongly influenced by Booth. Du Bois, who had a Ph.D. in history from Harvard, spent fifteen months in the city, studying the seventh ward particularly intensively. In that ward he made a canvass of every household, covering 9,000 people, using six schedules to collect data on household composition, housing conditions, institutions, servants, occupations and earnings, and literacy. His results were simply summarized and analyzed in tables and charts, including systematic black-white comparisons. Du Bois supplemented this survey data by participating in community life and attending meetings and gatherings in the city during his fieldwork period.[8] His work is a classic descriptive study without a reform orientation, but he had almost no influence on imitators. Du Bois, as a black, was excluded from appointment at a white university and found himself relegated to the periphery of the profession, spending the years 1897 to 1910 at Atlanta University. Even though he singlehandedly initiated serious sociological research on blacks in the United States, his attempts at Atlanta to mount an extensive research program foundered for lack of resources. He organized an annual series of conferences on the condition of urban blacks and succeeded in publishing sixteen monographs between 1898 and 1916 on topics such as black family life, religion, the Negro in business, the Negro artisan, and the health of the black population. Because of the difficulties he labored under, they were of uneven quality. Du Bois had to organize the work in intervals between his teaching and rely on voluntary unpaid, research assistance, mainly by graduates of black colleges whom he kept in touch with by correspondence. He had less than $500 a year available. Proper statistical and clerical assistance was lacking.[9] He appealed in vain for support from many sources, without result. "If Negroes were lost in Africa, money would be available to measure their heads, but $500 a year is hard to raise for Atlanta."[10] This experience contributed to his decision to abandon academic social science and turn to intellectual activism as editor of the NAACP's journal *The Crisis* in 1910.[11]

The most influential work of the social survey movement, with which Chicago graduates were thoroughly familiar, began a decade after Du Bois's fieldwork in Philadelphia, facilitated by outside support from a philanthropic foundation. The Pittsburgh Survey of 1909–14[12] was carried out by Paul U. Kellogg, at the time managing editor of the welfare magazine *Charities and Commons*.[13] The New York Charity Organization Society gave early support, but the main work was made possible by a grant of $47,000 from the newly established Russell Sage Foundation. Kellogg and his team covered industrial conditions—hours and wages, industrial conditions and accidents, public health, sanitation, housing, education, taxation, crime and justice, social welfare, and recreation. Loosely modeled on Booth's survey of London, the study was closer to investigative journalism than social science. Indeed, as in much of the social survey movement, the resemblances to Booth were less striking than the differences. Though Kellogg had taken one course with Giddings during a brief sojourn at Columbia, the limited use made of quantification was descriptive and exploratory, rather than analytic. When published, a civic exhibit was held in Pittsburgh to publicize its findings.

The early social survey was less a specific research methodology than a community movement to investigate local conditions and deal with social problems. It was distinguished by its dual emphasis upon the diagnosis of existing conditions and the organization of constructive programs for social change through local community action. The difference from the more scientific approach of Booth, Rowntree, Du Bois, and A. L. Bowley was very marked. The social survey movement, as it came to be called, flourished, aided by foundation support. In 1912 Russell Sage set up a Department of Surveys and Exhibits with Shelby Harrison as director. This financed many more local social surveys, including the Springfield Survey[14] carried out by Harrison himself. By the beginning of 1928, 154 general surveys and 2,621 surveys in specialized fields had been carried out in the United States.[15]

One sign of sociological interest in social surveys was Manuel C. Elmer's *Social Surveys of Urban Communities*.[16] Elmer, who as an undergraduate had studied biology, chemistry, and mathematics and had an M.A. from the University of Illinois in economics, apparently got the idea for his dissertation subject from attending a summer course at the University of Wisconsin taught by Lester Ward. According to his recollections, Small, Henderson, and Thomas were not very enthusiastic. Small thought he was on the wrong track, while Henderson opined that "to become a sociologist you must have a greater interest in human kindness in your efforts, rather than too much cold analysis." Thomas recommended he turn to business and industrial research. Only Ernst Freund was encouraging. Elmer recalled that "much of my work at Chicago was justifying my point of view."[17]

Interest in social survey work was stronger among academics teaching social welfare and social work than among sociologists. At Columbia, early collaboration between sociologists and the Charity Organization Society from 1894 to 1903 withered under Giddings's skepticism.[18] Most sociologists at this period maintained a considerable distance from community social surveys, though they were aware of them and recommended their students to read the results. Early social surveys found a much more receptive audience in social welfare. Between 1908 and 1920 Edith Abbott and Sophonisba Breckinridge at the Chicago School of Civics and Philanthropy carried out numerous studies of housing, child welfare, juvenile delinquency and other urban problems in Chicago.[19] Though Abbott taught part-time in the sociology department before 1920, after that date the gap between the department and the new Department of Social Service Administration widened. Indeed, the latter much more than the former was the standard bearer of the social survey in its original form. Abbott and Breckinridge conducted a great deal of empirical research into social problems during the 1920s, some of it under the auspices of the Local Community Research Committee (see chap. 8). The teaching of social work was related to the findings of research, and inquiry and advocacy went hand in hand. Though concerned with social conditions, the frame through which they were viewed was much more practical and action-oriented than that of the sociology department under Park and Burgess. Hence the gap between the Social Service Administration and the Department of Sociology was a widening one.[20]

It was not that Albion Small and Robert Park were uninterested in social reform, but that their interest was a rather olympian one. Park was a liberal in the sense that he believed in the natural movement of social events, in which public opinion had a considerable impact. He wished to enhance the efficacy of public opinion through the enlightenment that social science research provided. But this was very different from the orientation of academic social workers, who blurred science and social intervention in their own work. He was particularly disdainful of "do-gooders," partly a carry-over of his skepticism about the muckraking journalism he had encountered in his youth. One student recalled Park telling a seminar that the greatest damage done to the city of Chicago was not the product of corrupt politicians or criminals but of women reformers.[21] Park's personal relations with the Misses Abbott and Breckinridge were distant, and he discouraged students from taking their courses. Ernest Burgess was somewhat closer to them personally, but it does not seem to have brought the two departments closer together.

From the point of view of academic sociology, the social survey movement became something of a deadend. *Middletown* in 1929 had different origins, in the work of Galpin and the land-grant colleges, and was organized by the Institute of Social and Religious Research, which he had influenced intellectually. The development of the modern social survey in the work of Chicago political scientists and later in opinion research fed into sociology after 1940, particularly through the influence of Paul Lazarsfeld at Columbia. To use the same name for the social survey movement and the modern social survey is perhaps rather confusing, because they were so different. Even sociologists interested in quantitative methods at an early date, such as Giddings and his students, sought illumination elsewhere in the work of the English statisticians Pearson, Yule, and Bowley.[22] The effort to turn sociology into a science—whether pursued through general theory or more rigorous empirical research—involved the detached and objective study of society and allowed no room for an ameliorative approach, which involved explicit normative commitments. The new research methods that Thomas and Park developed diverged markedly from the approach of the social survey movement, even though they were well aware of it.

Indeed, both in his teaching and in one piece of research that he supervised Robert Park showed intimate familiarity. Beginning in 1916, Park taught for at least ten years a course on the social survey. In 1918, its syllabus read:

> An examination of current methods of social investigation, the diagnosis of social problems, and the formulation of community programs; the applications and limitations of the survey method; its relationship to statistical and case studies, the devices employed in the presentation and publication of social facts and survey findings; the role of the expert and the "survey committee"; the function of publicity as a means of social reform and social control.[23]

His surviving lecture notes show that Park was primarily concerned with the social survey as a social movement, combining two quite distinct motives, social reform and municipal efficiency. The publicity aspect of the survey was a major focus for Park's attention, interested as he was in public opinion and social control. The survey movement was a movement which

> manifests itself in an increasing disposition exhibited by people who are dealing practically anywhere with social problems. . . . to make them appeal to the public and seek their solution to social problems in an investigation of facts, in place of dogma or doctrine. Coincident with this, and corresponding to it, there has been an increasing distrust of politics.[24]

Surveys existed before the survey movement. The Pittsburgh Survey had added the notion of publicity. "It was publicity that made the survey investigation a means of social control." Park's interest was clearly in the social survey as a social movement, a method of publicity, a means of shaping public opinion. In his essay "The City," published in 1915, Park suggested that the Russell Sage Foundation surveys, the work of the New York Bureau of Municipal Research, and local social surveys across the country were really higher forms of journalism, dealing with existing conditions critically and seeking through the agency of publicity to bring about radical reforms. Their object is to shape public opinion. For "as a source of social control public opinion becomes important in societies founded on secondary relationships, of which great cities are a type." Fashion took the place of custom, and public opinion, rather than the mores, became the dominant form of social control.

> In any attempt to understand the nature of public opinion and its relation to social control, it is important to investigate first of all the agencies and devices which have come into practical use in the effort to control, enlighten, and exploit it.
>
> The first and most important of these is the press. . . . After the newspaper, the bureaus of research which are now springing up in all the large cities are the most interesting and the most promising devices for using publicity as a means of control. The fruits of these investigations do not reach the public directly, but are disseminated through the medium of the press, the pulpit, and other sources of popular enlightenment.[25]

Park was also interested in contrasting the development of the survey in America with earlier social investigations in Europe:

> Something corresponding to the survey there is to be sure in Germany and on the Continent. These are investigations and studies of social conditions, but where they seek to formulate programs they are undertaken by the government and are not addressed primarily, as they are here [in the U.S.] to the public. They are undertaken to inform the administration and not to instruct and inform the public.
>
> It is an interesting and singular thing that what we call a "movement" should connect itself with what is essentially a mere device, a device for investigating and reporting social facts. . . . It is interesting also that the survey, in the form that it has taken in recent years, is peculiar to America—at least, if not peculiar to America gained its greatest popularity here and to a lesser extent in England.[26]

Park directly linked the role of the social survey to pragmatist philosophy, underlining the part that school of philosophy had played in encouraging empirical social inquiry:

> Sociology seeks to analyze, describe, and explain just those social facts upon which we are now seeking more and more to conduct our common life together. It is a science only so far as it has sought to apply to our social life the same scientific methods which other sciences have applied in other fields. Heretofore we have sought to conduct our lives on a basis of

> history. History, however, is always an interpretation from a point of view already established. Every doctrine, every philosophy, every ism has its own historical point of view. It is another and more general fact upon which we are now seeking to base the conduct of our political and social organizations. I might with considerable propriety call this larger movement a sociological movement meaning by that the increasing disposition of men to conduct their common life on a basis of fact rather than doctrine; that is to say the dogmatic teaching of a school of thought.
>
> There has grown up in this same period a school of philosophy which is intimately associated with this movement. This is pragmatism. I can not undertake to interpret pragmatism here or indicate its deeper connections with this movement of which I speak. It again has insisted on the importance of fact as ever against mere speculation defining our larger views of life. It has insisted also that facts are through and through imbued with our own practical interests and points of view; that there are no pure facts. James's point that a distinction which does not make a difference to someone, somewhere is not only not worth making, it is not even a fact. I might call this larger movement, the pragmatic movement. I think I will. In this sense "pragmatic" would mean that a fact is never quite a fact merely because it is investigated and recorded. It only becomes a fact in the fullest sense of the term when it is delivered and delivered to the persons to whom it makes a difference. This is what the survey seeks to do. It seeks to get and deliver the facts; that is, to publish them and publish them in such a way that they get results.[27]

Park touched but lightly on the technical procedures of survey research. Certain questions recurred again and again in the survey. What was the character of the population? Are they foreigners? Are they a laboring population? What are the natural groupings? Who are their leaders? What are their sentiments? What are the lines of cleavage? Construction of the schedules themselves are a matter for the expert.

> Schedules are the forms in which he records the answers to the questions he has formulated in his questionnaire. The questions you can ask are limited by practical considerations. The form in which they are put is determined by exigencies. . . . The schedule grows with knowledge and experience. It uses index-standards; test questions; as the physician takes your temperature, measures your blood pressure, counts your pulse.[28]

Park in his lectures made a distinction between the more scientific, factual type of survey, such as those of Booth and Rowntree and represented by Elmer's text,[29] and the more publicity-oriented survey, represented par excellence by the Pittsburgh Survey and Aronovici's text.[30] He also distinguished between community surveys and surveys of a single topic over a wide area. The latter were more focussed.

> They abstract from the concrete human situation and the whole method of procedure becomes relatively technical. Such investigations are largely statistical, and the devices of presentation are not those of literature and description but of statistics. Maps, charts, graphic representation are used in presentation and interpretation of the findings.[31]

Both Park and Burgess were familiar with the range of surveys carried out and taught their students about them. Those mentioned by Park in his lectures in 1917–20 included the poverty studies of Booth and Rowntree, the Hull-House Papers, and Roberts's *Anthracite Coal Communities*. In 1921 Burgess taught a course on the causes and prevention of poverty, with the syllabus:

> The evolution of attitudes toward poverty; criteria of minimum standards of living; a survey of studies of poverty; an analysis of its causes; programs for the prevention of poverty.[32]

Chicago students in sociology in the 1920s have reported that they were made familiar with the classical poverty studies and other surveys. Writing in 1929, Park explicitly linked the urban studies in Chicago that he and his students had undertaken to a tradition of local surveys, while also making clear the differences. Among the studies referred to were those of Booth and Rowntree, surveys associated with the settlement house movement, the local work of Abbott and Breckenridge, and the Pittsburgh Survey. Park went on to refer to Harrison's *Springfield Survey* (1918–20), the *Survey of Criminal Justice in Cleveland* (1922) and *The Negro in Chicago* (1922). The latter were local case studies, but furnished materials that raised issues and suggested hypotheses that could be further investigated.[33]

The failure of Park and Burgess's students to conduct investigations in the manner of the social survey movement was thus a matter of quite deliberate choice. Its work was known, but the budding science of society should proceed using other research methods. This process of distancing may be traced in the career of Ernest W. Burgess, Park's collaborator in the period between 1916 and 1934. Burgess's influence has been underrated compared to Park, and yet his influence upon the research methods used was greater than Park's. Born in 1886 in Canada, he was brought up in the Middle West. He was a graduate student in sociology at Chicago from 1908 to 1912, gaining his Ph.D. in 1913 on a social-psychological topic related to the interests of W. I. Thomas. In 1912–13 he taught at Toledo University, Ohio; from 1913 to 1915 he was assistant professor of sociology at the University of Kansas; and from 1915 to 1916 assistant professor of sociology at Ohio State University. In 1916 at the age of thirty he was appointed assistant professor of sociology of the University of Chicago (advancing to associate professor in 1921 and full professor in 1927), where he remained until his retirement in 1952.[34] As a student Burgess had taken courses with Henderson on "modern communities," with Zueblin on "municipal sociology," and with Thomas, but his experience of survey work was gained at Kansas. While there,

> I had come in contact with the social survey movement under Shelby Harrison; I had made the recreation study for the Topeka Survey, had co-operated with the Health Department of the university in making a study of Belleville, Kansas, and then made a social survey of Lawrence.[35]

This last, published in 1917, was carried out under the supervision of the head of the Kansas department, F. W. Blackmar,[36] though Burgess provided the main research input.[37] It followed the conventional pattern for surveys of this period. It was a descriptive account, using data gathered with the cooperation of a committee of local notables, under such headings as land and people, city planning, municipal administration, public health and sanitation, housing, and charity. The chapters on delinquency and court cases did, however, show an interest in the potentialities of more rigorous measurement, including counts of the number of delinquent children in the city, their distribution by district, and the calculation of delinquency rates to show variation. The Lawrence Survey, limited though it was, represented an important step in Burgess's experience of research methods, which he later developed at Chicago.

As he arrived in Chicago, Burgess published an article on the social survey in the *American Journal of Sociology*.[38] His conception of the movement was little different from Park's. He said little about technical issues, and only in his remarks on its teaching function did he anticipate the research program he and Park were shortly to instigate. It was a summing-up of his experience in Kansas rather than an outline of what was to follow at Chicago, though he did emphasize its value as research training:

> Society is the laboratory of the sociologist. The social survey provides a unique opportunity both for investigation and for social construction, both for the analysis of mental attitudes and for the control of forces in seeming improvement. To the advanced student the social survey affords severe and stimulating training in the technique of investigation and in the art of social action.[39]

The main emphasis, however, was upon the value of the survey as a means of stimulating community consciousness. "Community self-study under expert direction is democracy being at school to the social scientist. The social survey is to the community what the demonstration station is to the farmer."[40] Once settled in the Chicago department, Burgess moved rapidly away from the social survey to what he came to consider more scientific methods such as firsthand observation, mapping, and the use of census tract statistics. His familiarity with the method, however, was even closer than Park's.

A surviving document in the Burgess papers showed that he and Park at one time, probably in the early 1920s, contemplated a survey of Hyde Park.[41] There is a two-page outline providing for the appointment of an executive secretary, research assistants, and stenographer at a cost of between four and eight thousand dollars for one year. The survey would be overseen by a local committee and after the first year would be a continuing activity. The main concern was to involve local people. The advice of the local clergy and their assistants should be sought. Parent-teacher associations, women's clubs, and men's organizations should be enlisted to discuss local problems and produce relevant facts. Old residents should be interviewed about changes in the community that they were aware of, and what current problems concern them. Consideration should be given to holding what might be called a "grand jury" of competent people meeting in private to air local grievances and matters of community concern. This work would draw upon available maps and statistical data, but was mainly framed with the self-help survey in mind. It did not represent any methodological advance upon what Burgess did in Lawrence, Kansas. In the event, the study was never carried out.

The influence of some elements in the social survey movement may, however, be traced in one notable early piece of research that was carried out, under Park's influence if not his actual supervision, by the black sociologist Charles S. Johnson. This was the massive study of the Chicago race riot of 1919, *The Negro in Chicago*.[42] This, unlike *The Polish Peasant*, was a work of applied, policy-oriented research for a commission of inquiry, which nevertheless was conducted in a scientific, detached manner. It followed none of the models provided by *The Philadelphia Negro*, the Pittsburgh survey or *The Polish Peasant*, but carried strong indications of Park's influence. The methods used blended and complemented each other. As a product of Chicago sociology, the work has been somewhat neglected and deserves closer attention.

The Chicago race riot of 27 July–8 August 1919, in which 38 people died (23 of them black) and 537 were injured (342 of them black), led to the setting up of the Chicago Commission on Race Relations, whose report of 672 pages, *The Negro in Chicago*, appeared in 1922, a large part of it based on original research. Race problems were comparatively new in the city. Detached, objective analysis seemed the way to deal with the issues. In point of fact, the report of 1922, like those of many other later riot commissions, had a negligible political impact. Yet it remains a major landmark in the social scientific study both of race riots and of the condition of the black population in American cities.[43]

The riot had not been unexpected by thoughtful Chicagoans—the City Club under its president George Herbert Mead and the Chicago Urban League under Robert Park had both warned of trouble earlier in 1919. Nevertheless, the loss of life and breakdown of order had been extremely serious. Though martial law was not declared, the South Side had resembled a beleaguered city.[44] The commission was established by the governor of Illinois three weeks after the riot in response to the urging of the powerful Union League Club.[45] Chaired by a white lawyer, six white and six black commissioners examined the course and causes of the riot. Both the reform orientation of its members and the problems of securing finance encouraged the commission to undertake a scholarly rather than a political analysis of race relations in Chicago.[46]

When looking for staff, Robert Park was among those considered, but the eventual choice was to appoint Graham Romeyn Taylor (son of Graham Taylor), a journalist, as executive secretary, and Charles S. Johnson, a twenty-six-year-old black graduate student in sociology, as associate executive secretary. Taylor's main role was to write and edit the report; Johnson, with the advice of Park, was the architect of its research program.[47]

Johnson had been born in Bristol, Virginia, on 24 July 1893, the son of a minister who was an emancipated slave. Johnson read widely as a child and worked his way up through the Virginia school system, graduating in 1917 from Virginia Union University, a private, denominational black college.[48] He then moved to the University of Chicago to begin graduate studies. There he came under the influence of Robert Park.

Johnson later recalled:

> I met Dr. Robert E. Park in my first quarter of study. His course on "Crowd in Public" seemed challenging, and I signed up for it with no prior intimation of his personality as a teacher. It was not long before he was on a basis of easy and stimulating exchange with individual members of the class and I was one of a great many who . . . had an opportunity to follow him to his office . . . as he continued to explore, with insightful clarity, the murky channels of our thinking.
>
> A first personal revelation came when I discovered through one of his excursions that it was possible to identify my own experience and thinking with a large and respectable fund . . . of social knowledge, thus providing some realism for the university experience. A second came when it dawned on me that I was

> being taken seriously and without the usual condescension or oily paternalism of which I had already seen too much. The relation of teacher and student grew into a friendship.[49]

Park was active in the Chicago Urban League, of which he was the first president. In 1917–18 Johnson ran the league's Bureau of Investigations and Records, collating published data and conducting original inquiries.[50] Several of the latter are noteworthy, including housing studies in Chicago and at Park's instigation, a field trip to Mississippi to gather data for Emmett J. Scott's study of black migration during the war.[51] Johnson also collected about 1,200 letters and projected a study (not carried out) on black migration along the lines of *The Polish Peasant*. The league's preference for proceeding on a basis of fact, not on theory and sentiment,[52] recalls Park's famous statement to graduate students predisposed to political reformism for black rights. He told them that the world was full of crusaders and that "their role was to be that of the calm, detached scientist who investigates race relations with the same objectivity and detachment with which the zoologist dissects the potato bug."[53]

The same approach, reflecting the orientation and methods of Park himself and of W. I. Thomas, were evident in the research conducted by Johnson for the commission. A number of research staff were hired to assist Johnson, one quarter of whom were students of Park. Park himself was closely involved in the research, providing advice on its conduct and on the writing-up.[54] This influence is shown most directly in the fact that one-quarter of *The Negro in Chicago* is devoted to two chapters on public opinion—one on the opinions of whites and negroes and the other on instruments of opinion-making (mainly the newspaper). Both topics were central to Park's life experiences and to his sociological work.

It is possible to reconstruct the research methods of the commission from the published report and the minutes of its proceedings.[55] The commission relied in part on a traditional means by which commissions of inquiry gather evidence: talking to and hearing evidence from members of the public, particularly those specially qualified on the subject in hand. In addition, the commission's staff interviewed leadership groups in industry, education, unions, social service agencies, and other walks of life.[56]

The commission also undertook its own original empirical research. Case-study materials were extensively used. *The Negro in Chicago* bears the mark of Park's influence in this respect strongly. Particular effort was put into the investigation of public opinion, much of the material being gathered by Park's university course called "The Crowd and the Public."[57] Personal documents characteristic of *The Polish Peasant* were used in the chapter exploring opinions of whites and negroes about each other. Fifteen whites and seventeen blacks answered detailed questionnaires about their beliefs, attitudes, and backgrounds.[58] The responses were presented in largely unanalyzed form, again in the manner of *The Polish Peasant*. The influence of the subjective orientation and Park's interest in exploring what lay "behind the faces of men" was apparent in the discussion of black attitudes.

> What are Negroes thinking? Few white persons know the intimate reactions of Negroes to problems which they face daily. Yet it is obvious that the conduct of Negroes in practically every phase of life is determined by these very sentiments, which for the white world remain a closed book.[59]

Case materials of a documentary kind were supplemented by direct observation. Park in his autobiographical writings placed considerable emphasis on the amount of time he had spent walking around the city, a habit acquired in his years as a newspaper reporter. This method was used to good effect in the housing part of the inquiry, where direct observation was used to map out the boundaries of areas of black residence and to look at the kinds of housing available to blacks. While Johnson was working on *The Negro in Chicago*, Park went around with him extensively in the Black Belt.[60]

The range of methods employed in the commission's research was broadened in the chapter on the instruments of opinion-making. Blacks pointed to the press as the main source of racial antagonism.[61] The analysis of the press focussed on three white and three black Chicago newspapers. An intensive content analysis was made of the white papers. "A careful study of the three selected white daily papers (the *Tribune*, the *Herald-Examiner*, and the *News*) was made covering 1918, the year preceding the riot, to note relative space, prominence, importance, and type of article on social matters."[62] The analysis of content was then blended with quotation from newspapers of the period, discussion of the events that are reported, and an evaluation of the biases and distortions found in the press in their treatment of blacks.

A repertoire of other methods was also used. The influence of the social survey movement was apparent in two large-scale surveys of the black population. In the field of housing, 274 families living in all parts of the city were interviewed.

> Three negro women, well equipped to deal intelligently and sympathetically with these families, gathered this information. These 274 families lived in 238 blocks, the distribution being such that no type of neighborhood or division of the Negro population was overlooked. The questionnaire employed contained five pages of questions and required an interview of about two hours. Special effort was made to secure purely social information without the aid of leading questions.[63]

The data was partly analyzed by simple frequency distributions, partly by extended quotation as illustrative case studies. The simple statistical analysis, it was noted, "takes away many of [the families'] human qualities. For this reason a selection has been made of various types of negro families in order that a rounded picture of the whole unit may be given."[64] There then followed seventeen detailed family histories of different types of Chicago black family, or different origins and occupations.

In the field of labor, the commission carried out personal interviews with black employees in selected industries—including meat packing, iron and steel, laundries, hotels, railroads, and the needle trades—to complement interviews with employers and the round-table conferences. Though a few details are given, 865 black employees were interviewed by a black investigator either at work or at home. Simple frequency distributions of their replies were given, together with extended quotations from individuals as illustrative case material.

In some respects these surveys were an improvement on those of the social survey movement. The avoidance of leading questions and the use of racially matched interviewers showed awareness of likely methodological pitfalls. The analysis of the data, on the other hand, was almost nonexistent, reflecting the lack of understanding of the potential of such individualized data for the study of interrelationships at the time. By contrast, the value of aggregate data was well appreciated. The commission made extensive use of official and preexisting statistics from administrative records. The 1910 and 1920 census data were used to show the growth in the size of the black population (a major factor in increasing the racial tension that led up to the riot) and its distribution ecologically, shown in a series of maps (highly characteristic of Chicago urban sociology at this period). Census data were also used in chapter 8 on the Negro in industry, together with extensive statistical data gathered from a questionnaire sent to 850 employers in the city. This was carefully analyzed in terms of type of industry, size, and proportion of blacks in the labor force.[65] An attempt was made to discover the extent of black and white trade union membership. Both in this study and in the survey of firms, the commission showed particular concern to achieve an adequate, representative, coverage of the phenomena being studied.

It is of considerable interest that Johnson and Park carried out such extensive inquiries in 1920. *The Negro in Chicago*, like *The Polish Peasant*, has been unjustly neglected in the Meadian and symbolic interactionist reconstruction and distortion of the history of the Chicago school. Looked at in retrospect, the study was imperfect in many ways. The quantitative data was scarcely analyzed, while much of the case-study data was raw and uninterpreted. The two sat uneasily side by side with abrupt transitions from numerical generalization to idiographic description without interpretive commentary. For all that, *The Negro in*

Chicago represented a considerable step forward. In the range of methods it drew upon, it was superior to *The Polish Peasant*. Census data were used (which Thomas and Znaniecki scarcely did), a systematic content analysis of newspapers was undertaken, and two firsthand local surveys were carried out. No attempt was made to set the materials within an explicit theoretical framework, even in the chapters on public opinion, but Park's influence provided one implicitly. Though traces of the influence of the social survey movement can be found, *The Negro in Chicago* was much more a scientific sociological study of a locality. It was a step in the process by which American sociology became emancipated from the early social survey.

The distancing of sociological research at Chicago from social survey work was explicit in Vivien Palmer's text on field studies, published in 1928. Miss Palmer, who worked under Burgess's supervision, distinguished between the social survey movement and the "sociological survey," emphasizing that the latter is not concerned with reform and amelioration, but with "the scientific discovery of how human societies function."[66] Though both social survey and sociological survey focussed on particular communities, the sociological survey did so in order to compare them with other communities and to abstract social processes and patterns. The sociologist was interested in normal as well as pathological phenomena. Unlike the reformers, he was not trying to prove particular points and could make an "unpartisan, unhurried stand that can lead to discoveries of scientific caliber."[67] The social survey provided a snapshot of existing social conditions, while the sociological survey aimed to penetrate beneath the surface to define problems for research and to abstract from the data the patterns of social organization and the processes that had produced these patterns. By comparison, the conventional social survey was a "stagnant backwater."[68] The sociologist should not pattern his work on the social survey, but develop his own type of research to meet his own particular needs.

Palmer's use of the term "sociological survey" was both broader and narrower than that of the earlier social survey movement. It was broader in being more scientific and general in its purpose, narrower in referring to "studies which take as their unit the community, or, in a more exact sense, a natural territorial group, and explore its total life." It was thus a tool of urban sociological study with a particular narrow geographical focus. Social phenomena were spatially located and to be studied as such, not abstracted and analyzed in terms of separate institutional topics such as belief, or power, or stratification, or deviance, as would be the tendency in modern sociological survey research.

Skepticism about the social survey movement was not confined to Park and Burgess. Others with stronger quantitative interests showed little interest. In 1929 William F. Ogburn, who had joined the Chicago sociology department, became director of research for President Hoover's Research Committee on Social Trends. Charles Merriam, of the political science department, was vice-chairman. The committee was charged to carry out a comprehensive survey of the nation's social resources, in accordance with Hoover's technical belief in the virtues of social planning. Though Shelby M. Harrison of the Russell Sage Foundation and a mainstay of the social survey movement was a member of the committee, their report *Recent Social Trends* (1933)[69] bore no trace of the old social survey tradition. It was a measure of the transformation of social science research in little more than a decade. Instead the committee pioneered work on social indicators, which they believed could be compiled in a purely objective manner. All commitment, bias, and indeed any partisanship were excluded rigorously from their study.[70] Merriam himself, of course, had pioneered at Chicago in the 1920s political science surveys of a modern kind, much closer to Lazarsfeld's later work than to Shelby Harrison's. Ogburn and Merriam's conception of social science embraced the definition and measurement of behavior, not the statistical correlation of disease, poverty, and housing conditions typical of the social survey movement and of their colleagues in the Chicago department of Social Service Administration. Waning academic interest in the social survey movement was an indication of the extent to which sociologists and political scientists saw themselves first and foremost as scientists.

The hiatus between the earlier social survey movement and the modern social survey using probability sampling methods (which developed from the late 1930s onward) in the United States was complete. In Britain, where academic sociology was almost nonexistent until after World War II, there was a much greater degree of continuity between the work of Booth and Rowntree, the interwar community self-study movement, and more recent developments.[71] American histories of survey research in some cases fail to refer at all to the social survey movement, so different is it thought to be from its modern namesake.[72] The Chicago department between 1915 and 1930 was very influential in bringing about this caesura. It was less that Park and Burgess underplayed the contribution to be made by the older form of the social survey, but that they and their students developed other methods of research which in practice were used as alternatives. These new methods, it was believed, were superior in use and fitted better with a scientific rather than a reformist approach to social investigation.

1 John D. Rockefeller, Sr., and William Rainey Harper at the decennial celebration of the University in 1901.

2 Albion W. Small

3 The Quadrangles, 1914

4 The east tower of Harper Memorial Library, where Robert E. Park and Ernest W. Burgess shared an office until 1929.

6 Robert E. Park

7 Ernest W. Burgess

5 W. I. Thomas

8 George Herbert Mead

9 Charles E. Merriam

10 Beardsley Ruml

11 The Social Science Research Building at 1126 East Fifty-ninth Street, shortly after its opening in 1929.

12 Harper Memorial Library and the Social Science Research Building, from the Midway.

13 The Harper Memorial Library bridges, looking toward the rear of the Social Science Research Building.

6 The Development of Field Research Methods

The reputation of the Chicago school of sociology rests less upon *The Polish Peasant* or *The Negro in Chicago*, which have been unjustly neglected, than upon a series of monographs published in the 1920s and early 1930s with evocative titles such as *The Hobo, The Gold Coast and the Slum, The Gang, The Taxi-Dance Hall,* and *The Pilgrims of Russian Town*. There is a list of the principal studies on pages 3–4. The research for these monographs was carried out under the supervision of Robert Park and Ernest Burgess during the 1920s. Taken together, they constitute the core contribution made by Chicago sociology between 1918, when Thomas left, and the early 1930s, when Park retired and the character of the department changed. These studies are sometimes characterized as falling within urban sociology. They do indeed share a common focus upon the city, within an overall theoretical framework which Park and Burgess provided in terms of human ecology, social process, and collective behavior. The theoretical framework, however, gave these efforts broader significance. Moreover, the studies made major contributions to other fields of sociology, such as criminology and deviance, the sociology of social problems, the sociology of the family, and the study of revolution. An excellent overview of their significance is provided by Robert Faris.[1]

Park and Burgess's urban studies were conceived within a scientific framework. Their view of sociology "emphasized science and the importance of understanding social problems in terms of the processes and forces that produce them."[2] In this they differed significantly from the earlier Chicago studies at Hull-House, or by Charles Henderson, Edith Abbott, and Sophonisba Breckinridge. Here, the aim was scientific generalization. The intellectual framework was provided initially by Park's article "The City" (1915),[3] followed in 1925 by Burgess's essay "The Growth of the City: An Introduction to a Research Project."[4] This classic paper set out the ecological theory of concentric zones, applied to the city of Chicago. The aim was to describe urban expansion in terms of extension, succession, and concentration; to determine how expansion disturbs the "metabolism" of the city; and to define mobility and measure it quantitatively. Studies by Anderson of the slum, Mowrer of family disorganization, Reckless of vice areas, Shideler of retail business,

Thrasher of gangs, and Zorbaugh of the lower North Side were cited as current sociological research examining the working out of these processes within the city.

Much more than *The Polish Peasant*, these studies involved their authors in firsthand acquaintance with the society around them. How was this accomplished in terms of their actual methods of working? What research methods were used in the monographs supervised by Park and Burgess? These questions are central to accounting for the transformation that Chicago brought about in conceptions of empirical research and in explaining why the Chicago school had such an influence upon the future direction of sociological research. This chapter is therefore concerned with the methods of field research used, which typically involved informal interviewing, observation, the collection of personal documents, and exploitation of other documentary sources. Few of the published studies contain very explicit or adequate statements about the research methods that were used. In part this may be attributed to lack of self-consciousness about research methods in sociology at that time; for example, there were few textbooks on research methodology published before 1930.[5] The statement of the methods used in an empirical monograph was not de rigueur at that time to the extent that it is today. Some archival evidence and scattered published sources permit a partial reconstruction of the methodological development of the Park and Burgess program of research.[6]

The distinctive blend of research methods used by Chicago sociologists in the 1920s—particularly their departure from the social survey movement—is partly explained by Robert Park's background in journalism.[7] Park was considerably influenced by his experiences between 1891 and 1898 as a newspaper reporter. The job of journalist gave him excellent opportunities to see high and low life in the city at first hand. By attending court sessions and investigating social problems for his paper, he gained intimate acquaintance with many features of the urban scene that academics like Chicago sociologist Charles Henderson were remote from, despite their interest in social welfare.

As Park recalled, "I wrote about all sorts of things and became in this way intimately acquainted with many different aspects of city life. I expect that I have actually covered more ground, tramping about in cities in different parts of the world, than any other living man. Out of all this I gained, among other things, a conception of the city, the community, and the region, not as a geographical phenomenon merely but as a kind of social organism."[8] Park stated that his earliest conception of sociology was to be a sort of superreporter, to report a bit more accurately and with more detachment "the big News." By this, he meant the long-term trends of what was actually going on.[9]

In later years, he was quite explicit about this influence:

> it was . . . while I was a city editor and a reporter that I began my sociological studies. . . . In the article I wrote about the city (1915) I leaned rather heavily on the information I had acquired as a reporter regarding the city. Later on, as it fell to my lot to direct the research work of an increasing number of graduate students, I found that my experience as a city editor in directing a reportorial staff had stood me in good stead. Sociology, after all, is concerned with problems in regard to which newspapermen get a good deal of firsthand knowledge. Besides that, sociology deals with just those aspects of social life which ordinarily find their most obvious expression in the news and in historical and human documents generally. One might fairly say that a sociologist is merely a more accurate, responsible, and scientific reporter.[10]

The comparison with the city editor is an illuminating one—pushing, suggesting, inquiring, rewriting, needling, scolding—in order to fulfill the plan of studying the city in all its aspects. This, rather than benign paternalistic guidance, seems to have been his characteristic as a supervisor.[11] One should not, however, exaggerate too much this journalistic influence upon the characteristic research methods of his students. Literature and sociology, in his eyes, were not very far removed from each other. Park also drew on novelists for insights into the urban condition.[12] He drew inspiration as a sociologist from a variety of sources, including his experience of public life as Booker T. Washington's secretary. It is a mistake to treat Park as if he simply derived his methods from his early experiences as a journalist, with the connotations of imprecision and casual and unsystematic inquiry that this carries.

Even before he was a journalist, Park had studied at Michigan with Dewey, who encouraged his intellectual curiosity about the world.[13] Park later returned to academic study. His work with William James, Royce, Santayana, and Munsterberg at Harvard and with Simmel, Windelband, and Knopp in Germany had a most powerful influence upon his methodological ideas. He derived from his philosopher teachers many of his views of the scope of the social sciences. For example, Munsterberg's lectures on the distinctions between history and the natural sciences and James's on human experience emphasized for Park how "the real world was the experience of actual men and women and not abbreviated and shorthand descriptions of it that we call knowledge."[14]

Park's work for Booker T. Washington and early contact with W. I. Thomas had made him familiar with some anthropological writing on race. In 1915, Park quite explicitly suggested that their methods could be used in urban research.

> Urban life and culture are more varied, subtle, and complicated,

> but the fundamental motives are in both instances the same. The same patient methods which anthropologists like Boas and Lowie have expended on the life and manners of the North American Indian might be even more fruitfully employed in the investigation of the customs, beliefs, social practices, and general conceptions of life prevalent in Little Italy on the lower North Side of Chicago, or in recording the more sophisticated folkways of the inhabitants of Greenwich Village.[15]

The influence of Park's German years was evident in his idea of the city as "a social laboratory" or clinic in which human nature and social processes might be conveniently studied. "The city magnifies, spreads out, and advertises human nature in all its various manifestations. It is this that makes the city interesting, even fascinating. It is this, however, that makes it of all places the one in which to discover the secrets of human hearts and to study human nature and society."[16] Another advantage of using the city as a laboratory was the rapid growth of urban institutions, which were open to observation and study. A clear parallel was drawn between the natural scientist in his laboratory at the university and the sociologist at work in his laboratory, the city.

Park had little use for experimentation in an artificial environment. He endorsed as "a particularly happy and accurate description"[17] James's characterization of laboratory psychology as "little more than an elaboration of the obvious." The sociologist had to go out and study people in their natural environment. As Burgess put it:

> There is at least one important difference between the laboratory of the physical scientist and that of the social scientist. In chemistry, physics, and even biology the subjects of study can be brought into the laboratory and studied under controlled conditions. This as yet, except on a small scale as with institutes of child research, is not feasible in the social sciences. The objects of social science research, as persons, groups, and institutions, must be studied if at all in the laboratory of community life.[18]

The idea of the city as a social laboratory was more than mere metaphor. Park's conception of scientific investigation was considerably more systematic than is sometimes implied in the inaccurate epithet "journalistic." In 1922, both he and Burgess were arguing the need to create an infrastructure for social research, providing the sociologist with facilities comparable to that of the natural scientist in his laboratory. In Burgess's judgment, with which Park concurred,

> research work in sociology should be oriented with reference to the utilization of the city of Chicago as a sociological laboratory. This means the collection of material upon the social life of the city; the organization of these materials; and their social analysis.[19]

Perhaps the most distinctive element in Park's methodological orientation was the emphasis he placed on the subjective point of view of the social actor. In this he had been greatly influenced by the teaching of William James at Harvard, particularly by "On a Certain Blindness in Human Beings,"[20] which affected Park profoundly:

> The "blindness" of which James spoke is the blindness each of us is likely to have for the meaning of other people's lives. At any rate, what sociologists most need to know is what goes on behind the faces of men, what it is that makes life for each of us either dull or thrilling. For "if you lose the joy you lose all." But the thing that gives zest to life or makes life dull is, however, as James says, "a personal secret," which has, in every single case, to be discovered. Otherwise we do not know the world in which we actually live.[21]

Park used to quote with approval a remark made by James, that "the most real thing is a thing that is most keenly felt rather than the thing that is most clearly conceived."[22] The formulation gave a new twist to the distinction between acquiring "acquaintance with" as distinct from "knowledge about" the social realm.

This teaching of James's influenced and reinforced Park's methodological ideas, but it also modified them. Park came to see that the detached and cynical observation from outside of the newspaper reporter was not enough. Real understanding also required imaginative participation in the lives of others, empathy as well as an acute eye. A few years later, Park had an opportunity to put his ideas into practice. While working for Washington, he collected material and wrote *The Man Furthest Down* (though it appeared under Washington's authorship), a description of the European peasantry, urban working class, and marginal social groups.[23] His ideas were also reinforced by meetings and collaborating with W. I. Thomas after 1912. The work that they did together for the Carnegie project on Americanization, beginning in 1917, published as *Old World Traits Transplanted*, used personal histories of immigrants to reveal the inner subjective life.[24] While carrying out the Carnegie work, Park lived for several months in Greenwich Village, where Thomas had moved after leaving Chicago. In a later review of *The Polish Peasant*, Park praised life histories as a means of penetrating into the subjective sphere, of mental and imaginative behavior, "which intervenes between stimulus and response [and] makes human behavior fundamentally different from that of the lower animals."[25]

The Negro in Chicago, under Park's influence, placed considerable emphasis on the subjective point of view, a recurring theme in the work of Park and his students in race relations. In his introduction to Johnson's classic study *The Shadow of the Plantation*, written at Fisk after Johnson's years as editor of *Opportunity* in Harlem,[26] Park quoted James again from "On a Certain Blindness" and emphasized its relevance to the methodology of studying "the customs and institutions of isolated and provincial peoples; peoples who, though they live close to, and depend upon us, as we upon them, are still outside the orbit of an ordinary life and understanding."[27] Park illustrated the point by the story of the old lady at the World's Fair, who visited the American Indian village and, in a friendly spirit, asked one of the residents: "How do you like our country?" The commonsense and ethnocentric assumptions of white Americans exposed the extent to which "we are all disposed to assume that other peoples, with other customs, are not quite human in the sense that we feel this is true of ourselves." The aim of sociology was to penetrate behind such exteriors, and to discover what is "behind their faces."[28]

Park's approach in guiding his students' research emphasized methods capable of catching this subjective element in human existence. The use of personal documents coupled with observational methods drawn from journalism and anthropology were designed to lay bare social processes in a way not hitherto achieved by social scientists.

The urban sociological studies for which Chicago sociology became famous owed much to Park's younger colleague, Ernest W. Burgess. On returning to Chicago in 1916, Burgess took over Henderson's course on modern communities and included in it some statistical and mapping materials.[29] Burgess's partnership with Park was of great importance for the development of departmental research. Although he was the junior in years, his interest in empirical research was stronger and more down-to-earth, and he sought actively to relate empirical studies to more general theoretical categories. His substantive interests, embracing social pathology, crime and delinquency, and, later, the sociology of the family, were also rather different from those of Park. Though as the younger man, Burgess was considerably influenced by Park, in the sphere of research methods Burgess was the more involved and original thinker, giving concrete form to Park's general methodological ideas.

Burgess and Park began to share an office in the East Tower of Harper Library and thus started a very close and fruitful collaboration, which continued for as long as Park remained at the University of Chicago. Park, Burgess later recalled, "lived and slept research. I never knew when I would get home for dinner because we would spend whole afternoons discussing both theoretical and practical aspects of sociology and social research."[30] Students recounted how, having gone for a conference with one of the two, they would get drawn into discussion with the other, perhaps because Burgess had passed some work over to Park for him to look at and he became interested. The intense intellectual climate of Chicago sociology in the early 1920s derived from this collaboration.

Its first product developed from an introductory sociology course, which they taught together. The "green bible" of those years, the Park-Burgess text, *Introduction to the Science of Sociology*,[31] emerged out of a series of prolonged conversations in which they argued through outlines for chapters. Then Burgess would try his hand at a first draft. Park would revise the draft, frequently rewriting whole sections, after which Burgess would complete the polishing.[32] Though a very influential general text, its influence on methodology was slight. In the mere sixteen pages on the subject was no reference at all to research strategies or techniques.[33] Only four works on "research methods" were cited in the bibliography, including Durkheim's *Rules*, Thomas and Znaniecki's *Methodological Note*, plus Small's *The Meaning of Social Science* (1910), which hardly qualified as a work on research methods. Their treatment of empirical research, however, was suggestive of a prolegomenon to future development.

The book did, however, emphasize the theoretical purposes underlying social inquiry. Park and Burgess compared the position of sociology in 1921 to that of psychology before the introduction of laboratory methods or medicine before Pasteur and the germ theory of disease.

> Facts have not been collected to check social theories. Social problems have been defined in terms of common sense, and facts have been collected, for the most part, to support this or that doctrine, not to test it. In very few instances have investigations been made disinterestedly, to determine the validity of a hypothesis.[34]

The main instrument Park and Burgess fashioned to stimulate empirical research was their graduate seminar on field studies, given by Park and Burgess from 1918–19 on, every quarter while Park was at the university, with the other teaching it if one was away. The syllabus in 1918 read:

> The mobility, local distribution, and segregation of the population within the urban and suburban areas of the city of Chicago; the cultural differences and relative isolation of different classes, racial, vocational, and local groups; resulting changes in institutions, e.g., the family, the church, etc.; in forms of recreation, uses of leisure time, in the organization and expression of public opinion, and in the traditional forms of social control.[35]

This does not convey the flavor of the course, which was structured to push the students out into the field to do empirical research. After a few introductory sessions, students would be sent out to gather data about some selected topic, conducting interviews, attending meetings, constructing spot maps and other small-scale exercises. This requirement to do empirical research was characteristic of many of the courses taught by Park and Burgess.[36] The underlying purpose, however, was scientific generalization. Park tried to clarify for students what it was they were trying to study. He once spent a seminar discussing for Norman Hayner the logical problems of defining a hotel. The sorts of questions Park asked were:

> What is a gang? What is a public? What is a nationality? What is graft? etc. I did not see how we could have anything like scientific research unless we had a system of classification and a frame of reference into which we could sort out and describe in general terms the things we were attempting to investigate.[37]

Though encouraging a systematic exploration of the social world, Park's interest in it was fundamentally theoretical rather than practical.

Subsequently, data gathered for seminar work formed the basis of term papers and might be suggestive of topics for later dissertation research. This seminar teaching exemplified the Germanic influence upon the developing graduate programs in the social sciences, combining elements of the advanced seminar and of laboratory work. In part it was also a response to the absence of an adequate American literature on urban phenomena.

To some extent this gap was filled by literature.[38] Just as students were encouraged to write their own life histories, so they were encouraged to read novels and autobiographies. Burgess, for example, encouraged his students in the 1920s to read Dreiser and Anderson. At the Summer Institute of the Society for Social Research in 1924, one session was devoted to the sociological use of literary materials. Whether naturalistic writers influenced sociologists to a greater extent is harder to determine.[39] Chicago novelist James T. Farrell studied sociology at the university during the 1920s and was influenced by the experience, though he retained a sense of irony. In one of the Lonigan novels a character studying at the university recounts for fellow students how he went to a brothel and discussed sociology with one of the prostitutes. His friends describe his adventures as a "sociological experiment" and suggest that he put it all down on 3 × 5 index cards as field work for his sociology course. There were marked affinities between journalism, naturalistic writing, and Chicago sociology, but they should not be exaggerated. Just as the work of Park and Burgess's students was not journalism, neither was it mere naturalistic description. The research procedures used resulted in a much more systematic attack on social reality than that of the novelists. Chicago sociologists conceived of themselves as scientists.

The line separating seminar teaching from individual graduate supervision by Park or Burgess was not a sharp one. Park's exceptional qualities as a teacher contributed largely to the success of their program of urban research.[40] Burgess was also an assiduous and careful supervisor, as well as an able manager and organizer of research. Everett Hughes recalled that "he always worked closely with students, whom he always treated as colleagues long before they had finished their work for a degree."[41]

Park devoted extraordinary amounts of time to guiding graduate students under his supervision, so much so that his own writing was neglected as a result. Not only did he spend long hours discussing thesis topics with them, but he took them on tours of exploration or gave them dinner. Norman Hayner, who was studying hotels under his supervision, recorded in his diary for 1922 that on Friday, 6 January, he went on a "tour of exploration" with Park which lasted from 9 A.M. to 5:30 P.M. It included a visit to the Chicago Real Estate Board, where the business manager suggested sources of information on land values, industries, buildings, hotels, and the like. They called at the City Library and consulted the most recently available city director, for 1917. At lunch at the City Club, Park told Hayner how he came to teach sociology. In the afternoon, the tour of the city continued, taking in South State Street, in the course of which Park gave "many interesting suggestions."[42] Such tours were sometimes reflected in the monographs, often by a chapter giving the reader a bird's-eye view of the milieu being studied, whether Cressey's "A Night in a Taxi-Dance Hall" or Zorbaugh's "In the Shadow of the Skyscraper."

Park emphasized the need above all to gather data at first hand.

> You have been told to go grubbing in the library, thereby accumulating a mass of notes and a liberal coating of grime. You have been told to choose problems wherever you can find musty stacks of routine records based on trivial schedules prepared by tired bureaucrats and filled out by reluctant applicants for aid or fussy do-gooders or indifferent clerks. This is called "getting your hands dirty in real research." Those who counsel you are wise and honorable; the reasons they offer are of great value. But one more thing is needful: first-hand observation. Go and sit in the lounges of the luxury hotels and on the doorsteps of the flophouses; sit on the Gold Coast settees and on the slum shakedowns; sit in the Orchestra Hall and in the Star and Garter Burlesk. In short, gentlemen, go get the seat of your pants dirty in real research.[43]

Like Malinowski in anthropology, Park turned social research toward a deeper and closer involvement in the world.

Nels Anderson's study of homeless men illustrated this process. Anderson came to Chicago in 1921 after an unsettled life in the Midwest and was taken on by Small as a graduate student.[44] He began to study the hobo in the field studies seminar. Through the intervention of a Chicago physician, Dr. Ben Reitman, he obtained a modest grant of $300, which enabled him to continue the work for a dissertation project. Burgess was his supervisor but most of his time was spent in the Madison-Halsted Street area, the heart of Chicago's "Hobohemia."[45]

Anderson recalled that the only instruction he ever remembered getting from Park was: "Write down only what you see, hear, and know, like a newspaper reporter."[46] He relied mainly on informal interviewing and reporting what he saw and heard. But the role he played was that of a hobo rather than of a research student. He did not identify himself as a researcher and kept the interviews informal. The term "participant observation" was not in use then, but even if it had been, this was not exactly what Anderson did.

> I did not descend into the pit, assume a role there, and later ascend to brush off the dust. I was in the process of moving out of the hobo world. To use a hobo expression, preparing the book was a way of "getting by," earning a living while the exit was under way. The role was familiar before the research began.[47]

In fact, Anderson felt more self-conscious with his middle-class fellow sociology students at the university than he did among homeless men on Madison Street. Life histories of homeless men were collected, though only brief extracts were included in the final, published version of the research. Living near the "main stem" of Chicago, as one of its habitués, Anderson was able to gather the information sometimes in a single conversation, sometimes in several conversations over a period of weeks. For several life histories, additional information was obtained from social agencies, missions, lodging houses and other sources.

As Anderson proceeded with the project, he began to write the material up. He passed this to Burgess for comment bit by bit, but felt he was getting no guidance. Burgess would ask seemingly innocent questions. It was only later that Anderson realized that the guidance was contained in these questions. When the final report was finished, he delivered it uneasily to Burgess. On returning a few days later to receive Burgess's comments, not only was Burgess very pleased with it, but he had passed it on to Park, who had immediately seen its possibilities for publication and had arranged with the university press to publish it. Park had already started editing the report for publication, and he and Anderson spent several hours going over the detailed editorial changes he suggested. Then Anderson had to do some rewriting, and over the next six days Anderson and Burgess got the manuscript ready for the press.[48] Thus was the first title in the University of Chicago Press Sociological Series, *The Hobo*, brought to publication.

This study illustrates many of the distinguishing features of Chicago sociology. The major empirical studies were carried out by graduate students. The role of Park and/or Burgess as supervisor was of great importance in guiding the conception of the study and suggesting methods of research. The use of informal and unstructured methods of interviewing and observation was characteristic. These were so time-consuming that Anderson had little time for anything else other than attending classes, illustrating another feature of the Chicago department, the extent to which students (and staff) "lived sociology." Some outside financial support was needed—provided in this case through Reitman's intervention by Dr. William Evans, head of the Public Health Department in the city—which paid for Anderson's living expenses while he was doing the research. When the research was written up, Park arranged for its publication. Park wrote a preface for the book, pointing out how the study aimed to see the hobo in the social milieu he had created for himself within the larger community by which he was surrounded, but from which he was in large part an outcast. Anderson had described a distinct and relatively independent local community, one of the Chicago urban worlds, the study of which the department made its hallmark.

Park and Burgess's plan, though it depended on graduate students pursuing individual projects, was rather more than simply two scholars pursuing a series of linked inquiries. From 1923, the creation of the Local Community Research Committee provided grants for the social science departments to pursue research. Park made the case for the creation of a modest infrastructure of support for research. The Department of Sociology was building up its courses mainly on the basis of original materials collected by instructors and students, including field studies by graduate students, case studies of local institutions, and other local studies. Assistance with this and with map-making was required. In addition, an archive of data about the city needed to be created:

> Very valuable data in regard to the city have been collected by various city commissions and private agencies—the telephone companies, the newspapers, and the Chicago Race Commission, etc.—data which has been gathered at very great care and which constitutes a fund of information of great permanent value.[49]

A plan was needed to organize these materials, to create a permanent data bank on the city. A grant was awarded, and in 1924 Vivien Palmer began work as a departmental research officer to collect basic data and advise graduate students on research materials. This formed an important underpinning to many of the individual pieces of research and is discussed further in the next chapter.

No individual study relied on a single method. Even Anderson's study of the hobo, which principally used informal interviews and observation, drew on the case records of social agencies where this was appropriate. A typical study would involve literature searches, the use of historical and current documentary materials, interviews with a wide variety of people, observation of relevant activities, and the collection of personal documents (usually life histories) from the subjects of the research, as well as the use of relevant statistical materials on ecological structure (discussed in chap. 9). A very wide variety of sources of data were tapped.

The archives of the Local Community Research Committee[50] show that during 1923–24, Harvey Zorbaugh began work on his study of the Near North Side, later published as *The Gold Coast and the Slum*. The documentary records he used included books, maps, and documents on file at the Chicago Historical Society; reports by various city departments and social agencies; and case records from various sources. Persons interviewed included old residents, influential people in the area, representatives of civic and social organizations, and people with useful specialized information. In addition, informal contacts were maintained with newspapermen, the night court, the nurses of the free ward of the hospital, and others familiar with the life of the area. He had also carried out block studies, making house-to-house surveys of rents, incomes, rooming houses, and related topics. Four kinds of analysis were being made. A social history of the area and its problems was being written. Graphic methods were being used to show the actual distribution of various types of phenomena by means of spot maps. Case studies were being used to characterize the members of different cultural groups in the area. And statistical analyses were being made of rents, incomes, land values, and population mobility.[51]

In the same period, Frederic Thrasher was beginning his study of the organization and habitat of one thousand boys' gangs in Chicago, one of the most important pioneering sociological studies of gang life. Again, there is little indication in the monograph of how Thrasher's data were gathered, other than a reference to its having taken seven years and acknowledgments of assistance.[52] In 1923–24, Thrasher obtained data from studies of boys' gangs and from various organizations coming into contact with gang members, such as the YMCA, settlement houses, schools, playgrounds, the Juvenile Court, and boys' clubs. He also had interviewed one hundred boys in the Cook County School for Boys, a smaller number in the Parental School, and individuals who were former members of boys' gangs. In addition, he had searched records and local studies in which reference was made to the existence of boys' gangs. The data were being analyzed to develop a classification of gangs and to show the relationship between gangs and their habitats.[53]

This multimethod approach was characteristic of many of the studies done by Park and Burgess's students. Their methods fell into distinct types, including a search of public documents, interviewing of various kinds, participant observation, and the use of personal documents. Only the first did not involve firsthand contact with the subjects of research. Most studies used at least three of these types of data together, without being explicit in the published monograph about how they did so.

A very wide range of documentary sources were used. Published materials could throw considerable light on certain subjects, as in Wirth's thesis on the ghetto or in Landesco's study of the literature on German and Italian racketeers. This was only a start, and the search usually ranged more widely. In his study of vice areas in the city, Walter Reckless consulted in 1923–24 the archives of the Chicago historical society; newspapers and newspaper files; records of the Morals Court, which dealt with vice offenses; and records of social agencies that dealt with vice and prostitution, such as the Committee of Fifteen, the Illinois Vigilance Association, and the Juvenile Protective Association.[54]

The sources typically used may be broadly divided into historical archives; newspaper files, both past and present; records of courts with jurisdiction relevant to the subject of study; records of social agencies dealing with particular groups, such as the hobo, the taxi-dancer, or the prostitute; and records of other organizations with information pertinent to the subject of study, as Norman Hayner's use of materials from the National Bureau for Research for the Study of Hotel Problems.[55] For different studies, documentary sources were of varying value. They were often particularly valuable in studies of crime and deviance.

An excellent example of the latter is provided by John Landesco's "Who's Who" of Chicago criminals in 1929 in *Organized Crime in Chicago*.[56] Landesco started with a content analysis of crime news in Chicago newspapers for a period of one year. From the current news, the names of gang leaders were noted and their gangs traced through newspaper archives for twenty-five years. Names of criminals were taken from the daily police bulletins, the Chicago Crime Commission records yielded 2,600 names from probation records, and the Illinois Association for Criminal Justice provided the names of persons regularly using habeas corpus. From these sources, documentary life histories of the gang leaders were compiled, and their geographical locations mapped. These documentary sources were supplemented by three and a half years' firsthand contacts with gang leaders and members by Landesco, but documentary sources provided the backbone of the card file of seven thousand criminals. From this list, four hundred names were selected for the *Who's Who of Organized Crime*. The criteria used for selection included the regular appearance of a name in the twenty-five years covered by the historical study of newspapers, the importance, prestige, or notoriety of a man in criminal news or criminal history, and the gang affiliations and involvements of particular individuals as judged by incidents such as gang warfare and killings.

These records compiled by Landesco were then checked against the records contained in the Bureau of Identification of the Police Department. Although in many cases this provided valuable additional data, it also showed that there were significant defects in the methods of police record-keeping, showing clearly the limitations of official police records.

Methods of data collection based on interviewing were featured as an important part of many of the Chicago monographs of the 1920s. Such interviews varied from the relatively formal to the informal. An example of the former was provided by Zorbaugh's study of the Near North Side (see schedules in fig. 2 and 3). Some of the interviews were carried out by students taking sociology courses. The schedules show how data were collected on rooming houses and family dwellings in the area and reveal the conceptions of wealthier residents about the area in which they lived.

A distinct role of social research interviewer was slow in emerging. Some studies relied on interviewing middle-class informants in a traditional manner. In others, no very sharp line was drawn between interviewing by the sociologist and by other middle-class professionals. This is confirmed by the frequency with which there are references to interview and life history data being cross-checked with records of social agencies as a matter of course. Paul G. Cressey argued that an interviewer of higher status than the respondent stood in a similar psychological relation to those he was interviewing as the doctor, social worker, personnel manager or reporter in relation to persons they interviewed. He reported a conversation with Clifford Shaw in which Shaw drew an analogy between the sociologist and the doctor. Shaw was quoted as saying that it was often desirable to take notes during an interview with a family. He had used a stenographer for this purpose, justifying her presence to the family by an analogy between sociology and medicine.[57]

A sharp distinction was not drawn between informal conversation and formal interviewing. Vivien Palmer's methods text of 1928 observed that "the interview is only a more specialized attempt to obtain efficiently through conversation the particular data which we want."[58] The kinds of interviewing characteristic of the Chicago department in the 1920s tended to be less formal rather than more formal. Unlike the political science surveys of Charles Merriam and Harold Gosnell, the role of the interviewer as conducting a large-scale, standardized survey was not clearly articulated. Interviewing was part of the case-study method, very much integrated with other objectives such as gathering personal documents.

A. INFORMATION TO BE SECURED CONCERNING EACH BUILDING

Block ____
Schedule No. ____
Investigator ____
Date ____

1. Street & no. ____ Condition of street ____
2. Condition of bldg. ____ Construction (frame, brick, etc.) ____
3. No. of floors ____ No. of apartments ____
   Back tenements ____ Heating ____
4. Name of landlord ____ Nationality of landlord ____
5. Does he live in community? ____ In the city? ____

B. INFORMATION FOR EACH FAMILY RESIDING IN ABOVE BUILDING

6. ____
   Name Nationality of head Nationality of father or head
7. ____
   How long in America In present community In present house Religion
8. ____
   No. of rooms Condition of apt. Telephone No. persons Rent per month
9. ____
   Industry in home Lodges Labor unions Political leaders

10. Family Status and Employment

Members of family & lodgers	Sex	Age	Present or usual employment	Place employed	Weeks unemployed last 12 months because of		Earnings 12 mos.	No. employers in last 12 mos.
					Sickness	Other reasons		
Father ____								
Mother ____								
Children:								
1.								
2.								
3.								
4.								
5.								
6.								
Lodgers:								
1.								
2.								
3.								

11. Other sources of income (specify) ____
12. Total family income last year ____ Surplus or deficit ____
13. How was deficit met? ____
14. Relief, extent ____ Source ____
15. Value of property owned ____ Encumbrance on same ____
16. Other indebtedness ____

(Remarks—over)

Fig. 2. Schedule used to gather data on dwellings in Zorbaugh's Near North Side study. Laura Spelman Rockefeller Memorial, Rockefeller Archive Center, Pocantico Hills, North Tarrytown, New York, Series III, sub 6, Box 70, Folder 749.

ROOMING HOUSE SURVEY

Block__________ Investigator__________
Address__________ Sign in window__________
Keep roomers___ Rooms: No. single ______ Rent single__________
Rooms: No. double__________ Rent double__________
No. light-housekeeping rooms__________ Rent on same__________
No. roomers when house is full__________ No. at present__________
No. single men______ No. single women ______No. married couples__________
No. Roomers accommodated in the course of a year__________
How long has keeper of house been at present address__________
Does she know neighbors__________ (Remarks over)

Fig. 3. Rooming house schedule used in study of the Near North Side. Laura Spelman Rockefeller Memorial, Rockefeller Archive Center, Pocantico Hills, North Tarrytown, New York, Series III, sub 6, Box 70, Folder 749.

The more informal type of interviewing is illustrated by Nels Anderson's experience on Madison Street:

> Wisely or not, I began with informal interviews, sitting with a man on the curb, sitting in the lobby of a hotel or flop house, going with someone for a cup of coffee with doughnut or rolls. I had to develop some system for this interview, as I had to devise some system in writing them down.[59]

An occasional question was in order, if asked casually, especially if promptings of his own about his own experiences were added:

> I discovered that one sitting next to someone else can effectively start conversation by thinking out loud. It invites attention, and one needs but to come out of his reverie, tell of the thought in mind. One must avoid causing those approached to feel that he is after something; the price of a beer, a cup of coffee, or a meal. One must expect to do some spending but must keep at the level of frugal spending.[60]

This detailed account of Anderson's informal interview technique emphasizes what today would be called the "participant observation" methods which he was using. Anderson had never heard the term used at the time.[61]

The blend of informal interviewing and observation mark several of the Chicago studies as pioneering works of participant observation.[62] Thrasher, for example, spent a great deal of time associating with gang members. A hint by Cressey suggests that a covert role was adopted.

Characteristic of all such studies was the ability to enter into different social worlds over an extended period. John Landesco, for example, was apparently adept at establishing relations with members of the criminal world, not an easy thing to do. Like Anderson, Landesco was well suited by his background to undertake studies in his chosen field. Born in Romania in 1890, he had spent his early teens in an immigrant neighborhood on Chicago's West Side. After a variety of work experience, including in an immigrant bank, he enrolled as an undergraduate at the University of Chicago in 1922, graduated in 1924, and was a graduate student (full-time or part-time) until 1929. During 1925–29, he very successfully developed extensive contacts with criminal groups in the city.[63]

> Landesco was a heavyset, outgoing individual, at ease in nearly any social situation. His experience as an immigrant boy on Chicago's West Side and his subsequent wide contacts with immigrant communities in a number of American cities gave him a background that made it possible for him to gain the confidence of the men he wished to study. He could speak their language as well as the language of academia. In short, his intellectual interests and personal traits were admirably suited to the research that he had undertaken.[64]

Anderson, in his study, did not identify himself to his subjects as a researcher. Paul G. Cressey, as well as using four student research assistants, himself adopted a role as covert observer in studying the taxi-dance halls. He contrasted the role of "sociological stranger" with that of "anonymous stranger," in which the sociologist pretended to be a taxi-dance hall habitué, mixing with the patrons on a basis of equality and concealment. Cressey believed that only Anderson and Thrasher had used the same strategy in their research. Its hallmark was identification with the group being studied, engaging in informal interaction in a situation of anonymity, and "exploring aspects of human nature not ordinarily revealed" in normal social intercourse. Cressey emphasized a number of features now recognized to be important aspects of participant observer research. It was necessary to speak the same "language" as those with whom one was interacting. The observer had to guide casual conversation in order to gather relevant data, which then had to be recorded "off-stage" from his performance. In playing a covert role, he invented various fictitious identities for himself, which sometimes posed problems when he met the same person on more than one occasion.[65]

Of the variety of research methods used in Chicago sociology in the 1920s, the personal document was perhaps the most characteristic, following the example provided by *The Polish Peasant*. Graduate students were encouraged to use every opportunity to gather personal documents.[66] Burgess wrote:

> I recall Nels Anderson telling me he was greatly bored by his landlady, in the roominghouse district where he was studying the homeless man, telling him her life history. I told him, "Why, this is valuable, you must get it down on paper." I still have this document; it is most revealing. Who becomes a roominghouse keeper? Who is the star boarder? How do you keep a roominghouse orderly against all the tendencies toward disorder in a roominghouse district? Out of this document you get more insight into how life moves in the roominghouse areas, and especially from the standpoint of the roominghouse keeper, than you do from a mountain of statistics that might be gathered.[67]

Several of the research students working with Burgess made extensive use of life-history materials. Cressey collected life histories of taxi-dance girls and patrons and reproduced extracts from them in his monograph. Anderson compiled life histories of homeless men whom he interviewed. Landesco collected a limited number of life histories of gangsters who were also ex-convicts. After the completion of *Organized Crime in Chicago*, he worked on a full-length life history of Eddie Jackson, the Immune Pickpocket.[68] Hayner collected life histories of permanent hotel residents.

The main criteria, in Burgess's view, for judging the usefulness of a personal document was that it should be revealing,

> that it penetrates beneath the conventional mask each human being wears, and that it freely admits one into the inner recesses of the memories and wishes, fears and hopes, of the other person. This sharing of the innermost feelings and thoughts of another person is what is offered by the secret diary, the intimate autobiography, the personal letter, and the confidential interview.[69]

The echo of William James thirty years before was strong. In his Preface to *The Jack-Roller*, Burgess compared the function of the life history in personality study to that of the microscope in the biological sciences, penetrating beneath the external surface of reality to show the hidden workings of the organism. "Like a microscope [the life history] enables [the student of personality] to see in the large and in detail the total interplay of mental processes and social relationships."[70]

The most assiduous collector of personal documents was Clifford Shaw, who began his research career in the Chicago sociology department in 1925, before moving to the Institute of Juvenile Research. His work, under Burgess's supervision, focused on juvenile delinquency and involved eventually the collection of over two hundred life histories of young offenders.[71]

The studies for which Clifford Shaw is probably best known among sociologists are two life histories which he published in 1930 and 1931, *The Jack-Roller: A Delinquent Boy's Own Story* and *The Natural History of a Delinquent Career*.[72] In *The Jack-Roller*, he presented the story of Stanley, a young male delinquent whose story is told in the first person by himself. Shaw first met Stanley when the boy was sixteen; he interviewed him and on the basis of that compiled a list of the main events in Stanley's life, including arrests, court appearances, and custodial treatment. This he put in chronological order and returned to Stanley, asking him to write "his own story," giving a detailed description of each event, the situation in which it occurred, and his personal reactions to the experience. This was a short document of about 3000 words. After Stanley had spent a period in prison, Shaw continued working with him, pointing out that his first attempt was a good summary of his life but lacked detailed descriptive material.

Shaw suggested that he write a fuller account, and he eventually produced a document of nearly 50,000 words. Shaw, however, took an active part in the process of its production. The main method of securing the document was a lengthy series of interviews, of which a stenographic record was kept, so that the story was recorded in the exact language of the interviewee. However, the subject's story was not taken at face value, but checked against "the usual family history, the medical, psychiatric, and psychological findings, the official record of arrest, offenses, and commitments"[73] and other material throwing light on the personality or career of the young offender. Where discrepancies occurred, the subject was confronted with these and asked to check his recollections.

Shaw's work showed how much progress had been made in standards of research since *The Polish Peasant*. He, unlike Thomas and Znaniecki, was well aware of the problem of representativeness. Shaw went to considerable lengths to verify the information given him.[74] And unlike the life history of Wladek, interpretation was provided. In a lengthy introduction (15,000 words) Shaw discussed the value of such material, the social and cultural background of Stanley's case, and a history of his behavior problems. Shaw justified the use of the life history on scientific as well as practical grounds, suggesting that it provided a source of hypotheses which could then be tested by further case histories and by statistical analysis.[75] Shaw, like Ernest Burgess,[76] saw life history and quantitative methods as complementary. Many aspects of delinquency were not susceptible to formal statistical treatment, though Shaw himself was involved in several studies of that type.

At the end of *The Jack-Roller*, Burgess provided a detailed methodological defense. The life history was more than merely good literary presentation. It was objective data about one person's own story of his career in delinquency. Its validity had, so far as possible, been checked against Stanley's work, court, medical, and other records, which showed that the events to which he referred took place, though he provided his own interpretation of them. It was internally coherent, and its spontaneity and freedom was some guarantee of its reliability. Data about third persons in the life history could not so easily be checked, but Stanley's view of others was important because it was his reaction to the events of his experience which was the focus of interest. The life history was an impressive demonstration of the importance of social (as well as individual) factors in delinquency, in the interplay between a person's environment and that person's own individual personality. Factors in the home and neighborhood, in delinquent and criminal groups outside and especially inside correctional and penal institutions had an influence on Stanley's attitudes and values so powerful as to control, in almost deterministic fashion, his behavior.[77]

Of the methods developed by the Chicago school, the personal document or life history is the least commonly used today, for various reasons.[78] What residue did the Chicago school leave, what impact did the studies have on the subsequent development of sociological research? Their influence was greater in some respects than others. The use of interviewing was an important step in establishing face-to-face contact between sociologist and research subject, but the full implications were not worked out. The use of personal documents declined in part because the modern social survey after 1940 showed to what good effect interviewing could be used. In the 1920s, Chicago sociologists did not move very far toward exploiting it.

The lasting influence of the field research methods of the Chicago school has been threefold. The use of documentary sources of all kinds has been stimulated, for example, by the use of newspapers as a source for the study of certain types of public behavior. Participant observation was established as a standard sociological research method, following Park's injunction to get the seat of one's pants dirty with *real* research. And a catholic, multimethod approach was characteristic. A common element in the various pieces of research was the reliance upon a combination of different research methods to build up a multifaceted picture of the problem under investigation: the basic reference to ecological structure and mapping; the reliance on personal interviews and observation; the importance of life histories and personal documents; and the subsidiary though not insignificant place of statistics. The metaphor of a mosaic seems appropriate, to represent both the way in which the different research techniques were meant to fit together and the part which each individual research study would play in the overall plan for the study of the city. This was part of the specific contribution to the broader movement toward theoretically informed empirical research in sociology which the Chicago school represented.

7 The Organization of Sociology by Park and Burgess

The success of the Chicago school of sociology was not due only to the fertility of Park's ideas, the receptivity of the urban milieu in which it flowered, or the power of the new methods of field research which it pioneered. The organization and institutionalization of the subject in the university was also an important explanatory variable, which has been unduly neglected. One of the conditions that favored the national dominance of the Chicago department by 1920 was the fact that it was a department in its own right. At other leading universities, the subject had a more marginal existence attached to other departments until a later date. At Harvard, for example, sociology was represented in the departments of social ethics and economics, a separate department not being created until 1930 (with the appointment of Sorokin), thirty-eight years after Chicago.[1] The institutional foundations that Albion Small established were sound and well constructed, his own lack of intellectual domination being in marked contrast to the ultimately stultifying influence of William Graham Sumner at Yale and Franklin Giddings at Columbia as institution builders.[2]

The base upon which the department rested was, nevertheless, a narrow one, and it was by no means obvious in 1915 that Chicago would in the following fifteen years come to dominate sociology in the United States. In the decade between 1915 and 1925, the number of teaching staff actually fell from eight to five. In 1915 it consisted of Small, Henderson, Thomas, and Frederick Starr (anthropology) as full professors, Park as a part-time professorial lecturer one quarter per year, Scott Bedford as associate professor, Clarence Rainwater teaching "playground and recreation work," and Edith Abbott as a part-time teacher. During 1915 Charles Henderson died; Clarence Rainwater left in 1916. Thomas was dismissed in 1918, and Edith Abbott resigned in 1920 when the School of Social Service Administration was founded. The only new appointments were Ernest Burgess in 1916 as assistant professor and Ellsworth Faris as professor in 1919 to teach Thomas's courses in social psychology.[3] The department in 1920 was reduced to six: Small, Starr, Park (part-time), Faris, Scott Bedford, and Burgess.

By the end of 1925, further changes had occurred. In 1923 Starr retired and went to live in Seattle. Small retired in 1925, being replaced as chairman of the department by Faris. Scott Bedford left in the same year.

Park was appointed to a full professorship after the new president, Ernest Burton, took office in 1923, though he still nominally held a part-time appointment. Burgess was advanced to associate professor in 1921 and to full professor in 1927. Fay Cooper-Cole was appointed as a social anthropologist to replace Starr and in 1925 was joined by Edward Sapir, whose appointment was made possible by a special grant from the Laura Spelman Rockefeller Memorial.[4] At a peak period of creative achievement, the teaching staff of the department thus consisted of only three sociologists—Park, Burgess, and Faris (as chairman), plus two anthropologists, Cole and Sapir.

The small size of the department had several consequences. It made contact between staff and graduate students easier and more intensive than it would have been with a larger staff group. It also encouraged contact among staff in different social science departments and between graduate students in sociology and staff in other departments, since the numbers involved were relatively small. And it meant that the research work of the department depended heavily upon the efforts of graduate students, since the teaching staff was so small, covering a wide range of courses and departmental administration. The ecology of scholarship at Chicago in the 1920s was not only a matter of physical propinquity, but of the relatively small size of the department of sociology.[5]

The leading members of the department, from Small onward, had a clear grasp of the organizational prerequisites for supporting a productive and stimulating intellectual environment. In this chapter and the next I will examine some of the institutional underpinnings of the Chicago school of sociology, in departmental administration, in teaching, in the organization of research, and in the social life of the department. Without an understanding of these features of the social sciences at Chicago, the picture is a partial one. Though not in themselves sufficient, they were necessary for the Chicago school to flourish as it did.

The importance and influence of Small as departmental chairman up to 1925 is shown in his dealings with Scott E. W. Bedford, a member of the staff from 1911 to 1925.[6] Early in 1924, Bedford pressed Albion Small for the reasons for the university's refusing to advance him beyond the minimum salary on the associate professor scale at which he had been held since his promotion in 1915. Small spelled out, in response to Bedford's pressing request, why he was not more highly appreciated by the university. The reasons throw important light upon Small's conception of how Chicago sociology should be organized.[7]

Bedford's first shortcoming had been his failure to support the American Sociological Society, of which he became secretary in 1913.[8] In 1920 Bedford had insisted upon resigning the secretaryship despite Small's urgent request. Burgess replaced him. "I tried to convince you that the position offered the best opportunity open to anybody to keep in close touch with the sociologists of the country and that it consequently gave you a unique vantage ground for service to the University. I failed."[9] In addition, no member of the department had been of less assistance in maintaining the *American Journal of Sociology*.

Second, Bedford had refused to cooperate with Burgess in teaching Bedford's subject, urban sociology,[10] as a result of which Burgess began collaboration with Park on a course that supplanted the one offered by Bedford. Moreover, his leave for educational work in the army had placed strains on the department which he had done nothing to accommodate. Since his return, Bedford complained of overwork, whereas in fact no one since the department opened had been as free of university responsibility outside the classroom.

The gravamen of Small's objections lay in Bedford's third, more general, characteristic, "the impression that you are an individual worker, not a team worker." There might be cases in which, by exceptionally outstanding individual work, a scholar's claim to advancement might be preferred over those of the cooperative type. This was not the case here, although Small appreciated the teaching Bedford was doing. A year later Bedford made the same request for advancement, and again was refused; six months after that he resigned from the university.[11] His case is not in itself of particular interest, except as showing the extent to which the university expected its teaching staff to achieve distinction in research, teaching, and administration,[12] and how very determined Small was to promote collaborative team effort in the department and to reward those who cooperated in this aim.

Small himself only laid the groundwork. Park and Burgess were the architects of the department's success in creating the Chicago school. They had Small's backing. In recommending Park's appointment in 1921–22 to teach throughout the year (without additional payment), Small told the president:

> Few men of my acquaintance are more conspicuous exhibits of the spirit which is described by the legend "science for science's sake." Mr. Park has experimented with residence at Harvard and at Columbia, but finds our environment more favorable than either for scientific work in our subject. His presence here during a part of the year in addition to the Summer Quarter, for which he has had several successive appointments, is a decided stimulus not only to the graduate students but to the members of staff.[13]

In 1921 Small also recommended Burgess for promotion after he turned down the chairmanship of the department of sociology at the

University of Kansas. His support was strong on grounds of teaching ability, promise as a researcher, and joint authorship of the "green bible." The latter would

> assure him a place among the most successful organizers of the material and methods of the subject. The book is such a decided advance upon anything previously produced as a college textbook that it cannot fail to be the foremost standardizer of college teaching of sociology for a long time to come.[14]

Small also placed Burgess in a key role nationally in 1920 as secretary of the American Sociological Society.

The Chicago school derived its strength, however, from organizational features of the department. Robert Park's genius as a teacher of graduate students has been well documented.[15] "Park saw himself as a captain of inquiry with a company of men and women who must be directed to a worthwhile topic, then given the energy required to complete their work."[16] Park's skills were not as a formal lecturer, but as a brilliant and original supervisor of graduate students, drawing out and encouraging them in long interviews in which the subject of their research was discursively explored. They covered the empirical particularities of the people whom the student was studying, but also sought to establish connections with broader categories and theoretical concerns. Park was fascinated by a whole range of topics, not confined to the study of the city, which would illuminate the nature and processes of social change. He sought to formulate the many general ideas that attracted his interest in a rather inarticulate fashion.[17] The most original aspects of his teaching were his insistence that students clarify the meaning of a concept by first identifying the class of things to which it referred and then seeking to distinguish very carefully this class of things and other classes of things that lay in the margin between them.[18]

In Everett Hughes's view,

> he was a man who meditated and reflected on his ideas continually. He never let an idea go without having worked it through very well indeed. Yet he was very interested in the news, in what was going on around him. The joining of these two qualities—the reflective philosophical quality and the alertness to the news and what was going on—the combination of these two made a very creative man.[19]

This interest in what was happening in the world was the key to his stimulation of the empirical research of his students, but he added to it the ability to extract generalizations and relate the particular observations to a broader conceptual scheme.[20]

Park's influence was attested by the fact that though some did, several of his students did not subsequently have particularly distinguished sociological careers after leaving Chicago. He helped many of his students to reach a level of achievement which they would not otherwise have done.[21] Herbert Blumer, who was not one of his students, observed that he attracted students of a wide range of ability and possessed a remarkable capacity

> to bring out from them a level of achievement which, paradoxically, exceeded what one could think to be the limit of their abilities. . . . He worked patiently, persistently, and hard with each, getting them interested in certain areas of group life, encouraging and guiding them and working out with them an analytical understanding of such areas of interest. . . . I have never seen any teacher who could be as successful as Park in awakening, mobilizing, and directing the talents of students and bringing them to their highest potentiality.[22]

These skills were extremely important in fostering a cumulative program of graduate research, complemented by Burgess, who could keep a check on Park's wilder flights of the imagination and guide students in the conduct of their research. The contrast with overbearing and dominant intellects such as W. G. Sumner and Giddings, who could brook no opposition, could hardly be clearer. Park directed his graduate students where to look, and pushed them hard to conduct effective research, but he did not impose an intellectual framework upon them or expect them to reproduce his own ideas. Rather he enabled them to realize their scholarly potential to the fullest within the program he and Burgess had devised. The Chicago school owed its success in part to their innovations in graduate supervision.

Park, however, also helped to create the broader institutional milieu in which graduate work would flourish. He recognized the educational value of interaction among the graduate student body, the way in which a group of peers can educate one another, in turning problems over together and sharing their reflections. The close propinquity and intensity of graduate student life and work in the 1920s has often been commented upon and documented.[23] One means by which this was achieved was through two Greek-letter dining clubs of graduate students in sociology, Zeta Phi and Sigma Theta. These were established in the early part of the decade as bodies to meet for discussion, dinner, and to hear a visiting speaker. Membership was by election and somewhat exclusive. Zeta Phi, which in its early years had an initiation ritual, consisted of men only; Sigma Theta also admitted women and was somewhat larger. Zeta Phi was organized on the initiative of E. T. Kreuger, who clashed as a result with Ellsworth Faris, who was opposed to the foundation of elite bodies within the student group. Members of both organizations recall them as stimulating settings for sociological discussion.[24]

Another departmental body was the Sociology Club, established in 1916 and open to undergraduates and postgraduates alike. It held regular lectures on sociological subjects through the year, open to all who wished to attend. It was separate from a more exclusive departmental organization, the Society for Social Research, which was fashioned by Robert Park as a means of strengthening the ties of graduate students to the department and to each other, but also as a means of maintaining contact with former Chicagoans elsewhere.

The role of the Society for Social Research has generally been neglected in histories of the Chicago sociology department, yet it was one of the most effective means of promoting collaborative scholarly effort. The society was founded in 1920 at the instigation of Park, who was its first president. Its stated purpose was "to stimulate a wider interest and more intelligent cooperation among faculty and students in a program of studies that focused investigation on the local community."[25] Membership of the society was open to teaching staff and advanced graduate students. Unlike the Sociology Club, it did not admit undergraduates and only admitted graduate students pursuing original research of their own. Its aim was to foster the orientation of the department toward serious research.

As such, it helped to generate and sustain the lively spirit of Chicago sociology during the 1920s and early 1930s. Writing in 1939, Robert Park recalled that its aim was

> to bring together students who had the interests and the competence that are developed only in those who have endured the pains of prolonged and patient research, not merely for facts but for the insights which contact with facts eventually brings. I believe the Society owed its first success to the fact that most of us, students as well as instructors, found ourselves working together in what seemed to us a virgin field because of our new frame of reference for approaching problems. There was, to be sure, an extensive literature on the subject of the city in existence, but no one up to that time had regarded the city as a natural phenomenon.[26]

The society was an integral part of the sociology department. Robert Park was president until 1929; the vice-president was Ellsworth Faris. In 1929 Faris became president and William F. Ogburn the vice-president. The key role, however, was that of secretary (originally secretary-treasurer), always filled by a graduate student or fellow in the department. The first secretary was a South African, George S. H. Rossouw, who obtained his Ph.D. in 1922 and returned to South Africa. He was followed by Ernest R. Mowrer (1921–22), Ernest H. Shideler (1922–24), Harry B. Sell (1924–25), Herbert Blumer (1925–27), Samuel A. Stouffer (1927–29), and Frederick F. Stephan (1929–30).[27] Blumer, Stouffer, and Stephan later became leading figures in the discipline.

If its origins lay in Park's desire to fashion an instrument with which to pursue the program of urban research, it soon developed into something more than this. Three main activities were promoted—evening meetings, the Summer Institute, and the *Bulletin*.[28] A wide range of speakers spoke to regular evening meetings throughout the year, at intervals of two to four weeks. Speakers from outside the university—city planners, heads of municipal agencies, social workers, real estate developers and others—came to talk about their work.

> Park, the father of the Society, placed great importance on the experience of such strategically-placed persons out in the "real" world. The Society sought to tap the knowledge and insights of such persons.[29]

Another feature of the society was the opportunity provided for interdisciplinary contact. In 1926, for example, the society was addressed by the neurologist Charles Manning Child. He depicted the nervous system of an organism (an insect of some sort), with its brain the receiving center whereon the outer world impinged. Impulses radiated from the brain center along the nerve pathways to all parts of the organism in a starlike pattern of gradients, the impulses growing weaker as the distance from the brain increased.

> Dr. Park and Dr. Burgess, who were at the meeting, almost on the spot adapted the Child scheme of impulse pathways to the city, where the pattern of big "through" streets was the analog of the nervous system. As in the organism, life in the city is most intense at the center, where new things, news and information, new populations and new styles, meet with least resistance; and it is least intense at the periphery. The indices with which we were working behaved as waxing or waning gradients running along the important thoroughfare.[30]

Other speakers from neighbor departments in the 1920s included George Herbert Mead and Edward S. Ames from philosophy, Harold Gosnell, Charles Merriam, and Harold Lasswell from political science, L. L. Thurstone from psychology, and H. C. Cowles from botany. (The effect of this exposure to other disciplines is discussed further in chap. 11.)

A third frequent type of meeting was one in which one or two graduate students in the department presented the results of their individual research. Formal papers by members of the sociology teaching staff were rare. A number of meetings were devoted to reports of conferences or to discussion and exchange of news. "The Society was notorious for its unrestrained criticism of what was presented in such talks."[31] In 1928–29, for example, T. C. McCormick and Herbert Blumer debated the logic and scope of statistical method in sociology.

The program of the society thus supplemented formal classroom instruction and individual supervision to emphasize the collective character of the Chicago research. The society's program of evening meetings was an informal and intense interactive setting in which research interests could be developed or discussed cooperatively between staff and students. It was, moreover, less stratified than the formal classroom setting, reinforcing the feeling of being engaged upon a collective research enterprise.

The society, however, also served Chicago-trained sociologists in other parts of the country. The network that linked sociologists of the Chicago school during the 1920s and early 1930s, enabling them to dominate sociology in the United States for a period, has often been commented upon.[32] The Society for Social Research was clearly one important means by which this network was sustained. Thus, in 1925–26 the society had 51 members in Chicago and 48 away from Chicago. In 1927–28 it had 53 local members and 97 out-of-town members. Most of the latter were Chicago sociology graduates teaching elsewhere. This widespread network connected all parts of the United States to the Chicago center.

The specific means by which contact was maintained was through the summer institutes of the society, held annually in Chicago from 1923 on. They brought together for one or two weeks former members of the department who wished to keep up with current research and meet current members of the Chicago department. All the speakers were Chicago staff, graduate students, or former graduate students, almost without exception. The second institute, in 1924, had a varied program including sessions of human ecology and migration, the study of personality, anthropological research, the sociological use of literary materials, and the study of social problems.[33] In later years, a single theme might dominate. In 1926, the theme was "personality," and in 1927, "the newspaper." Attendance was high in proportion to total membership. Familiarizing participants with current Chicago research was a main feature of each summer institute. Tours of the city were arranged under Park's leadership. Sessions were spent in the Local Community Research Laboratory. Participants were there to learn.[34] The summer institutes were an intense scholarly experience that helped strengthen the institutional ties of Chicagoans and keep them abreast of sociological work in Chicago. The summer institute gave actual physical form to the scholarly social network or "invisible college," the very strength of which was partly responsible for the revolt in the American Sociological Society in 1936.[35] The society ranked alongside the *American Journal of Sociology* as a most effective means of spreading the influence of the Chicago school throughout American sociology.

This aim was also achieved after 1922–23 by the society's regular *Bulletin*, which included news of meetings during the year of the summer institute, of the Chicago department (including Ph.D.'s awarded and visiting teachers and scholars), and the names of new members elected. More informal news also appeared of the activities of members, new appointments taken up, marriages, birth of children, and other items. The *Bulletin* was an important channel of communication among the membership that reinforced collegiate ties and the sense of belonging to a scholarly network, ties which were personal as well as intellectual. The society also attempted a publications program, though this petered out.[36]

When he created the society, Park had a clear notion of the institutional mechanisms necessary to consolidate and integrate a research group into a "school." Good supervision, a strong commitment to students, and intellectual excitement generated through a vigorous program of meetings were not sufficient, however, to sustain a research program. It is likely that Park by himself would not have established the Chicago research program successfully, had it not been for the support of Ernest Burgess. Park was the dominant figure intellectually. His was the more original and penetrating mind, the broader more synoptic sociological vision with greater theoretical acuity. Yet Burgess had qualities that complemented Park's and made an even more creative mixture when the two were combined. Burgess's commitment and skills were above all in the field of empirical research and its organization. Park's orientation to empirical study was strong, but liable to be weak on particulars, especially so far as the techniques of research were concerned. Burgess was sensitive to problems of empirical evidence, knew a good deal more than Park about methods of research, and possessed the administrative skills to run a research program which the untidy, somewhat disheveled but inspirational Park did not have. Burgess's approach to inquiry was much more through handling data and close attention to empirical materials, though he was far from being a raw empiricist.[37]

Thus Burgess was the sociology department's contact with the Local Community Research Committee, which financed a good deal of the early sociological research. Burgess had a primary role in maintaining contacts with individuals and city organizations which might prove useful in developing the urban research program. Throughout the 1920s, he was secretary-treasurer of the American Sociological Society as well as an associate editor of the *American Journal of Sociology*. Burgess, Herbert Blumer claimed in an obituary tribute,

> contributed more than any other person to the development of sociology in the United States. . . . Burgess was unstinting in his readiness to lay and expand the institutional basis of our discipline. In our preoccupation with theoretical and research achievements, we are prone to overlook the vital significance of basic organizational work on behalf of a scientific discipline, especially in its early period of struggle. Burgess played a role of paramount importance in implanting and entrenching sociological interests [both on the national scene and at the University of Chicago].[38]

Here his organizational contribution to the local research program is highlighted. The Park and Burgess course in field studies was backed up in several ways by his activities. One was the provision of census tract data for the city; another the employment of Vivien Palmer, from 1925 to 1930, as a senior research worker on the program of urban research. Her role was a threefold one. It included the creation of an adequate archive of detailed local data with the assistance of students in the department.[39] Second, Palmer's work included coordinating all the research being done in the department, organizing students to work in groups, and, if more than one group was working in the same community, making them aware of each other's existence. As a complement to this, she edited and prepared summaries of case studies and statistical data for the use of students in the department. For example, she put Paul G. Cressey in touch with Francisco Roque, who was interested in taxi-dance halls and who assisted Cressey with his research.[40]

Her third objective was to pool the experience of research fellows and students in order to build up gradually a manual of successful research methods, techniques, and practices.[41] According to Burgess, writing in 1928:

> In the course of [various] studies Miss Palmer undertook the experiment of inducting students into the theory and practice of sociological field studies. She believed that the study of a local community, of an immigrant colony, or of some small group like a boys' or girls' club might be advantageously carried on in connection with work in the courses in sociology. She planned the work as indicated in this manual in such a way that observations of group behavior in the field were timed to synchronize with the advance of the student in his reading of the textbook and in his class discussions. In this way he not only acquired some understanding of the principles and methods of research but he had at hand a growing fund of concrete materials to be organized and analyzed in terms of the concepts that he was studying.[42]

Palmer's work was carried on in connection with the course on field studies and involved the provision of materials for the course, the supervision of students' research, the creation of a data archive on the city, and the improvement of research techniques. In addition, research assistants were supervised, and some presentations made to interested local groups outside of the university.

Vivien Palmer also supervised the project, under Burgess's overall direction, which resulted in the definition of 75 exhaustive and mutually exclusive community areas for the city of Chicago. This classification of 75 "natural areas" not only formed the basis for the subsequent urban sociology of Chicago, but was and is widely used by city organizations as a means of distinguishing subdivisions within the city. (The local telephone books of the city, for example, still bear names and maps based on Burgess's classification.) Albert Hunter's recent study of Chicago's local communities showed that nearly half of the respondents interviewed gave the same name to their local area as that used in Burgess's classification.[43] "Natural areas" thus not only had a spatial reality in the 1920s, but possess an enduring spatial and symbolic reality into the present.

Completed between 1924 and 1930, the classification evoked a picture of Chicago as a complex metropolis, a mosaic of residential villages, industrial suburbs, immigrant areas, business and commercial zones, and hotel and apartment house areas. Each of the 75 "natural areas" and more than three hundred neighborhoods distinguished was

> a miniature society with its own history and traditions, its own individual problems, and its own conception of the future. Hyde Park, North Center, Bridgeport, South Chicago—these are not just names on a map. They represent distinct units within the city, each an integral part of it to be sure, but each playing its peculiar role in Chicago's destiny.[44]

Social and civic workers, educators, social scientists, and businessmen all recognized the existence of these areas and needed to have the facts about their population, institutions, economic status, and trends of development available.

The work began from the Social Base Map, on which communities were provisionally identified from the physical separation of different areas by rivers, elevated railways, industry, parks, and boulevards. Then some materials were collected from city libraries.

> Special reliance, however, was placed upon field work in the local communities, interviewing old residents and others, such as real estate men, who have much exact and complete knowledge about the community, its outstanding events, and the factors

> that are operating for social change. These interviews with old residents, real estate men and others, excerpts from daily papers, and historical accounts, were first subjected to an elaborate system of checks and then put in the form of documentary material. From these documents, aggregating from fifty to a hundred in number on each local community, an article or digest was prepared giving a descriptive and analytical account of community growth, and showing the different stages of social change through which each district had passed.[45]

The resulting classification of 75 "natural areas" subsequently formed the basis of the Chicago Local Community Fact Books.

Apart from the definition of "natural areas," the most enduring legacy of Vivien Palmer's work was her text *Field Studies in Sociology: A Student's Manual*, published in 1928 as a codification of the practices of the urban research program. One of the earliest research methods texts in American sociology, and only the second on field research,[46] this book is of particular interest because it shows the extent of methodological self-consciousness at the time. The influence Chicago exercised through the publication of *Field Studies in Sociology* was a product of Burgess's organizational skills just as much as the classification of the city into 75 "natural areas."

Palmer distinguished three main types of sociological method, the case study, the historical method, and the statistical method. The case study was defined as "a limited stage in the investigation of a research problem in which the investigator makes an exhaustive study of a case as an interacting whole, but confines himself to descriptive statements of the results."[47] Historical method was that of the historian—Langlois and Seignobos were quoted with approval.[48] Palmer, however, put some emphasis on the particular value of documentary sources such as letters, diaries, and autobiographies, giving insight into processes through which their writers have passed. The statistical method was distinctly different from the two other methods in its emphasis upon extensive enumeration and measurement.

Each method had its uses and limitations:

> Like a golfer with his bag of sticks, the investigator selects first one implement and then another in his drive towards the goal. Each implement has its specific use, with manifest limitations so the ultimate success depends upon both the selection and the skilful use of the right implement at each stage of the game. Each instrument is superior in its own sphere, and the variety of the problems encountered demands the interchanging use of first one tool and then another tool to insure the highest returns.[49]

A schematic outline of the typical relationship between the different methods ran as follows. First, the researcher studied the available statistics, historical narratives, and descriptive accounts that had any bearing on the subject. Second, a preliminary use was made of case-study methods to explore the problem. Then historical methods were used to secure a picture of the traditions and past of the group. Case-study methods were used in depth to study the present situation of the group exhaustively. Finally, the statistical method might be used to amplify and enlarge on the findings from the case materials. This emphasis upon the complementarity of research methods was characteristic of the Chicago school, reflecting the openness to different approaches and the emphasis on high quality in research.

Palmer's book was also notable for one of the earliest discussions in the literature of participant observation, a method that Chicago sociologists pioneered. In making an intensive study of an interest group, the investigator had to be a "participant observer"—either a person who has identified himself with a group for the purpose of studying it or one who already belonged to a group but studied it in an objective, detached manner. The smaller the group, the more carefully entrée would have to be negotiated. Records were needed in order to throw light on how group processes operate. Reflecting the extent to which Chicago students such as Nels Anderson engaged in "retrospective" participant observation, Palmer stressed the value of an active member of a group trying to study it scientifically.

> The effort of the investigator to study objectively social groups to which he belongs has exceptional value. . . . A participant observer can obtain more revealing data concerning a group than an outsider. And an individual can usually learn more sociology by getting a new point of view concerning groups with which he is already familiar through an impartial investigation of them, than by studying groups with which he has no intimate contacts.[50]

The final section of the book discussed four research techniques used within the case-study method: observation, the research interview, the diary, and the social research map. Each was discussed in the abstract without meaningful examples and not set in the context of actual research. A number of pertinent points were made. For example, the fact that the interview was a social situation was emphasized, as was the importance of rapport between interviewer and respondent. The opening, main part, and closing of the interview were discussed in detail, with suggestions on how to proceed. Proper records should be made of each interview. A minimum of notes should be taken during the interview, and a full record written down as soon afterwards as possible. Palmer recognized different types of interview, varying in formality, frequency, subject matter, type of person being interviewed.

In brief concluding chapters, Palmer discussed the presentation of data and, in a very cursory fashion, its analysis. A chart was recommended for analyzing material arranged chronologically in the vertical axis and broken down by topics in the horizontal axis. Essentially, this seemed to be a grid for the arrangement of data prior to comparison and classification, but these tasks could only be undertaken when considerable data had been collected.

In its day, Palmer's text was a brave attempt to systematize the practices of Park and Burgess's students. It was not completely successful, partly because too few examples were given from actual research. Nevertheless, it was one of the earliest attempts at the codification of sociological research methods and is a further example of Burgess's organizational ability in disseminating the Chicago approach more widely.

The book also suffered from the limitations of its general orientation, which was inductive and classificatory. The steps involved in any scientific study were identified as (1) the selection and definition of the problem, (2) the collection of data, (3) the classification and analysis of data, and (4) the formulation of scientific generalizations. Sociology differed from the reform-oriented social survey in proceeding to the third and fourth stages. What Palmer meant by generalization, however, was principally the formation of general concepts rather than testable hypotheses. This fitted closely with the characteristic emphasis in Chicago field studies, which were usually rich in empirical description and sought to develop "types" as generalizations drawn from the empirical data. There was a more ambitious overarching theory of social process adumbrated by Park, and the ecological theory most fully worked out by Burgess provided a general backdrop, but at the level of individual studies no very high-level generalizations were formulated. In Mowrer's study of family disorganization, for example, a central place in the analysis of case-study material was his classification of family tensions, which were identified as originating in incompatibility in responses, economic individualization, cultural differentiation, and individuation of life patterns. Such distinctions, Mowrer argued, permitted a transition to the aim of identifying causative factors. It also provided the logical consistency in the classification necessary for science by defining these factors in terms of attitudes.[51]

The weaknesses of this conception of science are apparent. The later decline of the Chicago school owed something to the lack of cumulative scientific force in the impressive body of studies carried out. Park "could not formulate a dynamic theory of behavior which would have unified his own classificatory and descriptive scheme and helped to systematize his rich aphoristic insights into modern social structure."[52] The failure to relate concrete studies to general abstract definitions and general explanations was a marked weakness, and it diminished the impact of the Chicago studies once Park had disappeared from the scene.

One field that is to some extent an exception to that generalization was criminology, including juvenile delinquency. Work in this area initiated and directed by Ernest Burgess was both intellectually and organizationally important for extending the influence of Chicago sociology. He shared Park's view that the sociologist's task was to pursue disinterested knowledge, but he was willing to cooperate actively with social agencies to show the relevance of sociology for their concerns and to secure research opportunities for graduate students. In the course of his work on the taxi-dance halls, for example, Paul G. Cressey was employed by the Juvenile Protective Association of Chicago.

Burgess's first published article was on juvenile delinquency,[53] and several of his research students in the early and mid-1920s worked in this field. Clifford Shaw was a graduate student in the department at this period, although he did not complete the Ph.D.[54] In the autumn of 1924, Shaw was working on a study of juvenile delinquency in relation to its local distribution and the movement of population, plotting on maps the distribution of delinquents and collecting some life histories from a small number of boys.[55] A year later Shaw was at work on three maps, showing the ecology of three particular gangs, the distribution of delinquency in relation to the natural areas of the city, and the ratio of delinquent boys to the total number of boys of the same age group in each of the natural areas of the city. He had also obtained six very extended and complete life-history documents, completed four case histories, and collected additional data on another fifteen cases.[56] He was one of several students studying problems in the field of delinquency: Murray Leiffer studied boys' courts in Chicago, Paul G. Cressey investigated the closed dance halls, and John Landesco examined criminal gangs as an entrée into the problem of organized crime.[57]

Burgess used the support of the Local Community Research Committee (LCRC) as "seed money" which later grew into larger projects. Shaw's work in the academic year 1925/26, for example, was funded partly by the LCRC and partly by the Women's Clubs of Chicago. In 1927 Frederick Zorbaugh (brother of Harvey) and Henry McKay (a new graduate student) were at work with Burgess. The famous collaboration of Shaw and McKay, their subsequent classic work at the Institute for Juvenile Research,[58] thus grew out of the Chicago Department of Sociology.

Burgess's role in the Institute for Juvenile Research (IJR) was also a central one. The IJR had been founded in Chicago as the Juvenile Psychopathic Institute in the first decade of the twentieth century, as a child study and guidance clinic. Its first director, William Healy, M.D., was a local man who at one time studied with William James at Harvard. The institute was then taken over by the State of Illinois and renamed, but it retained its clinical function and its association with the juvenile courts.[59] In the mid-1920s a group of local citizens calling themselves the Friends of IJR was formed to raise money for a behavior research fund. By May 1926, they had succeeded in raising $278,000 for a five-year period entirely from local sources and without recourse to the large foundations in the initial period. The friends were a roll-call of leading Chicago reform figures, including Mrs. Ethel Dummer, Jane Addams, and George Herbert Mead. Dr. Herman Adler, formerly professor of psychiatry at Johns Hopkins University, who had become director of IJR in 1917, had been keen to carry out research but had had few opportunities to do so. He became director of the fund, which operated as the research arm of IJR.[60]

The research program of the fund was wider than sociology, covering the biology of learning, physical growth, the emotions, personality disorders, and behavior problems of children. The studies of delinquency and crime carried out under its wing were, however, most important for the development of sociological criminology and owed a great deal to Ernest Burgess. On his recommendation a new sociological research section was created within IJR. Clifford Shaw was appointed its director in October 1926, and Henry McKay began work there in January 1927 as a clerical research assistant.[61] In addition to Shaw and McKay, the staff included for a period three other of Burgess's students, Frederick Zorbaugh, in 1928–30; Leonard S. Cottrell, Jr., in 1928–29; and Clark Tibbitts, in 1928. The main publications resulting from their work included Shaw, Zorbaugh, McKay, and Cottrell's statistical study of the distribution of delinquency, *Delinquency Areas*, Shaw and McKay's classic analysis, *Social Factors in Juvenile Delinquency*, for the Wickersham Commission in 1931, and their *Juvenile Delinquency and Urban Areas*. In addition Shaw produced *The Jack-Roller*, *The Natural History of a Delinquent Career*, and *Brothers in Crime* using life-history materials. By any standards this was a seminal contribution, one for which Burgess was the architect and the power behind the scenes.[62]

On Adler's resignation at the end of 1929, Burgess became the acting director and later the director of the Behavior Research Fund in order to facilitate a proposed merger with the University of Chicago. This did not come about, partly because funds were drying up. Although the Rockefeller Foundation granted $50,000 for 1931–34, the momentum could not be sustained, and in 1934 the fund was formally terminated.[63] Shaw, who was more of an activist and less academic than the more scholarly McKay, after 1932 threw his energies into the Chicago Area Project.[64] Burgess's own research interests in the mid-1930s were moving more into the area of marriage and the family. In the late 1920s, however, he brought into being within the IJR a notable group which made a major contribution to criminological research.

Nor did his organizational achievements end there. His work on parole prediction undertaken with Clark Tibbitts was the result of a request from the Parole Board of Illinois to the presidents of Illinois, Chicago, and Northwestern universities.[65] They established the three-man Committee on the Study of the Workings of the Indeterminate Sentence Law and of Parole in the State of Illinois, of which Burgess was a member.[66] John Landesco and Clark Tibbitts were employed as research assistants (on the strength of this work, Landesco was appointed a member of the Illinois Parole Board in 1933).[67] The committee's report was a classic document, but the best-remembered section is the chapter by Burgess on parole prediction. This pioneering predictive research was a notable example at the time of a successful piece of applied sociological research. It yielded "expectancy rates" of parole violation related to social background and personal characteristics, which Burgess argued could be used in parole administration.

One other notable study with which Burgess was associated involved the expansion of what was planned as a graduate thesis into a large project. John Landesco's research methods in studying organized crime were discussed briefly earlier. His classic work *Organized Crime in Chicago* was prepared for the Illinois Crime Survey sponsored by the Illinois Association for Criminal Justice, a body set up by civic leaders, lawyers, and academics in the city and the state in 1925.[68] A major crime survey was undertaken of which Landesco's study was merely a small part. Landesco's work, a landmark in the study of organized crime at any period, was based on his graduate research with Burgess between 1925 and 1929. (From 1925 to 1927 he was supported by the LCRC.) Landesco was a product of the Chicago school and of Burgess's supervision. His work, like that on parole prediction and on delinquency, also illustrates Burgess's capacity to obtain funding from within and outside the university to make such pathbreaking studies possible. The character and scale of sociological research was indeed changing at this period.

One further organizational outcome of the activities of Burgess and Park was the forging of strong links with members of other social science departments in the university. Burgess's role in the interdepartmental Local Community Research Committee was considerable. Both drew on ideas from related disciplines for their word on urban structure. The role of the Society for Social Research was mentioned earlier. But it was not only a process by which they drew on other disciplines to strengthen sociology, but one by which they influenced others.

Park's impact on colleagues and graduate students in other disciplines is shown by the cases of Harold Lasswell, Harold Gosnell, and Robert

Redfield. Lasswell, an undergraduate and graduate at the university before he joined the staff, took very few courses with Park, but got to know him when an undergraduate paper on Turner's frontier thesis was referred to Park for his comments. Thereafter they kept in contact. As a graduate student, Lasswell shared an office with Blumer, Wirth, and Redfield, from Park's department. He later recalled that he was very much stimulated by Park's concern for empirical methods of research, and assisted him on some of his urban studies.[69] They also shared common interests in the study of public opinion, propaganda, and social psychology. In a book published in 1935, after Park's retirement, Lasswell acknowledged his longstanding indebtedness to Park's "sagacious insight and my appreciation of his respect for creative interplay between hours of high abstraction and days of patient contact with humble detail."[70] According to Edward Shils, Lasswell had a genuine reverence for Robert Park.[71]

Harold Gosnell, also a graduate student and then teacher of political science, had been in Chicago longer than Lasswell, but got to know Park at his urging. The opportunity came in 1930 when he was starting work on a study of race relations in Chicago politics. Park advised Gosnell and suggested that he use Miss Frances Williams and Horace Cayton as research assistants,[72] suggestions which proved very satisfactory to Gosnell. Park helped in framing the questions to be tackled in his study.

> Dr. Park had an uncanny ability to propose questions which would help provide information to test significant hypotheses. . . . I had many conferences with [him] as the study progressed. I was greatly impressed with his emphasis upon the usefulness of life-history cases, the value of contemporary newspaper accounts, the place of the participant observer, the need for defining fundamental concepts, and the proper role for statistics. He had an unearthly horror of the use of statistics for trivial or unproductive purposes. I wish that I had recorded at the time his words of wisdom. Some of them have been preserved in the Introduction which he graciously wrote to my book *Negro Politicians: The Rise of Negro Politics in Chicago*. He helped me pick out the title for this book, saying slyly that the word "politician" would be intriguing.[73]

Robert Redfield, who married Park's daughter Margaret, was a graduate student in anthropology in the 1920s, in Park's department, and then a member of the staff of the separate department of anthropology created in 1929.[74] Redfield's interest in the structure of communities meshed with Park's on urban structure, and the older man had a considerable influence upon the ideas of the younger about types of society.

> Robert E. Park, impressed by W. G. Sumner's concept and book, *Folkways*, poured creative ideas into many of his students, including Howard Becker and myself. Becker began with the contrast between sacred and secular present in the dichotomies of Tönnies and of Durkheim and produced a complex and much differentiated typology of sacred and secular societies. My own efforts went to develop an imagined or ideal-typical folk society in considerable detail of characterization and to make use of the conception in describing, in more general and abstract terms than is usual in studies of changing primitive societies, some comparisons among tribal, peasant, and urban communities.[75]

All these social scientists were stimulated by Park, stimulated as his sociology students were by his unquenchable curiosity and inquisitiveness about the world and his capacity for linking general ideas and empirical particulars. The emphasis in this chapter upon the organizational consequences of Park and Burgess's work is not intended to suggest that personal qualities were unimportant. Without Park's academic leadership, Chicago sociology would not have been what it was. He led and managed and prodded, neglecting his own research and writing in the process. Edward Shils provides a vivid picture of his style of communicating from his last years at Chicago in the early 1930s.

> I remember Park growling as he paced up and back across the front of the room. He always looked into the distance when he spoke; he spoke slowly as if he were reading out his thoughts from a distant script which he could not easily decipher. Sometimes he spoke as if from the midst of the things he was talking about. . . . Park was not a lucid expositor of his own ideas; he proceeded by giving hints about glimpses, but his growling ruminations about what he had glimpsed were so vivid and so emphatic, so many-sided, that I understood things from him which he never said. . . . He continued to read the most miscellaneous books which seemed to bear on his interest in the unity of the crowd, the normative element in human action, the composition of conformity, the incessant disruptions of order in every sphere of social life. . . . He . . . paced back and forth . . . in a lumbering ursine movement, gesticulating with both hands outstretched in front of his chest, moving up and down. . . . I also came to understand why Park's writings are so incoherent. Wherever an idea came to him in the course of writing it, he transferred it to conversation, talking till he used up his stimulation. He would then go back to his manuscripts and would begin again where the conversation had left off. . . . [Hence] his penetrating but discontinuous essays.[76]

If Park was the dominant if somewhat disordered intellectual figure, Burgess's organizational skills were complementary. Some studies were supervised more by one, some by the other. *The Hobo, The Gang, The Gold Coast and the Slum, The Taxi-Dance Hall* and other monographs showed what empirical sociology could achieve. This achievement, however, had a solid institutional underpinning which assisted Park and Burgess in the creation of the Chicago school.

8 The Local Community Research Committee, 1923–30

The 1920s were a period of transition for the social sciences in American higher education between the older, nineteenth-century pattern of the lone scholar working with a few students on documentary and published sources and the newer type of larger-scale, collaborative, empirical research linked to organized graduate programs which was characteristic of the twentieth century. The contrast should not be overdrawn, for the older and newer styles have continued fruitfully to coexist. During the 1920s, however, the shift toward firsthand empirical investigation, evident at Chicago, became more marked in sociology and political science departments nationally, although the trend had started somewhat earlier in psychology.[1] It was associated with more extensive and coordinated programs of research, with more elaborate support facilities, with an expansion of graduate training, and with a greater emphasis on the publication of research results. Financial support for these activities was provided by the large philanthropic foundations, which played a key role in making such developments possible. Changes in the orientation of sociology and political science were associated with changes in the ways that social science research was organized and financed.

In explanations of the fertility of the Chicago schools of sociology and political science in the 1920s, these institutional developments have been largely ignored or underemphasized. In fact they were very important necessary conditions for the development of large-scale university social science as it is known today. The emphasis on graduate research that began with the establishment of Johns Hopkins, Clark, and the University of Chicago in the late nineteenth century was followed a generation later by an equally important but less well recognized shift in the scale, character, and professional orientation of the social sciences.[2]

If one had visited the University of Chicago in 1920, the manner in which research was conducted was not strikingly different from what it had been in the mid-1890s. Thomas and Park, it is true, had embarked upon significant firsthand empirical research, but each of them worked independently or at most with one or two research assistants or graduate students. The pattern of individual scholarship within departments was well established, even more so in political science where there were only three people on the teaching staff.[3] By 1930, however, the Chicago schools of sociology and political science enjoyed a stature they had not held in 1920. Chicago's was, by 1930, clearly the leading sociology department in the United States and the world, while its political science department was among the first three in the country and clearly the most original.[4]

The changes in the course of this decade were partly a result of the organization of programs of research over a wide field, all engaging the efforts of many individual teachers, graduate students, and research assistants. These programs of research took various forms. In some cases, they involved the loose integration of the work of graduate students on related problems. In most cases, however, there was more to it than this. Research supervisors such as Vivien Palmer and ancillary research staff were employed. Resources were made available for clerical, secretarial, and statistical support for research of a kind which in the previous decade was almost entirely absent from the university. Publication was supported financially. The research was conceived of as cooperative, directed to a common set of problems discerned in the local urban community.

In Chicago in the 1920s, an embryonic and loosely integrated organizational framework for empirical research was created. It was not the modern research organization with project directors, a division of research labor, and a very high degree of functional specialization, but it represented a significant departure from the model of the individual scholar working alone or with a research assistant or a couple of graduate students. Arguably it was a more effective system for linking empirical research to teaching departments than that later pioneered by Paul Lazarsfeld and Robert Merton at the Bureau of Applied Social Research at Columbia,[5] for it did not separate research so sharply from the other functions of a university department or group of social science departments.[6] What is certain is that for the social sciences it was an institutional innovation which was important in sustaining the Chicago schools of sociology and political science.

Albion Small was one of the main originators of the scheme which came to fruition in 1923, although his contribution was schematic rather than specific. Small had been profoundly influenced by his experience at Johns Hopkins, particularly in the interdisciplinary graduate seminar. In *The Meaning of Social Science*, published in 1910, Small sketched the possibility of an institute which would promote social science research without regard for disciplinary boundaries; to provide national leadership of the kind that Johns Hopkins had provided in the 1880s.[7] Small's vision of a university research institute had connotations of "social service," involving a moral elite of academics who would make agreed recommendations, based on scientific research for the resolution of social problems.

In the political science department a decade later, Charles Merriam was pondering the requirements if scientific methods were to be used for the study of political behavior. His approach was more empirical and less prescriptive than that of Small, but it pointed in the same direction. The organization of social scientific research, he considered, was palpably insufficient. The time available and the equipment required were deplorably inadequate. Most institutions failed to provide secretarial help, research assistance, or sufficient funds for research and publication. New initiatives were needed in order to promote research, both in the University of Chicago and over the country as a whole.[8] Early in the 1920s, Merriam proposed an institute of research on government, which would embrace not only political science but political economy, history, geography, psychology, law, and education. It would provide "for the broadest possible training in all branches of social science, and also the intensive work of more minutely specialized phases of the study of government." The scale of the proposed institute was far from modest, requiring funds in the order of $4 million.[9]

Economists, too, were turning their minds to the possibilities of organized, collaborative research programs. Leon C. Marshall, Laughlin's successor as head of the economics department and dean of the school of commerce and administration, submitted to President Judson in March 1922 a plan "to give our social science group a position of leadership."[10] The academic core of the plan involved "the improvement of teaching, a clear publication policy, and the fostering of interdisciplinary work. Group, departmental or individual research would foster training of students by having them gather cases and materials for class use, the provision for staff of clerical and mechanical aids, and making assistants available for research instead of routine marking of undergraduate papers. Such a shift would direct academic energies toward "productivity, improvement of methods, and contribution to knowledge rather than routine performance of habitual tasks."[11]

Six months later Marshall was pursuing the idea that Chicago was the ideal location for such a research program. Small told President Judson that he strongly supported such a move. "What I am thinking of is resolution of all the research men in our department, with all their graduate students, into genuine commissions of inquiry into problems of cardinal importance in our present stage of national life." Work would be blocked out and planned in advance, responsibility for particular projects being given to particular groups:

> The hack work of getting out and sorting materials, and of organizing them in accordance with the findings of their more experienced seniors, would be assigned to the graduate students.

> Regular sessions of the seniors would be held with the graduate students present for threshing out all the questions of principle involved in deciding what evidence is needed, where it may be obtained, and what its bearings are after it is in hand.[12]

Small alluded to a story of six quarrymen each individually trying for one hour to lever off a shelf a piece of stone too big for one man to handle, and all failing. They expended six man-hours with no result, whereas, "if they had formed groups of twos or at most threes, the whole job would have been easy in an aggregate of six minutes." It was a perfect illustration of the failings of social science groups in all American universities, of which Chicago was typical.[13]

The culmination of the campaign being coordinated by senior members of the social sciences faculty was reached early in 1923, when Small addressed a meeting of the faculty group in philosophy, political economy, history, political science, and sociology. For many years he had been criticizing the tendency of the social sciences to separate into watertight compartments.[14] As he neared retirement, his dream of the cooperative organization of and provision for social science research seemed to be drawing closer. Small's vision of "group study as opposed to departmental study or individual study" was closely tied to his conception of how a university such as Chicago should develop.

> Some University, sometime, somewhere, will realize this vision of a super-graduate school, with all that should surround and complete it. The contrast between that creation and our present type of school will be wider than the contrast between the Johns Hopkins that President Gilman projected and the old fashioned college.[15]

Recognizing that such proposals would encounter opposition, Small dealt with criticisms of such collaboration, suggesting that the plan for cooperative research was not without its critics, despite the powerful backing of senior men such as Small, Merriam, Marshall, and Tufts.

He stressed that it was not proposed to concentrate on a single problem or one research method: "I am arguing for a policy of organizing and concentrating on different research techniques, so that they will make an impression beyond the confines of our separate departmental constituencies."

> Full departmental autonomy, but intensive departmental cooperation, are the foundation courses of the ideal I am trying to suggest. . . . Unless we can show the people with money that we have the will and the competence to be and to do something

> of a higher order, only driblets of unsophisticated money will respond to our appeals.[16]

Nor did plans for collaborative research involve the suppression of individuality. The individual could still pursue his own research interests: "But research plans adopted by the group would offer inducements for selection of problems by individuals which would so reinforce and be reinforced by the work of the whole, that isolated, detached, unsupported studies would be relatively less inviting than they are now."[17] The influence of this conception of team research was evident in the Chicago school under Park and Burgess.

If Small addressed the general principles, Charles Merriam concerned himself with the practical arrangements that were necessary. Addressing the teachers of sociology, political science, history, political economy, and philosophy in 1922, he stressed the requirements of better research method, better equipment, and funds for publishing the results of larger inquiries not suitable for journals. Also needed were stenographic and clerical services, more adequate offices, funds for fieldwork and a building for the social sciences to provide proper working quarters.[18]

In May 1922, Merriam wrote to departments on behalf of an informal program committee of the departments of social science to canvass views on social science research with reference to two points:

> 1. Will you kindly give us your judgement of the minimum research facilities and equipment that research men in your department ought to have in order to carry on their work under the most favorable conditions.
> 2. Will you kindly indicate the lines of research in which you are most interested and what is needed in the way of additional equipment to make such inquiries feasible.[19]

In reply, Robert Park outlined the urban social research which was being developed, including the collection of original material through field studies and the reanalysis of data on the city collected by municipal commissions and private agencies. He urged the need for coordinated effort:

> Social investigations are expensive and at present there is much duplication and great waste. The problem of organizing present information so as to create a permanent fund of information upon which all future studies could draw and to which they could in turn contribute is a problem for the University. To create such a fund and make it available for future investigation is the very business, as I take it, of a science of sociology. Even-

> tually, mere information becomes in this way organized knowledge.[20]

Burgess, in his reply, suggested how this might be done.

> There should be a permanent research assistant to direct, in cooperation with the members of the staff, the graduate students engaged in collecting material. This research assistant should also direct the classification of this material. Stenographic and statistical assistance would also be necessary. Map-making, which we have already begun in the department, is a necessary part of the collection of materials, and requires expert assistance both in the direction of the actual work and in the classification and custody of map materials.[21]

These statements in May 1922 show that the architects of the Chicago school were acutely aware of the organizational prerequisites for the success of their plan of work. Merriam and Small also saw the research program as contributing to the improvement of research techniques and the instruction of a new generation of scholars. Merriam's views were presented to three national conferences on the science of politics at Madison in 1923, at Chicago in 1924, and at New York in 1925.[22] Small suggested that

> the minutes of each inquiry, properly filed, would form an object-lesson in the methodology of that type of inquiry and would be permanently instructive, both as to mistakes to be avoided in subsequent inquiries, and as to methods which proved to be useful. All this, in addition to the substantive results of the investigation.[23]

In February 1923, Small developed an analogy between social science and medicine or law. Group study, compared with departmental or individual research, required facilities analogous to those of the operating theater or court room, where students could participate in a forum in which staff would present the results of their research and have it criticized by their colleagues.

> The students will learn more of the social science craft by watching this procedure and occasionally taking part in it, than they ever acquire from our present ways of teaching. Here will be methodology alive.[24]

There was considerable imprecision in the use by Small, Marshall, and Merriam of the terms "collaborative" and "cooperative." All three thought that research must be organized by the social science group as a whole, with financial support from outside the university. They also believed, however, that to be fruitful the social sciences should be interdisciplinary in orientation. There was no doubt about the commitment to empirical inquiry among Chicago social scientists. Park and Burgess and their students were already at work. Charles Merriam's commitment to new techniques of investigation drawn from psychology and statistics was firm.[25] L. C. Marshall had a markedly empirical approach to institutional economics and business administration. How was the vision of interdisciplinary cooperation, large-scale projects, ancillary staff, and publication to be realized?

Matters were made easier by the retirement from the university in 1923 of the inflexible traditionalist President Judson, who was antagonistic to Merriam.[26] His successor Ernest D. Burton, professor in the school of divinity and a member of the university since its foundation, opened new doors. His dean of faculties and vice-president for academic affairs was James H. Tufts, the philosopher, who was keenly interested and involved in local social reform and had himself urged the necessity of local social research.[27] Such support was necessary but unlikely to be sufficient. The university did not dispose of a surplus of funds on the scale likely to be needed to finance such a research enterprise, though the president's backing would be essential in seeking external financial support. Universities such as Chicago were well used to seeking external support, but outside funding for social science research before 1920 was very rare.

The two main sources to which they looked were the large philanthropic foundations and wealthy members of the local community in Chicago. The university owed its existence to the personal munificence of John D. Rockefeller, Sr., though he and his family had refused to be involved in its administration or major policy issues. By the second decade of the century, however, he had abandoned personal giving in favor of the establishment of the Rockefeller Foundation in 1913.[28] The Carnegie Corporation had been founded three years earlier. Others followed suit: the Rosenwald Fund in 1917, the Commonwealth Fund in 1918.[29] These new creations were to play a most significant role in the development of academic social science just as they did in medicine and natural science.[30]

The foundations were unique in their wealth, intentions, and choice of beneficiaries. Their history is a fascinating and contested one.[31] They were independent corporations, with policies framed, increasingly, by the professional administrators who headed them, rather than by the trustees. Chicago social scientists tended naturally to look to the Rockefeller Foundation, whose president from 1917 to 1929 was Small's former colleague George E. Vincent. Personal ties were one thing, persuading the foundation to support social science was another. The main obstacle was Frederick Gates's "almost mystic belief in the promise and potency of medical research" and his suspicion of newfangled subjects like economics, as well as the Rockefeller experience of the Colorado coal strike. By 1920, the foundation supported public health and medicine to the total exclusion of social science.[32]

The Russell Sage Foundation supported the social survey movement, but outside academic social science. For a short while the Carnegie Corporation seemed a more likely source. Its president in 1920–21 was James R. Angell, formerly head of the psychology department at Chicago, but he moved on to become president of Yale. He did, however, during his brief tenure, bring Beardsley Ruml into the foundation world.

Ruml was born in Cedar Rapids, Iowa, in 1895 and was an undergraduate at Dartmouth, where he cut a lively figure. His teachers there encouraged him to go to the University of Chicago, where between 1915 and 1917 he completed a doctoral dissertation in psychology on the reliability of mental testing; Angell was one of his teachers. After Ruml's work at the Carnegie Institute and in Washington during the war on mental testing, Angell appointed him to the Carnegie Corporation in 1920 as his assistant. In 1922, on the recommendation of Angell and Abraham Flexner, John D. Rockefeller, Jr., appointed him, when he was only twenty-six, as director of one of the smaller Rockefeller foundations, the Laura Spelman Rockefeller Memorial (referred to usually as the Memorial).[33]

The Memorial had been founded in 1918 in memory of Mrs. Rockefeller, Sr. At about the time when Ruml became director, its endowment was increased to $74 million. The story of the Memorial under Ruml is the story of its transformation from an undistinguished social welfare charity into an instrument for the support of basic social science research throughout the world. By the time the Memorial was wound up in 1929, Ruml had distributed $40 million, half of it to support academic social science.[34]

A memorandum of October 1922 outlined his strategy for the promotion of social science. His basic argument was that

> [an] examination of the operations of organizations in the field of social welfare shows as a primary need the development of the social sciences and the production of a body of substantiated and widely accepted generalizations as to human capacities and motives and as to the behavior of human beings as individuals and in groups. Under the term "social sciences" we may include sociology, ethnology, anthropology, and psychology, and certain aspects of economics, history, political economy and biology. . . All who work towards the general end of social welfare are embarrassed by the lack of that knowledge which the social sciences must provide. It is as though engineers were at work with-

> out an adequate development in the sciences of physics or chemistry, or as though physicians were practising in the absence of the medical sciences. The direction of work in the social field is largely controlled by tradition, inspiration, and expediency, a natural condition in view of our ignorance of individual and social forces.[35]

Ruml suggested that there were three main reasons for the absence of a scientific basis for action with regard to social welfare. The social sciences were themselves very young: the first psychological laboratory had been established in Leipzig only fifty years earlier; the coefficient of correlation was developed only forty years earlier. The measurement of "intelligence" was a twentieth-century achievement. The subject matter of the social sciences was extraordinarily difficult to deal with. It could not be brought into the laboratory for study. Most important for the theme of this chapter:

> the universities have not been able so to organize their program as to afford favorable opportunities for social research. Facilities for the collection and tabulation of data are meager, and the requirements of classroom instruction limit markedly the possibilities of contact with social phenomena. As a result, production from the universities is largely deductive and speculative, on the basis of second-hand observations, documentary evidence, and anecdotal material. It is small wonder that the social engineer finds his social science abstract and remote, of little help to him in the solution of his problems.[36]

The task of the Memorial seemed clear. Here was a field and a task: "the development of the social sciences and the production of a body of fact and principle that will be utilized in the solution of social problems." Though the ultimate purpose was the practical one of improving human welfare, fundamental social science research was an essential foundation. Ruml proposed a series of initiatives which would promote empirical research in sociology, political science, anthropology, and psychology in particular. The Memorial itself would not conduct research, but would direct the initiatives to universities such as Chicago, Columbia, Wisconsin, Pennsylvania, Harvard, and Iowa, whose social science departments were already strong but whose own resources were insufficient for an enlargement of the scale of work. Initially funds would not be provided for scientific staff but for facilities. The provision of more adequate clerical, statistical, and field assistance, of essential materials and supplies, of supplementing funds for the purchase of books and documents, should be given precedence. This would increase the productivity of scholars already engaged in research, and the possibility of minor investigations by graduate students. Cooperation with local agencies would be encouraged. To increase the number of well-trained social scientists, fellowships for graduate study should be offered.[37]

This wide-ranging charter was of singular importance in the development of the social sciences in the United States in the 1920s. It sought to guide a philanthropic trust with large resources away from social welfare toward supporting basic and applied social science research. There was much in common with the ideas of Marshall, Merriam, and Small at Chicago. Ruml had been a graduate student of psychology and later an associate of James Angell. He knew Marshall and Merriam well. Yet it is unlikely in the extreme that Marshall, Merriam, and Small put forward their ideas simply because they thought Ruml would be well disposed. Small had been arguing the case for many years. Nor is it likely that Ruml was following them, for he was then—and remained—a brilliant and sparkling source of ideas, the most famous of which was his later idea for the "pay-as-you-go" scheme for the collection of the federal income tax. He was neither a bureaucrat nor an enunciator of commonplaces nor an echo of the ideas of other men.

The changing character of American sociology and political science in the 1920s may be traced in the grants which Chicago social scientists obtained from the Memorial. The University of Chicago was one of the most favored recipients of Memorial support. This support was used in part to create the infrastructure on which the Chicago schools of sociology and political science flourished. Though the details of this funding may appear mundane, even trivial, they represented a transformation as great as the establishment of the graduate school forty years before. The internal organization of the university was also somewhat modified by the advent of the program grant for empirical research.

In 1923, the University of Chicago, at the behest of the departments of political science, sociology and anthropology, and political economy, applied to the Memorial for and was awarded a grant of $21,000, for a study of the problems of the local community.[38] Memorial grants were given as block grants not tied to specific projects. It was up to the recipient institution to distribute them. To perform this function the university created the Local Community Research Committee, with representatives drawn from political science, sociology and anthropology, political economy, history, and philosophy. Thus came into existence one of the most important innovations in the organization of social science research in the period between the two wars.[39]

The first year's program of the research committee was primarily concentrated on empirical research by sociologists and political scientists. In sociology, the urban research of Park and Burgess and their students was the recipient. Of the $8,500 spent in the first year on sociological projects—40 percent of the total grant—$2,000 were spent on statistical and clerical assistance, $5,000 on research assistantships, and $1,400 on releasing teachers from teaching so that they could have time for research. The great bulk of the money was used to pay stipends or salaries for graduate students and auxiliaries, to enable them to conduct empirical research on a variety of small-scale projects dealing with life in Chicago.

Political science, by contrast, concentrated its resources on one project: $5,000, or 24 percent of the total grant, were devoted to the completion of the study *Non-Voting* by Merriam and Harold Gosnell. Almost all of this money was devoted to the cost of a survey; $3,000 were devoted to statistical, clerical and field workers, $1,300 to supervisors of field work, and $600 for supplies. Here the emphasis was on a large-scale project already under way.

Reviewing the first year's work, the members of the Local Community Research Committee (LCRC), Merriam, Small, Marshall, James Tufts, and Andrew McLaughlin (history), considered that the program had fostered the beginnings of a tradition of research, provided a training school for research workers, led to closer contacts with the local community, and encouraged interdisciplinary contact.[40] A new three-year program application for 1924–27 was prepared, after close consultation with Ruml, and submitted to the Memorial.

It was considered in the context of a broader review of Memorial strategy. Ruml pointed out to his trustees the value of building up certain centers of research. The development of such centers was

> best illustrated by the work of the University of Chicago. The plan here was to bring together the research capacities of the university in economics, sociology, and political science and, in co-operation with public and private agencies of the city of Chicago, to undertake a systematic investigation of the Chicago community. It was felt that such a program would be beneficial both to the City and to the University—that research and instruction in social science would flourish in the presence of opportunities for access to first-hand data and experience such as the City would provide—that the public and private agencies of the City would be aided in their programs for social betterment by the careful and impartial studies which the University would make. More fundamental, it is an experiment as to the possibility of a university assuming intellectual leadership based on scientific investigation in matters affecting the welfare of the community.[41]

The trustees of the Memorial agreed at the meeting to grant up to $225,000 to the University of Chicago for social research over a period of three years from 1924 to 1927. This consisted of an annual basic grant of $50,000, plus a commitment to "match" other funds obtained for research, up to a ceiling of $25,000 per annum. Thus if the research committee could raise at least $25,000 locally, they could receive from the Memorial another $25,000, which with the basic grant meant a maximum of $75,000 a year. The scale of the research program thus increased markedly. It rose from a budget of $21,000 in 1923–24, to approximately $100,000 in 1924–25; at that time, this was a very substantial sum indeed for one university to spend on social science research. The confidence which the Memorial trustees placed in developments at Chicago had major consequences for the scale of social science research at the university. Projects in the sociology and political science continued to be principal beneficiaries.[42]

The three-year program ran from 1924 to 1927. A further application was then made to the Memorial, which agreed to a further five-year program of research in the period from 1927 to 1932 on a considerably increased scale, with support for activities not hitherto included. The Memorial itself was wound up and merged with the Rockefeller Foundation in 1929, the foundation assuming its commitments to the University of Chicago.[43] Throughout the period the principle of a basic grant plus a commitment to "match" grants from other sources was continued (see table 4).

Over eight years, the Memorial allocated $451,000 in basic grants and a further $180,509 in matching grants to the University of Chicago for local community research, a total of $631,509. A further $180,509 was received in grants for research from other—chiefly local—sources. This was only part of the Memorial's total grant aid to the university, which totalled $3.4 million in all between 1923 and 1929.[44] The strength of the ties between the university and the city were apparent in the matching funds obtained. In most years the university managed to raise enough outside support to claim the full allocation of matching grant. No one source was predominant. They included three official sources, six city clubs, small grants from Chicago foundations, and a variety of special interest groups.[45] By comparison with the Memorial's, the scale of other grants was small and could not have provided the basis for rapid growth which the large foundation grant made possible. Merriam later pointed out that "the financing of local research inquiries from local funds is almost always a difficult if impossible undertaking, except perhaps on a matching basis."[46] Local pride, local sensitivities, and local special interests were prone to get in the way. Hence the importance of a disinterested donor such as the Memorial.

The Memorial explicitly adopted principles that ensured that it could not interfere in the research which was being conducted by an institution which it supported.[47] Ruml, although he met many of the academics involved on a regular basis, avoided formal contact with recipients of grants and asked that grants from the Memorial not be announced publicly.[48] The Memorial kept a very low profile, partly as a result of the

TABLE 4

Financial Support for Local Community Research at the University of Chicago, 1923–31, from the Laura Spelman Rockefeller Memorial and Other Sources (in dollars)

Year	LSRM basic grant	LSRM matching grant	Grants from other sources	Total grants received by research committee	Actual expenditure by research committee during financial year
1923/24	21,000	—	—	21,000	20,625
1924/25	50,000	21,376	21,376	92,752	59,644
1925/26	50,000	24,507	24,507	99,014	77,217
1926/27	50,000	15,374	15,374	80,748	111,301
1927/28	70,000	29,258	29,258	128,516	90,046
1928/29	70,000	29,994	29,994	129,988	137,752
1929/30	70,000	30,000	30,000	130,000	165,578
1930/31	70,000	30,000	30,000	130,000	152,880
Total	451,000	180,509	180,509	812,018	815,043

Source: Local Community Research Committee, University of Chicago, Reports to the LSRM, 1924–31.

Rockefeller Foundation's disastrous foray into industrial relations research at the time of the Colorado Coal Strike.[49]

During the 1920s, Chicago social scientists enjoyed considerable independence in deciding how the Memorial's grant was allocated. This policy of institutional support rather than providing project grants to individuals was pursued by the various Rockefeller foundations until the early 1930s, when it was abandoned and replaced by one much closer to that now operated by the National Science Foundation and the British Research Councils.[50] Memorial staff kept in close touch with universities in receipt of support, but more with a view to evaluating the climate of research at the university. On a visit to Chicago in March 1925, for example, Ruml's assistant, Lawrence K. Frank, emphasized the importance of openness to empirical observation and avoidance of dogmatism in graduate teaching, such as characterized "the way in which Giddings at Columbia and Carver at Harvard drill their ideas into their students' heads."[51] The Chicago social scientists were well aware that renewed support at the end of the period of grant depended on being able to show worthwhile results.

The Memorial's policy of lack of involvement in the university's affairs stemmed partly from the laissez-faire predilections of the Rockefellers and the trustees whom they had appointed, most of whom were conservative businessmen; partly from anxiety to avoid criticism for dictating the course of American scientific research; partly from the policy of concentrating resources in the most eminent national and regional centers, to serve as models for other institutions and "to make the peaks higher."[52]

The preeminence of Chicago social science in the 1920s owed much more to the intellectual qualities of its staff than to the mere fact of support from the foundation. Indeed, this was a primary reason why the Memorial chose Chicago as one of the centers of excellence at which it would help to promote organized social research. In 1927, Beardsley Ruml emphasized to his trustees the standing of the university as a center of academic excellence.

> The University of Chicago is the strongest privately controlled university in a large area where there has been a most vigorous development of higher education on a state university basis. There is no strong private institution *on the research and graduate instruction level* [my italics] in Indiana, Michigan, Kentucky, Kansas, Nebraska, the Dakotas, Iowa, Minnesota, or Wisconsin. In these states, the state university is the center of higher work. . . . this . . . places an increasing responsibility on the University of Chicago, which, as a private institution is able to set standards of freedom and quality of intellectual work of far-reaching influence. This responsibility has been assumed in past decades, and it would seem wise strategy in a national sense to

> assist in any appropriate way the University of Chicago in the continuance of this service.[53]

The University of Chicago was thus expected to take a lead and provide a national example. The broad outlines of the pattern of research expenditure and the way in which the committee operated show the innovations it made in the conduct of social science research. No longer was the norm the tradition of the single scholar teaching in the classroom and working in the library, paying research expenses from his own pocket or a small outside grant. Instead, a variety of types of expenditure (see table 5) were met by the LCRC, all of which made possible larger-scale and more extensive firsthand empirical research than ever before possible. The features of modern research departments today at leading American universities were first established at this period.

The practice of paying for part-time teaching to release regular teachers temporarily for full-time research prevailed in several departments through the period; it was largely a result of the belief that teachers should be given some time and some assistance in order that they might have a greater opportunity to make contributions to the creation of knowledge. In sociology the practice had begun with W. I. Thomas working on *The Polish Peasant*, but it assumed increasing importance during the 1920s.

The salaries of research assistants were a much larger part of the research committee budget. A variety of different sources of finance were available to graduate students; there were a few university studentships or fellowships, meager part-time teaching opportunities and part-time research work on the university budget, or part-time work of any kind. The importance of the availability of research committee funds for research assistance, therefore, did not simply lie in providing teachers with assistance in their investigation; it also provided an important source of part-time work and income for graduate students, making study more feasible for more students.

A prime objective of Memorial policy, implemented at Chicago, was to train future research workers by methods superior to those of the lone scholar tradition.[54] A thorough grounding in research was acquired by doing research. Among sociologists trained in this way were Ernest and Harriet Mowrer, Frederick Stephan, Louis Wirth, Andrew Lind, Clark Tibbitts, Helen McGill (Hughes), Paul F. Cressey, Ruth Shonle (Cavan), Frederic Thrasher, Harvey Zorbaugh, and John Landesco, all of whom left their mark on the discipline. The achievement of the Chicago school of sociology to a considerable extent rested on the studies of these graduate student part-time research assistants.

In the case of sociology, the strategy was deliberately one both of

TABLE 5
Classification of Research Expenditures of the Local Community Research Committee, University of Chicago, 1924–31 (in dollars)

	1924/25	1925/26	1926/27	1927/28	1928/29	1929/30	1930/31
Releasing instructors for work in research	250	1,600	3,077	4,650	7,825	4,725	5,583
Research assistants	23,043	36,832	41,742	25,973	17,608	15,833	19,316
Research employees	—	—	—	—	—	29,991	41,466
Supervision of research	6,750	6,720	10,687	11,810	20,195	26,610	16,867
Statistical, clerical, and field expenses	17,130	22,073	30,136	32,397	70,905	54,530	46,155
Supplies and equipment	2,384	4,739	8,312	8,210	12,550	13,487	12,031
Publications	5,857	1,200	12,761	1,507	3,452	13,621	4,232
General administrative expenses	4,231	4,053	4,586	5,499	5,217	6,781	7,230
Total	59,645	77,217	111,301	90,046	137,752	165,578	152,880

SOURCE: University of Chicago Social Science Research Council, Project Reports, 1924–42, 1126 Files.

providing the opportunity to gain a doctorate and of doing research of considerable scientific interest. As Park expounded it in 1926, the effects were cumulative:

> There are a great number of studies, which represent small increments in a larger study and they are constantly accumulating, and out of these accumulations we are building up our courses for one thing. The material in a good many of our courses where there are no textbooks as yet, is made up by materials collected by students. The same way with studies of the city. They represent an accumulation of materials gathered by students over a number of years. Every student that takes up a new project has access to the materials that have gone before, and so the accumulation goes on from year to year. . . . As a mere matter of economy and getting the work well done, it is very much the best way to do it. It takes a longer time, but we get it more thoroughly done, things are more thoroughly thought out, the supervision is more complete. You don't have to formulate your project so far in advance.[55]

Through a loosely organized research program, many members of a generation of Chicago sociologists received at least part of their training in research under the aegis of the LCRC.[56] In sociology, supervision of research by Vivien Palmer was made possible by LCRC funds. In political science, major pieces of research, such as Merriam and Gosnell's *Non-Voting* (1924) and Gosnell's *Getting Out the Vote* (1927), involved interviewing by graduate students and coding, punching onto cards, and analyzing in a counter-sorter. The costs involved were paid by the LCRC.

The expansion of statistical facilities and support of cartographic work (chap. 9) was an important development. This was a major item of expenditure at a time when the most sophisticated mechanical aid to computation was a machine like the counter-sorter. Most complex calculations and analyses of data which would today be handled by computer had to be carried out by hand with the aid of various types of simple calculating machines.[57] Park and Burgess's urban research required extensive map-making facilities.

Publication of the results of research was given considerable weight. Merriam and Gosnell's *Non-Voting* appeared later in 1924, the first in the Studies in Social Science series, published under the auspices of the committee by the University of Chicago Press. A range of studies from political science, economics, and social service administration followed,[58] also including Palmer's methods text discussed in the previous chapter and Burgess and Newcomb's volume of 1920 census data. The policy adopted by the LCRC of supporting publication on a significant scale by subsidy was a most important step in disseminating the results of research and gaining public recognition of Chicago as a center of social science research.

In the LCRC series, twenty-one titles appeared in eight years, almost all of them receiving some subsidy. The main sociological studies appeared in a second series (which started slightly earlier), the University of Chicago Sociological Series. In 1927 Thrasher's *Gang* and Mowrer's *Family Disorganization* appeared in it with due acknowledgment to the research committee. In eight years, eighteen titles appeared in the Sociological Series.[59]

The Memorial's support was influential also in relation to the scholars whom the university was able to appoint to its staff. In the previous chapter the small size of departments at this period was emphasized. The Department of Sociology and Anthropology expanded in 1925, when Edward Sapir was appointed associate professor of anthropology, with a special grant from the Memorial.[60] The major grant in 1927 permitted the university to make appointments to research professorships. The first three made were L. L. Thurstone in psychology, Simeon Leland to work on public finance, and Henry Schultz to work on the measurement of demand and other problems out of which developed the subject of econometrics.[61] In 1928–29 further appointments made were Chief of Police August Vollmer of Berkeley, California as professor of police administration, Clarence Ridley as associate professor of political science to work on city management, and Bessie Pierce as associate professor of history to work on the history of Chicago.[62] In 1930, Edwin Sutherland was appointed as professor of sociology specializing in criminology for five years under the same scheme.[63] None of the research professors were required to do any teaching, though some did. They devoted themselves whole time to research. No clearer indication could be given of the importance the Memorial and the university attached to advancing the cause of empirical social science research.

The progress of the research committee's program was demonstrated most dramatically by the building and opening in 1929 of the Social Science Research Building (chap. 11). To the five original departments represented in the LCRC, Social Service Administration had been added. Merriam, Burgess, and Edith Abbott were members of the committee throughout the 1920s. L. C. Marshall was a member until he failed to get "local community" dropped from the committee's title and he left the university in 1928.[64] J. H. Tufts and T. V. Smith alternated as representatives from philosophy. Leonard D. White was part-time executive secretary from 1926 to 1930.[65]

The impact of the LCRC upon social science in the university was considerable. The program of research in the sociology department could not have developed without its support, particularly in supporting graduate students, providing ancillary help and materials, and aiding with the typing of manuscripts. Burgess's work in criminology was materially helped by the LCRC before and during the period in which the IJR was set up. The path-breaking empirical research of political scientists under Merriam's tutelage—men such as Harold Gosnell, Leonard D. White, and Harold Lasswell—was made possible in many cases only as a result of the support of the Memorial. Major pieces of research were also carried out on regional planning in the Chicago area; on social welfare problems in the city, under the direction of Edith Abbott and Sophonisba Breckinridge; by L. L. Thurstone on the measurement of attitudes; by Henry Schultz in building the foundations of modern econometrics; and in Simeon Leland's studies of public finance. Quincy Wright's studies of the causes of war were also supported.[66] Not all projects reached a successful conclusion, but the rate of completion was high, as was the quality of achievement. A survey in 1925 by R. M. Hughes, president of Miami University, showed that Chicago was regarded as in the first, second, or third place nationally in each of the five subjects in the social science group; 80 percent of graduate work in political science in America was done at the University of Chicago; one third of all graduate students in sociology were registered at the university.[67]

Behind the scenes of the LCRC there was more dissatisfaction, particularly from L. D. White, who was in day-to-day charge. From 1927 onward, a number of critical questions were raised about its effectiveness. White considered that the LCRC lacked initiative, cohesion, and planning capacity. The program of research was too diffuse and too few of the projects set out to test hypotheses rigorously. The burden of these criticisms was that the LCRC lacked an overall strategy and coordinated program.[68] White's argument was justified. Disciplines cleaved to their own interests and would not cooperate with each other. The most successful work supported by the LCRC was carried on within particular disciplines, by Park and Burgess in sociology, Merriam, Gosnell, Wooddy, and White in political science, Thurstone in psychology, and Schultz in econometrics. As it turned out, the interdisciplinary character of the Chicago program had more reality in its form of organization than in the research carried out. Relatively few projects were truly interdisciplinary, and efforts to promote them did not meet with success.

The considerable emphasis upon interdisciplinary work at this period had a number of sources. One was the fact that the different disciplines were only gradually becoming sharply differentiated, departments were small and often combined disciplines—as in the Chicago Department of Sociology and Anthropology up to 1929—and in smaller centers members of the teaching staff taught more than one subject. Another was part of the reaction against overemphasis on their own distinctiveness in each of the disciplines. As political science and sociology became more empirical in orientation, research workers sought help—particularly with methodological problems—from neighboring disciplines. Merriam's interest in psychology is a good case in point. A further reason was the more practical, applied, orientation of many social scientists at this period, pointing toward interdisciplinary cooperation and receiving clearest endorsement by Ogburn and Goldenweiser in 1927.[69] The belief that practical research with direct usefulness must be interdisciplinary received endorsement from the philanthropic foundations,[70] in part reflecting and in part reinforcing the same beliefs among social scientists who were to be the objects of their beneficence. There was more interdisciplinary cross-fertilization at Chicago than in most universities of the period, but the barriers between disciplines remained quite high. Park, for example, referred to his colleagues in Social Service Administration as "do-gooders." They, for their part, regarded Park and Burgess's courses as "too much up in the air," theoretical, and vague.[71] Park noted in 1926:

> As soon as you take up more abstract problems, it seems to me you fall apart into all your several disciplines. It is only when you are taking up some rather practical problem, applying your methods of research to that problem, that you are likely to have any opportunity for cooperation. I am not sure that it is so, but it seemed to me so in reflecting upon the efforts to bring about cooperation in the social sciences.[72]

From the Memorial, Lawrence Frank shared with Merriam at the end of the decade some of his pessimism about the integration of the social sciences. Schemes for its realization required that the people involved grasp what the objectives in view were.

> Merely the expression of a desire and willingness to cooperate does not mean anything until you know whether the would-be cooperator understands the extent to which his habitual thinking and procedures will have to be modified and adjusted and frequently reoriented, both on the intake and on the output side.[73]

Perhaps the aim of interdisciplinary cooperation at this period was a chimera, one that nevertheless created a research organization and supported some very good research almost as an unintended consequence.

The end of the decade marked changes both for the Rockefeller philanthropies and the University of Chicago. In January 1929 the Memorial was consolidated with the Rockefeller Foundation as its social science division.[74] Ruml retired, though he remained director of the new Spelman Fund of New York, with a capital of $10 million, which he and Merriam used in the early 1930s to create the Public Administration Clearing House south of the Midway.[75] The university's new president Robert Hutchins justly claimed at the opening of the Social Science

Research Building that the Memorial "in its brief but brilliant career did more than any other agency to promote the social sciences in the United States."[76] The culmination of Chicago's close association with Ruml came in 1931, when he became for three years dean of the new division of social sciences and professor of education at the university.

Arguments about how cooperation could be achieved continued.[77] The opening of the Social Science Research Building, symbolic though it was, led to some critical questioning. Hutchins hinted that the social sciences had not yet lived up to their promise.[78] Ruml observed that vested academic interests resisted the breaking down of academic boundaries.[79] Even Merriam expressed some self-doubt about what all the elaborate organization he had helped to create could achieve.

> We appreciate only too well that neither excellence of equipment nor strength of personnel is a guarantee of ultimate success, and it may well be that in some top floor, in some rear alley in Vienna, or elsewhere, some half-starved genius may see and state what has escaped us with better facilities for seeing and stating.[80]

The ceremonies of 1929 put the seal of approval upon what Chicago social scientists were trying to do; yet afterwards the early spirit was more difficult to re-create. Hutchins's commitment to social science research was lukewarm. Some of the new faces, notably Mortimer Adler, were outright hostile. Certain departments, too, particularly sociology, had passed their peak of creative achievement. As departments grew larger, they also became more differentiated, a process most clearly observable in economics. Yet the Local Community Research Committee between 1923 and 1930 was a prototype for the organization of university-based social science research, not only in America but throughout the world. Just as Chicago had established the first department of sociology in the world by Small's appointment in 1892, so in the 1920s it pioneered an organized effort to promote empirical social research and it did so with support obtained outside the regular university budget. This support was a necessary condition for the success of the research which Park and Burgess directed.

The university tried to maintain the same criteria as before in terms of excellence of scholarship, the training of graduate students, specialization and academic professional standards, but added to it several new dimensions. These included the solicitation of large-scale external financial support for research, both from foundations and local sources; the initiation of large-scale collaborative projects, some of them interdisciplinary; a significant increase in the scale and quality of graduate teaching, linked to the growth of research and using research funds in part to finance graduate study; an important emphasis upon publication of the results of research and the use of external funds to subsidize publication; some emphasis upon the development of systematic research techniques and self-conscious attention to the procedures and practices of research. It did all this while maintaining a strong commitment to high academic quality of achievement, rigorous standards in assessing the quality of scholarship, and a desire to maintain the national preeminence of the Chicago social science group.

The gap even between the way in which W. I. Thomas studied the Polish peasant and Merriam and Gosnell studied nonvoting was quite wide in terms of organizational complexity. Chicago in the 1920s did not achieve the high degree of specialization and division of labor later established in centers such as the Columbia Bureau of Applied Social Research.[81] The Chicago pattern of the 1920s was important, however, because it was intermediate between a collection of lone scholars (which was traditionally the character of a social science department) and a separate and highly differentiated research institute.[82] It provided a means of blending teaching and research in the university without substantially separating them, yet providing support and services for research on a very considerable scale. There is little doubt that on the Midway in the 1920s, a new conception of the role of the social sciences in the university was being successfully institutionalized.

9 The Development of Quantitative Methods in the Early 1920s

"When you cannot measure ◉ your knowledge is ◉ meagre ◉ and ◉ unsatisfactory ◉ Lord Kelvin."[1] The irony of the inscription carved below the bay window of the Social Science Research Building, 1126 East 59th Street, is considerable. Erected in 1929, the building is tangible evidence of the fruitfulness of the program of collaborative research organized by the Local Community Research Committee, as well as of the strengths of the Chicago "schools" of sociology and political science.[2] Yet the triumph of Lord Kelvin over the favored alternative of Aristotle's *Anthropos Zoon Politikon*, which was engineered by William F. Ogburn, chairman of the subcommittee on symbolism,[3] emphasizes concretely the centrality of quantitative methods in Chicago social science. How does this square with the familiar contrasts that are drawn between the Chicago and Columbia schools of sociology?[4] How does this fit in with the predominant identification of Chicago social science with "soft" ethnographic methods in the 1920s and 1930s? Why was such a paeon to social measurement carved so prominently upon the building that embodied the research achievements of the 1920s in sociology, political science, economics, psychology, and other social sciences?

The neglect of this quantitative tradition in Chicago social science in the 1920s and 1930s is manifest, and its significance misunderstood. Henrika Kuklick, for example, has asserted that the hiring of William F. Ogburn by the Department of Sociology in 1927 brought a "vehemently scientistic sociologist who prescribed a research program for sociology which in many ways violated Chicago ideals."[5] Norbert Wiley, in a recent comparison of Chicago in the 1920s and Columbia in the 1940s states that:

> The thread running through [Chicago] methods was the study of the single case whether an individual or a group, with special attention to the symbolic culture and subjective definitions of the case. They were looking, not for laws but for patterns, ideal types and gestalts, and they used the insights of case analysis, not primarily for defining variables and pursuing later statistical analysis but for enlarging the case and searching for bigger patterns.[6]

Paul Rock's interpretative history of symbolic interactionism more or less identifies the approach with the University of Chicago.

> The interactionist perspective was first given its distinctive structure by a community of psychologists, philosophers, and sociologists who were centered on the new University of Chicago at the beginning of the century. . . . The position took form in a distinct intellectual community. Indeed one sociologist who confronted the task of defining it preferred not to allude to its structure or substance but to its anchorage in the world of Chicago. Its location and history represented its most tangible and identifiable facets.[7]

Intensive field research, the collection of personal documents and life histories, and an approach to social behavior from the subjective point of view of social action were all very important strands in the work of the Chicago school of sociology in the 1920s.[8] This is the legacy that has been left to the discipline when it reconstructs its history today.[9] Edward A. Tiryakian, for example, wrote in a recent general discussion of sociological schools that the influence of the Chicago school carried on into the present "in the continuing use of field research, participant observation, urban sociology, and the attention given to social psychological or intersubjective features of social organization and social processes."[10] This image is reinforced by recent controversies over the correct historical interpretation of the origins of symbolic interactionism and sociological social psychology, largely focused on the thought of figures active at Chicago.[11]

No comparable attention is devoted to the quantitative emphasis in Chicago social science—indeed it is largely forgotten[12]—partly because of the fact that the history of quantitative research methods is fragmented between different academic disciplines and between the academic world and nonacademic research bodies in government and market research.[13] The history of the social sciences tends to be written around developments in its constituent disciplines. Developments that cut across disciplines, such as the diffusion of the idea and practical use of random sampling, are much more difficult to trace and to account for coherently.[14] Yet one preeminent feature of Chicago social science in the 1920s—the extent and fruitfulness of genuine interdisciplinary collaboration—is either lost sight of or viewed through distinctly partial lenses. The links between sociological social psychology and philosopher G. H. Mead are now well known, but one hears much less of the important ties of sociologists with political scientist Harold Gosnell, or with psychologist L. L. Thurstone, or with the economist Henry Schultz, or that throughout the 1920s Chicago's graduate students in sociology took courses in statistics with the economist James A. Field. One reason for the confusion about the history of quantitative methods is that as a topic it falls somewhere between statistics, sociology, political science, psychology, and economics as academic disciplines and social survey research and market research as areas of (both nonacademic and academic) social inquiry. An adequate history of the development of quantitative methods in American social science is still a long way off, and the lines of development are very crossed.

In this chapter and the next I consider what Chicago contributed to the development of quantitative methods in social science. My main focus is upon sociology and political science, but psychology, economics, and the interdisciplinary setting are also considered.

There is no evidence that W. I. Thomas took any particular interest in statistical work or the collection of quantitative data. There are scarcely any figures at all given in *The Polish Peasant*, and none of his other writings make much use of quantification. In this respect he was in marked contrast to Franz Boas, whose work on racial difference has a firm statistical basis. Robert Park is likewise thought not to have been much interested in quantitative data. The course on field studies he taught with Burgess put the emphasis on firsthand acquaintance with the social world. Park's general methodological position emphasized the importance of studying the meaning of action and understanding social processes. He was not proficient in quantitative methods and in his later years at Chicago, perhaps provoked by the advent of Ogburn, was sometimes disparaging about them.[15] Park was certainly not a strong advocate of the statistical approach to the study of society, yet it would be a mistake to see him as strongly antiquantitative. He was skeptical, but he also encouraged a certain amount of quantitative work himself. The two surveys carried out by Charles S. Johnson with his advice for the Chicago Commission on Race Relations are a case in point.

Park was familiar with the classic urban surveys of Booth and Rowntree, Kellogg and Shelby Harrison, which were prominently mentioned in the final section of Louis Wirth's bibliography on the study of the city in *The City* in 1925.[16] Park's main emphasis in urban theory was upon processes of invasion and succession and the natural histories of groups and areas within the city. He wrote in 1926: "In so far as social structure can be defined in terms of position, social changes may be defined in terms of movement; and society exhibits, in one of its aspects, characters that can be measured and described in mathematical formulas."[17] He took an interest in land values, or street-car transfers, or the volume of traffic at intersections, as indexes for underlying social processes. Thus his student Helen McGill studied land values as an ecological index in the community of south Chicago, relating values to land use and distance from the center.[18] Andrew Lind used street-car transfers as an index of physical mobility. The street-car company gave him all the transfers collected at certain intersections at a specified day and time.[19] Such measures were indicative in quantitative terms of the intensity of social process.

In his work on the Survey of Race Relations in the Pacific, Park was closely associated with Emory Bogardus (of the University of Southern California, who received his Ph.D. at Chicago in 1911), well known as the originator of the Bogardus social distance scale. Bogardus attributed the origin of the idea of his scale to Park:

> Park was aware of the weaknesses of social research methods. None seemed entirely satisfactory or reliable. He wanted us to obtain subjective data and present them objectively. One day he drew some vertical lines and crossed them with horizontal lines, and set me at work on developing a scale for measuring racial attitudes. This was the origin of my work in developing a racial distance scale and in measuring racial and other social attitudes of groups of persons. Each time that I presented a new version of the scale to Park, he pointed out its weaknesses, a discussion followed and later a revised scale appeared. It was this persistence on illuminating errors in research that was one of Park's strong characteristics, and the one for which I am most indebted to him.[20]

It is worth remembering that Park, despite his antiquantitative tendencies, was associated with the inception of one of the earliest attitude scales.

If Park's interest in these methods was relatively minor, Ernest Burgess's was not. Although the growth of quantitative methods at Chicago is often dated from the appointment of William F. Ogburn in 1927, in fact it more properly began eleven years earlier with the appointment of Burgess, whose role has been understated and the richness and range of whose concerns are not reflected in the generalized image of the department as committed to field research. One of the first courses Burgess taught at Chicago was on social pathology, and for this he had students prepare maps of the distribution of social problems throughout the city. "From this began to emerge the realization that there was a definite pattern and structure to the city, and that many types of social problems were correlated with each other."[21] Burgess's ecological ideas about urban structure, which culminated in the theory of concentric zones in 1925 and his concept of natural area, grew out of this work, which was associated with the seminar on field studies.

> In every course I gave I am sure there were one or two students who made maps. I think the maps of juvenile delinquency were the first ones undertaken. They were followed by maps showing the distribution of motion picture houses. Then came maps showing the distribution of patrons of the public dance halls. . . We were very impressed with the great differences between the

> various neighborhoods in the city, and one of the earliest goals was to try to find a pattern to this patchwork of differences, and to "make sense of it." Mapping was the method which seemed most appropriate for such a problem.[22]

Burgess cultivated his connections with city organizations partly as a way of obtaining data. The students made maps with any data they could find, and often these were obtained from the city organizations that Burgess cultivated, such as the Juvenile Court, the Health Department, the Association of Commerce, and the urban transport and telephone companies. In 1923–24 the *Social Research Base Map* of the city of Chicago was produced, showing physical features and political boundaries, but in addition zoning of land for different purposes, the location of residential, industrial, railway, and business property and vacant areas.[23] Social data were then plotted on the base map to disclose patterns.

As Vivien Palmer wrote:

> Plotting cases of social phenomena on a map according to the locality in which they occur is one form of statistical procedure for classifying large numbers of cases. The spot map classifies the data spatially, making it possible to bring the phases of group life which are being studied into juxtaposition with other social phenomena, thus classifying many different types of phenomena into the constellations in which they occur, and suggesting possible relationships between them.[24]

Mapping was a basic tool of urban research, and ecological analysis rested on its use. In Helen McGill Hughes's recollection:

> We were given seven-foot-long blank maps of Chicago, where only the community boundaries had been entered. On these we each plotted the index we were dealing with. [These maps were then] superimposed upon spot maps made by others of us—locating alcoholics, or divorced couples, or persons of a specific ethnicity, for instance,—one could instantly see that these indices were lacking on some parts of the city, while in other local communities they clustered. Thus personal pathology was an index of community disorganization.[25]

No monograph was complete without its map or maps. Particularly extensive use of them was made in Reckless's *Natural History of Vice Areas*, Thrasher's *Gang*, Cavan's *Suicide*, Helen McGill's M.A. thesis on land values, Shaw's *Delinquency Areas*, and Mowrer's *Family Disorganization*. Mowrer indeed recalled that it was difficult as a Chicago sociologist in the 1920s to get a Ph.D. without doing a spot map.[26]

Base maps were constructed to show different kinds of variables, such as population density, distribution of nationalities, land values, business, religious groups, and occupational distribution. Rates were calculated for the incidence of different social characteristics to permit "a comparison, so far as possible statistically, of the play of social forces and trends in the different local communities of the city."[27] The measurement of gradients was an integral part of Chicago urban research. Thus male juvenile delinquency rates were calculated along lines radiating from the Loop, to show the declining rate from center to perhiphery. There were similar rates of change for parallel indices of family disorganization, population change, adult crime, and so on.[28] Both Burgess and Park were keenly interested in such quantitative measurement, which was an integral part of their theory of urban structure.

Mapping work received essential support from the LCRC. In June 1925 Frederick F. Stephan, then a graduate student, was appointed for nine months to take charge of cartography.[29] Map exhibits formed part of the material on display at summer institutes of the Society for Social Research and at the opening of the Social Science Research Building in 1929. In the new building, three rooms were set aside for the map drawing office and map collection library.[30]

Such work nowadays would tend to be the preserve of social and statistical geographers, which is one measure of the extent to which disciplinary boundaries shift over time. So long as ecological studies flourished, mapping was an important, if simple, quantitative technique. With growing criticism of ecological theory, and then the discovery of thc ecological fallacy, human ecology was eclipsed both as a general theory and as a method of data analysis, outside the specialized area of urban sociology.[31] With it, mapping as a technique lost the prominence in sociology which it still retains in geography.

At Chicago in the 1920s, mapping was complementary to the use of other research methods. It was emphasized to students that data on maps should be carefully compared with statements derived from documents, personal observation, and statistical materials. One prime source of statistical data on the city was the census, and Burgess's influence in greatly improving the availability of census data for the city of Chicago was one of his more notable contributions to quantitative research. His developing interest in zones and "natural areas" called for comprehensive, finely broken-down, base-line data, which only the census could provide. In the early 1920s, he set about obtaining these, in a remarkable initiative that emphasizes the catholicity of methodological approaches within the Chicago department. Burgess saw the process as a necessary scientific step.

> What is meant by the phrase, the city as a laboratory for social science research? If it is anything more than a metaphor, it must

> mean the establishment of a control over observation and experimentation in urban behavior essentially the same as that provided by the physical, chemical, or biological laboratory. In the study of the city this control can perhaps only be secured through comparable statistical data, not merely for the city as a whole but for its local area.[32]

Burgess, it may be fairly claimed, was the father of modern census tract statistics, both by example and as a coordinator of pressure on the Bureau of the Census to make data available in that form. He did not invent the census tract, a distinction which belongs to Dr. Walter Laidlaw, a New York public health specialist around the turn of the century,[33] but he was their modern progenitor and midwife, helping to bring into being a type of statistical data entirely taken for granted today.

Potentially, the census was a valuable source for the study of local areas. Topics covered included total population, its age and sex structure, household composition, race and nationality, mother tongue, citizenship, literacy, housing conditions, occupation of those employed, and school attendance, among others. It thus provided unrivaled data on many social topics, if the data could be made available. However, for a large city like Chicago such data for the city as a whole were relatively useless, except for comparisons with other major cities. A few data were published for wards, but these were too large (in Chicago in 1920 an average of 77,000 people in each) for detailed analysis.

Burgess saw that the best prospect lay in making proper use of the data available for census *tracts*, much smaller areas than wards. A city is subdivided (more or less arbitrarily) into areas with a population between three thousand and eight thousand for statistical purposes. Tracts today are permanently established, so that comparisons may be made from year to year and from census to census. They are laid out with a view to approximate uniformity in population and with some regard for uniformity in size; and each is designed to include an area fairly homogeneous in its population characteristics. The availability of such data owes a great deal to Burgess.

The census tract in the United States originated with Dr. Laidlaw's initiative in New York in 1902. This led to the Census Bureau's compiling data for New York and seven other cities by small areas in the 1910 census, and again for the same cities—New York, Chicago, Philadelphia, Cleveland, Saint Louis, Baltimore, Boston, and Pittsburgh—in the 1920 census. Only Dr. Laidlaw in New York paid for these data actually to be tabulated, in itself a very laborious task requiring a great deal of clerical work by the Census Bureau.[34]

When census tracts were first established for Chicago in 1910, they had been laid out on the basis of square miles and subdivisions of square miles with increasing density of population; the smallest unit was one-eighth of a square mile (or 80 acres). In the central part of the city the majority of census tracts were one-eighth of a square mile, around these were tracts of one-quarter of a square mile, still further out tracts of one-half of a square mile area, and at the outskirts the tracts were one square mile or even larger.

Burgess's contribution to the sociological use of census data was at least twofold. In the first place, with funds from the LCRC, Burgess negotiated with the U.S. Bureau of the Census in 1924–25, to produce, at a cost of $3,500, census data for the 486 census tracts in the city of Chicago.[35] The data had to be specially extracted over several months.[36] From 1925 on, they formed part of the basic data used by social science researchers at the university. Similar data from the 1910 census were also obtained. Burgess was determined to publish the data to make it more widely available, which, with a subsidy from the LCRC and the assistance of Charles Newcomb, he was able to do in 1931.[37] Earlier stages of the work were assisted in 1926–27 by Frederick F. Stephan. An example of the detailed breakdown of data for each tract is shown in figure 4.

Burgess also had the Census Bureau extract the 1910 census tract data but comparability with 1920 data was very problematical. In both years the tracts were based on ward boundaries. These were irregular, determined primarily by political considerations.[38] Moreover, the city government regularly altered them, making accurate between-census comparisons of smaller areas of the city impossible. Since ward boundary changes were a regular feature of Chicago political life, there was little value in trying to produce local census data standardized for wards.

From a scientific point of view this variability in boundaries from census to census was clearly unsatisfactory. Burgess's second contribution was to organize in 1924 the Chicago Census Committee, consisting of twenty representatives from a very wide range of Chicago civic bodies, including the city government, voluntary associations, local newspapers, and local industries, such as the Bell Telephone Company. Burgess was elected chairman, to pursue the main objective of promoting and carrying on "the collection, correlation, tabulation, and publication of statistical data concerning Chicago in a manner that would insure their maximum usefulness to social, civic, and governmental bodies in Chicago. In particular, the committee aimed to secure the collection and publication of census data according to relatively small permanent areas."[39] In June 1924 the committee adopted a recommendation that "the *Census Tracts*, used for tabulating statistical data concerning Chicago, should be defined in terms of the established section lines and section areas; the latter to be further sub-divided, into halves, quarters, and eighths, as the density of population increases." In addition, "*enumeration districts* should be laid out in uniform minimum fractional parts of the Tracts," except as modified by such barriers as rivers, lakes, or railroads.[40]

The real test of the effectiveness of the committee came before the 1930 census. There was complete agreement on the value of tracts, but a difference of opinion over what boundaries the tracts should have. Some favored ward lines, others square miles and subdivisions of square miles,

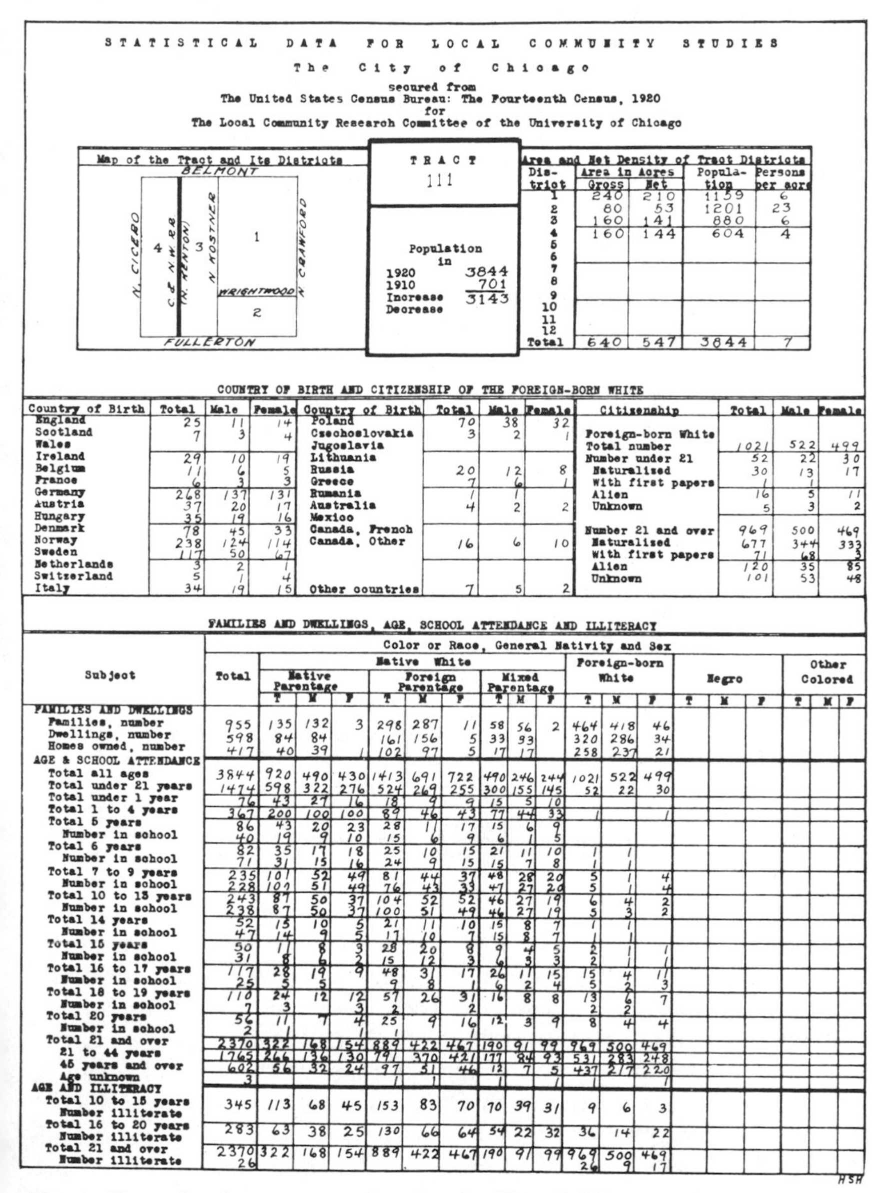

STATISTICAL DATA FOR LOCAL COMMUNITY STUDIES

The City of Chicago

secured from
The United States Census Bureau: The Fourteenth Census, 1920
for
The Local Community Research Committee of the University of Chicago

Map of the Tract and Its Districts

TRACT 111

Population in

1920	3844
1910	701
Increase	3143
Decrease	

Area and Net Density of Tract Districts

District	Area in Acres: Gross	Area in Acres: Net	Population	Persons per acre
1	240	210	1159	6
2	80	53	1201	23
3	160	141	880	6
4	160	144	604	4
5				
6				
7				
8				
9				
10				
11				
12				
Total	640	547	3844	7

COUNTRY OF BIRTH AND CITIZENSHIP OF THE FOREIGN-BORN WHITE

Country of Birth	Total	Male	Female	Country of Birth	Total	Male	Female
England	25	11	14	Poland	70	38	32
Scotland	7	3	4	Czechoslovakia	3	2	1
Wales				Jugoslavia			
Ireland	29	10	19	Lithuania			
Belgium	11	6	5	Russia	20	12	8
France	6	3	3	Greece	7	6	1
Germany	268	137	131	Rumania	1	1	
Austria	37	20	17	Australia	4	2	2
Hungary	35	19	16	Mexico			
Denmark	78	45	33	Canada, French			
Norway	238	124	114	Canada, Other	16	6	10
Sweden	117	50	67				
Netherlands	3	2	1				
Switzerland	5	1	4				
Italy	34	19	15	Other countries	7	5	2

Citizenship	Total	Male	Female
Foreign-born White			
Total number	1021	522	499
Number under 21	52	22	30
Naturalized	30	13	17
With first papers	1	1	
Alien	16	5	11
Unknown	5	3	2
Number 21 and over	969	500	469
Naturalized	677	344	333
With first papers	71	68	3
Alien	120	35	85
Unknown	101	53	48

FAMILIES AND DWELLINGS, AGE, SCHOOL ATTENDANCE AND ILLITERACY

Subject	Total	Native White: Native Parentage T	M	F	Native White: Foreign Parentage T	M	F	Native White: Mixed Parentage T	M	F	Foreign-born White T	M	F	Negro T	M	F	Other Colored T	M	F
FAMILIES AND DWELLINGS																			
Families, number	955	135	132	3	298	287	11	58	56	2	464	418	46						
Dwellings, number	598	84	84		161	156	5	33	33		320	286	34						
Homes owned, number	417	40	39	1	102	97	5	17	17		258	237	21						
AGE & SCHOOL ATTENDANCE																			
Total all ages	3844	920	490	430	1413	691	722	490	246	244	1021	522	499						
Total under 21 years	1474	598	322	276	524	269	255	300	155	145	52	22	30						
Total under 1 year	76	43	27	16	18	9	9	15	5	10									
Total 1 to 4 years	367	200	100	100	89	46	43	77	44	33	1		1						
Total 5 years	86	43	20	23	28	11	17	15	6	9									
Number in school	40	19	9	10	15	6	9	6	1	5									
Total 6 years	82	35	17	18	25	10	15	21	11	10	1	1							
Number in school	71	31	15	16	24	9	15	15	7	8	1	1							
Total 7 to 9 years	235	101	52	49	81	44	37	48	28	20	5	1	4						
Number in school	228	100	51	49	76	43	33	47	27	20	5	1	4						
Total 10 to 13 years	243	87	50	37	104	52	52	46	27	19	6	4	2						
Number in school	238	87	50	37	100	51	49	46	27	19	5	3	2						
Total 14 years	52	15	10	5	21	11	10	15	8	7	1	1							
Number in school	47	14	9	5	17	10	7	15	8	7	1	1							
Total 15 years	50	11	8	3	28	20	8	9	4	5	2	1	1						
Number in school	31	8	6	2	15	12	3	6	3	3	2	1	1						
Total 16 to 17 years	117	28	19	9	48	31	17	26	11	15	15	4	11						
Number in school	25	5	5		9	8	1	6	2	4	5	2	3						
Total 18 to 19 years	110	24	12	12	57	26	31	16	8	8	13	6	7						
Number in school	7	3		3	2		2				2	2							
Total 20 years	56	11	7	4	25	9	16	12	3	9	8	4	4						
Number in school	2	1		1	1		1												
Total 21 and over	2370	322	168	154	889	422	467	190	91	99	969	500	469						
21 to 44 years	1765	266	136	130	791	370	421	177	84	93	531	283	248						
45 years and over	602	56	32	24	97	51	46	12	7	5	437	217	220						
Age unknown	3				1	1		1		1	1		1						
AGE AND ILLITERACY																			
Total 10 to 15 years	345	113	68	45	153	83	70	70	39	31	9	6	3						
Number illiterate																			
Total 16 to 20 years	283	63	38	25	130	66	64	54	22	32	36	14	22						
Number illiterate																			
Total 21 and over	2370	322	168	154	889	422	467	190	91	99	969	500	469						
Number illiterate	26										26	9	17						

HSH

Fig. 4. Example of census tract data for the City of Chicago, 1920, extracted by the Bureau of the Census. Ernest W. Burgess Papers, University of Chicago Archives, Box 3, Folder 12.

yet others the seventy-five local community areas worked out by the LCRC. The problem was solved by a plan of tracts designed to meet the needs of all organizations, reconciling the various requirements.[41]

This scheme was embodied in the U.S. Census Bureau's plans for the 1930 census, giving Chicago the most flexible and comprehensive system of census tracts of any city in the United States. Nationally, tract data were produced in 1930 for another eight cities in addition to the eight in 1920. A comparison volume of 1930 census tract data for Chicago was published in 1933.[42] This contained data collected from 2,508 enumeration districts, assembled and published for 935 census tracts, and for these tracts combined into the 75 community areas. It is noteworthy that collaboration between city and university was so far advanced that an academic classification could be used as the basis for official categorizations. In 1931 the 75 community areas were adopted by the Chicago Department of Public Health as 75 health districts for the reporting of births, deaths, and morbidity.

The commitment of Burgess to the usefulness of census data was shown by his strong support for the idea of a special Chicago city census in 1934. Indeed, he was its originator.

> The idea came to me of having a city census. The data could be contrasted with those of 1930 and, later, with those of 1940. I got in touch with the Department of Health and the mayor of the city. I wrote the ordinance under which the census could be conducted. We had the promise of the W.P.A. that they would furnish the enumerators. I attended the meeting of the council because I was afraid if any questions were to be asked of the mayor by the aldermen he would not be able to answer them. This fear showed my naïveté, because Mayor Kelly made a short speech in which he spoke of all the persons out of work. He said the census would give 1,000 unemployed men jobs. And I heard the aldermen say: "pass, pass." No formal vote was taken.[43]

The census was conducted by a commission, chaired by the mayor. Its director in charge of operations was Charles Newcomb, a sociology graduate student and Burgess's associate, assisted by another graduate student, Richard Lang. It had full city backing. Financial assistance was provided by the Civil Works Administration and by the University of Chicago Social Science Research Committee (successor to the LCRC). The results of this 1934 census, which used the 1930 census tracts and the 75 local community areas as the basis for tabulation, were published late in the year that it was taken.[44]

In 1935, the Chicago Recreation Commission published a *District Fact Book*, edited by E. L. Buchard and M. J. Amin, based in part on the 1934 census. In 1938 the commission followed this by publishing an improved and expanded version, perhaps the best-known of the Chicago statistical publications, the *Chicago Local Community Fact Book*, edited by Louis Wirth and Margaret Furez. The volume was intended to be "a compendium of reliable information, . . . an index of local community life, . . . a measure for dealing more effectively with local problems, and . . . a basis for the formulation of more enlightened programs and policies."[45] Burgess again was a notable influence acknowledged by the editors.

The *Local Community Fact Book*, based on the 1930 and 1934 censuses, contained statistical data for the 75 local community areas of the city. In several respects, however, it was a departure from the earlier volumes of data. It incorporated data from other sources (chiefly from Chicago sociologists) on topics such as fertility and mortality (P. M. Hauser), insanity rates (Faris and Dunham), delinquency rates (Shaw and McKay), and family structure (Burgess). It included data for both 1930 and 1934. And in addition to the statistical tables for each of the 75 areas, it included for each a descriptive page of text, incorporating information on its history, boundaries, social characteristics, schools, churches, recreational facilities, registered voters, selected morbidity rates, social agencies, and civic organizations, drawn from a variety of sources. Its detail was less fine—for 75 areas as opposed to nearly 1000 tracts—but for each area it provided considerably more information. This volume and the later volumes for the 1940, 1950, and 1960 censuses were established on the foundations Ernest Burgess laid in the early 1920s.[46] He was not the only pioneer—Howard Whipple Green at the Cleveland Health Council was active in urging the formation of "tract committees" around the country[47]—but he was most influential both in Chicago and at the Census Bureau. Appropriately, the 1960 Local Community Fact Book was dedicated to him.

> His pioneering work, more than 40 years ago, helped to make census tract statistics for Chicago possible. Moreover, he is largely responsible for the delineation of the community areas in Chicago, and for leadership in indicating how information for such areas may be utilized in policy formation and administration for the common good.[48]

The influence of Burgess was important in substantive areas of sociology. A 1926 paper on gradients in city growth exemplified the use of census tract data to test hypotheses about the zonal structure of the city.[49] His 1928 paper on residential segregation used census tract data to test hypotheses about racial segregation in the city in the light of the concentric zones model.[50] This type of analysis was taken further by some of his students. His contribution lay both in the use of such data in substantive analysis and in taking practical steps to make such data available. The importance he and Park attached to such data demonstrates the diversity of methodological approaches in the department and the inadequacy of equating Chicago sociology with nonquantitative methods.

The word "statistics" is ambiguous. It can refer to numerical data collected by the state, as in the census, or to a body of ideas enabling one to analyze numerical data, whatever its source. In the late 1920s, following William F. Ogburn's arrival in 1927, Burgess became interested in statistics as a body of ideas and set of techniques.[51] He attended at least one of Ogburn's courses while a full professor and subsequently made or supervised several notable further studies of crime and the family using what at the time were more advanced statistical procedures. He and Clark Tibbitts analyzed detailed records of 1000 men paroled from three Illinois penal institutions. They related a variety of background factors, personal characteristics, and criminal records to experience of parole. Each offender was scored on the combined influence of 21 factors, and violation rates compared for low and high scores, showing that high scorers had a low rate and low scorers a high rate. The method could be used to derive expectancy rates of parole violation and nonviolation for use in parole administration. Similar methods had proved to be of value in insurance and other areas where forecasting was necessary.[52]

Burgess made notable contributions to criminology through his association with the Institute for Juvenile Research. It is ironic that one of the most vigorous proponents in the late 1920s of the case study method in social research—Clifford Shaw—headed an organization which at the same time was carrying out what were, for the period, sophisticated types of quantitative analysis, within an ecological framework. The early results of this research appeared in *Delinquency Areas* in 1929, which included a partial correlation analysis of the relation between rates of delinquency in certain areas and rates of recidivism.[53] More impressive still for its analytical contribution was the work Shaw and McKay did for the National Commission on Law Observance and Enforcement of 1931. *Social Factors in Juvenile Delinquency* was a landmark in criminology and for the time a very sophisticated causal analysis of a particular phenomenon, using ecological data and case studies.[54]

These works had a major impact on subsequent criminology.[55] Chicago sociology had a marked quantitative strain, due, to a considerable extent, to Burgess's influence. In the controversy over case studies versus statistics in the later 1920s, he took a middle position. "If statistics and case study are to yield their full contribution as tools of sociological research," he wrote, "they should be granted equal recognition and full opportunity for each to perfect its own technique. At the same time, the interaction of the two methods is certain to prove fruitful."[56] This hardly squares with the view that Chicago sociology was preeminently concerned with the study of the single case. Burgess quietly got on with his own work and encouraged younger members of the department with an interest in quantification in spite of Park's skepticism.[57] He adopted a catholic and statesmanlike position on "hard" as against "soft" methodology.

The teaching of statistics also showed that the sociology department took quantitative methods seriously. Small had clashed with Laughlin over the economist's claim to teach the subject in the 1890s. Edith Abbott taught a methods course using published statistical material prior to 1920.[58]

Of much greater importance were Field's courses in statistics in the Economics Department. James A. Field, a Harvard graduate, taught in the Department of Political Economy at Chicago from 1908 until his early death at the age of forty-seven in 1927.[59] His research interest in population had brought him into contact with Karl Pearson in London in 1906. His main contribution was as a teacher, particularly of graduate students, with whom he was popular for his clarity and politeness.[60] As early as 1911 sociology students were directed in the university handbook to take his courses, for several substantive seminars "rest in great part on a statistical basis."[61] These courses, which covered only sources, tabulation and graphics, and averages, were supplemented in 1913 by a more advanced course in statistical theory and method, which involved the simple application of correlation methods,[62] and in 1914 by a course in vital statistics.

In 1919, after war service in London (where he renewed contact with Karl Pearson and met, through an interest in standards of living, A. L. Bowley), Field returned to revamp both his introductory course and his advanced course. The former dealt with simple descriptive statistics and some elementary ideas about association. It was complemented by another course on statistical presentation, which considered how to produce maps, diagrams, and tables. His more advanced course included (in 1922) some probability theory, simple sampling, the normal distribution, and the logic of inference, together with the Pearsonian correlation coefficient.[63] Field also advised the Local Community Research Committee, suggesting the establishment of a statistical division with staff to do calculations and suitable equipment.[64] His deteriorating health meant that he did no teaching after 1926. One secondary reason for the appointment of Ogburn was to replace Field in the teaching of statistics to sociology students.

Of sociology students in the early 1920s, Ernest R. Mowrer, Ruth Shonle, Norman Hayner, and Walter Reckless all recalled having courses with Field.[65] Mowrer remembered that he was "the only sociology student during the period that had all the courses he gave. As a matter of fact, I think I was the only one . . . who took any courses beyond the introductory one in statistical methods. Therefore I was a little bit off color, because of my statistical interest."[66] Others such as Henry McKay and Frederick Stephan may have taken courses with Field. His most notable influence was on the pioneering political scientist Harold Gosnell: "He did not publish much but was an excellent teacher and gave me sound advice on the nonvoting and getting-out-the-vote studies,"[67] two of the most innovative quantitative studies carried out at Chicago in the 1920s. Gosnell took two courses with him and learned from him of the work of Yule, Pearson, and Bowley.[68]

It was in political science that some of Chicago's most important quantitative research was carried out in the early 1920s. Political science under Charles Merriam became, much more explicitly than sociology, the leading center for the promotion of a scientific social science. The quantitative surveys and field experiments conducted there in the mid-1920s are well known to political scientists,[69] but do not feature prominently in histories of survey research. They were part of a wider pattern of interdisciplinary influence, discussed in the next two chapters.

The main methodological contribution was made by Merriam's younger colleague, Harold Gosnell, in Merriam and Gosnell's *Non-Voting* (1924) and Gosnell's *Getting Out the Vote* (1927).[70] Both used what would today be called social survey methods; both used questionnaires not unlike modern ones; they showed awareness of sampling methods; and the latter employed quite a sophisticated type of experimental design. The training of interviewers for such studies prefigured modern survey organization, as did the insistence on quality control. Yet few sociologists are aware of them, again because of the barriers separating disciplines.

In a series of papers between 1921 and 1925, Merriam spelled out his view of the scientific direction the study of politics should take.[71] Statistics and psychology were singled out as having a particularly important contribution to make. He took various steps to promote these aims, including inviting L. L. Thurstone to speak to a national conference.[72] His presidential address to the American Political Science Association in 1925 was on the same theme. One of the most promising substantive fields for the application of quantitative methods was the study of voting. A series of studies of voting behavior (and of nonvoting) carried on under controlled conditions would reveal much regarding the political interests of the voter in different situations.

Merriam was a strong advocate of quantitative methods, but he did not himself know a great deal about how such work was actually conducted.[73] He sparked the ideas and found the wherewithal to implement them, but relied on his younger colleagues to carry out the work. This was the case with Harold Gosnell, who was well-versed in methodology and made several notable contributions to political science. He is one of the neglected pioneers of social survey research in the United States.

Gosnell had studied economics, mathematics, history, and psychology at the University of Rochester.[74] In 1919 he came to Chicago as graduate student and fellow, completing his Ph.D. in 1922 on Boss Platt and the New York machine.[75] He was a research fellow and instructor from 1922 to 1924, spent 1924/25 in Europe on an SSRC fellowship, and was appointed assistant professor in 1925, remaining at Chicago until 1942. Gosnell became interested in quantitative methods as a graduate student under the influence of Merriam (or "The Chief," as he was known). In 1921 Gosnell published his first article, which included a discussion of the use of psychological tests in the army in World War I.[76] He took courses with Field in the economics department and with Freeman on educational tests and measurement, "which helped me in the construction of questionnaires used in the voting studies." L. L. Thurstone came to Chicago in 1924, and Gosnell had discussions with him on psychology and politics.[77] He first met W. F. Ogburn in Paris in 1925 and thus began a long association, which culminated in Ogburn writing a preface to the classic *Machine Politics: Chicago Model*, in which Gosnell acknowledged his obligation to Ogburn "for an inspiring example of pioneering statistical work in the field of American politics."[78]

The problem tackled in *Non-Voting: Causes and Methods of Control* was the varying propensity of Chicago residents to participate in elections. Significant proportions of the population, particularly among immigrants, did not register to vote; of those registered, not all exercised their right to vote. Elections in the years immediately after 1920, moreover, showed a fall in voting participation. The study focused on the Chicago mayoralty campaign of 1923. Six thousand nonvoters throughout the city were interviewed. Though not selected by probability methods, the respondents' characteristics were very carefully analyzed from the point of view of representativeness. A control group of 5,000 voters was studied from documentary sources and compared with nonvoters on a number of characteristics. A structured schedule of 31 questions was used, including both "face-sheet" variables and questions about reasons for nonvoting (see fig. 5). The questions were printed on two sides of a small card. This schedule is of particular interest, since it was clearly framed in an objective and scientific manner. An organized, paid, field force was used. Detailed guidance was provided for the interviewers, most of whom were graduate students. For those who did not speak English, the interviewers were matched by language with those whom they were interviewing.[79]

Non-Voting was a quite different kind of survey from those of the social survey movement. It was one of the earliest modern studies of American political behavior using survey methods. According to the historians of American political science,

SCHEDULE FOR INTERVIEWING ADULT CITIZEN NON-VOTERS IN CHICAGO

THE UNIVERSITY OF CHICAGO — Investigator ____

SOCIAL RESEARCH COMMITTEE — Ward ____ Precinct ____ Date ____

1. Name ____ Address ____
2. Term of residence ____
   at present address — County — Illinois — United States
3. Date of naturalization ____ Place ____
   Individual — Marriage — Parents
4. Sex ____ Occupation ____ Age ____ Color ____
   M. F. — Kind — Place — White — Colored
5. Relation to head of family ____
   Head — Wife — Son — Daughter — Boarder — Roomer
6. Place of birth ____
   of non-voter — of father — of mother
7. Type of neighborhood ____
   very good — good — fair — poor
8. Type of dwelling ____
   House — Apartment — Flat — Store — rent per month
9. Have you ever voted in Chicago? ____
   yes or no — date of last voting
10. Have you ever voted elsewhere? ____
    yes or no — place — date

    Reasons for not registering ____ *for not voting* ____

11. Illness ____ 12. Absence from city ____
    give cause
13. Insufficient legal residence. (See 2.) ____
14. General indifference ____
    to all elections — to the last election
15. Disbelief in woman's voting (for female citizens) ____
    anti-suffragist — Objections of husband
16. Belief that one vote counts for nothing ____ 17. Neglect—intended to vote but failed ____
18. Fear of loss of business or wages ____

[FRONT]

SCHEDULE FOR INTERVIEWING ADULT CITIZEN NON-VOTERS IN CHICAGO

19. Fear of disclosure of age________ 20. Fear of jury duty________

21. Disbelief in all political action________

22. Congestion at the polls________ 23. Poor location of polling booth________ (Explanation)

24. Belief that the candidates are equally good________

25. Disgust with politics________

26. Objection to own party candidate and objection to vote for other party candidate________ (General / Special)

27. Ignorance or timidity regarding elections________

28. Belief that the ballot box is corrupted________

________ (give examples)

29. Failure of party workers________

30. Detained by helpless member of family________ (to call at all / to furnish transportation to the polls)

31. Additional reasons or detailed explanations given by non-voter________

____

____

____

____

____

32. Investigator's comments________

____

[Back]

Fig. 5. Interview schedule used for study of adult citizen nonvoters in Chicago, 1923–24. Reprinted from Charles E. Merriam and Harold F. Gosnell, *Non-Voting* (Chicago: University of Chicago Press, 1924), pp. 264–65.

> the significance of this book would be hard to overestimate. The problem itself was one about which little of a systematic character was known, and the study provided a means of introducing a bevy of young graduate students to field research. More to the immediate point . . . it was based on a survey rather than aggregate data. . . . Interviewers were trained for their assignments, the schedules were carefully structured, and Hollerith cards and counter-sorters were used in data processing. With *Non-Voting* the Chicago department took a giant step towards establishing itself as the national center for the scientific study of politics.[80]

It held that position for most of the period between World War I and II.

During 1924 Gosnell carried out another study—to see to what extent factors associated with nonvoting could be controlled in a particular election; published in 1927, *Getting Out the Vote* was the "classic experiment in stimulated voting" and a rare early example of a social science field experiment.[81] Over 3,000 respondents were interviewed in 12 selected districts of the city. The respondents were then divided, within each district, into two groups. The experimental group was sent stimulus material consisting of individual nonpartisan appeals to vote to encourage registration; the control group received nothing. At the final stage, data were gathered from poll books and the list of registered voters to check whether individuals were registered. As a check, however, all persons originally canvassed who were not on the list of registered voters were canvassed again. The overall finding was that the experimental stimulus had the effect of increasing the proportion of nonvoters registered by 10 percent.

It is important to emphasize how rigorous and elegant was the design of this study for the time. The division into experimental and control groups was done within areas along geographical lines within blocks. Comparisons showed that the characteristics of both groups were practically the same on a number of variables. Special efforts were made to reduce nonresponse to a minimum.

The innovations pioneered by Gosnell did not end at the design stage. Both this study and a study carried out in the same year on nonnaturalization[82] illustrate the care with which the field force were recruited, trained, and briefed. Gosnell's comments on the qualities that interviewers needed were remarkably modern: "It requires persons of tact, good physique, perseverance, amiability, linguistic ability, ingenuity, and intelligence, who have a sympathetic feeling toward the canvass which is being undertaken, to do this work successfully. Such persons are not any too plentiful."[83] An introductory letter was provided, interviewers were instructed in how to approach respondents, the sensitivity required was emphasized, confidentiality was to be stressed, and specific times of day to call were suggested.[84]

The Local Community Research Committee supported these studies and made them possible, in three ways. It provided $5,000 for each study to finance data collection and analysis. The cost per interview in *Non-Voting* was estimated by Gosnell at 26¢ plus 20¢ for statistical handling and 10¢ for paper. Although recognizing the expense of this, he was clear that it was much superior to a survey relying on volunteer student assistance. "The principal drawback to a study on this basis is that the work would be less thorough and scientific. Volunteer student help would be much more difficult to organize and supervise."[85] The employment of supervisors of field workers (at a cost of $1,300) is indicative of the care that went into the planning and execution of the study.

Data from the nonvoting study were put onto Hollerith cards and a counter-sorter was then used to produce cross-tabulations. As no machines were available in the university, Gosnell had to pay the Comptroller's Office at City Hall from the grant to use their card-tabulating machine.[86] The second contribution of the LCRC was to acquire such equipment in 1925 jointly with the departments of psychology and education, permitting analysis to be carried out on the premises. The third contribution was to employ support staff for computational work. Tasks now routinely carried out by computer were then done by hand, very laboriously. The Hollerith machine, first developed to cope with the volume of data from the 1890 U.S. census, was the most advanced form of mechanical aid available. Calculating machines were simple. Quantitative data analysis required much more intensive use of manpower than is the case today.

These pioneering studies by Gosnell establish Chicago's claim to be regarded as one of the originators of the scientific social survey in the United States. It was one of several signs that, by the middle of the decade, the social sciences were changing, facilitated by the existence of the LCRC bringing together staff from separate departments, encouraging their research activities, and providing concrete help in the form of clerical assistance and statistical and computational facilities. The first results of research were being published. The appointment of L. L. Thurstone to the psychology department (discussed in the next chapter) gave a further boost to quantitative methods. And in sociology the trend toward more quantitative work was given a decisive push by the appointment in 1927 of William F. Ogburn to a senior professorship. There is evidence that Ogburn was attracted to Chicago partly by the facilities that the LCRC offered. What, on the other hand, did Chicago sociologists expect to achieve by his appointment?

This is a significant question in relation to the development of quantitative methods, because it has been suggested that Ogburn's appointment was some sort of aberration on the part of sociologists committed to case-study methods.[87] This is not born out by the evidence and represents a major misunderstanding of methodological currents in the 1920s. An examination of the circumstances surrounding the invitation to Ogburn illuminates not only the place of quantification in sociology at the period but also the true character of Chicago sociology in the 1920s. The diversity of the department's interests and its collective commitment to excellence are shown by this episode.

In 1926 Small had retired and Scott Bedford's post was vacant. The only sociologists were Faris, the chairman, and Park and Burgess. In 1925/26, Floyd N. House held a one-year appointment, leaving to head the new department at the University of Virginia. With more than seventy graduate students in residence, finding a new senior sociologist was a matter of urgency.[88]

The department's choice fell upon William F. Ogburn at Columbia, in order to strengthen the quantitative side of the department's work and ensure that Chicago retained its strength as the leading department of sociology in the country. Trained at Columbia under Giddings in the early part of the century (where he had had courses in statistics from the economist Henry L. Moore), Ogburn had then taught economics, history, statistics, and sociology at Reed College. During World War I he worked on cost-of-living statistics on the staff of National War Labor Board and the Bureau of Labor Statistics in Washington. He returned to Columbia in 1919. His best-known work was *Social Change*, published in 1922, but he had also done quantitative work on political behavior (with aggregate data), standards of living, and the family.[89] He was clearly identified as a proponent of quantitative methods.

In June 1926 Faris wrote to Ogburn to see if he would be responsive to an invitation to move from Columbia to Chicago. The aim was clearly to strengthen the department on the quantitative side. "We are weak in statistical work and you would have full charge of as much of that as you cared to cultivate with courses of a general theoretical nature in so far as it would appeal to you." Mention was also made of the strength of the economics department, and of the political science department under Merriam, "whom of course you know well."[90] Ogburn replied noncommittally in July, emphasizing his interest in quantitative research (which was explicitly spelled out) and his lack of interest in administration. "I am most interested in freedom and support for research."[91]

Quantitative research required support and organization on the same basis as work in natural science. This was not always recognized by university administrators. Whether or not Ogburn moved would depend on developments at Columbia. He had been away for a year, and plans for the future of sociology were uncertain. "It is possible that there may be many difficulties in the way against the development of sociology, and that sociology may not be supported at Columbia in the manner in which I think the situation calls for, in which case an offer from the University of Chicago would be especially attractive."[92]

At a staff meeting of the sociology department held in a private dining room at the Quadrangle Club on 14 October 1926, attended by Faris, Park, Cole, Burgess, Sapir, Eyler N. Simpson, and Louis Wirth (the last two instructors), it was unanimously agreed to make an offer to Ogburn,[93] though there was no certainty, in the light of counter-offers from Columbia, that he would accept it. Faris then pressed Vice-President Woodward to act on behalf of the university. He made clear that there were two main considerations, apart from Ogburn's personal qualities. Ogburn was an outstanding man in the field of quantitative sociology "whose research has been in the statistical subject. . . . The statistical aspect of sociology is obviously of the highest importance. The development of statistics in all fields has been very rapid and our work here needs such a man imperatively."[94] His appointment would also help to ensure that Chicago remained the strongest graduate sociology department in the country, as it had been shown to be in 1922.[95] On Ogburn's part, support of the kind he was seeking at Columbia was not forthcoming, and he accepted the university's offer in January 1927. He came in July of that year and remained at Chicago until he retired in 1951.

The *Bulletin* of the Society for Social Research announced his appointment in March 1927. "Professor Ogburn's chief interest in research is in the quantitative aspects of sociology. He plans to develop the statistical approach in a way not hitherto done at the university."[96] In making the appointment, it was clear at every stage what Ogburn stood for and why he was being appointed. It reflected the desire to retain the department's preeminence as the foremost sociology department in the country. Sociologists in the Chicago department might have different methodological predilections, but these did not determine who was considered the best man for the job. Ogburn was approached in quite self-conscious recognition of current trends toward quantitative empirical research within the social sciences coupled with a determination to maintain the strength of the department. Ogburn's arrival in the summer of 1927 did alter the balance in the department between those who favored "softer" and those who favored "harder" methods of research, but it was a shift which its members intended that he should bring about, and a conscious decision to further encourage diversity.

10 Quantitative Methods in the Later 1920s

If the growth of quantitative work in the early part of the 1920s was gradual, in the second half of the decade the pace quickened. One impetus was the appointment of Ogburn, another the appointment of L. L. Thurstone and Henry Schultz to research professorships funded by the memorial. The number of graduate students working in quantitative fields increased. At the end of the decade a lively controversy was waged among members of the sociology department over the merits of case studies as opposed to statistics. Diversity was manifest, while the collective spirit among the sociologists remained strong.

Ogburn's arrival gave a strong impetus to the development of quantitative methods, transforming the teaching of research methods within the sociology department and ending the reliance on service teaching. In 1927/28 Ogburn introduced three new courses on methods of research for sociology students. Introduction to Statistics replaced Field's introductory course. It covered simple descriptive statistics, basic ideas of sampling, and types of statistical fallacy.[1] Statistical Methods, taught in the second quarter, dealt with correlation and the theory of errors.[2] Statistical Problems, taught in the third quarter, was concerned with "special studies in sampling, curve fitting, determination of trend lines, cyclical and seasonal variation." The following year, 1928/29, Ogburn added a seminar for three quarters, Quantitative Sociology, for graduate students, thus strengthening the methods component in graduate teaching.[3]

Looking back to 1915, one can see clearly the shift toward a diversified and demanding range of graduate courses which became characteristic of graduate education in sociology by the middle of the twentieth century. At first there had been Edith Abbott's rather old-fashioned methods course and Field's introductory statistics. As time went on Park and Burgess began their stimulating and innovative course on field studies, which was more of a research practicum than formal instruction. The scope of Field's courses expanded at the beginning of the decade. By the end of the 1920s the range and depth of the courses offered had increased considerably. The practical element was retained through Burgess's course based on the work of the LCRC fellows. The seminar on research methods taught by Park placed considerable emphasis on the philosophy of science and the methodological foundations of sociological knowledge. He used as texts at this period A. D. Ritchie's *Scientific Method* and

Morris Cohen's *Reason and Nature*. Topics covered included the distinction between knowledge about and acquaintance with scientific knowledge as a form of knowledge, the nature of facts, the relation between fact-finding and scientific research, concepts and categories, the formulation of concepts, frames of reference, and society as an object of scientific research.[4] This more explicit attention in teaching to the philosophical foundations of social knowledge may well have been stimulated in part by the arrival of Ogburn.

The impact Ogburn had on graduate teaching in the sociology department was considerable. He was a large, personally impressive man who left his mark on those he taught.[5] He attracted a number of first-rate students. Leonard Cottrell recalled: "When Ogburn came, [he] set the tone pretty much for quite a while . . . [he] made quite a splash and attracted some very good students like Sam Stouffer, Clark Tibbitts, Fred Stephan and people like that. Pretty soon he had a coterie of students, but they became less and less the journalistic Parkian-oriented sociologist and more and more the quantitative orientation."[6] According to Robert Faris, a graduate student in the late 1920s, Ogburn "brought statistics and an appreciation of statistics and therefore a more rigorous method, and added it to the Chicago tradition." As an undergraduate, Faris, together with Stouffer, had taken a statistics course in economics taught by Henry Schultz. In his first year as a graduate student he took another from Ogburn. "The realization came up that it was an important subject."[7]

The change brought about by Ogburn should not be exaggerated, nor should the influence of Burgess be forgotten. Both Stephan and Tibbitts had worked with Burgess, Stephan on census materials, Tibbitts on the parole prediction study. Nevertheless, Ogburn gathered around him an able group, some of whom later made notable contributions to quantitative methods. Some of these, like Gosnell, who occupied an office next to Ogburn after 1929, were on the teaching staff; Tibbitts was his research assistant for three years; Stouffer, Hauser, Stephan, Dollard, Mueller, and McCormick were graduate students.

Clark Tibbitts collaborated with him on various pieces of work on voting behavior, crime, and social trends.[8] A good example of their work together was an unpublished memorandum from 1929/30 prepared for the Wickersham Commission, On the Nativity of Certain Criminal Classes Engaged in Organized Crime, and of Certain Related Criminal and Non-criminal Groups in Chicago.[9] It was a meticulous, objective, factual study on a most sensitive subject, using a wide variety of sources including prison and police records, Landesco's *Who's Who of Organized Crime* (containing 20,000 names), the Chicago Crime Commission record of all felony cases for the past twenty years, and the files of the U.S. attorney in Chicago. Not all these sources contained data on nativity, which was deduced where missing, through a variety of ingenious methods, including inferences from the areas of Chicago in which people lived which were then checked against police and probation records. Because of its sensitivity, only a few, numbered, copies of the report were produced and it was never published.

Of Ogburn's graduate students, T. C. McCormick (Ph.D., 1928) was later an outstanding teacher of research methods, statistics, and demography at the University of Wisconsin for twenty years.[10] Another graduate student of the period, J. H. Mueller (Ph.D., 1928) translated Durkheim's *Rules of Sociological Method* with Sarah A. Solovay in 1938; after World War II, he authored a major social statistics text.[11] John Dollard was a tennis friend of Ogburn's and took up graduate work at his suggestion to complete a quantitative dissertation on the American family in 1931.[12]

Frederick F. Stephan had been an M.A. student at Chicago from 1924 to 1926 and an LCRC research assistant in 1926/27. He taught sociology for a year at the University of Pittsburgh, but returned to Chicago on leave for the year 1929/30, taking courses with Ogburn. From 1934 to 1940 he was secretary and editor for the American Statistical Association (whose president he was in 1966). From there he moved to Cornell and then to Princeton. He was an influential teacher of students such as Leo Goodman. He died in 1971.[13] To what extent Stephan's interests in quantitative methods were developed in Chicago is unclear, but to some extent their foundations were clearly laid in the Chicago department. In 1936 he wrote an article on sampling in sociological research, for the *American Sociological Review*, apparently stimulated by A. L. Bowley.[14] His subsequent career was more in social statistics and demography than in sociology.[15] Dollard recalled him as an active graduate student. "Stephan . . . was one of Ogburn's really best students, too. He didn't have the tremendous energy and social thrusts that Stouffer had, but he was intellectually very able."[16]

Philip Hauser was also a graduate student at the University of Chicago between 1929 and 1932 and an instructor in sociology between 1932 and 1934. Later in the 1930s he moved to the Bureau of the Census in Washington, D.C., returning in 1947 to the Chicago faculty, where he remained for the rest of his career. Hauser was taught by both Burgess and Ogburn and also by Park. Hauser's major career interest in population studies was stimulated by Ogburn's teaching at this period.[17]

Ogburn's most brilliant and distinguished student was Samuel Stouffer. He took all Ogburn's graduate seminars in quantitative sociology as well as Park's course in methods of social research before submitting his dissertation in 1930.[18] Stouffer is so much identified with *The American Soldier* and his later career at Harvard that his graduate origins at Chicago are frequently overlooked. With Stephan and Hauser, Stouffer made major contributions to the advance of quantitative methods in his career. The foundations for this work were laid while he was studying with Ogburn.

Ogburn had been attracted to Chicago partly by the opportunity that the LCRC afforded to improve the physical facilities and equipment for quantitative work.[19] This he set about doing vigorously, playing a major part in planning the new Social Science Research Building (opened in 1929) and equipping its statistical laboratory.[20] Ogburn's arrival crystallized the organization of quantitative social research in Chicago.

Ogburn's impact came, in addition, through his research. His interests embraced statistics both in the headcounting sense and as interpretive tools. With the former, he sought to develop systematic statistical indicators of social conditions. From 1927 to 1934, Ogburn edited annually an issue of the *American Journal of Sociology* entitled "Social Change in 19–," which reviewed the year in statistical terms. His best-known work in this field was in the early 1930s as research director of President Hoover's Committee on Recent Social Trends, which reported in 1933 and whose massive compendium of data was one of the first pieces of social indicator work.[21] This statistical policy research had an important influence on the discipline in the long run, even if the aim of developing a sociological analogue to time series data in applied economics proved difficult to realize.[22]

But Ogburn was also a statistician, who between 1915 and 1920 had carried out a number of pioneering statistical studies, particularly of wage levels and the cost of living and of voting behavior.[23] In 1929 he carried this further by a statistical study of the presidential election of 1928.[24] For each of 173 counties he had five variables: (1) the foreign-born population, (2) the percent urban, (3) the percent of adults who were catholic, (4) the percent voting "wet", and (5) the percent of voters regularly voting Democratic. Each of these factors was then correlated with the percent of the vote in each county for Al Smith, the Democratic candidate, who was a Catholic.

Simple correlations were first computed, from which it appeared that the "wet" issue and the religious issue were most important in determining the election. But since there were interaction effects between the variables (e.g., urban and "wet"), partial correlation was used to control statistically for the effects of the other factors. It still appeared that voting "wet" was most important, followed by religion, followed by the Democratic factor. There was a negative correlation with the urban vote; the urban voter only seemed to be more pro-Smith because he was Catholic, Democratic, and "wet." When these influences were removed, the urban voter was somewhat anti-Smith.

This demonstration of the potential of the statistical method relied on ecological data. This was not unusual. For example, much of the work of the political scientist, V. O. Key, Jr., who was trained at Chicago in the

1930s, made use of aggregate rather than individual level data. Ogburn demonstrated how far multivariate analysis could progress when skillfully handled. His work also suggests the influence upon sociological reasoning and analysis of English statisticians such as Pearson, whose work has had a profound influence on the methodology of scientific research, but whose impact upon sociology has been thought rather slight. At this period the main guide to correlation analysis was Ezekiel's text published in 1930.[25] The logic of the methods of analysis that Ogburn used was not very different from that later developed by Lazarsfeld for tabular analysis, except that the data Ogburn used was aggregate rather than individual-level data from a sample survey. This meant that cases could not be directly subdivided into groups suitable for the application of significance tests. Indirect methods such as partial correlation gave rise to various problems, which Stouffer identified (using Ogburn's election study as an example) in 1934.[26] Later work has shown the limitations of the method for the problem Ogburn tackled.[27] Nevertheless, for its day, Ogburn's approach to multivariate analysis was advanced for sociology.

A feature of Chicago social science was the extent of interdisciplinary influence. This was particularly marked in quantitative methods. Ogburn and Gosnell were close colleagues, while from psychology L. L. Thurstone came to have a considerable influence on certain sociologists and political scientists. Thurstone, born in 1887 in Chicago, had studied mechanical engineering as an undergraduate at Cornell, later enrolling as a graduate student in psychology at Chicago in 1914, at the age of twenty-seven. Before completing his doctorate in 1917, he took up an appointment with Walter Bingham in the Carnegie Institute of Technology's division of applied psychology, where he rose to be chairman of the department before he left in 1923. During the First World War he worked under Beardsley Ruml in the trade test division of the army testing program (see chap. 3). From 1923–24 he worked in Washington on objective tests for civil service examinations before being offered an appointment at Chicago, where he taught and did research from 1924 to 1952.[28] His initial appointment as associate professor of psychology may have owed something to Merriam. In 1927, on Merriam's recommendation, he was promoted to one of the first three research professorships in social science created with memorial support, and moved into the orbit of the social sciences.[29]

For the next three or four years he worked intensively on the measurement of attitudes, making a major contribution to social science research in a field that is now an integral part of social psychology and social survey research.[30] His interest in the subjective measurement of social attitudes and opinions arose from his work in psychophysics, when he became dissatisfied with the sorts of examples used in experimental work and began to look at the possibilities of asking subjects questions about their attitudes on social issues.[31] This led to his development of attitude *scales*, considerably extending thereby the scientific study of attitude, which in Chicago in particular had been dominated by the quite different conception adumbrated by Thomas and Znaniecki in *The Polish Peasant*.[32] He brought with him in 1927 three projects attempting to construct scales for the measurement of attitudes and opinions on prohibition, on militarism and pacificism, and on the church.

Using methods developed in psychophysics for the measurement of discrimination of physical stimuli, he represented the attributes to be measured on a linear continuum of more or less. The base line represented a range of opinions from those at one end who are most strongly in favor of the issue to those at the other end of the scale who are strongly against it. Somewhere between is a neutral zone representing indifference to the topic. The measurement is carried out by asking respondents to accept or reject statements of opinion.

The central problem was the definition of the unit of measurement and the construction of the linear scale. The method used to design scales to measure attitudes toward prohibition, the church, blacks, militarism, and pacificism was that of the equal appearing interval. The scales were constructed as follows: several hundred persons were asked to sort a hundred or so statements of opinion into ten piles that ranged from the most favorable to the most unfavorable opinions. Subjects were asked to make the steps in attitude as nearly equal as possible so that the ten piles could be regarded as an equally graduated series. The series of ten piles was then regarded as series of ten class-intervals in a continuous scale, and each opinion was assigned a scale value which was the median point on the scale at which it had been allocated by the several hundred judges. Attitude on the issue was measured on a final scale consisting of forty opinions selected so as to make up an evenly graduated series of scale values. The subject responding to the scale was asked to tick those statements the burden of which he agreed with. His or her attitude was then assigned a numerical value equal to the average scale value of all the opinions which he endorsed.

Thurstone was not the only scholar trying to measure attitudes at this period. Bogardus's scale was mentioned earlier, and in 1932 Rensis Likert began trying out a different method at the Department of Agriculture. But Thurstone "commanded a level of mathematical facility that made him one of the towering figures in the quantification of psychology."[33] In a period of less than five years, he made a major impact upon social research. Thurstone and Professor Chave, of the Divinity School, collaborated to develop a scale for measuring attitudes toward the church, published in 1929 as *The Measurement of Attitude*, the most comprehensive statement of the methods that he developed.[34] The previous year he published an article in the *American Journal of Sociology* entitled "Attitudes Can Be Measured," which was criticized by those who thought that the essence of social attitudes was by definition something unmeasurable.[35] "Instead of gaining some approval for this effort, I found myself in a storm of criticism and controversy."[36]

In the early 1930s, however, Thurstone abandoned attitude measurement in order to concentrate on the development of multiple factor analysis, despite widespread interest in the application of his attitude measurement techniques to all sorts of issues and groups.[37] One example of Thurstone's impact on those in other disciplines was the study of political scientist L. D. White, carried out in 1927, of the prestige of public employment in the city.[38] White's aim was to discover as precisely as possible the degree of prestige attached to the Chicago public service by the population of Chicago. The design of the study involved a questionnaire, designed with Thurstone's advice, showing twenty pairs of occupations, one public and one private,[39] such as janitor at the First National Bank or janitor at City Hall and library assistant at the Chicago Public Library or library assistant at the Crerar Library. The 4,680 subjects of the inquiry were asked to tick the occupation for which they had the higher esteem. The pattern of response was then analyzed by sex, age, education, occupation, years of residence in Chicago, race, nationality, and economic status, data gathered in the second part of the schedule. Responses were converted to a scale, and the variations in rating by the factors compared. All showed significant differences, linked to economic status, except year of residence in the city.[40] This rather simple scaling exercise, which today would seem jejeune, was a step forward in the quantitative study of politics.

When appointed to a research professorship, Thurstone opted to continue to teach one course each quarter, taking the view that to do research exclusively was stultifying and isolating.[41] His most distinguished student, and the one on whose Ph.D. he had the most marked influence, was Samuel Stouffer in sociology. Stouffer took three of his courses as a graduate student,[42] including The Theory of Psychological Measurement, for which the syllabus included "psychological scale construction, the problem of measuring cognitive and affective values, the measurement of attitude on social issues."[43] Stouffer's dissertation involved a comparison of statistical and case study materials for the assessment of attitudes, partly taking up the challenge implicit in Thurstone's 1928 article and partly addressed to controversies then raging in the sociology department.[44] It was a fine piece of work and a model of elegant and rigorous methodology. The study involved comparison of judges' coding of 238 students' personal documents describing their lives and views on prohibition with the results of the same students' completion of one of Thurstone's attitude scales (Mrs. Hattie Smith's scale on prohibition). The four judges to code the personal documents—Leonard S. Cottrell,

Jr., Robert Faris, Everett V. Stonequist, and Edgar T. Thompson—were chosen by a committee of the sociology teachers to be those best equipped, technically and theoretically, to perform the task. Stouffer's comparison showed a high degree of agreement between the two procedures. By implication, case studies were more time-consuming and less efficient than the most rigorous quantitative methods. Though supervised by Faris, the dissertation bore the marks of Thurstone to a greater extent than Ogburn, but Stouffer's interests were catholic. He also collaborated with political scientist Carroll Wooddy in a study of local option and public opinion published in the *American Journal of Sociology* in 1930.[45]

Stouffer was an instructor in sociology at Chicago in 1930/31. He then accepted an appointment at the University of Wisconsin, but spent the year 1931/32 in England, studying with Karl Pearson, G. Udny Yule, R. A. Fisher, and A. L. Bowley at the University of London. This link to the intellectual tradition of statistics is of great importance in understanding the development of quantitative methods before Lazarsfeld and one that is frequently overlooked, perhaps because Stouffer's further work in the 1930s, after he returned to Chicago in 1935 as a full professor, was on demographic topics such as migration.[46] He later took part in Myrdal's study of the American Negro, and in 1940, when Myrdal was kept in Europe by the war, brought the work to completion in the senior author's absence.[47] All this happened before *The American Soldier* group assembled in 1941, and yet it is neglected. By the early 1930s, Stouffer had published a series of papers on significance tests, correlation and sampling,[48] doing distinguished work well before Paul Lazarsfeld appeared on the scene. The impact of his year in England was great, taking him in a direction more influenced by academic statistics than was Ogburn in the 1930s, but he was also influenced as a graduate student by Ogburn and, as his Ph.D. shows, by Thurstone.

One further major influence upon quantitative work in the late 1920s came from Henry Schultz, appointed to the economics department in 1926, and the next year to a memorial research professorship alongside L. L. Thurstone. He had done graduate work at Columbia and had spent most of 1919 in London at the London School of Economics and University College, working with Cannan in economics and with Pearson and Bowley. His Ph.D. thesis and later work (up to his death in a car accident in 1938) was on the theory and measurement of demand.[49] Schultz continued to teach courses previously taught by Field.[50] His main statistical publications dealt with curve fitting, sampling errors, and correlation methods.[51]

Schultz's interests in the statistical analysis of time series complemented the interests of Ogburn, with whom he was closely associated. Both shared a common admiration for their statistics teacher at Columbia, Henry L. Moore. In the early years of the century Moore and

Richmond Mayo-Smith had trained a number of sociologists, including Ogburn, Howard Odum, and Stuart Chapin.[52] There was a simple statistical laboratory and encouragement from Giddings, but the impetus was not maintained, because of the fact that Giddings's reputation for quantification was out of all proportion to his accomplishments. In the new Social Science Research Building, opened in 1929, Ogburn and Schultz's offices were side by side.

The historical importance of Schultz's work in mathematical economics lies in the foundations it laid for econometrics.[53] He continually stressed that economic theory and data should be integrated.[54] Schultz established links with quantitative researchers in other departments, not only with Ogburn but also with his friend the biometrician Sewall Wright, who first developed path analysis.[55] The economist's use of simple, partial, and multiple correlation analysis also complemented the interests of quantitative sociologists. The marked shift toward a more quantitative approach evident in sociology, political science, and (through Thurstone) social psychology, was encouraged in econometrics by Henry Schultz.

In political science, Merriam's own work lacked the sound methodological grasp that the work of Thurstone or Schultz showed. Merriam's genius was clearly to create the conditions under which fruitful research could flourish and to encourage the work of the younger members of his department such as Gosnell and L. D. White. Carroll Wooddy and Harold Lasswell also made contributions to the quantitative study of politics, the former in collaboration with Stouffer,[56] the latter in the area of content analysis.[57] In the early 1930s, a new wave of graduate students in political science, including V. O. Key, Jr., Gabriel Almond, David Truman, Herman Pritchett, and slightly later Herbert Simon, was introduced to the quantitative study of politics as part of the study of a discipline in which in Chicago "science" was the watchword.[58] Merriam's skill lay in creating the conditions to nourish the next generation:

> He provided exceptional opportunities for some of the younger faculty to obtain supplementary training, to do research, and to have a hand in advanced teaching. Recognizing that many new techniques call for large-scale data gathering and processing, Merriam took the initiative toward consolidating a central services staff to provide consultation in research design, in the development of research instruments (like questionnaires and tests), and in analyzing and storing data.[59]

This is a further reminder of the sheer hard slog that quantitative research at this period required in the way of routine calculations and data manipulation. The demands the new techniques could make was most clearly illustrated in the early 1930s by Thurstone's work to develop multiple factor analysis, which required thousands of hand calculations and major outside research support to fund the costs of data handling and processing.[60] These tasks were much greater than those involved in library or even field research using observational methods. The relation between advances in analytic methods and the available technology deserves more attention. The underanalyzed data of the early political science surveys owed something to the limitations imposed by technical means upon Gosnell.

By the late 1920s, Chicago was becoming a major center for quantitative social science research. Ogburn and Thurstone were creating statistical and psychometric laboratories such as Harper had envisaged for the natural sciences.[61] Ogburn taught statistics, did research with the assistance of Nell Talbot and Clark Tibbitts, and influenced the next generation through graduate students such as Samuel Stouffer, Frederick Stephan, Philip Hauser, John Dollard, and Tom McCormick. Burgess, meanwhile, was working with Tibbitts and John Landesco on parole prediction and with Richard Newcomb to make available 1920 and 1930 census tract data for the city, while encouraging McKay, Cottrell, and Frederick Zorbaugh to study quantitatively the ecological distribution of delinquency. Palmer maintained a repository of local data. In political science, Gosnell was pioneering quantitative work, alongside Harold Lasswell, Leonard White, and Carroll Wooddy. In psychology, L. L. Thurstone's work on attitude measurement was closely followed, particularly influencing Stouffer and L. D. White. Henry Schultz in economics was a close associate of Ogburn's.

This was not a tightly knit network, but rather a loose association of teachers and graduate students, with ties between particular teachers and particular students (as between both Ogburn and Thurstone and Stouffer), between teachers themselves (as between Ogburn and Gosnell and Ogburn and Schultz) and among the students themselves, arguing the merits of different approaches in a forum such as the Society for Social Research. The network was not only loose-knit, with nodes centered on particular teachers, but it was not methodologically exclusive. The relative advantages of case study materials, historical records, and contemporary documents were not only recognized by people such as Burgess, Stouffer, Lasswell, Wooddy, and White, but they were used in their own research.

At this period, the controversy in the sociology department between statistics and case studies was at its height. Ogburn was, to all appearances, one of the most outspoken on behalf of quantitative methods. On coming to Chicago, he later recalled, he found a much more hostile attitude to statistics than had existed at Columbia.[62] He fought strenuously on its behalf at first, most explicitly in his presidential address to the American Sociological Society in 1929, entitled "The Folkways of a

Scientific Sociology." "Sociology as a science," he proclaimed, "is not interested in making the world a better place in which to live, in encouraging beliefs, in spreading information, in dispensing news, in setting forth impressions of life, in leading the multitudes or in guiding the ship of state. Science is interested directly in one thing only, to wit, discovering new knowledge."[63] He predicted a decline in the intellectuality of sociology and the prestige of theory; proofs, records, and measurement would assume greater importance. All universities would have statistical laboratories and individual workers plenty of machines. "Statistics will disappear as a distinct field of knowledge because it will be almost universal, not only in sociology and in economics, but perhaps in social psychology and political science also."[64]

Ogburn put considerable emphasis on the need to control emotional involvement and bias, because of the greater temptation in the social sciences to distort conclusions in the interest of emotional values.[65] He later clashed fiercely with Robert Lynd over the chapter Lynd wrote for *Recent Social Trends*, attempting to insist that all evaluative statements and policy recommendations be removed.[66] When *Middletown* was published, he allegedly remarked that it was "too interesting to be science."[67]

The strident, prescriptive tone of the presidential address mixed prescience with prejudice. He correctly predicted that increasing wealth would increase the amount of social research carried out, more and more being done outside the universities, particularly by government, less single-handed by the lone researcher.[68] His scorn for social theory was considerable. It lacked a sound base in data and, like the superstitions of primitive cultures, was based on wishful thinking.[69] Though the gap between research and theory remains a wide one, his wish for the abandonment of social theory has not come about, partly indeed because of the fruitfulness of the work that was going on around him at the time in Chicago.

The most visible triumph of Ogburn's standpoint was when the committee on symbolism for the new Social Science Research Building, agreed to have inscribed above a first floor bay window fronting on the Midway the motto: "When you cannot measure ◉ your knowledge is ◉ meager ◉ and ◉ unsatisfactory ◉ Lord Kelvin."[70] Ogburn had spent some time distilling this from the original longer quotation, in Lord Kelvin's lecture in 1883 to the Institution of Civil Engineers in London:

> In physical science a first essential step in the direction of learning any subject is to find principles of numerical reckoning and methods for practically measuring some quality connected with it. I often say that when you can measure what you are speaking about, and express it in numbers, you know something about it; but when you cannot measure it, when you cannot express it in

> numbers, your knowledge is of a meager and unsatisfactory kind: it may be the beginning of knowledge, but you have scarcely, in your thoughts, advanced to the stage of *science*, whatever the matter may be.[71]

Like Ogburn's presidential address, the motto bordered on overstatement. Merriam was furious when he returned after the summer vacation to find the inscription in place.[72] How most of Ogburn's other colleagues responded to this flourish is not recorded. Thurstone no doubt approved, but skepticism and outright disagreement was more the order of the day, for the case study method was not without its proponents.

Floyd House, who taught at Chicago in 1925/26, defined the method (citing Sombart and Max Weber on *verstehen*) as a means of "establishing knowledge of the processes of social and personal behavior, a method rendered necessary . . . by the fact that such behavior can be made most intelligible to us when it is explained in terms of the psychic, or subjective, processes and motives by which it is determined."[73] The "case study" drew on the field research methods used by Park and Burgess, but emphasized more the use of life histories such as those Clifford Shaw was collecting to interpret behavior.[74] Charles Horton Cooley defined it as "a direct and all-round study of life histories" in his influential essay on the case study published in a collection that Burgess edited in 1929. Cooley argued that measurement was only one kind of precision. A motion picture was precise, but it was not quantitative. What was needed was the ability to record living wholes, "the complete perception, record, and understanding of fundamental acts." The sociologist's aim was to make us see human life as a dramatic activity and "to participate in those mental processes which are a part of human function and are accessible to sympathetic observation by the aid of gesture and language." The method could be applied to persons, families, and groups. He cited Robert C. Angell at Michigan as having made a study of campus life as a "participant observer," relying on his own firsthand experience as well as on statistics "and so able to animate his facts by authentic interpretations."[75]

Among the advocates of case study methods was Herbert Blumer, whose dissertation was on problems of method in social psychology.[76] Issue was joined in the late 1920s with the proponents of statistics—principally Ogburn, McCormick, and Stouffer—in the meetings of the Society for Social Research.[77] In 1928, the society heard Thurstone speak on an experiment with the measurement of attitudes. "An interesting discussion followed centering especially on the underlying problem of just what such a test measures and what it does not measure, granting the validity of the statistical superstructure." Early in 1929 the limitations and problems of using statistics in sociology and social psychology took up two meetings. Herbert Blumer and T. C. McCormick debated the logic and scope of statistical method in sociology, followed at the next by critical consideration of life history documents as data in social psychology. Guests at a valedictory dinner for the society's president before his departure for Asia at the end of 1928/29 heard Park urge sociologists "not to lose their human interests while amidst their abstractions and their measurements."[78] Philip Hauser recalled that at softball games at departmental picnics during the period teams tended to be formed of proponents of case studies or of quantification.[79]

In the methodological controversies, Burgess acted as an integrating and soothing force. He had a singularly open-minded and catholic approach to methodology. His early quantitative work was with census data, but he took pains (by attending one of Ogburn's courses after his arrival) to learn about statistics as a body of ideas and techniques. He encouraged the delinquency area studies and later sent Leonard Cottrell to attend Thurstone's course on multiple factor analysis so that they could use the method in their work on the family.[80] At the same time, he also attended meetings of the Psychoanalytic Institute in order to understand Freud.

> Burgess was very instrumental in encouraging students who had been brought up on making case studies and getting close to your data . . . to try to translate them into more quantifiable form and pay some attention to the statistics.[81]

The terms of the discussion had changed a good deal since *The Polish Peasant*. Burgess took a particular interest in the reliability and validity of life history materials.[82] In advising Clifford Shaw, he urged that statements made in life histories be checked by interviews with parents, siblings, friends, associates, teachers, probation officers, and social workers.[83] Account of delinquencies should be checked against official records. Burgess's contributions to *The Jack-Roller* and *The Natural History of a Delinquent Career* were sensitive to the method's possible deficiencies.[84] His concern with representativeness led Shaw to collect a large number of delinquent histories.

Similar preoccupations were apparent in Paul G. Cressey's work on taxi-dance halls, which Burgess supervised. The regular accounts Cressey wrote of the progress of his research show a continual preoccupation with cross-checking information that he was given, if possible from another observer, patron, or dancer and/or from official records. He stressed the large number of observations he himself made and the use of eight assistants whose data could be used as a means of ensuring reliable data.[85]

Such concerns were part of a conscious effort to avoid methodological polarization. Floyd House, who received his Ph.D. in 1924 and taught in the department in 1925/26, commented:

> The impression that Columbia stands for statistical method in sociology, Chicago for the case study, cannot be conclusively documented; the writer found it widely prevalent among graduate students in sociology at the University of Chicago in 1922, although the contrast was somewhat deprecated by members of the sociological faculty there. Subsequently, during the period 1925–1927, the members of the existing sociological faculty strove to counteract the impression that Chicago sociology was in any sense anti-statistical through the move that resulted in the addition of Ogburn to the staff.[86]

Burgess's 1927 paper on statistics and case studies represented a determined attempt to achieve a rapprochement. Burgess quoted with approval Bowley's definition of statistics as "the science of the measurement of the social organism, regarded as a whole in all its manifestations."[87] Statistics could be used comparatively; they could be used to show correlations between variables and to provide crude indices of underlying sociological variables. Case studies, from Thomas and Znaniecki onward were a means of getting behind figures to the meaning of men's lives and a method of overcoming the social atomism inherent in a statistical approach.

> The methods of statistics and of case study are not in conflict with each other; they are in fact mutually complementary. Statistical comparisons and correlations may often suggest leads for research by the case study method, and documentary materials as they reveal social processes will inevitably point the way to more adequate statistical indices. If, however, statistics and case study are to yield their full contribution as tools of sociological research, they should be granted equal recognition and full opportunity for each to perfect its own technique. At the same time, the interaction of the two methods is certain to prove fruitful.[88]

Stouffer's dissertation research, which germinated in the departmental debates of the time, took the issue of the effectiveness of different methods considerably further. It was a carefully balanced and meticulous comparison of case study methods using the life history and Thurstonian attitude measurement to study the same subject. He took pains to ensure that the case studies were coded by competent observers. The initial pilot phase of the study used Ellsworth Faris and Ernest Burgess as two of the six judges. The four judges used in the main study to code the qualitative materials were chosen "by a committee of the faculty in the Department of Sociology as among those best equipped by technical experience in the interpretation of case materials, knowledge of the theoretical literature on attitudes, and quality of insight into human experience, to make the judgements."[89] The department was thus brought in both to select the judges and through the use of graduate students to participate in the research. Other students at the time, such as Ruth Shonle Cavan and Philip Hauser, did work on related problems.[90]

Stouffer succeeded in demonstrating the greater efficiency, cheapness, and elegance of more formal measurement methods, reflecting Thurstone's push toward more scientific methods derived from his background in engineering, mental testing, and psychophysics. Stouffer may not have dented the conviction of those who favored case study methods, but he did win the argument on points in terms of the efficiency of particular research techniques. His later career in research in quantitative methods, following study with the English statisticians in London in 1931/32, may give the impression that he was antipathetic to case study methods. Yet in 1934 one finds Stouffer, in an article on sampling, discussing statistical data on the causes of delinquency and the sorts of further statistical analysis which it would require.

> Yet it is hard to conceive of a mathematical equation, however complicated, which will be of very much value unaccompanied by juvenile delinquency data of a nonquantitative nature, including, perhaps, documents whose interpretation is essentially an artistic procedure. And why, indeed, should we care whether or not our methods are copies of those used in the more nearly exact fields of natural science? *The Jack-Roller* may more nearly resemble art than science, as the word science is conventionally used by scientists, but if the study helps us understand delinquency for a few years, it ought to be good sociology. Why not, one ventures to suggest, declare a moratorium on the use of the word "science" as applied to studies of social phenomena? To limit ourselves to measurement would sterilize research. . . . We should be free to borrow as we like from [the] logic and techniques [of natural science] and to add logic and techniques of our own, without having to waste time in the scholastic futilities of discussing about a piece of research, "Now is this science or isn't it?"[91]

The battle lines were not quite what they appeared to be. Cooley, after all, had once been on the staff of the Census Bureau.[92] Even Ogburn, apparently so strident an advocate of quantification, was a more complex figure. His admiration for Lord Kelvin squared oddly with his deep interest in psychoanalysis and close friendship with Franz Alexander.[93] His friend Beardsley Ruml once ribbed him that in a conversation on the train between Washington and Chicago, Ogburn had said that the reason he had stuck to the quantitative method in social analysis was because he was afraid that his imagination would lead him into expositions for which he would not want to be responsible.[94] Ogburn had become interested in psychoanalysis around 1918 and had himself been analyzed; this had had a major impact on his view of bias in the social sciences. One of his students, John Dollard, later made major contributions to case study work in sociology. But in 1929–31, he completed a quantitative dissertation under Ogburn's supervision.[95] Ogburn's influence lay less in his classroom teaching or Dollard's work for him as a research assistant than at an informal level.[96] The seeds of Dollard's subsequent dramatic shift of orientation were sown at Chicago under the influence of Sapir perhaps more than Ogburn, leading to a well-known book on the life history in 1935 and an ethnographic case study in 1937 of race relations in the South, *Caste and Class in a Southern Town.*[97] In the latter Dollard quoted favorably Burgess's argument that case studies should treat an individual as a specimen of a group rather than one of a mere aggregate of individuals, as in a statistical study.[98]

Ogburn always insisted that insight was needed as well as figures. Which of the two he emphasized was partly dependent on his audience. His presidential address to the American Statistical Association in 1931, entitled "Statistics and Art," recognized that "hypotheses have to be formulated and . . . there is a drive back of research which calls for the constructive imagination of an artist, without which there could be no research."[99] Everett Stonequist considered that "there was a richness in Ogburn, that was unquestionably there. It might not be felt by many people."[100] Moreover, he was a southern gentleman and the whole debate was conducted with considerable good humor.[101] His sense of humor is revealed in a remark about Burgess:

> Burgess is a quite unique person. He teaches a course on recreation and he never plays, he teaches a course on the family and he isn't married, and he teaches a course in criminology and he never committed a sin.[102]

The commitment in the department to a wide variety of approaches to sociology is evident in a reference Ogburn wrote in 1930 about Herbert Blumer, whose methodological standpoint was far removed from his own and who had been an outspoken defender of case study methods.

> Blumer has a remarkably good critical mind, a fine personality and a sense of scholarship. He is not as statistical as I like and has a liking for the psychological type of work such as Cooley has done. He is pretty familiar with the German sociologists. . . . His thesis was a very scholarly piece of work.[103]

In retrospect, Blumer believed that the point at issue in the case studies versus statistics controversy was not so much the individual versus the aggregate. It was necessary to transcend individual cases to build a science. The problem was rather the issue of how one derives generalizations. According to Park and Faris, generalizations had to be based upon a rather faithful depiction of what was actually taking place in the experiences and action of people. Those who worked with the statistical approach, on the other hand, felt that in order to achieve an objective, quantitative account, focused upon the product of action, as it were, instead of dealing with the whole process whereby that action came into being.[104]

There was certainly controversy between the proponents of qualitative and those of quantitative research methods among Chicago sociologists in the late 1920s. At this period, there were several attempts to bring the two styles of research together and a degree of methodological eclecticism which prevented lines hardening between rival methodological camps. The decline of the Chicago school (discussed in the next chapter) may have led to a change in the situation. There is some suggestion that the lines of antagonism in the later 1930s between Ogburn and Stouffer on one side and Wirth, Hughes, and Blumer on the other grew sharper. Burgess, although committed to rapprochement, was not an expansive or striking enough personality to keep them in check.[105]

Before 1930, however, this stiffening of methodological positions had not taken place. The holders of opposing points of view were not intransigent. The department self-consciously sought to uphold its position as the leading graduate department of sociology in the country. One consequence of this policy was a catholicity of approaches to research methodology throughout the department, which meant that it fostered both qualitative and quantitative methods at the same time. An emphasis on field research and personal documents, though certainly a distinctive feature, is far from the whole story about Chicago sociology and other social sciences at this period. Notable developments in early quantitative methods took place which tend to have been ignored in histories of sociology, for various reasons.[106]

As the discipline changes over time, advances in research methodology render certain approaches and techniques out of date. The methods used in Chicago in the 1920s in many respects seem somewhat antiquated to a contemporary observer. There tends, however, to be a difference between quantitative and qualitative sociologists. As Jones and Kronus have demonstrated, interest in quantitative methods and interest in the history of sociology seem to be antithetical. The more committed a social scientist is to the "scientism" of his discipline, the more likely he is to adopt an ahistorical approach to the subject.[107] Progress over time is seen as cumulative; there is less desire to examine the origins of the methods used or to teach their history. Qualitative sociologists, on the other hand, cultivate an understanding of the historical origins of their approach and treat it as an integral part of their writing and teaching. It is impossible to discuss symbolic interactionism or the use of participant observation methods or the influence of Herbert Blumer or Everett Hughes apart from Chicago. Yet who would associate Chicago sociology with the first use of census tract data, with attitude measurement, with partial correlation analysis, or with the careers of Samuel Stouffer or Frederick Stephan?

The tendency for quantitative methodologists to write off the relevance of the history of such methods for present practice is not the whole story. A clear view of the growth of quantitative methods in the social sciences is hampered by their interdisciplinary character, as well as by the split between academic and nonacademic worlds. An adequate history must embrace not only the developments in many different academic disciplines but also the role of the foundations, of independent research bodies, of research and statistical activity within the federal government, and of private industry. Some aspects of interdisciplinary contact in quantitative methods are dealt with in this book, but the whole subject requires much fuller examination in the period between 1930 and 1950.

This discussion of the place of quantitative research in sociology and nearby disciplines during the 1920s has emphasized the way in which the unique character of the Chicago department, the growing intellectual significance of empirical research, and the institutionalization of research with foundation support flowed together both to produce several important advances and to train as graduate students scholars who made major future contributions to quantitative methods in sociology and political science. Though this may not correspond to many sociologists' image of Chicago sociology, it has to be taken account of. Doing so also makes it a little easier to understand how Lord Kelvin's dictum came in 1929 to be given such prominence and permanence on the Social Science Research Building on the Midway.

11 The Chicago Manifold

Sociology became a differentiated subject in the United States in the late nineteenth and early twentieth century. In exploring the process by which it did so there is a particularly strong tendency to view the subject from the standpoint of the present. The contemporary academic scene in the social sciences is generally marked by sharp disciplinary boundaries. Departments are established as the setting in which an academic discipline is pursued, providing the organizational and intellectual frame of reference for academic activity and intercourse. Those who identify themselves with a discipline tend to seek out others in the same discipline and to pursue their interests in terms of the standards and criteria of that discipline.[1] The Chicago schools of sociology and political science developed to the extent that they did in part because they were established in separate departments. The extent of disciplinary isolation, however, was much less than in the contemporary university. Even though its internal organization was from the outset departmental, the University of Chicago was characterized by less rigid disciplinary boundaries than many universities. This goes some way to explaining how and why the university produced two such distinguished schools.

One of the most important characteristics of Chicago social science up to 1930 was the fostering of interdisciplinary links, of what Lasswell later called the "cross-disciplinary manifold."[2] A few members of the university—Mead, Park, until his departure W. I. Thomas—could command an audience across departments of the university. It was, however, the common characteristics of the Chicago setting, rather than just individual personalities, which fostered interdisciplinary contacts. The extent of interdisciplinary exchange and cooperation owed much to the small size of the teaching staff of social science departments, mentioned earlier. In departments like sociology and political science with half a dozen or fewer staff, ecology alone encouraged contact with neighboring and even with more distant disciplines.[3] The tendency was also encouraged by the interest in local research on the city of Chicago, the pragmatist orientation widely diffused through the university, and the success of the LCRC in attracting funds and mounting a vigorous research program. Faculty met and talked at the Quadrangle Club. Students were exposed to speakers from many other disciplines at the Society for Social Research.

Interdisciplinary course work was encouraged among students. Members of different disciplines were aware of the relative lack of prestige of the social sciences and sought to strengthen their scientific claims. It also had something to do with the character of the university as an institution of higher learning and the intensity of intellectual life there. The University of Chicago was a relatively small university, with a high ratio of graduates to undergraduates. This had the effect of focusing attention upon the intellectual substance of graduate work and encouraging teachers to exchange ideas with each other across disciplinary boundaries.

One example of this is provided by the influence of the physiologist Jacques Loeb. Loeb taught biology, distant from the social sciences, yet over a long period had an important influence upon a number of scholars including Veblen,[4] W. I. Thomas, and Park. In his early years in the department, Thomas was influenced less by Small, Henderson, and Vincent than by others such as Loeb, with whom he studied physiology and experimental biology, and Adolf Meyer, the prominent psychiatrist who at that time gave courses on brain anatomy. The effect of this influence was to turn him away from the vestiges of Christian belief he still held toward a mechanistic—that is, a materialistic—conception of life.[5] Park, too, came under Loeb's influence and took up his biological ideas to apply in the study of the city, just as Park did with the ideas of a number of biologists. Park used Loeb's work on ant societies to make generalizations about processes of communication and social control in human societies.[6]

Testimony of contemporaries shows that in the 1920s and early 1930s, interdisciplinary contacts were strong in Chicago. Everett Hughes wrote of Park:

> I see Park in my mind sitting in the Quadrangle Club at a table full of men talking. The men might be zoologists. He would be there talking about how it was possible for animals to form groups. Or he might be talking about Greek epics. He was especially interested in the *Odyssey*. Or it might be Chinese philosophy. He was, of course, very interested in Merriam and in the psychologists and the theologians and the philosophers. (He was, of course, very much interested in the work of Mead.) He was not a departmental man. The Quadrangle Club was a pretty chummy place. Park was very much a club man. He didn't play cards or billiards, but he throve on intellectual talk. Where he was—was a seminar. He could talk of any subject. Merriam was a very genial man and he, like Park, paid no attention to the departmental boundaries. The University of Chicago was not at that time a really departmentalized place. Your colleagues were where you found them.[7]

Of the twenty-five sociologists interviewed by James Carey in 1972 who had been students in the department in the 1920s, all were encouraged or required to take graduate courses in other departments. The most frequently mentioned field was philosophy, followed (in rank order) by anthropology, political science, economics, and psychology. The significant teachers outside the department most frequently mentioned were Mead (11 times), Charles Merriam (7), Edward Sapir (7), James Field (6), L. C. Marshall (4), James Tufts (3), Edward Scribner Ames (3) and L. L. Thurstone (3).[8] Carey's sample was composed of survivors of the period whom he was able to reach and cannot be regarded as representative. His data does, however, give some indication of the range of interdisciplinary contact as experienced by graduate students.

Early in the 1920s, Ernest Mowrer found that graduate students were encouraged to take courses in other departments.

> I think one of the most outstanding features of the department [of sociology], as of that time, was this interchange between the departments. . . . Because, after all, the points of view of different departments harmonized to a very appreciable extent, and those students found that to be true and therefore were encouraged to take courses.[9]

Herbert Blumer, a contemporary of Hughes's, has also emphasized the importance of interdisciplinary links.

> There was a considerable amount of crossing over from one discipline to another by both faculty people and students so that I had a feeling that when one comes to identify what might be regarded as the sources of stimulation of the period, one has to recognize that this stimulating milieu, if I might use that expression, was by no means confined to sociology—it was in a wider context there.[10]

Political scientist Harold Lasswell confirmed Blumer's view of the importance of interdisciplinary links:

> A leading characteristic of the rejuvenation of political science [at Chicago] was an emphasis on the subject that was both cross-disciplinary and scientific. . . . The University of Chicago was relatively well prepared for a cross-disciplinary program by an interlocking network of intellectual and personal friendships that cut across departmental lines and found nourishment in informal groups.[11]

The economist Henry Schultz formed a hiking group on the Indiana and Michigan dunes with close friends from other disciplines—George

Link, Sewall Wright, Benjamin Willier, Arthur Dempster, and Samuel Allison. On these walks the group, consisting of an embryologist, a geneticist, a pathologist, an economist, and two physicists, took a book or a journal article and discussed its contents en route, or drew diagrams, curves, and equations in the sand or snow, depending on the weather.[12]

The extent to which boundaries were somewhat artificial is shown by Frank Knight's interest in Max Weber. Knight, a brooding, learned, stimulating presence in the economics department, translated Weber's *General Economic History* in 1927 at a time when Weber was only slightly known in the English-speaking world. Edward Shils attended his lectures in the early 1930s, in which he never mentioned sociology or sociologists, except Max Weber.

> Although he had not himself studied very much sociology—he was by training an economist—Frank Knight offered a great deal to a sociologist. He had reflected profoundly about the market and he was aware that the behavior of human beings was not exhaustively described when one has described the market.[13]

The most self-consciously interdisciplinary efforts were made in the department of political science. Merriam's calls for closer cooperation with other disciplines, particularly psychology and statistics, were part of a move to turn the subject in a more scientific direction:

> The cross-disciplinary merits of identifying and organizing the "social sciences" into one body . . . was understood to be a means of accelerating useful cross-disciplinary interchanges of two kinds: first, among the social sciences themselves, which would presumably accelerate the diffusion of sophisticated procedures with the physical and biological sciences, which would presumably result, at least initially, in upgrading the social sciences.[14]

One part of Merriam's strategy, already mentioned, was to encourage the appointment of sympathetic figures in other departments in the university, notably those of L. L. Thurstone and William F. Ogburn. Merriam was also acutely aware of the importance of providing an intellectual frame of reference to inspire, guide, and justify his cross-disciplinary and scientific aims. One step to encourage this was the cross-disciplinary "roundtables" of the American Political Science Association, organized in the mid-1920s. In the department, he assembled a small group of fellow teachers—Quincy Wright, L. D. White, Harold Gosnell, Harold Lasswell, among others—who could provide a stimulating and technically competent environment in which advanced students could cultivate the "new" politics. At the local level, cross-disciplinary work was pushed through the LCRC. Nationally, the Social Science Research Council, composed of nominees from seven constituent social science disciplines, was Merriam's chosen instrument.[15]

The influence of other disciplines, notably statistics, was to be seen in Harold Gosnell's work, discussed earlier. It was also apparent in the work of Harold Lasswell, a graduate student in the department from 1923 to 1926, when he was appointed to an assistant professorship. Lasswell's was an inquisitive, inquiring, and wide-ranging mind which drew its inspiration from several disciplines.[16] In his first year as a graduate student, he shared an office with Robert Redfield, Eyler N. Simpson, and Louis Wirth, all in the sociology department. He soon got to know Park, Burgess, and Mead and was particularly influenced by Park. He paid several visits to Europe, in 1923/24, in 1925, and in 1929/30 on an SSRC fellowship, which deepened his cross-disciplinary interests. "I have never known a more remarkable master of words and ideas," was Harold Gosnell's later judgment. "Merriam sent him to England and he came back with an English accent, he sent him to Vienna and he came back with a full-grown psychoanalytic vocabulary, he sent him to the Soviet Union and when he came back he showed that Marx could be reconciled with Freud."[17]

He began to develop a considerable reputation for his studies of the propaganda strategies of dominant elites and subversive counterelites; the destabilizing impact of technological change on citizen loyalties; and the private pathological motives that sparked off political movements.[18] In the 1920s many of his publications were in journals catering to economists, sociologists, social psychologists, or journalists as much as to political scientists. His case is somewhat unusual in the breadth of his interests. He possessed imagination and insight of a high order, even if his books lacked the quality of continuous, coherent exposition.[19]

Developments in political science show very clearly the influence exercised by other disciplines. One important aspect of this was the example other disciplines provided for moving the social sciences in a more scientific direction. To the extent that political scientists drew on statistics and scientific psychology, their work was likely to become more empirical and more rigorous. These tendencies were not quite so strong in sociology initially, but were greatly strengthened after the arrival of Ogburn.

The involvement of staff and graduate students in the Society for Social Research encouraged these interdisciplinary links. So, too, did the Local Community Research Committee. This was not merely a funding body, but had its own office building which housed office and support staff, equipment, research fellows, and graduate students. The fostering of interdisciplinary contacts was a deliberate part of the policy of the LCRC. Research seminars were an integral part of its work; the research committee also arranged dinners at which teachers and research assistants met and listened to the presentation of papers.[20] These social activities played an important part in creating a feeling of solidarity among those participating in the work of the LCRC.

The physical arrangement of university buildings has implications for the extent, nature, and frequency of academic interchange. The commitment of the LCRC to interdisciplinary objectives was shown in the plans that developed to rehouse the departments in the social science group. As the program expanded, it became apparent that the physical accommodation of the local community research program was not ideal. The building that the LCRC occupied at Sixtieth Street and Ellis Avenue was inadequate and remote from the teaching departments, which were also short of space. In 1927, therefore, in seeking renewal of its grant from the Memorial, the social science departments asked for funds totalling $1 million to build a new center for social science research.[21] A case was made for the creation of a single building, with ample room for research and for intra- and interdepartmental collaboration. One of the prime reasons for such a building would be to foster cross-disciplinary contacts: "Each department, adhering to its own sphere of activity, should be so housed as to permit greater co-ordination with the other social sciences." The aim was also the more mundane one of improving the day-to-day effectiveness of teaching and research.[22]

The Memorial approved the application and planning for what became "Eleven Twenty-Six"; the Social Science Research Building could begin. The plans that were developed embodied both the belief in interdisciplinary cooperation and the absolute priority given to research.[23] The building was to be used for the research activities of the LCRC, including the research professors, research laboratories and materials, offices for teaching staff involved in LCRC research, and accommodation for the six journals published by the group.[24] Certain functions would not be housed in the building: offices of members of staff engaged exclusively in undergraduate teaching, departmental administrative offices, and student activities. Larger rooms for group meetings would not be available for undergraduate teaching, unless part of an approved research project. Only research courses and seminars were to be held in the building. In addition to offices, seminar rooms, and a common room, the original plan also included two card-sorting machine rooms, two drafting rooms, one map display room, a statistical laboratory and four statistical data rooms, a "psychological-psychiatric laboratory," an anthropological-archaeological laboratory, eight storerooms, and two vaults.[25]

The enhanced facilities these specialized rooms provided can be illustrated by provision for statistical work, planned by Ogburn who corresponded with social scientists all over the country to secure the best possible design for the new accommodation.[26] Ogburn proposed that

$25,000 from the generous budget be spent in equipping the building with statistical machines and $15,000 on the purchase of census materials, reports, and the like.[27] These are shown in table 6. The significance of this equipment has to be seen in terms of the technological limitations of quantitative analysis at this period. Without benefit of computers, laborious hand calculations were required needing staff and time. The equipment provided in the new building greatly facilitated more extensive quantitative work, though it did not amount to a technological breakthrough such as that achieved by the Hollerith machine in the 1890s or the electronic computer in the 1950s.

The exceptional character of Chicago social science was shown by the allocation plan. This represented a departure from two norms for the allocation of space in contemporary universities, separation along departmental lines and relative separation of teaching staff from research workers. Both had been exemplified in the arrangements at Chicago before 1929. In the new building the barriers between departments were deliberately broken down, with teaching staff and research staff members located side by side in adjacent rooms. Thus, when the building opened, the fourth floor housed—in addition to the statistical laboratory, three machine rooms and a room holding census data—W. F. Ogburn, of the department of sociology, and Harold Gosnell, of the department of

TABLE 6
Equipment and Source Materials for
Social Science Research Building, 1929

A. Equipment	Cost
1 Harmonic analyser	$4,000
1 Adding machine	1,000
4 Hand Monroe calculators	700
18 Electric Monroe calculators	9,000
1 Millionaire calculator	800
1 Mercedes Euclid	800
5 United multiplying machines	5,000
1 Mathematical typewriter	135
1 Tabulator typewriter	150
1 Mechanical integraph	300
12 Electric adding machines	1,800
8 Hand adding machines	480
1 Planimeter	750
B. Source Materials	
U.S. government statistical data: Census, etc.	2,200
Texts, tables, and formulas	1,700
Yearbooks	500
American Statistical Association and Royal Statistical Society Publications	900
League of Nations and International Labour Organization data and studies	3,000
Various other international and foreign statistical publications (and British census)	1,500
Public health and other data	1,500
Other headings	3,400

SOURCE: Ogburn Papers, Special Collections Department, Joseph Regenstein Library, University of Chicago, Box XXXI.

political science, in adjacent rooms, Henry Schultz, Harry Millis, and Simeon Leland, economists, Herbert Blumer, a sociologist, L. D. White, a political scientist, together with the project on the economics of meat-packing and research assistants to White and Blumer. On the third floor were found the psychological laboratory, four experimental rooms, L. L. Thurstone, and Harold Lasswell. Further along the corridor were Merriam, Jernegan, an American colonial historian interested in "debtor and servant classes," Vollmer, in police administration, Burgess, Park, and Faris, who were all sociologists, together with research projects on organized crime, regional planning, leadership and personality studies, the local communities project, and three rooms for map display, map storage, and drafting.[28]

At a social level, too, the building served to bring colleagues in the social sciences together. Until World War II, all the social scientists in the university were housed in it, with one or two exceptions. It encouraged easy contact between generations and easy contact between disciplines. The building made a difference to the ethos of the social sciences at Chicago. Members of the social science departments

> saw their colleagues when they came in the morning, they saw them when they went to lunch—they often walked to lunch together, not by prearrangement but by the pleasant accident of being in the lobby at the same time.[29]

There was a common staircase and elevator, a common room where tea was served every afternoon, and regular series of well-attended public lectures (also held in the building) where the results of recent research and reflection were presented.

The social science departments at the University of Chicago were thus brought together both by their common involvement in local community research and through the construction of the Social Science Research Building. Sociology and anthropology were a joint department until 1929, although in separating the anthropologists stressed their strong links to departments other than sociology.[30] The vogue for interdisciplinary work was in part a response to doctrines of social usefulness, powerfully pushed by Ruml and the Memorial. Yet this utilitarian influence is insufficient to account for the strength of belief in the value of cooperation. Small's strongly held views, for example, were maintained for a long period before there was any prospect of foundation support at Chicago.

Three influences seem to have been particularly important. One was the marked shift in several subjects at about the same time toward empirical research, whether in sociology, institutional economics, experimental psychology, or empirical political science.[31] The emphasis on first-hand inquiry tended to highlight common elements shared by different disciplines, particularly in methodology, and the value of shared research facilities, as in the new building. A second, linked development was the greater interest in applied research carried out from within particular disciplines, such as economics and sociology. This tended to bring home the extent to which social problems required the strengths of more than one discipline for their effective treatment.

The third, more intangible, factor was the optimism generated by a period of self-confident expansion in the 1920s. Both at Chicago and Columbia at this period, there were new initiatives and growth in the social sciences generally (even if sociology at Columbia languished). The departments concerned were small, the younger members in particular lively and open to varied intellectual influences. At graduate level, smallness of size meant that courses in other disciplines were a required part of graduate study. The growing emphasis upon research methodology which encouraged the teaching of statistics and psychology also exerted some influence. The collection of essays on *The Social Sciences and Their Interrelationships*, edited by Ogburn and Alexander Goldenweiser, published in 1927, bore the influence of Columbia.[32] At Chicago, the intellectual basis of interdisciplinary cooperation was not so clearly spelled out in written form, but the ecology of scholarship tended to produce a similar cross-disciplinary effect. Its organizational form was, however, much clearer in the LCRC and the building at 1126 East Fifty-ninth Street.

In the 1920s at the University of Chicago, interdisciplinary work did not become completely preeminent in the way that Small and Merriam sometimes envisaged. Indeed the LCRC, as L. D. White had observed in 1929, failed to overcome the powerful barriers between disciplines. Even so, different studies did both carry traces of the influence of other disciplines and themselves influence other disciplines in turn. The more limited interdisciplinary influences, which were widespread at the period, did result in significant cross-disciplinary borrowings and a greater degree of cross-fertilization than has generally been common among the social sciences later in the twentieth century. Park in particular drew eclectically from ideas and insights of other disciplines in developing ecological theory. Ogburn was considerably influenced, particularly in methodology, by economics and statistics. Burgess took a strong interest both in social psychology and quantitative measurement. Several graduate students, notably Stouffer, were influenced by teachers outside sociology. The influence of George Herbert Mead from philosophy was not insignificant.

It is true that the ideal of interdisciplinary work, as adumbrated by Small, had very little content to it. In practice, however, a great deal of cross-fertilization went on, without merging the identities of the different disciplines. Ogburn's contention that "the natural meeting ground of the social sciences and the sphere par excellence of their interrelations are in their common *sociological level*"[33] would have been strongly disputed by colleagues in economics, anthropology, or psychology, but disciplinary differentation at Chicago *was* attenuated in the belief that different social sciences could learn from each other. The fertility of sociology and political science during the 1920s owes a good deal to this. The LCRC, moreover, had demonstrated the scope for collaboration between different disciplines within a common organizational and financial framework sharing common equipment and facilities. It institutionalized a loosely integrated program of research within a linked network of scholars and studies. The social sciences at the University of Chicago by 1930 had gone well beyond the pursuit of uncoordinated individual interests.

The influence of Chicago social science lay not only in the achievements of the 1920s, but in the development of younger scholars who would reach their prime elsewhere, while retaining the traces of their Chicago years. In sociology, Samuel Stouffer, Frederick Stephan, and Herbert Blumer all in different ways carried the influence of other disciplines with them through their later work. In political science, Gabriel Almond recalled that as a graduate student in the early 1930s he had as strong personal relationships with anthropologists and sociologists as he did with political scientists.[34] Intellectually, too, the enterprise depended on other social sciences. "Political science at Chicago, even at its peak, had always depended more on the quality of the other social sciences at the university than the rhetorical stance of the department tended to concede."[35]

The process may be followed in psychiatry, not a field one immediately associates with Chicago social science. There was in fact sufficient interest in psychoanalysis and dynamic psychiatry to leave its mark for the future. This example also shows the openness to new ideas characteristic at Chicago and the inadequacy of simplified delineations in terms of particular standpoints.

Harold Lasswell was one of the earliest American social scientists to show a sustained interest in psychoanalysis and for many years was the foremost writer on the psychology of politics. While in Berlin in 1929/30, he underwent some months of therapy with Theodore Reik. He was interested in trying to make scientific use of these insights. On his return he exposed volunteers to a stressful interview in the laboratory and measured physiological changes such as pulse rate, skin resistance, and body movement.[36] Leonard Cottrell was one of his subjects.[37] In *Psychopathology and Politics*, published in 1930, Lasswell used clinical material to examine the private motives and personality characteristics that influenced political actors and energized political movements.[38]

One of those influenced by Lasswell was John Dollard, who was also a friend of the anthropologist Edward Sapir, himself interested in psychoanalysis. Even though he was doing a quantitative dissertation with Ogburn, Dollard belonged to a social discussion group with Lasswell, Frank Knight, and Philip Miller in the medical school.

> Analysis was up for discussion all the time. Lasswell represented it in our midst. Then [Franz] Alexander [the Berlin psychoanalyst] came and actually was a professor on the grounds for a year, and indeed gave his chief course in sociology, believe it or not [in 1930/31]. So it was raging all the time. . . . I was very much interested in psychoanalysis during the time I was in Chicago and had a piece of an analysis while I was in graduate school and . . . really had some plans to develop that side of my life. . . . That's where social interaction led me, to a deeper definition of interstimulation and response, and how your immediate stimulus reverberated in the personality.[39]

The most sympathetic member of the sociology department, according to Dollard, was, of all people, Ogburn.[40] Before he went to Columbia, Ogburn had been involved in various social reform movements on the West Coast, but came to the view that the ideological component of reform movements was largely rationalization of wishes. Seeking to understand this, he read widely in psychoanalysis and himself underwent analysis.[41] In a paper published in 1922, he discussed the value of psychoanalysis in controlling bias and trying to make the social sciences less unscientific.

> The way of becoming less unscientific is to know the etiology of our own desires and the mechanisms of their behavior. . . . The study of abnormal psychology and of psychoanalysis is doing a great deal to acquaint us with the ways our desires disguise themselves, how they originate, how they are conditioned, and the part they play in forming specific opinions.[42]

Despite holding that measurement was essential for the social sciences, Ogburn did briefly use psychoanalytic material in his teaching. At Barnard College in the early 1920s, Margaret Mead took one of his courses on psychological aspects of culture, "one of the first courses in which Freudian psychology was treated with respect."[43] A. A. Brill, the leading psychiatrist, credited him with being the first American sociologist to recognize the value of Freudian concepts in the teaching of sociology.[44]

On coming to Chicago, Ogburn kept this interest and his scientific work in sociology strictly separate. His deep interest in analysis was, nevertheless, a striking demonstration of the catholic interests of teaching staff. Everett Hughes said of him:

> He was . . . a man of very broad interests. It is not generally known that he was the president of the Chicago Psycho-Analytical Society. He was very much interested in analysis and believed it was an important thing. But he wanted to make it clear that he did not think that was science. Science was verifiable facts that could be tabulated statistically.[45]

Reviewing Freud's influence on American sociology in 1939, Ernest Burgess, who had himself taken some interest in psychoanalysis in the late 1920s and early 1930s, included Ogburn and himself in a list of nine established sociologists who had used psychiatric classifications in publication prior to 1927. Among younger sociologists, Burgess named seven who had made use of such classifications and methods, of whom four (Cottrell, Dollard, Lasswell, and Willard Waller) had done graduate work at the university and a fifth (Kimball Young) had studied for the master's with W. I. Thomas.[46]

As well as influences from Freudian psychoanalysis, there were contacts with dynamic social psychiatry, particularly through Harry Stack Sullivan. Like W. I. Thomas, Sullivan had been influenced by the psychiatrist Adolf Meyer.[47] In the late 1920s he had a number of contacts with Chicago school sociologists, including W. I. Thomas, Park, Burgess, and Clifford Shaw, trying to bring social psychiatry closer to the social sciences.[48] At Chicago, Sullivan's closest links were to two men on the margins of sociology, the anthropologist Edward Sapir and Harold Lasswell. Before moving to Chicago, Sapir's first wife had died after a long illness, leaving him with three children. She had also suffered from mental problems. The whole experience had been deeply disturbing to Sapir, who consulted Sullivan professionally in the fall of 1926. Out of this meeting developed an immediate and close friendship which continued until Sapir died, in 1939 at the age of fifty-five.[49]

In 1931 Sapir accepted an invitation from President James Angell to move to Yale and found the department of anthropology there. Though his main impact on anthropology was through his linguistic studies, he was also a "principal pathfinder"[50] in the field of culture and personality, where he sought to blend sociology and anthropology with the insights of social psychology and psychiatry. Sapir's work in this area had a particularly strong influence on the sociologist John Dollard (whom he brought to Yale), as well as on Ruth Benedict and Margaret Mead.[51] Later, beginning in 1933, Lasswell and Sapir were closely associated with the formation by Sullivan of the William Alanson White Psychiatric Foundation in Washington, D.C., which later nurtured the Washington School of Psychiatry and the journal *Psychiatry*.[52]

The Chicago of the late 1920s thus showed significant interest in psychiatry, which was reflected at the time or later in the writings of

Lasswell, Sapir, and Dollard. Ogburn was also heavily involved but kept his involvement separate. Burgess was mildly interested in the insights psychoanalysis had to offer. The presence of Franz Alexander on the campus for a year was a further sign of the interest that was shown in these new intellectual tendencies. The importance and influence of psychoanalysis and psychiatric ideas should certainly not be exaggerated. It was a minor tributary, which influenced a few considerably, but the majority little or not at all. Some, indeed, were quite antagonistic to Lasswell's ideas. It does, however, make apparent the intellectual diversity, the extent of interdisciplinary contact and the degree to which Chicago social scientists (such as Ogburn, Burgess, and Dollard as a graduate student) could not be easily compartmentalized. The residue, moreover, particularly through Sapir and Dollard, was influential later.

Consideration of the influence of Chicago years on careers pursued elsewhere is a reminder that universities do not remain static. The end of the 1920s and the opening of the Social Science Research Building in late 1929 marked the apogee of the Chicago schools of philosophy, sociology, and political science. The developments of the 1920s coincided with the presidencies of Ernest D. Burton and Max Mason, followed by the acting presidency of vice-president Frederick Woodward after Mason's sudden resignation in 1928.[53] Burton and Woodward, in particular, were closely involved in developing a strategy for social science research in collaboration with their senior colleagues Small, Merriam, and Marshall. The University of Chicago, the social sciences included, was profoundly affected by the appointment as president in 1929 of the young dean of the Yale Law School, Robert Maynard Hutchins. Though the reasons for the decline of Chicago sociology lay elsewhere, Hutchins pursued policies which, coupled with generational change, affected the departments of philosophy and political science detrimentally.

Philosophy suffered most directly, plunging immediately into fierce conflict between the new president and senior professors such as Tufts and Mead over appointments.[54] At one point the whole department threatened en bloc to resign.[55] Mead made arrangements to spend the 1931/32 academic year at Columbia, but died in April 1931 before he could do so.

> It seems typical of the University of Chicago that the close of that important era did not take place with the quiet retirement of the remaining patriarchs, after appropriate academic celebrations, but instead was marked by a flurry of resignations amidst considerable uproar.[56]

Tufts, in partial retirement, left Chicago to teach briefly at UCLA. Three members of the department, Burtt, Murphy, and Hall, resigned and went elsewhere. Mead was dead. Moore had retired in 1929. By 1932, only Ames and T. V. Smith remained of the original Chicago school of philosophy.

One of the sources of conflict had been that Hutchins appointed his friend Mortimer Adler, from Columbia, to teach philosophy. Soon after his arrival, Adler disturbed the fairly calm atmosphere of the social science departments by propounding in a controversial manner his views about the deductive and a priori character of social reasoning. In the autumn of 1930 he proclaimed that "current research programs in the social sciences are misdirected and methodologically ill-advised because of erroneous conceptions of the nature of science which comprise the 'raw empiricism' characteristic of contemporary social science." The distinction between exact (natural) and inexact (social) science was likened to that between good and bad science. Theoretical and mathematical economics were singled out for praise; sociology in particular was condemned as unscientific. Adler's mode of argument, as he himself later acknowledged, was counterproductive and tended to alienate many of his listeners by his dogmatism.[57]

The spirit of the 1920s, in which independent disciplines actively cooperated, was fractured by both Adler and Beardsley Ruml (dean of social sciences from 1931 to 1934, before he left for New York and a successful business and public career) advocating the dissolution of conventional academic disciplines. At the dedication of the Social Science Research Building in 1929, Ruml described traditional disciplinary categories as anachronisms, promoting sterile divisions and isolation on the conduct of empirical research. Learned societies were criticized for stimulating mainly trade union consciousness and sectarian politics.[58] A year later, addressing the SSRC, he advocated a much greater infusion of firsthand practical experience, organized interdepartmentally, in place of the "highly intellectualized, bookish and abstract" offerings in social science courses.[59]

In October 1933, Ruml chaired and Adler presented a seminar to the Social Science Division entitled Systematic Social Science devoted to Ruml's objective of producing a unified social science. Adler lectured on the prerequisites for such a move, as he saw them—pure and applied logic, including the theory of probability, and philosophical psychology. After a number of meetings, exasperation with the mode of argument and the idea of a unified social science led to an outright attack by Frank Knight, Louis Wirth, and three graduate students.[60] Chicago social scientists knew what they stood for, and it was not the abstract metaphysics that Adler expounded.

In political science, by comparison with philosophy, the early 1930s were something of a golden age, particularly among graduate students.[61] Though Merriam was aging, his influence carried forward through the students who were trained in his department, including Gabriel Almond, V. O. Key, Jr., David Truman, Herman Pritchett, and Herbert Simon. Writing to Harold Gosnell in 1980, David Truman observed:

> It was a wonderful group of graduate students who taught each other a great deal, but the real stimulus and the challenging atmosphere were created by you and your colleagues. . . . There has not been another department of political science like it since, at Chicago or anywhere else.[62]

In the longer term, however, Hutchins's impact was felt severely, for he was generally unsympathetic to the empirical approach to the study of politics and did not favor Merriam's protégés. Hutchins told Merriam that his department was full of "monuments to his passing whims," a remark apparently directed against Gosnell and Lasswell.[63] It was an unmerited and unjustifiable judgment, but Hutchins's veto of Lasswell's promotion to a full professorship led directly to his resignation in 1938.[64] Gosnell's final departure for Washington in 1942 had a similar origin. He, too, quite clearly did not receive the advancement he deserved because of the influence of the president. The author of two classic empirical studies, *Negro Politicians* and *Machine Politics: Chicago Model*, was another victim of the president's prejudices about the social sciences.[65]

Under Hutchins two departments experienced a considerable strengthening in personnel and intellectual quality. In anthropology, when Sapir moved to Yale in 1931, Radcliffe-Brown was appointed. Paradoxically until his departure for Oxford in 1937, the anthropology department became more sociologically oriented than it had been within the sociology department before 1929. Robert Park described the British functionalist school, which Radcliffe-Brown represented, as "nothing more or less than sociology, with the qualification that it is mainly concerned with primitive peoples."[66] Lloyd Warner's appointment in 1935 jointly to the departments of anthropology and sociology also strengthened social anthropology.

Chicago economics, too, was in the ascendant, though it is doubtful if it is useful to speak of a Chicago school of economics before the 1950s. The hallmark of the department in the 1920s was its institutionalist orientation, represented by Harry Millis and Simeon Leland. In the 1930s, the department expanded and grew in stature around Jacob Viner and Frank Knight. Other important staff were Paul Douglas, Henry Simons, John U. Nef, and, after 1939, Oscar Lange. A group of graduate students and young teachers around Frank Knight, including Simons, Lloyd Mints, Aaron Director, Milton Friedman, George Stigler and Allen Wallis, was particularly important. The department flourished in a way that it had not done in the 1920s, characterized particularly by the rigor of its graduate training program, which produced scholars with distinctive habits of work and thought through a process of professional acculturation.[67] Internal controversy was not absent, but it did not seem to have an inhibiting or weakening effect, as it had in the sociology department.

The decline of Chicago sociology during the 1930s owed little to Hutchins, who was neutral toward the department while pursuing his interests in the College and the general education program.[68] Several factors contributed, the principal one being the absence of Robert Park. Park was on leave traveling around the world for much of 1931 and 1932, and when he retired in 1934, he went to live in Nashville, Tennessee, near his old friend, Charles S. Johnson, head of the social science department at Fisk University.[69] With his departure, the department began to falter, lacking the stimulus derived from the intellectual integration he provided. No one else could supply the compelling overview, the insistent movement between the particular and the general, the curious and penetrating questioning, the devotion to students, which he did. He and Burgess complemented each other admirably, but Burgess on his own threw out fewer ideas to students, and in the 1930s concentrated more on the area of marriage and the family, while ecological studies became more pedestrian and mechanical.[70] Ogburn maintained a national orientation and in the early 1930s was much preoccupied with working for the President's Committee on Recent Social Trends. Ellsworth Faris played a supporting role as chairman through to 1939, but was not able to provide intellectual leadership of the caliber of Thomas or Park. The appointment of Edwin Sutherland from 1930 to 1935 as a research professor was not as fruitful as the earlier ones of L. L. Thurstone and Henry Schultz; Sutherland moved on to Indiana University.[71] New strength was brought by Samuel Stouffer's appointment as full professor in 1935 from Wisconsin and Everett Hughes's coming from McGill in 1938. With Louis Wirth and Herbert Blumer also on the staff, the composition of the department changed. It remained diverse, but the new mixture did not gel as before. Disagreements over methodology and orientation became more salient. To some extent the decline after 1932 was due to Park's failure to interest himself in administration and to devote more attention to appointments to the department during the 1920s.[72]

The caliber of sociology students may have had something to do with the decline. The political science department in the early 1930s trained several scholars who subsequently made creative contributions to their discipline.[73] Park and Burgess extracted very good work from many of their students, but a considerable number of them published little or nothing subsequently.[74] The department produced a small number of scholars who made a major contribution to American sociology—the most outstanding were Everett Hughes and Samuel Stouffer—but

> only a few of the students who produced publishable dissertations continued to carry out research or publish after they left the university. Perhaps Park was so dominant in his expectations that students became too dependent on him to be able to function independently later.[75]

Certainly the decline of Chicago sociology at the national level owed a good deal to the failure to produce outstanding successors, as well as to resentment over the Chicago dominancc. The crisis in the American Sociological Society in 1935–36, the severance of the connection between the society and the Chicago-based *American Journal of Sociology*, the establishment of the *American Sociological Review* as the society's own journal, and the setting up of the rival (Chicago-oriented) Sociological Research Association, were signs that American sociology was changing.[76] The crisis in the academic job-market resulting from the Depression also played some part.

During the 1930s, too, America was becoming less of a local and regional, more of a national, system. The loss of intellectual impetus in the 1930s—which occurred before the rise of Columbia after the late 1930s or of Harvard after 1945—partly derived from the weakness of a local orientation in a period more preoccupied with national issues and problems of national integration.[77] The new methods of survey research were better suited to studying the effects of the Depression or the impact of mass communications than field research or aggregate statistics.

The strength and reputation of universities and of departments tend to go in cycles. Departments can rarely perpetuate themselves in the same form for long periods, as Chicago sociology in the 1930s clearly showed. Academic succession can be influenced by a university president, but it is also a matter of personality, of the good judgment of senior members of the department, of the quality of younger scholars, and of chance. The Chicago schools of sociology and of political science declined for different reasons, but to some extent their disappearance was to be expected. Older scholars influence younger scholars but rarely perpetuate their ideas and approach in quite the same way. Those who try hardest—like Sumner and Giddings—are often the least successful.

What these Chicago schools left behind—to a significant extent common to several social sciences—was a changed orientation toward their subject. The emphasis on graduate training of a rigorous kind linked to empirical research marked a continuing trend toward professionalization of preparation for an academic career. The marriage of theory and adequate evidence became a hallmark of fruitful work in the discipline. Along with it, there was an attenuation of the interdisciplinary ideology which was so strong during the 1920s. In the cross-disciplinary manifold, the boundaries between different parts of the social sciences emerged as stronger than the flow of ideas and data between them. To be sure, the social science departments now occupied a single building, and social and intellectual intercourse among their members was frequent. Social scientists at Chicago remained more committed to interdisciplinary contact than at many institutions. The demands of graduate study were not as exigent as they have subsequently become, but increasingly these focused the attention of students upon developments within their own disciplines and made command of issues internal to the discipline the prerequisite for achieving professional standing as a scholar. Comparing 1940 with 1915, a very considerable transformation had taken place.

12 The Conditions of Creativity

In the history of sociology, "schools" that effectively combined general ideas and firsthand empirical inquiry are altogether exceptional. The Durkheim school is an example, with a greater emphasis than Chicago's upon the theoretical ideas of the master and the use of empirical materials gathered at second hand. The closest comparisons to the Chicago school of sociology are the schools of social anthropology of Bronislaw Malinowski, at the London School of Economics in the 1920s and 1930s, and of Max Gluckman, in Northern Rhodesia and Manchester in the 1940s and 1950s.[1] Like Chicago sociology, these schools were characterized by the pursuit of a program of empirical research carried out by graduate students and junior research workers, meshed with a concern to generalize and theorize about social processes. In political science, too, the Chicago school is unusual if not unique. Why are such collective research programs so rare, comparatively, in social science?

The undoubted preeminence of Chicago social science during the 1920s, particularly in sociology and political science, is not explained merely by an account of its own internal development. Why did Chicago forge ahead in the decade while other universities stood still or failed to develop these same social sciences? At a later period, after 1945, Columbia and Harvard rivaled or surpassed Chicago in sociology.[2] Why did they not do so at the earlier period? Was it really the case that developments at the University of Chicago were so outstandingly different from those at other leading institutions?

Among Chicago's early rivals, Clark University had soon faded from eminence and Johns Hopkins had undergone a relative decline. Neither, in any case, were centers of sociology teaching. Sociology was established at a number of state universities, where the emphasis was almost entirely upon undergraduate teaching, with little encouragement or opportunity for research. In the period between 1915 and 1940 only Harvard and Columbia had strong graduate schools which could compete on anything like equality with Chicago in the social sciences. At both, particularly at Harvard, the conception of the university as a center of research had to do battle with an ingrained commitment to teaching and the ideal of the college.

Sociology suffered a double handicap in being a new discipline which had difficulty in becoming established at older institutions. Until 1930 Harvard lacked what Chicago had had since 1892, a departmental structure within which the discipline of sociology could be nurtured.[3] The subject had been taught after 1893 in the department of economics and from 1906 to 1930 was also taught in the department of social ethics.[4] The pall of moral philosophy was lifted with the arrival of Pitirim Sorokin in 1930, but until that time there was fragmentation and lack of significant impact. The advances that were made in the late 1920s, including the bringing of Elton Mayo to set up an industrial fatigue laboratory in 1927 in the Business School and the creation of the new sociology department three years later, owed a good deal to the energy of a single individual, the biochemist L. J. Henderson, who also had an important influence upon the youthful George Homans, Talcott Parsons, and William F. Whyte.[5] Even in the 1930s, under Sorokin, the Harvard faculty teaching sociology in no way rivaled Chicago.

At Columbia sociology had, or had had in the early years of the century, a more impressive presence in a separate department. Its main weakness lay in Franklin Giddings, under whom sociology was in relative decline in the 1920s. Despite his earlier influence on students such as Ogburn, Chapin, and Odum, the increasing dogmatism of his views and his dominating personality undermined any attempt to build a strong department and led to resistance to sociology among his colleagues in other departments.[6] Indeed, shortly after he retired it was seriously suggested by President Butler that the department of sociology should be closed down, a proposal which John Dewey and Robert MacIver successfully resisted.[7] Moreover, Giddings lacked any leading idea or vision of society that could become the focus for a school in the way that Thomas and Park's ideas did. New York, too, did not have a large plutocratic elite concerned to any extent with local problems. Its local elite had a national orientation, while there were too many other distracting activities for its faculty members to pursue, particularly public service at the national level.[8]

In the 1920s, Columbia sociology did not rival Chicago to any degree. Ogburn's move in 1927 was prompted by dissatisfaction with research opportunities. On taking over the department in 1929, Robert MacIver inherited a mess.

> The department of sociology was in a parlous state . . . [Giddings's] staff appointments were determined less by ability than by the virtue of discipleship, a quality in strong men that has not infrequently had deleterious effects. The reputation of the department had fallen. It did not attract many able students. Leadership had passed to other institutions, notably the flourishing sociology department at the University of Chicago. . . . I confine myself to saying that the department lacked the quality and was wholly without the distinction one might expect in the graduate department of a great university.[9]

During the 1930s, MacIver and Robert Lynd restored its fortunes somewhat, but it was only with the appointment of Robert Merton and Paul Lazarsfeld at the end of the decade that Columbia began to overtake Chicago.

The competitive edge Chicago possessed over Columbia in political science owed something to generational differences. Merriam and his colleagues led the movement toward a new "science of politics." Combining intellectual innovation with considerable appeal to younger scholars, it gave political science at Chicago an élan which the older, less venturesome schools at Columbia and Harvard lacked.[10]

Few other universities apart from Columbia or Harvard had established centers of social science research that could rival Chicago in the early 1920s. One of the few was the University of Pennsylvania, with its Wharton School of Business and the Bureau of Industrial Research organized by Joseph Willitts,[11] where Elton Mayo first worked in the United States. Pennsylvania, nevertheless, failed to develop a research program embracing the social sciences. Another growing center was the University of North Carolina at Chapel Hill, where Howard Odum began to teach sociology in 1920, founded the journal *Social Forces* in 1922,[12] and in 1924 established the Institute for Research in Social Science, with the support of the memorial.[13] The university, however, was a struggling institution in a rural backwater of the South. North Carolina became a strong regional center, precariously dependent on foundation support.

Perhaps only the London School of Economics and Political Science during the 1920s resembled the social sciences at the University of Chicago in the scope of its work and the international stature of its staff. These included the political scientist, Graham Wallas, the economist Edwin Cannan, the statistician A. L. Bowley, the sociologist L. T. Hobhouse, and the comparative ethnologist, E. A. Westermarck.[14] It was just entering a period of consolidation and expansion under its new director William Beveridge.[15] The London School of Economics was one of the few centers of concentrated social science research in Europe that could in any way rival Chicago or Columbia.

Even so, in 1920 it was a small and rather marginal part of the University of London, with many part-time staff, a relatively small student body (many of them evening students) and few postgraduates. By comparison with leading American universities, the LSE was impoverished, lacking even secure and adequate premises for its growing numbers of staff and students. Research took second place to teaching and was in any case very much an individual effort, rather than being conducted on an organized or collaborative basis.[16] Social research was not institutionally established there in the way that it was at Chicago. Various initiatives by Beveridge, such as Lancelot Hogben's work in social biology and the *New Survey of Life and Labour in London* (a replication of

Booth),[17] were intended to promote the empirical study of society, but were flawed by a failure to connect empirical data with a significant body of theoretical ideas, as Park was able to. Only Malinowski's developing school of anthropology was in any way comparable to the achievement at Chicago.

Part of the explanation for Chicago's exceptionality lay in the character of the university. From its foundation, particular emphasis was placed on the performance of research and standards of scholarship. Significant research was expected from its faculty, publication was fostered, and greater importance was attached to training graduates in research than to undergraduate teaching than was then common in universities in the English-speaking world. It faced little competition from the reformed colleges of Oxford and Cambridge, the numerous undergraduate colleges across North America, or even the colleges of distinguished universities such as Yale and Harvard. In the 1920s and early 1930s, for example, President James Angell at Yale, influenced by his years at Chicago, was trying to strengthen graduate work and wean the university away to some slight extent from its devotion to teaching undergraduates and building character.[18] It was an uphill battle. The values of college education were strongly held and resonant, as even Chicago found when Robert Hutchins became president in 1929 and began to press through a greater emphasis on college teaching, in part influenced by his own experiences as a student and teacher at Yale.

The commitment to research and publication united teachers and graduate students in a common effort. Writing of a later period, Harry Johnson suggested that the Chicago economics department was a department in a different sense from those at Harvard and Yale. It stressed publication, its main emphasis was upon graduate teaching, and its core was an intellectual and social community of professional economists. Most members lived within a mile of the campus and shared one floor of a single building in which they met one another regularly informally and in passing.[19] Something of the same was true of sociology and political science in the late 1920s, reinforced in the case of the sociologists by the Society for Social Research, the Greek letter societies, Local Community Research seminars, and the opportunity and requirement to gain experience of firsthand empirical research.

This contributed to the sense of intellectual seriousness among the student body. Sociology graduate students of the period have testified to the extent to which they "lived sociology" and were preoccupied with their studies much of the time.[20] The small size of the teaching staff made contact with teachers straightforward. Park and Burgess were skilled institution builders who created the conditions for the successful flowering of empirical social science. Support from the memorial and good local contacts facilitated empirical inquiries. There were adjunct institutions, such as the Institute for Juvenile Research, the Juvenile Protective Association, and the Chicago Crime Commission, to which students could be attached. When the research was completed, staff and equipment provided by the outside funds could help with analysis and report-writing, and with subsidies for publication by the university press. The *American Journal of Sociology*, published from the department, was another prestigious outlet to which the abler could aspire. Sociology did not achieve national dominance alone, but as part of a collective enterprise shared by several social science departments.

The explicit attention given to research methods, both in conducting research and in creating an adequate institutional structure for research to take place in, has been examined in previous chapters. The limitations of the research methods in use in the 1920s will be obvious to the reader in the light of subsequent advances. Even so, the relative modernity of some of the field studies by sociology students or Thurstone's work on attitude measurement is quite striking. For reasons discussed in chapter 10, many of the innovations that were made during the decade have been lost sight of in the onward march of quantitative research.

Some methodological issues current at the time endure, particularly contention over measurement or case studies versus statistics. "When you cannot measure ◉ your knowledge is ◉ meagre ◉ and ◉ unsatisfactory ◉ Lord Kelvin" no doubt found favor on the fourth floor on the new building after 1929, but it can hardly have been equally satisfactory to many others. At the official dedication of the building, Merriam made a speech in which he referred to Ogburn having been "threatened with a ride for omitting Machiavelli, Aristotle, and Plato from the stone faces." ("Ride" was a euphemism used by Chicago gangsters for murder.) He also expressed caution lest the adaptation of Kelvin's statement should be taken too literally: "The translation of Lord Kelvin's brave words concerning quantitative methods into scientific actualities will require much longer work on much harder stone. Experimental techniques require not only laboratories but inventive and continuing spirits undismayed by failure and frustration."[21] Frank Knight was heard to mutter in the 1930s, while contemplating Ogburn's inscription: "And if you cannot measure it, measure it anyhow."[22] Jacob Viner reportedly said: "If you can measure . . . your knowledge will still be meager and unsatisfactory."[23] Tensions between proponents of measurement (such as Thurstone) and its fiercer opponents (such as Knight) reflected enduring controversy within the social sciences about the scope for extending the methods of the natural sciences into the human domain. Differences of this kind came to assume more importance in the sociology department during the 1930s.

A university like Chicago committed to graduate work provided the institutional context for professional training of scholars, research, and publication and the advancement of the discipline. Edward Shils has observed that

> the University of Chicago, practically from its beginning in the 1890s had conducted its affairs with a genuine—some would say grim—conviction of the supreme importance of scientific and scholarly learning. The teachers were serious and so were the students, both undergraduate and graduate. Those who recall the University of Chicago in the 1920s, or who like myself come upon memories of it in the 1930s, testify to the vigor and intensity with which ideas were pondered. They were however ideas which arose out of or in connection with scientific research. "Idle speculation" was not well looked upon.[24]

Mortimer Adler looked back at the end of the 1930s at a decade of controversy at the university and compared Chicago with his previous ten years at Columbia. He acknowledged without qualification "the exceptional character of Chicago's intellectual vitality. . . . there has been more real tangling over basic issues at Chicago than has occurred at a dozen other places during the same time, or at some places during their whole existence."[25] The vigor owed something to the physical propinquity of the university's members on and around the campus, the social life of whom resembled that of officers and wives in an army camp. At Columbia, teachers lived far from the campus and moved in social circles that were predominantly nonacademic.[26]

Unlike an army camp, however, the university was not isolated from the city in which it was located. Members of the university staff were heavily involved in local affairs, providing an orientation and a set of connections that helped to stimulate the local community research program, which was central to the social sciences in the 1920s.[27] A characteristic of Chicago social science at this period was its local focus, which gave those involved a delimited frame within which to work. Park and Burgess's program of urban research, in many ways rather diffuse and unfocused, gained coherence and importance from being carried out within a specific local setting. Similarly the political science surveys were made manageable (and to some extent sidestepped sampling problems) by being studies of political behavior within the city.

It has been argued by Milton Friedman that as a city Chicago has been more tolerant of intellectual diversity than New York City.

> The great good fortune of our university was that it was not established on the East Coast. . . . Fortunately we were established in Chicago, a new, raw city, bursting with energy, far less sophisticated than New York, but for that very reason far more tolerant of diversity, of heterodox ideas. . . . Chicago [was]

> characterized by diversity in every dimension, by a willingness to experiment, to judge people by their performance rather than their origins, to judge ideas by their consequences rather than their antecedents.[28]

In economics, this fostered at a later period the growth of a school whose major tenets were considerably at variance with those of major universities on the East Coast.

One can only partially account for the tendency of Chicago to produce schools in social science in terms of the distinguishing qualities of the university and the city in which it was located. At the heart of any academic school are one or two individuals with a body of ideas or a compelling vision that attracts others, binds the group together, and gives it a greater degree of intellectual cohesion than is usual among colleagues in academic social science departments. A "school" is ultimately the product of that personal quality of intellectual passion or self-confidence that emanates from one or two individuals who stand out at some distance from their colleagues. In sociology, for example, leadership was shared, initially between Thomas and Park, then between Park and Burgess. Park was the key figure, however, after whose retirement the school rapidly declined. Thomas alone would not have created the Chicago school, and Burgess alone could not have sustained it. In political science, Merriam was the single source of inspiration. The Chicago school of economics matured later. Its origins lay in the 1930s, when it hardly yet constituted a school.[29] At that stage, the most influential figures were Jacob Viner and Frank Knight, with Henry Simons. At a later period Milton Friedman and George Stigler were the dominant influences.

One of the common characteristics of the leaders of these schools was to be inspiring and effective teachers. Park aroused the curiosity of his students, built on their capacities, and pushed them toward the empirical study of phenomena in which he was interested, complemented by Burgess's more practical skills. Burgess himself, particularly in criminology, initiated research of note by playing a similar role. Merriam did not have Park's intellectual curiosity or sharp insight. At the core of his thought, there was a rhetorical element which diminished its impact. But he was able to seek that quality of curiosity in others, such as Lasswell and Gosnell, and foster it. Coupled with his vision of a quantitative, scientific, political science and his administrative and organizational capability (which was far superior to Park), he created single-handed the school of political science. In economics slightly later, Frank Knight gathered about him an informal group of students and protégés, including Simons, Friedman, Director, Stigler, and Wallis, which in time came to constitute a school.[30]

Intellectual dominance could take various forms. Later schools such as those of Malinowski and Gluckman had a more explicit theory at their center than those around Park and around Merriam had. Chicago sociology and political science had nevertheless an implicit general theory and a clear intellectual vision. The way in which this vision was propagated was through the seminar. Park and Burgess's Field Studies seminar has distinct parallels with Malinowski's later postgraduate fieldwork seminar at the LSE, with the difference that the anthropologist's "field" was not close at hand in the city. In economics, the crucible in which graduate students in the 1930s received their professional induction was Jacob Viner's tough, demanding, and rigorous graduate course 301 on economic principles.[31]

Dominance, however, did not mean at all that students were expected to reproduce the views of their teacher. There was a degree of openness about the Chicago schools of sociology and political science which in part explains their success. Park provided a loose framework for research in his essay "The City," which Burgess developed with the theory of concentric zones. Within this framework, students were encouraged to investigate undogmatically. Merriam's framework was more in the nature of a general methodological orientation, but had this same quality of openness. The contrast could not be greater with those who were not successful in promoting sociology, such as Giddings.

> His personal dogmatism, conceit and prejudices alienated many prominent and influential members of the Columbia faculty, who saw to it that sociology would not be expanded there before Giddings retired. Giddings himself contributed to it by surrounding himself with second-rate men who were no threat to his leadership. According to those who knew him personally, he was anti-Semitic and had poor relations with outstanding Columbia social scientists like Boas and Seligman because they were Jewish.[32]

Park, by contrast, was infinitely curious about the sociological relevance of ideas from other disciplines, on cordial personal relations with colleagues in other departments, and through his interest in ethnic groups free from many of the conventional prejudices of the time. It was no accident that two of the most outstanding early black sociologists, Charles S. Johnson and E. Franklin Frazier, were his students.[33]

There is, moreover, a direct connection between this openness and Chicago sociology's commitment to foster the best of contemporary sociology, whatever its methodological orientation. The term "school" sometimes has the connotations of clique or cult, yet what was remarkable about the groups of scholars around Park and Merriam was their freedom from narrowness.

> Not isolation and uniformity, but tolerance for diversity, stress on scientific quality as the decisive criterion for appointments, and success in identifying and attracting future leaders of their profession—these are the sources of the Chicago proclivity to generate "schools." . . . Balance and diversity have been and will continue to be valuable by-products of an undeviating emphasis on quality alone. They are not objectives to be sought directly.[34]

The dependence of schools upon their leading figures is very striking. Schools do not come into existence before they have appeared on the scene. Small created the conditions, but it was not until Thomas brought Park to Chicago that the Chicago school began to develop. In Merriam's case the start was even less propitious, due to Judson's antagonism to him. And schools do not last beyond the generation of their founders. The decline of sociology and political science in the 1930s was traced in the previous chapter. The local influence of other dominant social scientists, for example, Lazarsfeld at Columbia, Max Gluckman at Manchester, was dissipated almost immediately after their death. An interesting exception to this generalization is the Chicago school of economics, which has endured over a longer period. Though it did not really come into existence until the 1940s and 1950s, it was never so dependent as sociology and political science on one or two individuals throughout. It had more of a collective leadership.[35]

In explaining the coming into being of schools, the role of financial support deserves consideration. The role of the Laura Spelman Rockefeller Memorial during the 1920s was a major innovation which accompanied the academic transformation of the social sciences, encouraging a more differentiated and ambitious type of social science research. To what extent did such support nurture the Chicago schools? Lack of support could clearly be a decisive obstacle, as Du Bois's attempts at Atlanta to initiate serious research on black Americans showed.[36] His difficulties in obtaining funding derived from Booker T. Washington's tight control over philanthropy among the black population. There may clearly be some association between institutionalized research and the coming into being of schools. The LCRC assisted at the birth of two schools in Chicago, the Rhodes-Livingstone Institute in Northern Rhodesia, of which Gluckman was director, made possible the creation of his school of anthropology.[37]

Critics of the type of research encouraged by the Memorial certainly thought that it was altering the character of the social sciences. In the late 1920s, the LSE political scientist Harold Laski roundly attacked the role of foundations in fostering these new developments.

> No university today is complete without its research institute; no foundation is worthy of the name unless its directors are anxiously scanning the horizon for suitable universities which can be endowed with such institutes. There are few universities where the movement is not away from the discussion of principle to the description and tabulation of fact. Everything is being turned into material for quantitative expression, since this best yields to cooperative effort.[38]

Laski's doubts were threefold. He did not believe that creative scholarship was born of committees. Great discoveries had been a matter of a lone thinker brooding in solitude upon the meaning of facts and gaining some sudden illumination. He feared an increasing drift from basic principles toward concrete facts. With Chicago in mind, he criticized fieldwork as

> taking the student's mind away from essentials; it is teaching him not to inquire and evaluate, but to describe. It is computer's work made better only to the degree that the teacher later explains what meaning he attaches to the result.[39]

Laski's critique of empirical research was typical of one strand in English social science, represented in a distinct but related way by L. T. Hobhouse, the country's first professor of sociology.[40] Third, intentionally or not, gifts from foundations altered the character of universities. They influenced directions of research interests. They might make those who attract funds more significant members of staff than those who did not. The institution developed along lines the foundation approved.

Criticism of the role foundations have played vis-à-vis universities has persisted. It has been alleged, for example, that bodies such as the Memorial and the Rockefeller Foundation were instruments by means of which private capitalistic business enterprises and entrepreneurs exercised domination over intellectual life.[41] One of the adherents of this view, Donald Fisher, says that philanthropy was a means of distributing surplus wealth which would otherwise have gone in taxes in order to produce knowledge that would help preserve the economic structure of Western society.[42] The officers of the Memorial and other foundations might be progressive, change-oriented, and to a degree radical (as indeed they were) but they were (it is argued) really "sophisticated conservatives."

In the case of the Memorial, the evidence for this view is not very compelling. Ruml pursued a radical and innovative policy with scarcely any interference from the trustees, let alone John D. Rockefeller, Jr. Far from being "conservative," he and the most active trustee, Raymond B. Fosdick, were Democrats with a strong belief in the reformist influence of social science.[43] The most powerful negative evidence is provided by the twelve principles drawn up by Ruml in 1924, which guided the practice of the Memorial. These stipulated that the Memorial would not support organizations involved in political or social reform, would avoid concentrating on particular institutions and thereby incurring the danger of bias, and would neither conduct research itself nor attempt to influence investigations through direct or indirect means. This latter objective was achieved by block grants made to institutions without strings, a policy pursued by all the Rockefeller boards until its replacement in 1934 by the move to project grants of a more specific kind.[44] The main positive principle was that scientific research should be carried out "when responsible educational or scientific institutions initiate the request, sponsor the research, and assume responsibility for the selection and competence of the staff and the scientific spirit of the investigation."[45]

The influence of Ruml and the Memorial was considerably more subtle than the articulation of the class interests of donors or of foundation officials.[46] Influence was exerted upon the character of sociology, and social science more generally. Ruml's strongest views about the role of sociology related to the need to be empirical, the need for scientific method, the scope for the application of the results of research, and the value of interdisciplinary work. These matters were not a question of furthering the class interests of his philanthropic employers, but of influencing the development of the subject in universities in a more scientific direction. Radical critics of the social role of foundations assume all too easily that the causal influence was unidirectional, from foundations to the character of scholarship. The Memorial as a grant-giving body was a great innovator, but the changes in the social sciences which it encouraged by no means came from Ruml alone, who was a brilliant intellectual entrepreneur, identifying and encouraging tendencies already present in American academic social science.

Laski was right to the extent that the impact of the foundations *was* helping to transform academic social science. Through the grants made, foundation support was a necessary condition for the movement toward "empirical" observation, toward fieldwork, interviews, questionnaires, efforts to standardize observations in the form of "tests," the use of unpublished governmental statistics, and the development of quantitative methods, but it was not a sufficient condition. Just as in colonial central Africa, the support available to Gluckman as director of the Rhodes-Livingstone Institute made possible the development of his school, the creation of the LCRC facilitated the programs of Park and Merriam in important ways. In neither case, however, did the financial support bring the school into being. Many research institutes are established without a school being created around them.

The Chicago school of sociology did not owe its existence to outside funding. Support from the Memorial was a facilitating factor, but foundation support was not responsible for the fact that sociology was changing, becoming less evangelical, less devoted to abstract theorizing, more empirical in orientation, and curious about the world outside the university. The creativity of the Chicago department under the influence of Thomas and Park and then of Park and Burgess had other sources and would have been likely to develop in the direction that it did even without the support of the Memorial. The more interesting question in relation to foundation support is, Why did academic scholars at the time accept what the foundations had to offer? This puts the emphasis more upon the changing character of the social sciences at the period. The gravamen of Laski's charge was that the integrity of universities was being demeaned by outside influences that were intellectually inferior, though economically more powerful. But again this begs the question of the direction of the causation. If this was the case, why did the universities so willingly acquiesce in seeking foundation support for their research?

An explanation of the trend toward more rigorous empirical research is complex.[47] The social sciences were perpetually on the defensive, vis-à-vis the natural sciences, and trying to show that their work was truly scientific in the sense that natural scientists understood the term. The influence was strongest upon psychology and economics, but had some influence on sociology at Chicago particularly through the work of W. F. Ogburn and L. L. Thurstone. Trends in biology and behaviorist psychology toward a more mechanistic and positivist approach had their influence upon social science. So, too, did advances in statistics—particularly those advances made by the English statisticians—which were absorbed by a few economists, sociologists, and political scientists (such as James Field, Samuel Stouffer and Harold Gosnell) and given wider currency. Robert Park, unusually, drew upon his experience as a newspaperman.

Another contributory factor evident in the approach of Park and influencing Merriam during the 1920s (though not earlier) was a degree of disenchantment with politics as a solution to national problems. Merriam was more reform-oriented than Park, but both shared a belief that empirical knowledge of the state of society was a means to achieve "social control" (in the original sense of that word).[48] The need for such an approach was underlined by the evident problems of rapid urbanization and building a new nation from a more and more ethnically heterogeneous population. Both Merriam's research on nonvoting and Park's on race relations were concerned with different aspects of this diversity.

The older more theoretical and library-based studies in sociology and political science were inadequate tools with which to grapple with these insistent social conditions. Yet sociologists and political scientists approached these problems as scientists, not as social reformers. Park had little use for "do-gooders," and Merriam's students (though not Merriam himself) were generally free from active political involvements.

As the limitations of an evolutionary viewpoint became apparent, the solution to the value problem which was represented by theories such as Sumner's social Darwinism came to seem increasingly deficient. The social sciences in the late nineteenth century had a strong ethical component and still bore traces of the Protestant village culture whence many of its academic practitioners came. This strand was influential generally on the University of Chicago through Chautauqua and the Baptist affiliations of many of its early staff. The generation of Small still sought to fuse science and values.[49] The generation of Merriam, Wesley Mitchell, and J. B. Watson, proponents of scientific method in social science, all broke decisively with such confusions of fact and value, while the marginally older generation of Thomas and Park reached the same conclusion by a slightly different route.

Another powerful if intermittent influence was the demands of public policy. A number of social scientists in major positions in the 1920s had some experience of work for either government or the foundations, which had had implications for policy. Park, for example, collaborated closely with Charles Johnson on the work of the Chicago Commission on Race Relations and had worked on the Carnegie-financed Americanization study in 1918–19. Wesley Mitchell, at Columbia, had worked in government during World War I before setting up the National Bureau of Economic Research.[50] Scientific psychology had been boosted by the impact of psychological testing in the army during the war, an experience reflected directly in the counsels of the social sciences in the 1920s through Beardsley Ruml. The scope for the application of social science was still extremely limited, but demands were beginning to be made which contributed to turning social scientists more in the direction of firsthand empirical inquiry.

All these influences contributed to the intellectual climate in which the Local Community Research Committee was established. The type of research fostered by the LCRC was different from what had gone before. Was it, contemporaries wondered, better or not? Laski obviously thought it was worse, and he reserved particular scorn for the idea of team research. For Laski, the very conception of a school was a check on creative individual scholarship. Viewed in retrospect, he was clearly wrong, for Chicago produced a number of notable works in the 1920s.

This book has not provided a systematic summary of the substance of the research conducted in the 1920s, but the highlights may be mentioned. Park and Burgess's program of sociological studies made a major contribution to the study of urban structure, race and ethnic relations, criminology, and the sociology of social problems. W. I. Thomas laid the foundations of sociological social psychology, while symbolic interactionism may be traced back to George Herbert Mead. In political science, Merriam, Gosnell, and White's studies of political behavior and Lasswell's studies of political psychopathology were of lasting significance. Thurstone's work on attitude measurement, Henry Schultz's work on the theory and measurement of demand and Quincy Wright's studies of the causes of war all helped to give substance to the claim that Chicago was the leading center of the social sciences throughout the world in the 1920s. To be sure, some of the work could be accused of triviality.[51] Not all of the projects financed by the LCRC provided useful or interesting results. As L. D. White complained in 1929, too many lacked clear criteria of research design. This was true of several of the studies by Abbott and Breckinridge, of Palmer's work collating urban research material, and of some of the studies of the institutional economists. Taken as a whole, however, the work of the decade, particularly in sociology and political science, turned social science in a new and fruitful direction.

The Chicago schools of sociology and political science showed that firsthand empirical social inquiry could be successfully integrated into an academic discipline, as opposed to being pursued outside academia, for example in the social survey movement. Not only did sociology and political science become more differentiated (as they had done increasingly since the 1880s), but detailed empirical inquiries became an integral part of their concerns at the same time that more general theories and perspectives were pursued. During the 1920s, sociology and political science began to take on their modern form. Whereas in 1915, their nineteenth-century character was still marked and their stature at the University of Chicago was not firmly established, by the time of the opening of the Social Science Research Building in 1929 their position was secure. In sociology this was achieved by fertile empirical research within a loose general theory, pursued by a community of scholars committed to intellectual excellence and a catholic receptivity to diverse approaches.

The Chicago school made by far the most important American contribution to dissolving the stratification of sociology into theoretical sociologists and empirical sociologists.

> There is still a distinction between theory and research, and some division of labour, but it is no longer a hierarchy the upper and lower strata of which do not mingle with each other. They have found a common task and a common ancestry.[52]

Thomas and Park played a crucial role in bringing about that transformation, through conducting empirical research but seeing the phenomena they studied theoretically and introducing this theory and aphoristic observations. The old type of fact-finding study continued after the Chicago school—represented at the end of the 1920s by *Middletown* and in 1933 by *Recent Social Trends*—but increasingly the most interesting sociological work was that which embodied a theoretical element explicitly or implicitly. Notable studies of this kind by former Chicago graduate students included John Dollard's *Caste and Class in a Southern Town* (1937), Everett Hughes's *French Canada in Transition* (1938), and the pioneering work on the army during World War II directed by Samuel Stouffer, *The American Soldier*. Gunnar Myrdal's *An American Dilemma*, in which Stouffer also played a considerable role, was a synthesis of material rather than original research, but it bore very markedly the traces of the research of Park and his students and his macrosociological approach to sociological understanding of race in the United States. Meanwhile, at Chicago, Lloyd Warner was organizing a number of studies of race relations in the South and encouraging St. Clair Drake and Horace Cayton in their research for *Black Metropolis*.

By no means all of the major empirical studies of the 1930s and early 1940s bore the influence of the Chicago school directly. The study of Marienthal in Austria, the Hawthorne studies, the Lynd's restudy of Middletown, Paul Lazarsfeld's early audience research, all had different roots. Moreover, there were very significant gaps in the coverage of Chicago research. Major aspects of social structure such as social stratification, bureaucratic organization, and the determinants of political behavior received scant attention. Sorokin's *Social Mobility* (1927), *Management and the Worker* (carried out between 1927 and 1932 in Chicago, published in 1939), or later Lazarsfeld and Berelson's *The People's Choice* were exploring areas of the discipline that Chicago sociologists had left largely untouched. Nevertheless, their influence was felt indirectly through the extent to which they had advanced methods of empirical research and dissolved the duality of "theory" and "research." On the Continent, Durkheim and Weber had achieved the same objective, but their work was only slightly known by American sociologists before the late 1930s and the 1940s.[53] Park, though well-read in Simmel and Toennies, virtually ignored Weber and Durkheim. The example and influence of the Chicago school was therefore of particular significance in bridging the gap between theory and research.

The repertoire of research methods available to sociologists was considerably broadened by the achievements of the Chicago school. Personal documents began to be collected by sociologists. Census tract data began to be used systematically for urban studies at the local level. More rigorous kinds of attitude research, developed by L. L. Thurstone, were applied. And above all field research, involving participant observation, the use of informants, and informal interviewing, was introduced to become in future a standard sociological research method. The Chicago approach to methodology was a catholic and tolerant one. Though there was debate about the merits of case studies versus statistics, the lines did not harden and studies typically employed a range of methods. The attention given to quantitative methods was particularly noteworthy, reinforcing the point about the diverse commitment of the department to excellence of whatever kind.

Ecological analysis of aggregate data was limiting, a characteristic which became apparent with the rise of survey research. Though Gosnell in political science was an important forerunner, the subsequent development of social survey methods in the U.S. government and in media and public opinion research had its main origins elsewhere. Little direct influence was apparent in Lynd's study of *Middletown*, though he had received methodological advice from L. C. Marshall and Burgess of the LCRC.[54] Even so, Thurstone's work on attitude measurement carried through, and Stouffer later became a leading practitioner of the new survey methodology. Sociological research as it was practiced in the 1930s and 1940s would have been very different if the Chicago school had not existed. The influence of the school was decisive in breaking away from the social survey movement and establishing an independent repertoire of methods for sociologists to use. Not all of those methods proved equally useful, but they helped to establish sociology as an autonomous research-based discipline. The slow development of sociological research in Britain, by contrast, showed how little could occur in the absence of a stimulus such as that provided at Chicago.

In the longer term, the new direction that Chicago established for American sociology had a major impact on what sociological theorists thought they were doing. Apart from W. G. Sumner, the generation of Ward, Ross, Cooley, and Small did not conceive of their work as being particularly illuminated by empirical evidence. They were concerned with abstract general classificatory schemes and generalized explanations, tinged with social philosophy. By contrast, the Chicago school seemed very empirical and has indeed been misread as atheoretical, because the vague and inchoate theoretical ideas of Thomas and Park were not made very explicit. An important transformation that they helped to bring about was to make general theorists aware of the empirical dimension.

> No theorist, however abstract and however preoccupied with fundamental concepts . . . can any longer carry on his work

> without feeling that empirical sociologists are looking over his shoulder and that sooner or later he must answer to them. He knows now that his work can no longer be self-sustaining but that it must justify itself by what it contributes to research.[55]

The Chicago school tends to attract admirers and critics who are very ready to read into its history tendencies within the discipline which they either like or dislike. Often such accounts of the Chicago school entail considerable distortion of the historical record in order to fit the thesis being argued. It is the contention of the present study that the principal characteristics of the Chicago school were its collective commitment to excellence in empirical research and its considerable intellectual and methodological diversity, rather than the embodiment of a particular kind of sociology. The overall significance of the Chicago school lies in its success in institutionalizing within a collective research program a kind of sociology which successfully bridged the gap between, and combined together, theory and empirical research.

A Note on Documentary Sources

Original documentary sources for the study of the social sciences at the University of Chicago between 1915 and 1930 vary considerably in their comprehensiveness. The main series of papers consulted for the present work are located at the University of Chicago. The most comprehensive collection is in the Special Collections Department of Joseph Regenstein Library, University of Chicago (referred to in footnotes as the "University of Chicago Archives"), whose staff under the curator, Mr. Robert Rosenthal, pursues an active policy of trying to preserve the papers of leading scholars connected with the university and of other material relating to the university.

Two major series, the official Papers of the President of the University of Chicago for 1889–1925 and for 1925–45 contain some material about the development of the social sciences, principally letters between heads of departments and the president, more rarely letters between individual members of staff and the president. This material is, however, scattered through this very large collection and does not of itself provide a comprehensive picture of developments in the period. The Harold H. Swift Papers may also be consulted.

The Albion W. Small Papers are sparse and disappointing, throwing little light on the period being considered and containing little correspondence for the later period of Small's time at the university. The James H. Tufts Papers are more substantial and contain useful material on the early years of the university. But there is little for the period 1923–25, when Tufts was vice-president of the university and a member of the Local Community Research Committee.

From W. I. Thomas, there are no papers at all and only very occasional correspondence in other series. The Robert E. Park Papers are, by comparison with other series, fragmentary and disappointing, including some lecture notes, notebooks from his Tuskegee period, and correspondence. Some of the material was sent to the university by Winifred Raushenbush and includes useful memoranda prepared for her by social scientists who had known Park at the University of Chicago, either as colleagues or graduate students. By comparison with the Park Papers, the Ernest W. Burgess Papers are much more substantial and would provide the basis for a full biographical study, which Burgess deserves. Material from these papers on the 1920s is not, however, abundant, for much of it relates to the later stages of Burgess's career. Nevertheless, there is valuable information about the Local Community Research Committee, Burgess's census work, and the organization of research.

The single most comprehensive archive for developments in Chicago social science in the 1920s contains the three hundred boxes of the Charles E. Merriam Papers. This archive includes general correspondence with many important figures inside and outside the university, material about the social sciences at the University of Chicago in the 1920s, records of Merriam's dealings with the Laura Spelman Rockefeller Memorial, records of the workings of the Local Community Research Committee, and the transcripts of some of the Dartmouth conferences held by the Social Science Research Council. For the purposes of this work it also contains within it a most valuable source, the Papers of Harold F. Gosnell for the 1920s and 1930s, which provide invaluable information on the development of quantitative research methods. Many other topics lying somewhat outside the scope of this work are covered in the Merriam Papers, such as his participation in President Hoover's Research Committee on Social Trends, 1929–33, of which he was a member.

The research director of the Hoover committee was William F. Ogburn, and his papers were also deposited in the Special Collections Department. They provide some information about his early years in the Department of Sociology, for example, on teaching methodology, but, like the Burgess Papers, are much fuller for the later years of his time at the university. Other series of papers of University of Chicago social scientists consulted include the Philip M. Hauser Papers, the Robert Redfield Papers and the Louis Wirth Papers. Of these the most useful were the Hauser Papers. Hauser was a graduate student in the Department of Sociology in the late 1920s and kept notes on the courses he attended, including some given by Park.

The records of the Social Science Research Committee, 1923–64 are also now held in the Special Collections Department. (At the time of this research, they were housed under closed access in the basement of the Social Science Research Building, University of Chicago, 1126 East 59th Street, and are referred to here as the "1126 Files.") This committee was formed in 1930 out of the Local Community Research Committee (1923–30), discussed in chapter 8, and includes the administrative records of the LCRC for the 1920s.

One other series contains interesting though sparse information, the Beardsley Ruml Papers. Mainly covering the later decades of his life in business in New York, they do contain some scattered information about his career and his role as director of the Laura Spelman Rockefeller Memorial. Also kept in the Special Collections Department are the Faculty (Staff) Meeting Minutes of the Department of Sociology from

October 1926 to August 1939. What appears to be a promising source is in fact of relatively little interest, containing principally a record of routine business and administration, much of it concerning students for higher degree and junior teaching appointments. Throwing much more light on the collective life of the Department of Sociology in the 1920s are the records of the Society for Social Research, an organization of staff and students run by graduate students, which was at the center of the intellectual life of the department.

Two other sources are of particular value. In 1972, Professor James T. Carey, of the University of Illinois at Chicago, interviewed twenty-five surviving sociologists and other social scientists who had studied at the University of Chicago in the 1920s. These interviews formed the basis of his book *Sociology and Public Affairs* (1975), but the full verbatim typewritten transcripts of these interviews are deposited at the Special Collections Department. They vary in length from 24 to 51 pages. Those interviewed were Kenneth E. Barnhart, Herbert Blumer, Ruth Shonle Cavan, Harriet M. Bartlett, William P. Carter, Leonard S. Cottrell, Jr., John Dollard, Robert E. L. Faris, Norman S. Hayner, Mrs. Howard Jensen, Guy B. Johnson, Fay Berger Karpf, Samuel C. Kincheloe, Franc L. McCluer, Henry McKay, Ernest and Harriet Mowrer, Raymond E. Nelson, Martin H. Neumeyer, Ruth Newcomb, Laura Pederson, Walter C. Reckless, Antony Stephan, Everett V. Stonequist, Edgar T. Thompson, and Ellen Black Winston. Professor Carey used a list of standard questions for each interview, so some comparability is possible. These interviews provide a particularly valuable source on a number of aspects of Chicago sociology in the 1920s.

Also deposited in the Special Collections Department are letters sent to Fred H. Matthews in response to inquiries he made while preparing his study of Robert Park, *Quest for an American Sociology* (1977). Though briefer, they contain very helpful insights. His correspondents included Saul D. Alinsky, Nels Anderson, Jessie Bernard, Emory Bogardus, Pitrim Sorokin, Harold Lasswell, Leslie A. White, and Bernard L. Hormann.

Elsewhere, the main collection consulted has been the archives of the Laura Spelman Rockefeller Memorial, 1918–29, located at the Rockefeller Archive Center, Pocantico Hills, North Tarrytown, New York. This very large collection provides a comprehensive overview of the support the Memorial provided for the social sciences during the 1920s. Its records concerning the University of Chicago complement those contained in the Papers of the President of the University, the Charles E. Merriam Papers, and the records of the Social Science Research Committee (LCRC) prior to 1930.

Notes

Preface

1. Marianne Weber, *Max Weber: A Biography* (1926; New York: Wiley, 1975), p. 286.

2. Lincoln Steffens, quoted in Henry Steele Commager, Foreword to Jane Addams, *Twenty Years at Hull-House* (New York: Signet, 1961), p. x.

3. Charles Philips Trevelyan, *Letters from North America and the Pacific* (London: Chatto & Windus, 1969), pp. 36–50.

4. From Carl Sandburg, "Chicago," in *Chicago Poems* by Carl Sandburg (New York: Henry Holt, 1916), pp. 3–4, copyright 1916 by Holt Rinehart and Winston, Inc., copyright 1944 by Carl Sandburg. Reprinted by permission of Harcourt Brace Jovanovich, Inc.

Chapter 1

1. The earliest use of the term "Chicago school" is in L. L. Bernard, "Schools of Sociology," *Southwestern Political and Social Science Quarterly* 11 (September 1930):133, though the term was not in use at the University of Chicago in the 1920s: Ruth Shonle Cavan, "The Chicago School of Sociology, 1918–1933," *Urban Life* 11 (January 1983):408. For an account of the contrasting French school of sociology of Emile Durkheim, see Philippe Besnard, *The Sociological Domain: The Durkheimians and the Founding of French Sociology* (Cambridge: Cambridge University Press, 1983). On the failure of sociology to become institutionalized in Britain, let alone develop schools, see Philip Abrams, *The Origins of British Sociology, 1834–1914* (Chicago: University of Chicago Press, 1968) and Martin Bulmer, ed., *Essays on the History of British Sociological Research* (Cambridge: Cambridge University Press, 1984).

2. Edward A. Tiryakian, "The Significance of Schools in the Development of Sociology," in William E. Snizek, Ellsworth R. Fuhrman, and Michael K. Miller, eds., *Contemporary Issues in Theory and Research: A Metasociological Perspective* (Westport, Conn.: Greenwood Press, 1979), pp. 216–17.

3. See Carl W. Condit, *The Chicago School of Architecture* (Chicago: University of Chicago Press, 1964); Hugh D. Duncan, *Culture and Democracy: The Struggle for Form in Society and Architecture in Chicago and the Middle West during the Life and Times of Louis H. Sullivan* (Totowa, N.J.: Bedminster Press, 1965); Hugh D. Duncan, "The Chicago School: Principles . . . ," and Carl W. Condit, "The Chicago School: . . . and Practice," in Arthur Siegel, ed., *Chicago's Famous Buildings* (Chicago: University of Chicago Press, 1969), pp. 3–26.

4. Tiryakian, "The Significance of Schools," pp. 218–19.

5. See Morris Janowitz, *The Last Half Century* (Chicago: University of Chicago Press, 1980), pp. 1–43.

6. Robert E. L. Faris, Foreword to J. David Lewis and Richard L. Smith, *American Sociology and Pragmatism: Mead, Chicago Sociology, and Symbolic Interaction* (Chicago: University of Chicago Press, 1980), p. xiv.

7. William Isaac Thomas and Florian Znaniecki, *The Polish Peasant in Europe and America* (5 vols.; Boston: Badger, 1918–20).

8. Chicago Commission on Race Relations, *The Negro in Chicago* (Chicago: University of Chicago Press, 1922).

9. Clifford Shaw and Henry D. McKay, *Social Factors in Juvenile Delinquency*, vol. 2 of National Commission on Law Observance and Enforcement, Report on the Causes of Crime (Washington, D.C.: U.S. Government Printing Office, 1931).

10. Robert E. Park, "The City: Suggestions for the Investigation of Human Behavior in the Urban Environment," *American Journal of Sociology* 20 (1915):577–612.

11. William F. Ogburn, *Social Change: With Respect to Culture and Original Nature* (New York: B. W. Huebsch, 1922).

12. President's Research Committee on Social Trends, *Recent Social Trends* (2 vols.; New York: McGraw-Hill, 1933).

13. Issues of the *American Journal of Sociology* for July 1928 and May 1929–35.

14. See Werner J. Cahnman and Rudolph Heberle, eds., *Ferdinand Toennies on Sociology: Pure, Applied, and Empirical* (Chicago: University of Chicago Press, 1971); W. J. Cahnman, ed., *Ferdinand Toennies: A New Evaluation* (Leiden: E. J. Brill, 1973).

15. Edward Shils, *The Calling of Sociology and Other Essays on the Pursuit of Learning* (Chicago: University of Chicago Press, 1980), p. 264.

16. Ibid., pp. 168–69.

17. See Fred H. Matthews, *Quest for an American Sociology: Robert E. Park and the Chicago School* (Montreal: McGill-Queens University Press, 1977); Winifred Raushenbush, *Robert E. Park: Biography of a Sociologist* (Durham, N.C.: Duke University Press, 1979); and Barry D. Karl, *Charles E. Merriam and the Study of Politics* (Chicago: University of Chicago Press, 1974); see also Darnell Rucker, *The Chicago Pragmatists* (Minneapolis, Minn.: University of Minnesota Press, 1969); Paul Rock, *The Making of Symbolic Interactionism* (London: Macmillan, 1979); Robert E. L. Faris, *Chicago Sociology, 1920–1932* (Chicago: University of Chicago Press, 1970); and James T. Carey, *Sociology and Public Affairs: The Chicago School* (Beverly Hills: Sage, 1975).

18. See Thomas L. Haskell, *The Emergence of Professional Social Science: The American Social Science Association and the Nineteenth-Century Crisis of Authority* (Urbana, Ill.: University of Illinois Press, 1977).

19. Shils, *The Calling of Sociology*, pp. 265 ff.

20. See Anthony Oberschall, "The Institutionalization of American Sociology," in A. Oberschall, ed., *The Establishment of Empirical Sociology* (New York: Harper, 1972), p. 225.

21. Roscoe C. Hinkle, *Founding Theory of American Sociology* (London: Routledge & Kegan Paul, 1980), pp. 68–72.

22. On Ward, see Hinkle, *Founding Theory*, and Harry Elmer Barnes, ed., *An Introduction to the History of Sociology* (Chicago: University of Chicago Press, 1948), pp. 173–90.

23. George Christakes, *Albion W. Small* (Boston: Twayne, 1978), pp. 53–54.

24. On Sumner, see Barnes, *Introduction*, pp. 155–72.

25. Ibid., p. 171.

26. Oberschall, "Institutionalization," pp. 215–32.

27. On Giddings, see Hinkle, *Founding Theory*, and Barnes, *Introduction*, pp. 744–65. On Giddings at Columbia, see Seymour Martin Lipset, "The Department of Sociology," in Robert G. Hoxie et al., eds., *A History of the Faculty of Political Science, Columbia University* (New York: Columbia University Press, 1955), pp. 284–303, and Robert M. MacIver, *As a Tale That Is Told* (Chicago: University of Chicago Press, 1968), pp. 98–99.

28. Barnes, *Introduction*, p. 819.

29. For a full account, see Mary O. Furner, *Advocacy and Objectivity: A Crisis in the Professionalization of American Social Science, 1865–1905* (Lexington: University of Kentucky Press, 1975), chap. 10.

30. On Ross, see Hinkle, *Founding Theory*, and Barnes, *Introduction*, pp. 819–32 (by William Kolb).

31. On Cooley, see Hinkle, *Founding Theory*; Barnes, *Introduction*, pp. 833–52 (by Richard Dewey); Shils, *The Calling of Sociology*, pp. 216, 226; and Charles Horton Cooley, "The Development of Sociology at Michigan," in C. H. Cooley, *Sociological Theory and Social Research* (New York: Henry Holt, 1930), pp. 3–14.

32. Publication of *The Polish Peasant* is perhaps "the most apt indicator-barometer of basic intellectual change. . . . The interval of years around World War I (i.e., 1915–18) seem to represent a crucial temporal boundary setting off the first period from the second and the second from the first in the history of American theory"; Hinkle, *Founding Theory*, p. 20.

Chapter 2

1. Hugh Dalziel Duncan, *Culture and Democracy: The Struggle for Form in Society and Architecture in Chicago and the Middle West during the Life and Times of Louis H. Sullivan* (Totowa, N.J.: Bedminster Press, 1965), p. 45.

2. Ibid., pp. 3–13.

3. On demographic growth, see Ernest W. Burgess and Charles Newcomb, eds., *Census Data of the City of Chicago, 1920* (Chicago: University of Chicago Press, 1931), pp. 1–6. On the physical growth of the city, see Harold M. Mayer, and Richard C. Wade, *Chicago: Growth of a Metropolis* (Chicago: University of Chicago Press, 1969).

4. On the growth of the black population, see Allan H. Spear, *Black Chicago: The Making of a Negro Ghetto, 1890–1920* (Chicago: University of Chicago Press, 1967).

5. Carl Sandburg, "Chicago," *Chicago Poems* (New York: Henry Holt, 1916), pp. 3–4.

6. Lincoln Steffens, quoted in Henry Steele Commager, Foreword to Jane Addams, *Twenty Years at Hull-House* (New York: Signet, 1960; first published 1910), p. x.

7. See John Maxon, *The Art Institute of Chicago* (London: Thames & Hudson, 1971). Some of the reasons for the extent of support for cultural institutions are discussed in Kathleen D. McCarthy, *Noblesse Oblige: Charity and Cultural Philanthropy in Chicago, 1849–1929* (Chicago: University of Chicago Press, 1982), pp. 75–96, and in Helen L. Horowitz, *Culture and the City: Cultural Philanthropy in Chicago from the 1880's to 1918* (Lexington: University of Kentucky Press, 1976).

8. Duncan, *Culture and Democracy*.

9. The rough, uncivilized, raw qualities of the city were celebrated in Dreiser's novels *Sister Carrie* and *The Titan* (modeled on the life of Chicago businessman Charles Yerkes), as in Sandburg's *Chicago Poems*. On Dreiser's view of Chicago ("Hail, Chicago! First of the daughters of the new world!"), see Morton White, *The Intellectual versus the City* (Oxford: Oxford University Press, 1977), pp. 124–31.

10. Duncan, *Culture and Democracy*, pp. 385–86.

11. Steven J. Diner, *A City and Its Universities: Public Policy in Chicago, 1892–1919* (Chapel Hill: University of North Carolina Press, 1980), p. 74.

12. Robert E. Park, "The City: Suggestions for the Investigation of Human Behavior in the Urban Environment," *American Journal of Sociology* 20 (1915):577.

13. On the early history of the University of Chicago, see Thomas W. Goodspeed, *A History of the University of Chicago: The First Quarter-Century* (Chicago: University of Chicago Press, 1916), and Richard J. Storr, *Harper's University: The Beginnings* (Chicago: University of Chicago Press, 1966). A useful short overview of the university's history is: Special Collections Department, Joseph Regenstein Library, *A Retrospective View of the University of Chicago Based on Records in the University Archives: An Exhibition, 1973/74* (Chicago: University of Chicago Library, 1973).

14. Thomas W. Goodspeed, *William Rainey Harper* (Chicago: University of Chicago Press, 1928).

15. Goodspeed, *A History of the University*, p. 130.

16. Ibid., p. 145, quoting a draft of his first annual report, 1892.

17. Ibid.

18. There is a good short discussion of the university's foundation in Darnell Rucker, *The Chicago Pragmatists* (Minneapolis: University of Minnesota Press, 1969), chap. 1.

19. Goodspeed, *A History of the University*, pp. 145–46.

20. Roger W. Shugg, *The University of Chicago Press, 1891–1965* (Chicago: University of Chicago Press, privately printed, 1966), p. 7.

21. Edward Shils, "The Order of Learning in the United States from 1865 to 1920: The Ascendancy of the Universities," *Minerva* 16 (Summer 1978):171.

22. See Laurence R. Veysey, *The Emergence of the American University* (Chicago: University of Chicago Press, 1965), pp. 125 ff.; Jurgen Herbst, *The German Historical School in American Culture: A Study in the Transfer of Scholarship* (Ithaca, N.Y.: Cornell University Press, 1965).

23. Hugh D. Hawkins, *Pioneer: A History of Johns Hopkins University, 1874–1889* (Ithaca, N.Y.: Cornell University Press, 1960); Francesco Cordasco, *Daniel Coit Gilman and the Protean Ph.D.* (Leiden: Brill, 1960).

24. Veysey, *The Emergence of the American University*, p. 164.

25. On Dewey's years at Hopkins, see Neil Coughlan, *Young John Dewey* (Chicago: University of Chicago Press, 1975), pp. 18–54.

26. Josiah Royce, "Present Ideals of American University Life," *Scribner's Magazine* 10 (1892):383.

27. See Dorothy Ross, *G. Stanley Hall: The Psychologist as Prophet* (Chicago: University of Chicago Press, 1972).

28. Veysey, *The Emergence of the American University*, pp. 166–70.

29. Ibid., pp. 164–65.

30. Samuel E. Morison, ed., *The Development of Harvard University since the Inauguration of President Eliot, 1869–1929* (Cambridge, Mass.: Harvard University Press, 1930). For an illuminating account of how one department at Harvard blossomed as a result of this policy in the 1890s, see Bruce Kuklick, *The Rise of American Philosophy: Cambridge, Massachusetts, 1860–1930* (New Haven, Conn.: Yale University Press, 1977), pp. 233–59. The expansion of the graduate program in philosophy was directly inspired by competition from Johns Hopkins, which in 1890 had no peer as a graduate center. By 1900 the two schools were neck and neck, and then Harvard took over the lead. Though Kuklick does not mention it, the growth of philosophy at Chicago under Dewey, much admired by William James, was a further spur to the developing professional orientation in the Harvard graduate faculty.

31. Robert G. Hoxie et al., eds., *A History of the Faculty of Political Science at Columbia University* (New York: Columbia University Press, 1955).

32. Shils, "The Order of Learning," p. 172.

33. Ibid., p. 173.

34. "In the 1870s research played no important role in American higher education"; Veysey, *The Emergence of the American University*, p. 174.

35. Veysey, *The Emergence of the American University*; Shils, "The Order of Learning."

36. Veysey, *The Emergence of the American University*, pp. 153–58.

37. See Robert W. Rieber, ed., *Wilhelm Wundt and the Making of a Scientific Psychology* (New York: Plenum, 1980), and Wolfgang G. Bringmann and Ryan D. Tweney, eds., *Wundt Studies: A Centennial Colloquium* (Toronto: C. J. Hogrefe, 1980).

38. Albion W. Small, *The Meaning of Social Science* (Chicago: University of Chicago Press, 1910), pp. 35–36.

39. Joseph Ben-David, *The Scientist's Role in Society: A Comparative Study* (Englewood Cliffs, N.J.: Prentice-Hall, 1971), pp. 139–68.

40. Storr, *Harper's University*, p. 159.
41. Quoted in ibid.
42. Ibid., p. 160.
43. Shils, "The Order of Learning," pp. 186–87.
44. Storr, *Harper's University*, p. 368.
45. Ibid., pp. 367–68.
46. Diner, "Department and Discipline," pp. 516–18.
47. For an account, see Dorothy M. Livingstone, *The Master of Light: A Biography of Albert A. Michelson* (Chicago: University of Chicago Press, 1973), pp. 163–70.
48. Coughlan, *Young John Dewey*, p. 150.
49. Storr, *Harper's University*, p. 76.
50. See Goodspeed, *A History of the University* and *Harper*; Storr, *Harper's University*; and Frederick T. Gates, *Chapters in My Life* (New York: Free Press, 1977), pp. 189–98.
51. Ibid.
52. See the experiences of James Breasted described in Charles Breasted, *Pioneer to the Past: The Story of James H. Breasted, Archaeologist* (New York: Charles Scribner's, 1943).
53. Edward Shils, quoted in Christopher Driver, *The Exploding University* (London: Hodder & Stoughton, 1971), p. 58.
54. Quoted in Muriel Beadle, *Where Has All the Ivy Gone: A Memoir of University Life* (Garden City, N.Y.: Doubleday, 1972), p. 162.
55. Veysey, *The Emergence of the American University*, p. 172.
56. "When University of Chicago sociology graduates meet they do not say 'how are you?' but 'what are you working on?' " Walter Reckless at a summer institute of the Society for Social Research, late 1930s, quoted in a personal communication by Edward Shils.
57. Shils, "The Order of Learning," pp. 185–86.
58. For a discussion of the impact of Chautauqua upon Harper and through him on the University of Chicago, see Joseph E. Gould, *The Chautauqua Movement: An Episode in the Continuing American Revolution* (Albany: University of New York Press, 1961).
59. Duncan, *Culture and Democracy*, p. 212.
60. Robert Morss Lovett, *All Our Years: The Autobiography of Robert Morss Lovett* (New York: Viking, 1948), p. 54.
61. Morris Janowitz, Foreword to Albert Hunter, *Symbolic Communities: The Persistence and Change of Chicago's Local Communities* (Chicago: University of Chicago Press, 1974), p. xv.
62. Diner, *A City and Its Universities*.
63. Marianne Weber, *Max Weber: A Biography* (New York: Wiley, 1975; first published 1926), p. 286.
64. Steven J. Diner, "Department and Discipline: The Department of Sociology at the University of Chicago, 1892–1920," *Minerva* 13 (Winter 1975):524–26.
65. Jane Addams, *Twenty Years at Hull-House* (New York: Macmillan, 1919), and Allan F. Davis, *American Heroine: The Life and Labor of Jane Addams* (New York: Oxford University Press, 1973). The general context is treated in Allan F. Davis, *Spearheads for Reform: The Social Settlements and the Progressive Movement, 1890–1914* (New York: Oxford University Press, 1967).
66. Diner, "Department and Discipline," p. 550. See also Albert Hunter, "Why Chicago? The Rise of the Chicago School of Urban Social Science," *American Behavioral Scientist* 24 (November–December 1980):215–27.
67. Diner, *A City and Its Universities*, pp. 57, 69–70.
68. Ibid., esp. pp. 123–28; Mary Jo Deegan and John S. Burger, "George Herbert Mead and Social Reform: His Work and Writings," *Journal of the History of the Behavioral Sciences* 14 (1978):362–73; personal communication from Professor Harold L. Orbach, Kansas State University, 30 December 1981.

69. See Storr, *Harper's University*, esp. pp. 83–85, 96–98; Mary O. Furner, *Advocacy and Objectivity: A Crisis in the Professionalization of American Social Science, 1865–1906* (Lexington: University of Kentucky Press, 1975), pp. 163–98.

70. Storr, *Harper's University*, pp. 109, 324–25, 338; Mary Jo Deegan, "Women and Sociology, 1890–1930," *Journal of the History of Sociology* 1 (Fall 1978):11–32; Meyer Weinberg, *A Chance to Learn: A History of Race and Education in the United States* (Cambridge: Cambridge University Press, 1977), pp. 274, 291; Rhett S. Jones, "Black Sociologists, 1890–1917," *Black Academy Review* 2 (Winter 1971):43–67. The obstacles faced by even the most distinguished black scholars at this period are portrayed in Kenneth R. Manning, *Black Apollo of Science: The Life of Ernest Everett Just* (New York: Oxford University Press, 1983).

71. Rucker, *The Chicago Pragmatists*, p. 15.

72. Ibid., pp. 14–15.

73. Robert Herrick, *Chimes* (New York: Macmillan, 1926), pp. 7–8.

Chapter 3

1. The personal networks linking leading pragmatists are illustrated by the relationships between Dewey, Mead, Tufts, and Angell. Dewey brought Mead with him to the University of Chicago, was preceded by Tufts, and encouraged the appointment of Angell, but the links go further back. Dewey and Angell both came from Vermont families who were close friends, and Angell's father subsequently became president of the University of Michigan at which Dewey, Tufts, and Mead all taught. Angell took his bachelor's and master's degrees at Michigan, under Dewey and Tufts.

2. William James to Mrs. Henry Whitman, 29 October 1903, *The Letters of William James* (Boston: Atlantic Monthly Press, 1920), 2:201–2. James expressed a similar view publicly at the same time without mentioning Harvard and Yale by name. "The rest of the world has made merry over the Chicago man's legendary saying that 'Chicago hasn't had time to get round to culture yet, but when she does strike her, she'll make her hum.' Already the prophecy is fulfilling itself in a dazzling manner. Chicago has a School of Thought!—a school of thought which, it is safe to predict, will figure in literature as the School of Chicago for twenty-five years to come"; William James, "The Chicago School," *Psychological Bulletin* 1 (15 January 1904):1. James's prediction of the twenty-five-year life span for Dewey's school was almost exactly correct. See the discussion of the break up of the Chicago school on pages 202–3.

3. Darnell Rucker, *The Chicago Pragmatists* (Minneapolis: University of Minnesota Press, 1969), pp. 25–27; David L. Miller, *George Herbert Mead: Self, Language, and the World* (Chicago: University of Chicago Press, 1973), pp. xxxvii–xxxviii; Mortimer J. Adler, *Philosopher at Large* (London: Weidenfeld & Nicolson, 1977), pp. 128–34.

4. Richard J. Storr, *Harper's University: The Beginnings* (Chicago: University of Chicago Press, 1966), pp. 296–302, 339–41.

5. Rucker, *The Chicago Pragmatists*, pp. 4–6.

6. Tufts took over the chairmanship of the philosophy department from Dewey in 1904 and held it until he retired in 1930. Mead died in 1931, Moore retired in 1929 and died in 1930. Ames took over the chairmanship from Tufts's retirement until his own in 1935.

7. See Anselm Strauss, ed., *George Herbert Mead on Social Psychology* (Chicago: University of Chicago Press, 1964); Robert E. L. Faris, *Chicago Sociology, 1920–1932* (Chicago: University of Chicago Press, 1970), pp. 95–100; Herbert Blumer, *Symbolic Interactionism* (Englewood Cliffs, N.J.: Prentice-Hall, 1969); Paul Rock, *The Making of Symbolic Interactionism* (London: Macmillan, 1979); J. David Lewis and Richard L. Smith, *American Sociology and Pragmatism: Mead, Chicago Sociology, and Symbolic Interaction* (Chicago: University of Chicago Press, 1980).

8. The best short discussion of Chicago philosophy is in Rucker, *The Chicago Pragmatists*.

9. See Neil Coughlan, *Young John Dewey: An Essay in American Intellectual History* (Chicago: University of Chicago Press, 1975), esp. pp. 18–53; Rock, *The Making of Symbolic Interactionism*, pp. 59–82.

10. Coughlan, *Young John Dewey*, pp. 37–68.

11. John Dewey, *Psychology* (New York: Harper Bros., 1887).

12. Coughlan, *Young John Dewey*, p. 67.

13. William James, *Pragmatism* (New York: Meridian Books, 1955), p. 24.

14. Storr, *Harper's University*, pp. 296–302; Rucker, *The Chicago Pragmatists*, pp. 4–5.

15. Rucker, *The Chicago Pragmatists*, pp. 83–106.

16. Anselm Strauss, *George Herbert Mead on Social Psychology*, p. xii.

17. Faris, *Chicago Sociology, 1920–1932*, p. 158.

18. John Dewey, "The Need for Social Psychology," *Psychological Review* 24 (1917):266–77; Ellsworth Faris, *The Nature of Human Nature* (New York: McGraw-Hill, 1937). For a discussion of the influence of Dewey and Faris (and of W. I. Thomas) on instinct theory, see Hamilton J. Cravens, *The Triumph of Evolution: American Scientists and the Heredity-Environment Controversy, 1900–1941* (Philadelphia: University of Pennsylvania Press, 1978), esp. pp. 191–223.

19. Lewis S. Feuer, quoted by Morris Janowitz, Review of N. Coughlan, *Young John Dewey*, *American Journal of Sociology* 83 (1978):1282.

20. Letter from W. I. Thomas to L. L. Bernard, 10 January 1928, reproduced in Paul J. Baker, "The Life Histories of W. I. Thomas and Robert E. Park," *American Journal of Sociology* 79 (1973):245.

21. Personal communication from Edward Shils.

22. Fred H. Matthews, *Quest for an American Sociology: Robert E. Park and the Chicago School* (Montreal: McGill-Queens University Press, 1977), pp. 87–89. At the university's memorial service for Park on his death in 1944, Ames was one of five speakers, together with John U. Nef, Louis Wirth, Charles S. Johnson, and Everett Hughes. *Robert Ezra Park, 1864–1944: Appreciations Read at the Memorial Service Held in the Joseph Bond Chapel of the University of Chicago, February 9th 1944* (Chicago: privately printed, 1944; copy in University of Chicago Library).

23. See Lucy Sprague Mitchell, *Two Lives: The Story of Wesley Clair Mitchell and Myself* (New York: Simon & Schuster, 1953), pp. 84–89.

24. T. V. Smith and William K. Wright, eds., *Essays in Philosophy by Seventeen Doctors of Philosophy of the University of Chicago* (Chicago: Open Court Publishing Co., 1930), pp. xiii–xiv. See also Rucker, *The Chicago Pragmatists*, pp. 166–67.

25. Steven J. Diner, "Department and Discipline: The Department of Sociology at the University of Chicago, 1892–1920," *Minerva* 13 (Winter 1975):516.

26. Small quoted in ibid., p. 517.

27. Ibid.

28. George Christakes, *Albion W. Small* (Boston: Twayne, 1978), chap. 1.

29. Albion W. Small, *Introduction to a Science of Society* (Waterville, Maine: Colby University; privately printed, 1890).

30. See letter from Small to Harper, 25 April 1895, reprinted in Vernon Dibble, *The Legacy of Albion Small* (Chicago: University of Chicago Press, 1975), pp. 163–68.

31. Christakes, *Albion W. Small*, pp. 20–23, 54–57.

32. Diner, "Department and Discipline," p. 523.

33. Albion W. Small and George E. Vincent, *An Introduction to the Study of Society* (New York: American Book Co., 1894).

34. The following account relies upon Dibble, *The Legacy of Albion Small*; Christakes, *Albion W. Small*; and Roscoe C. Hinkle, *Founding Theory of American Sociology, 1881–1915* (London: Routledge & Kegan Paul, 1980).

35. Its most explicit statement was in Albion W. Small, *The Meaning of Social Science* (Chicago: University of Chicago Press, 1910).

36. Charles R. Henderson, "The Ministry of Today—Its New Equipment," *University of Chicago Record* (20 January 1899):281.

37. Diner, "Department and Discipline," pp. 523–25.

38. Ibid., pp. 525–26.

39. Ernest W. Burgess, "A Short History of Urban Research at the University of Chicago before 1946," in Ernest W. Burgess and Donald J. Bogue, eds., *Contributions to Urban Sociology* (Chicago: University of Chicago Press, 1964), p. 3.

40. Diner, "Department and Discipline," p. 526.

41. Biographical details are drawn from: W. I. Thomas, "Life History," *American Journal of Sociology* 79 (1973):246–50 (written in 1928); Robert E. L. Faris, "W. I. Thomas, 1863–1947," Ernest Burgess, "W. I. Thomas as a Teacher," and Florian Znaniecki, "W. I. Thomas as a Collaborator," *Sociology and Social Research* 32 (March–April 1948):755–67; Emory S. Bogardus, "The Sociology of W. I. Thomas," *Sociology and Social Research* 34 (September–October 1949):34–48; Morris Janowitz, ed., *W. I. Thomas on Social Organization and Social Personality* (Chicago: University of Chicago Press, 1966); and Lewis A. Coser, *Masters of Sociological Thought* (New York: Harcourt Brace Jovanovich, 1977), pp. 511–59.

42. Janowitz, *W. I. Thomas*, p. viii.

43. A full bibliography of the work of W. I. Thomas appears in Janowitz, *W. I. Thomas*, pp. 307–10.

44. William I. Thomas, *Sex and Society: Studies in the Social Psychology of Sex* (Chicago: University of Chicago Press, 1907).

45. Donald Fleming, "Attitude: The History of a Concept," *Perspectives in American History* 1 (1967):324.

46. William I. Thomas, ed., *Source Book for Social Origins* (Chicago: University of Chicago Press, 1909).

47. See George W. Stocking, Jr., *Race, Culture, and Evolution* (New York: Free Press, 1968), pp. 260–64.

48. Cravens, *The Triumph of Evolution*, pp. 145–47, 180–82.

49. William I. Thomas and Florian Znaniecki, *The Polish Peasant in Europe and America* (5 vols.; Boston: Badger, 1918–20). Its publication history is described in chap. 4, note 1.

50. Robert E. Park, "Notes on the Origin of the Society for Social Research," *Bulletin of the Society for Social Research*, August 1939, pp. 3–5 (copy in the records of the Society for Social Research, University of Chicago Archives).

51. See Mary Jo Deegan and John S. Burger, "W. I. Thomas and Social Reform: His Work and Writings," *Journal of the History of the Behavioral Sciences* 17 (1981):114–25.

52. For biographical data on Robert Park, see R. E. Park, "Life History," *American Journal of Sociology* 79 (1973):251–60; Matthews, *Quest for an American Sociology*; Winifred Raushenbush, *Robert E. Park: Biography of a Sociologist* (Durham, N.C.: Duke University Press, 1979); and Ralph H. Turner, ed., *Robert E. Park on Social Control and Collective Behavior* (Chicago: University of Chicago Press, 1967), pp. ix–xlvi.

53. See Matthews, *Quest for an American Sociology*, pp. 1, 97–103. Thomas, who came from Tennessee, was drawn to the study of ethnic and race relations by an academic route. Park's background in the study of race relations was a practical one, as secretary to Booker T. Washington in the years immediately before he came to Chicago. See St. Clair Drake, "The Tuskegee Connection: Booker T. Washington and Robert E. Park," *Society* 20 (May–June 1983):82–92; and Louis R. Harlan, *Booker T. Washington: The Wizard of Tuskegee, 1901–1915* (New York: Oxford University Press, 1983), pp. 270–71, 290–94.

54. See Jurgen Herbst, *The German Historical School in American Scholarship: A Study in the Transfer of Culture* (Ithaca, N.Y.: Cornell University Press, 1965).

55. Robert E. Park, *The Crowd and the Public* (English translation of *Masse and Publikum*; Chicago: University of Chicago Press, 1972; thesis submitted 1899, first published in Germany by Lack & Grunan, Bern, 1904). See also Matthews, *Quest for an American Sociology*, pp. 31–56.

56. On the career of Small, see Christakes, *Albion Small*, pp. 15–23. On W. I. Thomas, see Janowitz, *W. I. Thomas*, pp. vi–xviii. On Charles Zueblin and Charles Henderson, see Diner, "Department and Discipline"; on Park, see Matthews, *Quest for an American Sociology*, pp. 33–56. On Mead, see Miller, *George Herbert Mead*, pp. xi–xxxviii.

57. Diner, "Department and Discipline," pp. 540–43.

58. See Steven J. Diner, "Scholarship in the Quest for Social Welfare: A Fifty-Year History of the *Social Service Review*," *Social Service Review* 51 (March 1977):1–68.

59. See George W. Stocking, Jr., *Anthropology at Chicago: Tradition, Discipline, Department* (Special Collections Department, Joseph Regenstein Library, University of Chicago, 1979).

60. "Autobiography of James Rowland Angell," in C. Murchison, ed., *A History of Psychology in Autobiography* (New York: Russell & Russell, 1961), 3:1–38. David Cohen, *J. B. Watson: The Founder of Behaviorism* (London: Routledge & Kegan Paul, 1980), pp. 24–50; James H. Tufts, "Dr. Angell, the New President of Yale," *Worlds Work* 42 (August 1921):387–400.

61. Alfred Bornemann, *J. Laurence Laughlin: Chapters in the Career of an Economist* (Washington, D.C.: American Commission on Public Affairs, 1940).

62. A. W. Coats, "The Origins of the 'Chicago School(s)'?" *Journal of Political Economy* 71 (October 1963):492–93.

63. Diner, "Department and Discipline," pp. 545–46.

64. Karl, *Charles E. Merriam and the Study of Politics* (Chicago: University of Chicago Press, 1974), pp. 44–45, 58–59, 140–45.

65. Karl, *Charles E. Merriam*, and Diner, *A City and Its Universities: Public Policy in Chicago, 1892–1919* (Chapel Hill: University of North Carolina Press, 1980), pp. 14 ff.

66. Manuel C. Elmer, *Social Surveys of Urban Communities* (Menasha, Wis.: Collegiate Press, 1914; printed version of University of Chicago Ph.D. thesis, 1914).

67. Personal communication from Manuel C. Elmer, 3 October 1980.

68. Edward Shils, *The Calling of Sociology and Other Essays on the Pursuit of Learning* (Chicago: University of Chicago Press, 1980), pp. 183 ff.

69. This is based upon the more comprehensive data provided in Hinkle, *Founding Theory*, p. 14. Estimates differ. An earlier survey calculated that 56 Ph.D.'s in sociology had been awarded by American universities by 1915; 27 by Chicago, 8 by Columbia, 11 by Pennsylvania, 2 by Yale, and 8 by New York University. G. Albert Lunday, *Sociology Dissertations in American Universities, 1893–1966* (Commerce: East Texas State University, 1969). Lunday does not indicate the sources of his data. The discrepancy is partly accounted for by the fact that in many universities sociology was not established in a separate department until quite a late date, rendering the identification of Ph.D.'s in sociology much more problematical. Out of 19 Ph.D.'s awarded in sociology before 1900, 11 were from Chicago and 2 from Columbia. Columbia had a greater number of graduate students in sociology in the last decade of the nineteenth century (39 out of 125 in the United States) than did Chicago (25), but prepared most of them for the master's degree. J. Graham Morgan, "Preparation for the Advent: The Establishment of Sociology as a Discipline in American Universities in the late Nineteenth Century," *Minerva* 20 (Spring–Summer 1982), pp. 46–53.

70. Seymour Martin Lipset, "The Department of Sociology," in Robert G. Hoxie et al.,

eds., *A History of the Faculty of Political Science, Columbia University* (New York: Columbia University Press, 1955), p. 292.

71. Shils, *The Calling of Sociology*, p. 187.

72. Calculated from Robert E. L. Faris, *Chicago Sociology, 1920–1932* (Chicago: University of Chicago Press, 1970), pp. 135–50.

73. Data from Howard Odum, *American Sociology: The Story of Sociology in the United States through 1950* (New York: Longmans, 1951).

74. Albert Somit and Joseph Tanenhaus, *The Development of American Political Science, from Burgess to Behavioralism* (Boston: Allyn & Bacon, 1967), pp. 102–8.

75. Coats, "The Origins of the 'Chicago School(s)?' "

Chapter 4

1. William Isaac Thomas and Florian Znaniecki, *The Polish Peasant in Europe and America*. The five-volume edition was published in 1918–20, the first two volumes by the University of Chicago Press and then (after Thomas's dismissal by the University of Chicago), the whole five volumes by Richard Badger, a Boston publishing house, after the University of Chicago Press broke the contract on the instructions of the president of the university. In 1926 Alfred Knopf of New York purchased the plates and copyright and brought out in 1927 a two-volume edition, an unabridged version of the first edition with slight transposition of material, repagination, and the addition of an index. This was reprinted by Dover in New York in 1958. All references in this chapter are to this two-volume edition. At the time of writing (1983), *The Polish Peasant in Europe and America* is out of print.

2. Lewis Coser, *Masters of Sociological Thought* (New York: Harcourt Brace Jovanovich, 1977), p. 381. See also Robert K. Merton, *Social Theory and Social Structure* (2d ed.; New York: Free Press, 1957), p. 62, note 69.

3. Donald Fleming, "Attitude: The History of a Concept in America," *Perspectives in American History* 1 (1967):325.

4. Edward Shils, *The Present State of American Sociology* (Glencoe, Ill.: Free Press, 1948), p. 26, note 33.

5. W. I. Thomas, "Life History," *American Journal of Sociology* 79 (1973):248 (written in 1928).

6. W. I. Thomas, ed., *Sourcebook for Social Origins* (Chicago: University of Chicago Press, 1909).

7. Morris Janowitz, Introduction to *W. I. Thomas on Social Organization and Social Personality* (Chicago: University of Chicago Press, 1966), p. viii.

8. See Shils, *The Present State of American Sociology*, p. 25.

9. Upton Sinclair, *The Jungle* (New York: Jungle Publishing Co., 1906).

10. Ellsworth Faris, "W. I. Thomas, 1863–1947," *Sociology and Social Research* 32 (March–April 1948):757.

11. W. I. Thomas, speaking on 10 December 1938, quoted in Herbert Blumer, *Critiques of Research in the Social Sciences, vol. 1: An Appraisal of Thomas and Znaniecki's "The Polish Peasant"* (New York: Social Science Research Council, 1939), p. 103.

12. William Isaac Thomas to Dorothy Swaine Thomas, January 1935 memorandum "How *The Polish Peasant* came about," Dorothy S. Thomas correspondence, University of Chicago Archives, p. 1.

13. Thomas W. Goodspeed, *A History of the University of Chicago: The First Quarter-Century* (Chicago: University of Chicago Press, 1916), p. 273. Helen Culver's interests in race and ethnic relations went back to her Civil War work with the Sanitary Commission and post–Civil War experiences with blacks in the South. See Rudolf K. Haerle, Jr. "William

Isaac Thomas and the Helen Culver Fund for Race Psychology: Foundation for *The Polish Peasant*" (Middlebury College, Vermont, 1984).

14. W. I. Thomas, "How *The Polish Peasant* came about," pp. 1–2.

15. Ibid., pp. 2–3.

16. Ibid., p. 3.

17. Ibid.

18. Robert E. Park and Herbert A. Miller, *Old World Traits Transplanted* (New York: Harper, 1921).

19. W. I. Thomas to Samuel N. Harper from Berlin, 30 June 1912, Samuel N. Harper Papers, University of Chicago Archives, Box 1, Folder 15.

20. Ibid., outline of projected study attached to letter.

21. Thomas, "How *The Polish Peasant* came about," p. 1.

22. A full bibliography of the published works of Florian Znaniecki in both Polish and English is to be found in the Introduction (by Helen Znaniecki Lopata) to F. Znaniecki, *Social Relations and Social Roles: The Unfinished "Systematic Sociology"* (San Francisco: Chandler, 1965).

23. These and other biographical details of Florian Znaniecki are drawn principally from Robert Bierstedt, ed., *Florian Znaniecki on Humanistic Sociology* (Chicago: University of Chicago Press, 1969), pp. 1–5; Lewis A. Coser, *Masters of Sociological Thought* (2d ed.; New York: Harcourt Brace Jovanovich, 1977), pp. 511–59; and Helena Znaniecki Lopata, "Florian Znaniecki: Creative Evolution of a Sociologist," *Journal of the History of Behavioral Sciences* 12 (1976):203–15.

24. Contrast Janowitz, *W. I. Thomas*, p. xxv, and Bierstedt, *Znaniecki*, p. 2.

25. Thomas, "How *The Polish Peasant* came about," p. 2.

26. Ibid., p. 3.

27. Janowitz, *W. I. Thomas*, p. xxv.

28. Coser, *Masters of Sociological Thought*, p. 539.

29. Thomas, "How *The Polish Peasant* came about," p. 4.

30. Ibid.

31. Ibid.

32. In part the explanation for the greater credit which tends to have been given to Thomas lies in his much greater visibility in American sociology. While Znaniecki returned to Poland and remained there until 1939 (apart from a visiting appointment at Columbia in 1931–33), Thomas continued to be active in America and was president of the American Sociological Society in 1927. His social psychological writings were widely read in the 1920s, particularly in Chicago, and the tendency to attribute the principal authorship of *The Polish Peasant* to him may have stemmed partly from this greater influence. In addition, the history of American sociology has been written principally by American sociologists, some of whom were ardent admirers of Thomas. The most extreme example of favoring Thomas is to be found in Edmund H. Volkart's edition of Thomas's papers, *Social Behavior and Personality* (New York: Social Science Research Council, 1951), which reprints twenty pages of the "Methodological Note" as if it were exclusively the work of Thomas. More justly, Bierstedt, *Florian Znaniecki*, includes the whole of the "Methodological Note." For a discussion of rival interpretations of the relative influence of Thomas and of Znaniecki, see Konstantin Symmons-Symondewicz, "*The Polish Peasant in Europe and America*: Its First Half-Century of Intellectual History, 1918–68," *Polish Review* 13, no. 2 (1968):14–27.

33. Florian Znaniecki, *Cultural Reality* (Chicago: University of Chicago Press, 1919). For a critical view of the relationship between sociology and philosophy in Znaniecki's work, see Z. A. Jordan, *Philosophy and Ideology* (Dordrecht, Holland: D. Reidel, 1963), pp. 63–68.

34. *The Polish Peasant* 1:74–75. All references are to the two-volume edition published in New York by Knopf in 1927 and reprinted by Dover in 1958.

35. Maldwyn A. Jones, *American Immigration* (Chicago: University of Chicago Press, 1960).

36. *The Polish Peasant* 2:1511.

37. For an excellent summary of the book, see John Madge, *The Origins of Scientific Sociology* (London: Tavistock, 1963), pp. 52–87. Coser, *Masters of Sociological Thought*, pp. 511–59, provides a sympathetic critical assessment. Janowitz, *Thomas*, and Bierstedt, *Znaniecki*, are companion volumes in this series.

38. Thomas to S. N. Harper, 30 June 1912, Outline of Projected Study.

39. Thomas, quoted in Blumer, *An Appraisal*, p. 104.

40. Thomas, "How *The Polish Peasant* came about," p. 3.

41. Thomas, in Blumer, *An Appraisal*, p. 104.

42. Ibid., p. 105.

43. Ibid., and Thomas, "How *The Polish Peasant* came about," p. 3.

44. Thomas, in Blumer, *An Appraisal*, p. 105.

45. Coser, *Masters of Sociological Thought*, p. 533.

46. Thomas, "How *The Polish Peasant* came about," p. 4.

47. *The Polish Peasant* 1:76.

48. Herbert A. Hodges, *William Dilthey: An Introduction* (London: Routledge, 1944), p. 29. See also Kenneth Plummer, *Documents of Life* (London: Allen & Unwin, 1983), p. 52.

49. Thomas, "How *The Polish Peasant* came about," p. 4.

50. For further discussion, see James Bennett, *Oral History and Delinquency: The Rhetoric of Criminology* (Chicago: University of Chicago Press, 1981), pp. 123–50; Plummer, *Documents of Life*, esp. pp. 39–63.

51. *The Polish Peasant*, 2:1852, 1834–35.

52. Ibid., pp. 1122–23.

53. This use was later extended in the work that Thomas and Robert Park conducted for the Carnegie project on Americanization; see p. 93.

54. W. I. Thomas, "Race Psychology: Standpoint and Questionnaire with Particular Reference to the Immigrant and the Negro," *American Journal of Sociology* 17 (May 1912):771.

55. Max Weber, "Die Verhaltnisse der Landarbeiter im ostelbischen Deutschland," *Schriften des Vereins für Sozialpolitik*, vol. 55 (Berlin, 1892). See also Reinhard Bendix, *Max Weber* (New York, 1959), chap. 2, and Anthony Oberschall, *Empirical Social Research in Germany, 1848–1914* (The Hague: Mouton, 1965), pp. 21–27. Weber was concerned, at a slightly earlier period, with a phenomenon studied by Thomas and Znaniecki, the very large-scale seasonal migration of agricultural workers from Poland to Prussia, which reached a peak of 600,000 per year in 1913.

56. *The Polish Peasant* 2:1832–33.

57. Thomas, in Blumer, *An Appraisal*, p. 107.

58. *The Polish Peasant* 1:68.

59. Ibid., 2:1831.

60. Ibid., 1:38.

61. Ibid., 2:1846–47.

62. Bierstedt, *Florian Znaniecki*, p. 11; Coser, *Masters of Sociological Thought*, p. 539.

63. In *Cultural Reality*, published in 1919, Znaniecki wrote: "Of all my later debts, none is as great as the one I owe to pragmatism, of which, in fact, I am inclined to consider myself a disciple"; pp. iii–iv.

64. *The Polish Peasant* 1:21.

65. Ibid., p. 22.

66. Ibid., p. 44.

67. Ibid., p. 27–28.

68. The idea was developed further in W. I. Thomas, *The Unadjusted Girl: With Cases and Standpoint for Behavior Analysis* (Boston: Little, Brown, 1923), and in W. I. Thomas and Dorothy Swaine Thomas, *The Child in America: Behavior Problems, and Programs* (New York: Alfred A. Knopf, 1928).

69. *The Polish Peasant* 1:32–33.

70. See p. 61.

71. This was demonstrated most convincingly in Blumer, *An Appraisal*, in 1939. See also Blumer's Introduction to the reprint of *An Appraisal* (New Brunswick, N.J.: Transaction Books, 1979), pp. v–xxxviii.

72. Florian Znaniecki, in Blumer, *An Appraisal*, p. 90.

73. Janowitz, *W. I. Thomas*, pp. xxxiv–xxxviii.

74. See William I. Thomas, "The Psychology of Race Prejudice," *American Journal of Sociology* 9 (1904):593–611.

75. Fleming, "Attitude," pp. 326–27.

76. George W. Stocking, Jr., *Race, Culture, and Evolution: Essays on the History of Anthropology* (New York: Free Press, 1968), pp. 258–64.

77. Edward B. Reuter, "Racial Theory," *American Journal of Sociology* 50 (1945):456, and Hamilton Cravens, *The Triumph of Evolution* (Philadelphia: University of Pennsylvania Press, 1978), p. 181.

78. Janowitz, *W. I. Thomas*, pp. xiv–xx.

79. See Mary O. Furner, *Advocacy and Objectivity: A Crisis in the Professionalization of American Social Science, 1865–1905* (Lexington: University of Kentucky Press, 1975).

80. See W. I. Thomas, *Sex and Society: Studies in the Social Psychology of Sex* (Chicago: University of Chicago Press, 1907).

81. *Chicago Examiner*, 10 June 1915; *Chicago Tribune*, 12 June 1915.

82. Thomas to Small, 17 June 1915, 23 June 1915, 5 July 1915, and Small to Judson, 21 June 1915, 6 July 1916, Papers of the Presidents of the University, 1889–1925, University of Chicago Archives, Box 64, Folder 4.

83. Thomas to Dean Shailer Mathews, 5 October 1917, Divinity School Papers, University of Chicago Archives, Box 17, Folder 1.

84. Janowitz, *W. I. Thomas*, pp. xiv–xv.

85. Fred H. Matthews, *Quest for an American Sociology: Robert E. Park and the Chicago School* (Montreal: McGill-Queens University Press, 1977), pp. 102–3.

86. Barry D. Karl, *Charles E. Merriam and the Study of Politics* (Chicago: University of Chicago Press), p. 87.

87. David Cohen, *J. B. Watson: The Founder of Behaviorism* (London: Routledge & Kegan Paul, 1980), pp. 53–54.

88. Ibid., p. 159.

89. Karl, *Charles E. Merriam*, p. 87.

90. Robert M. Hutchins to Edwin B. Wilson, 4 January 1930, Harold H. Swift Papers, University of Chicago Archives, Box 135, Folder 20.

91. Harold H. Swift to Robert M. Hutchins, 11 January 1930, Swift Papers, Box 135, Folder 20.

92. Swift to Hutchins, 17 January 1930, Swift Papers, Box 135, Folder 20.

93. Robert E. Park and Herbert A. Miller, *Old World Traits Transplanted* (New York: Harper, 1921). The book was actually written by Thomas but could not be published in his name because of the controversy surrounding his dismissal. W. I. Thomas, *The Unadjusted Girl* (Boston: Little, Brown, 1923); W. I. Thomas and D. S. Thomas, *The Child in America* (New York: Knopf, 1928).

94. See Dwaine Marvick, *Harold D. Lasswell on Political Sociology* (Chicago: University of Chicago Press, 1977), pp. 32–34; Edward Shils, "Some Academics, Mainly at Chicago," *American Scholar* 50 (Spring 1981):195.

95. William J. Goode, Frank Furstenberg, Jr., and Larry R. Mitchell, eds., *Willard W. Waller on the Family, Education, and War* (Chicago: University of Chicago Press, 1970), pp. 72–79.

96. See Earl Rubington and Martin S. Weinberg, *The Study of Social Problems: Five Perspectives* (New York: Oxford University Press, 1971), pp. 47–79.

97. Harvey Zorbaugh, *The Gold Coast and the Slum* (Chicago: University of Chicago Press, 1929), p. 223.

98. Ernest Mowrer, *Family Disorganization* (Chicago: University of Chicago Press, 1927), pp. 188–93, 256–57.

99. Frederic Thrasher, *The Gang* (Chicago: University of Chicago Press, 1927), p. 68.

100. Nels Anderson, *The Hobo* (Chicago: University of Chicago Press, 1923).

101. Paul G. Cressey, *The Taxi-Dance Hall* (Chicago: University of Chicago Press, 1932).

102. Fred H. Matthews, *Quest for an American Sociology*, p. 1.

103. Winifred Raushenbush, *Robert E. Park: Biography of a Sociologist* (Durham, N.C.: Duke University Press, 1979), p. 68.

104. Ibid., p. 74.

105. Ibid., p. 69.

106. W. I. Thomas to R. E. Park from Berlin, 3 July 1912, in Robert E. Park Papers, University of Chicago, Additional Papers II, Box 1, Folder 3.

107. Raushenbush, *Robert E. Park*, p. 69.

108. Park and Miller [Thomas], *Old World Traits*.

109. Janowitz, *W. I. Thomas*, p. xvii.

110. See Matthews, *Quest for an American Sociology*, pp. 97–103.

111. Quoted in Helen Snick Perry, *Psychiatrist of America: The Life of Harry Stack Sullivan* (Cambridge, Mass.: Belknap Press, Harvard University Press, 1982), pp. 255–56.

112. Robert E. Park, "Notes on the Origin of the Society for Social Research," *Bulletin of the Society for Social Research*, August 1939, pp. 3–5, at p. 3. It has been published with an introduction by Lester R. Kurtz, "Robert E. Park's 'Notes on the Origin of the Society for Social Research,' " *Journal of the History of the Behavioral Sciences* 18 (October 1982):332–40. See also Martin Bulmer, "Chicago Sociology and the Society for Social Research: A Comment," *Journal of the History of the Behavioral Sciences* 19 (October 1983):353–56. The *Bulletin* was a quarterly mimeographed newsletter distributed to members of the society (see chap. 7).

113. Ibid., p. 3.

114. Ibid.

115. See Robert E. Park, "The Sociological Methods of William Graham Sumner and of William I. Thomas and Florian Znaniecki," in Stuart A. Rice, ed., *Methods in Social Science: A Casebook* (Chicago: University of Chicago Press, 1931), pp. 154–75, reprinted in Robert E. Park, *Society* (Glencoe, Ill.: Free Press, 1955), pp. 243–66.

116. Park, "Notes on the Origins of the Society for Social Research," p. 4.

Chapter 5

1. Anthony Oberschall, "The Institutionalization of American Sociology," in A. Oberschall, ed., *The Establishment of Empirical Sociology: Studies in Continuity, Discontinuity, and Institutionalization* (New York: Harper & Row, 1972), pp. 225–32.

2. See Dorothy Ross, "The Development of the Social Sciences," in Alexandra Oleson and John Voss, eds., *The Organization of Knowledge in Modern America, 1860–1920* (Baltimore, Md.: Johns Hopkins University Press, 1979), pp. 125–30.

3. See G. Duncan Mitchell, *A Hundred Years of Sociology* (London: Duckworth, 1968), chap. 10; Claus Moser and Graham Kalton, *Survey Methods in Social Investigation* (London: Heinemann, 1971), chap. 1; Catherine Marsh, *The Survey Method* (London: Allen &

Unwin, 1982), chap. 2; Martin Bulmer, *The Uses of Social Research* (London: Allen & Unwin, 1982), chap. 1; Martin Bulmer, ed., *Essays on the History of British Sociological Research* (Cambridge: Cambridge University Press, 1984).

4. Pauline V. Young, *Scientific Social Surveys and Research* (New York: Prentice-Hall, 1939), pp. 55–64.

5. On the social survey movement, see Young, *Scientific Social Surveys and Research*, chaps. 1 and 2; Jessie F. Steiner, "The Sources and Methods of Community Study," in Luther L. Bernard, ed., *The Fields and Methods of Sociology* (New York: Farrar & Rinehart, 1934), pp. 303–12; Allen F. Davis, *Spearheads for Reform: The Social Settlements and the Progressive Movement, 1890–1914* (New York: Oxford University Press, 1967); and Michael Gordon, "The Social Survey Movement and Sociology in the United States," *Social Problems* 21 (1973):284–98.

6. See Robert Bremner, *From the Depths: The Discovery of Poverty in the United States* (New York: New York University Press, 1956), p. 71.

7. Davis, *Spearheads for Reform*, p. 173.

8. W. E. B. Du Bois, *The Philadelphia Negro: A Social Study* (Philadelphia: University of Pennsylvania Press, 1899; reprinted with an Introduction by E. Digby Baltzell, New York: Schocken, 1967), pp. 1–4.

9. Elliott Rudwick, "W. E. B. Du Bois as a Sociologist," in James E. Blackwell and Morris Janowitz, eds., *Black Sociologists: Historical and Contemporary Perspectives* (Chicago: University of Chicago Press, 1974), pp. 38–50. The Atlanta studies are listed in Dan S. Green and Edwin D. Driver, eds., *W. E. B. Du Bois on Sociology and the Black Community* (Chicago: University of Chicago Press, 1978), pp. 12–13. They were republished as a set by Arno Press of New York in 1968. On Du Bois as a sociologist, see Rudwick, pp. 22–55, Green and Driver, pp. 9–20, and Elliott M. Rudwick, *W. E. B. Du Bois: A Study in Minority Group Leadership* (Philadelphia: University of Pennsylvania Press, 1960), pp. 27–53.

10. W. E. B. Du Bois, "The Laboratory in Sociology at Atlanta University," *Annals of the American Academy of Political and Social Science* 21 (May 1903):162.

11. Rudwick, *W. E. B. Du Bois*, p. 52; Dan S. Green and Edwin D. Driver, "W. E. B. Du Bois: A Case in the Sociology of Sociological Negation," *Phylon* 37 (December 1976):308–33; Allison Davis, *Du Bois and the Problems of the Black Masses* (W. E. B. Du Bois Institute for the Study of the American Black, n.d., mimeo).

12. Paul U. Kellogg, ed., *The Pittsburgh Survey* (6 vols.; New York: Charities Publications Committee and Survey Associates, 1910–14).

13. C. A. Chambers, *Paul U. Kellogg and the Survey* (Minneapolis: University of Minnesota Press, 1971). See also Steven R. Cohen, "Reconciling Industrial Conflict and Democracy: The Pittsburgh Survey and the Growth of Social Research in the United States" (Ph.D. diss., Columbia University, 1981).

14. Shelby M. Harrison, *Social Conditions in an American City* (New York: Russell Sage Foundation, 1920).

15. A. Eaton and Shelby M. Harrison, *A Bibliography of Social Surveys* (New York: Russell Sage Foundation, 1930).

16. Manuel C. Elmer, *Social Surveys of Urban Communities* (Menasha, Wis.: Collegiate Press, 1914; printed version of Ph.D. thesis, University of Chicago, 1914).

17. This paragraph draws on a personal communication to the writer from Professor Elmer, 3 October 1980.

18. Oberschall, "Institutionalization," pp. 226–27.

19. See Steven J. Diner, *A City and Its Universities: Public Policy in Chicago, 1892–1919* (Chapel Hill: University of North Carolina Press, 1980), esp. pp. 44–47.

20. Steven J. Diner, "Scholarship in the Quest for Social Welfare: A Fifty-Year History of the *Social Service Review*," *Social Service Review* 51 (March 1977):1–13, 63.

21. Winifred Raushenbush, *Robert E. Park: Biography of a Sociologist* (Durham, N.C.: Duke University Press, 1979), p. 97.

22. Oberschall, "Institutionalization," pp. 229–32.

23. Circular of the departments of political economy, political science, history, sociology, and anthropology, 1918, *Official Publications of the University of Chicago* (Chicago: University of Chicago Press, 1918).

24. Robert E. Park, "Notes on the Social Survey," 1917, Robert E. Park Papers, University of Chicago Archives, Box 5, Folder 1 (hereafter Park Papers).

25. R. E. Park, "The City: Suggestions for the Investigation of Human Behavior in the Urban Environment" (first published 1915), in Robert E. Park and Ernest W. Burgess, *The City* (Chicago: University of Chicago Press, 1925), p. 38.

26. "Notes on the History of the Social Survey," 1917–20, Park Papers.

27. "The Social Survey and Pragmatism," Park Papers, Box 5, Folder 1.

28. "Further Notes on Surveys," 1917–21, Park Papers, Box 5, Folder 1.

29. Manuel C. Elmer, *The Technique of Social Surveys* (Minneapolis: Minnesota University Printing Co., 1917).

30. Carl Aronovici, *The Social Survey* (Philadelphia: Harper, 1916).

31. "Further Notes on Surveys," 1917–21, Park Papers, Box 5, Folder 1.

32. Official Publications, 1921, Course 61.

33. Robert E. Park, "The City as a Social Laboratory," in T. V. Smith and Leonard D. White, eds., *Chicago: An Experiment in Social Science Research* (Chicago: University of Chicago Press, 1929), pp. 1–19.

34. Biographical details of Ernest W. Burgess from Leonard S. Cottrell, Jr., Albert Hunter, and James F. Short, Jr., eds., *Ernest W. Burgess on Community, Family, and Delinquency* (Chicago: University of Chicago Press, 1973), esp. pp. 325–29; Ernest W. Burgess, "Research in Urban Society: A Long View" in E. W. Burgess and Donald J. Bogue, eds., *Contributions to Urban Sociology* (Chicago: University of Chicago Press, 1964), pp. 2–14; and Donald J. Bogue, ed., *The Basic Writings of Ernest W. Burgess* (Chicago: Community and Family Study Center, University of Chicago, 1974), pp. ix–xxv.

35. Burgess, "Research in Urban Society," p. 3.

36. Frank W. Blackmar and Ernest W. Burgess, *The Lawrence Social Survey: Report to the Lawrence Social Survey Committee* (Topeka: Kansas State Printing Plant, 1917).

37. Ernest W. Burgess, "Frank Wilson Blackmar, Pioneer Sociologist," *Sociology and Social Research* 16 (January–February 1932):322–25; see also Alan Sica, "Sociology at the University of Kansas, 1889–1983: An Historical Sketch," *Sociological Quarterly* 24 (Autumn 1983):605–23.

38. Ernest W. Burgess, "The Social Survey: A Field for Constructive Service by Departments of Sociology," *American Journal of Sociology* 21 (1916):492–500.

39. Ibid., p. 499.

40. Ibid.

41. Ernest W. Burgess, "Plan for Survey of Hyde Park, according to the Following Outline and Suggestions by Professor Robert E. Park," no date, Ernest W. Burgess Papers, University of Chicago Archives, Box 187, folder 2.

42. Chicago Commission on Race Relations, *The Negro in Chicago: A Study of Race Relations and a Race Riot in 1919* (Chicago: University of Chicago Press, 1922).

43. For a fuller discussion amplifying points made here see Martin Bulmer, "Charles S. Johnson, Robert E. Park, and the Research Methods of the Chicago Commission on Race Relations, 1919–22: An Early Experiment in Applied Social Research," *Ethnic and Racial Studies* 4 (July 1981):289–306.

44. On the history of the riot, see *The Negro in Chicago*, pp. 1–52; Arthur I. Waskow, *From Race Riot to Sit-In: 1919 and the 1960s* (New York: Doubleday, 1967); and William M. Tuttle, Jr., *Race Riot: Chicago in the Red Summer of 1919* (New York: Atheneum, 1970).

45. *The Negro in Chicago*, p. 24.

46. Diner, *A City and Its Universities*, p. 32.

47. Bulmer, "Charles S. Johnson," pp. 292–93.

48. Richard Robbins, "Charles S. Johnson," in Blackwell and Janowitz, *Black Sociologists*, p. 59.

49. Raushenbush, *Robert E. Park*, p. 101.

50. See Arvarh E. Strickland, *History of the Chicago Urban League* (Urbana: University of Illinois Press, 1966).

51. Emmett J. Scott, *Negro Migration during the War* (New York: Oxford University Press, 1920); Charles S. Johnson to Robert E. Park from Indianola, Mississippi, 19 November 1917, Park Papers, Additional MS II, Box III, Folder 3.

52. See Nancy J. Weiss, *The National Urban League, 1910–1940* (New York: Oxford University Press, 1974), p. 220.

53. Ernest W. Burgess, "Social Planning and Race Relations," in Jitsuichi Masuoka and Preston Valien, eds., *Race Relations: Problems and Theory—Essays in Honor of Robert E. Park* (Chapel Hill: University of North Carolina Press, 1961), p. 17.

54. Waskow, *From Race Riot to Sit-In*, p. 81.

55. Documentary material relating to the research programme no longer exists, having been destroyed in a fire at the Chicago Urban League, where it was deposited (Waskow, *From Race Riot to Sit-In*, p. 82). So one series of tantalizing questions remains unanswered about the precise details of the methods of research employed.

56. Waskow, *From Race Riot to Sit-In*, p. 84.

57. Ibid., p. 87.

58. *The Negro in Chicago*, pp. 459–75, 493–519.

59. Ibid., pp. 493–94.

60. Walter Reckless interview with James Carey, 28 June 1972, James Carey Interviews, University of Chicago Archives.

61. *The Negro in Chicago*, p. 520.

62. Ibid., p. 531.

63. Ibid., p. 152.

64. Ibid., p. 170.

65. Ibid., pp. 359–85.

66. Vivien Palmer, *Field studies in Sociology: A Student's Manual* (Chicago: University of Chicago Press, 1928), p. 48.

67. Ibid., p. 49.

68. Ibid., pp. 49–51.

69. President's Research Committee on Social Trends, *Recent Social Trends in the United States* (New York: McGraw-Hill, 1933). See also Barry D. Karl, "Presidential Planning and Social Science Research: Mr. Hoover's Experts," *Perspectives in American History* 3 (1969):347–409.

70. See Martin Bulmer, "The Methodology of Early Social Indicator Research: William F. Ogburn and *Recent Social Trends*, 1933," *Social Indicators Research* 13 (1983):109–130.

71. Mitchell, *A Hundred Years of Sociology*; Marsh, *The Survey Method*; Bulmer, *The Uses of Social Research.*

72. For example, Morris H. Hansen and William G. Madow, "Some Important Events in the Historical Development of Sample Surveys," in D. B. Owen, ed., *On the History of Statistics and Probability* (New York and Basel: Marcel Dekker, 1976), pp. 75–102.

Chapter 6

1. Robert E. L. Faris, *Chicago Sociology, 1920–1932* (San Francisco: Chandler, 1967). On Park's theoretical ideas, see Ralph H. Turner, Introduction to R. H. Turner, ed., *Robert E. Park on Social Control and Collective Behavior* (Chicago: University of Chicago Press, 1967), pp. ix–xlvi. For a recent sympathetic overview, see Ulf Hannerz, *Exploring the City* (New York: Columbia University Press, 1980), pp. 19–58.

2. Ernest W. Burgess, "Research in Urban Society: A Long View," in E. W. Burgess and Donald J. Bogue, eds., *Contributions to Urban Sociology* (Chicago: University of Chicago Press, 1964), p. 4.

3. Robert E. Park, "The City: Suggestions for the Investigation of Human Behavior in the Urban Environment," *American Journal of Sociology* 20 (1915):577–612, reprinted in R. E. Park and E. W. Burgess, eds., *The City* (Chicago: University of Chicago Press, 1925), pp. 1–46.

4. E. W. Burgess, "The Growth of the City: An Introduction to a Research Project," in Park and Burgess, *The City*, pp. 47–62.

5. The earliest textbooks on social survey methods (providing guidance for conducting surveys in the manner of the social survey movement) were Shelby M. Harrison, *Community Action through Surveys* (New York: Russell Sage Foundation, 1916), Carl Aronovici, *The Social Survey* (Philadelphia: Harper, 1916), Manuel C. Elmer, *The Technique of Social Surveys* (Minneapolis, Minnesota: University Printing Co., 1917), and Carl C. Taylor, *The Social Survey: Its History and Methods* (Columbia: University of Missouri, 1919). The first textbook in sociological research methods identified is by Giddings's student F. Stuart Chapin, *Field Work and Social Research* (New York: Century Co., 1920). This was followed by a former Chicagoan Emory S. Bogardus's *The New Social Research* (1926), Vivien M. Palmer's *Field Studies in Sociology: A Student's Manual* (Chicago: University of Chicago Press, 1928), Howard W. Odum and Katherine Jocher's *An Introduction to Social Research* (New York: Henry Holt, 1929), and George A. Lundberg's *Social Research* (New York: Longmans Green 1929).

6. Particularly from the records of the Local Community Research Committee, set up at the University of Chicago in 1923.

7. Fred H. Matthews, *Quest for an American Sociology: Robert E. Park and the Chicago School* (Montreal: McGill-Queens University Press, 1977), pp. 8–30.

8. Robert E. Park, "An Autobiographical Note," in R. E. Park, *Race and Culture* (Glencoe, Ill.: Free Press, 1950), p. viii.

9. Ibid., p. ix.

10. Robert E. Park, "A Note on the Origins of the Society for Social Research," *Bulletin of the Society for Social Research*, August 1939, p. 4 (copy in papers of the Society for Social Research, University of Chicago Archives).

11. Matthews, *Quest for an American Sociology*, p. 109.

12. Park, "The City," p. 3.

13. Robert E. Park, "Life History," *American Journal of Sociology* 79 (1973):253 (written 1928); Matthews, *Quest for an American Sociology*, pp. 6–8, 24–30.

14. Park, "Life History," p. 255.

15. Park, "The City," p. 3.

16. Robert E. Park, "The City as a Social Laboratory," in T. V. Smith and Leonard D. White, eds., *Chicago: An Experiment in Social Science Research* (Chicago: University of Chicago Press, 1929), p. 19.

17. Park, "Life History," p. 256.

18. Ernest W. Burgess, "Basic Social Data," in Smith and White, *Chicago*, p. 47.

19. Ernest W. Burgess to Charles E. Merriam, 4 June 1922, letter in Charles E. Merriam Papers, University of Chicago Archives, Box CXX, Folder 7.

20. William James, "On a Certain Blindness in Human Beings," in William James, *Talks to Teachers of Psychology: And to Students of Some of Life's Ideals* (New York: Henry Holt, 1899), pp. 229–64.

21. Park, "An Autobiographical Note," pp. vi–vii.

22. Matthews, *Quest for an American Sociology*, p. 33.

23. Booker T. Washington, *The Man Furthest Down: A Record of Observation and Study in Europe* (Garden City, N.Y.: Doubleday, Page, 1918).

24. The project was concerned with the adaptation of European immigrants to life in the United States and traced the process by which immigrants accommodated to the new society and culture in which they were living. See William S. Bernard, "General Introduction to the

Republished Studies," in Frank V. Thompson, *The Schooling of the Immigrant*, vol. 1 of Americanization Studies: The Acculturation of Immigrant Groups into American Society (Montclair, N.J.: Patterson Smith, 1971), pp. vii–xliii; Milton M. Gordon, "The American Immigrant Revisited," *Social Forces* 54 (1975):470–74. See Robert E. Park and Herbert A. Miller, *Old World Traits Transplanted* (New York: Harper, 1921), though Thomas was the principal author. For the story of Thomas's involvement, and why his name was not originally put on the book, see Donald R. Young's Introduction to the republished edition by Patterson Smith of Montclair, N.J., 1971, pp. vii–xv. Park also completed another study as part of the project: R. E. Park, *The Immigrant Press and Its Control* (New York: Harper, 1922).

25. Robert E. Park, "The Sociological Methods of W. G. Sumner and of W. I. Thomas and F. Znaniecki," in R. E. Park, *Society* (Glencoe, Ill.: Free Press, 1955), p. 257.

26. Charles S. Johnson, *The Shadow of the Plantation* (Chicago: University of Chicago Press, 1934). On Johnson's work in New York, see Richard Robbins, "Charles S. Johnson," in James E. Blackwell and Morris Janowitz, eds., *Black Sociologists: Historical and Contemporary Perspectives* (Chicago: University of Chicago Press, 1974), pp. 60–62, and Chidi Ikonné, *From Du Bois to Van Vechten: The Early New Negro Literature, 1903–1926* (Westport, Conn.: Greenwood, 1981), pp. 91–97. On Johnson at Fisk, see Robbins, "Charles S. Johnson," pp. 62–84 and, for a critical view, August Meier, "Black Sociologists in White America," *Social Forces* 56 (1977):259–70.

27. Robert E. Park, Introduction, to Johnson, *Shadow of the Plantation*, p. x.

28. Ibid., p. xxi.

29. Albert Hunter, Introduction, in Leonard S. Cottrell, Jr., Albert Hunter, and James F. Short, Jr., eds., *Ernest W. Burgess on Community, Family, and Delinquency* (Chicago: University of Chicago Press, 1973), p. 5.

30. Burgess, "Research in Urban Society: A Long View," p. 3.

31. Robert E. Park and Ernest W. Burgess, *Introduction to the Science of Sociology* (Chicago: University of Chicago Press, 1921).

32. Donald J. Bogue, Introduction to D. J. Bogue, ed., *The Basic Writings of E. W. Burgess* (Chicago: Community and Family Study Center, University of Chicago, 1974), p. xiv.

33. Park and Burgess, *Introduction to the Science of Sociology*, pp. 43–59.

34. Ibid., p. 44.

35. Syllabus of Course 43b, 1917 (and same course in subsequent years with different number), *Official Publications of the University of Chicago* (Chicago: University of Chicago Press, 1917).

36. Bogue, Introduction to *The Basic Writings*, p. xv.

37. Robert E. Park, quoted in Howard Odum, *American Sociology: The Story of Sociology in the United States through 1950* (New York: Longmans, 1951), p. 132.

38. "We are mainly indebted to writers of fiction for our more intimate knowledge of contemporary urban life"; Park, "The City," p. 3. This statement was particularly pertinent in Chicago. See Carl S. Smith, *Chicago and the American Literary Imagination, 1880–1920* (Chicago: University of Chicago Press, 1984).

39. The most explicit discussion of the relationship between literature and Chicago sociology is in James T. Carey, *Sociology and Public Affairs: The Chicago School* (Beverly Hills: Sage, 1975), pp. 179 ff., where the issue was probed in interviews with graduate students from the 1920s, with rather inconclusive results. See also Frederic Thrasher's Introduction to James Farrell's novel *Young Lonigan* (1932) and James T. Farrell, "Some Observations on Literature and Sociology," in *Reflections at Fifty and Other Essays* (New York: Vanguard, 1954), pp. 186–87.

40. Matthews, *Quest for an American Sociology*, pp. 105–10; Raushenbush, *Robert E. Park*, pp. 96–106.

41. Everett Hughes, "The First Young Sociologist," in *Ernest Watson Burgess, 1886–1966: Four Talks Given at a Memorial Service* (privately printed, University of Chicago, 1967), p. 5.

42. Norman Hayner, Diary, Friday, 6 January 1922, from copy kindly made available by Mrs. Una Hayner of Seattle, Washington. A copy may now be consulted in the University of Chicago Archives.

43. The words of Robert Park in the 1920s recalled by Howard Becker, quoted in John C. McKinney, *Constructive Typology and Social Theory* (New York: Appleton-Century-Crofts, 1966), p. 71.

44. Nels Anderson, "A Stranger at the Gate: Reflections on the Chicago School of Sociology," *Urban Life* 11 (January 1983):398–99.

45. For accounts of this research, see Nels Anderson, Introduction to the Phoenix Edition, in N. Anderson, *The Hobo* (1923; Chicago: University of Chicago Press, 1961), pp. v–xxi; and N. Anderson, *The American Hobo: An Autobiography* (Leiden: E. J. Brill, 1975), pp. 160–70. Anderson reveals in the latter that he could not talk to fellow-students about his own background and deliberately omitted any personal material from the original edition. "I let them believe that all the material in *The Hobo* had been assembled in Chicago's 'Hobohemia' " (p. 2).

46. Anderson, Introduction, p. xii.

47. Ibid., p. xiii.

48. Anderson, *The American Hobo*, pp. 168–69.

49. Letter from Robert E. Park to Charles E. Merriam, 1 June 1922, Charles E. Merriam Papers, Box CXX, Folder 7.

50. In the University of Chicago Archives. The LCRC provided financial support for part-time research assistantships for graduate students. Those in receipt of awards were required to provide quarterly reports on their progress, and these reports throw interesting light on the research methods used in many of the studies. From them, it is possible to obtain an impression of the research methods actually used, despite the absence of information in the published works.

51. Harvey Zorbaugh, "The Lower North Side: A Study in Community Organization," in Reports, 1923–24, Ernest W. Burgess Papers, University of Chicago Archives, Box 13, Folder 3.

52. Frederic Thrasher, *The Gang: A Study of 1,313 Gangs in Chicago* (Chicago: University of Chicago Press, 1927), pp. xii–xiii.

53. F. Thrasher, "One Thousand Boys Gangs in Chicago: A Study of Their Organization and Habitat," Reports, 1923–24, Burgess Papers, Box 13, Folder 3.

54. Walter C. Reckless, "The Natural History of Vice Areas in Chicago," in Reports, 1923–24, Burgess Papers, Box 13, Folder 3.

55. N. Hayner, "The Hotel as an Index of City Life," Reports, 1923–24, Burgess Papers, Box 13, Folder 3.

56. John Landesco, *Organized Crime in Chicago: Part III of the Illinois Crime Survey, 1929* (Chicago: Illinois Association for Criminal Justice, 1929), republished with an Introduction by Mark H. Haller (Chicago: University of Chicago Press, 1968).

57. Paul G. Cressey, untitled manuscript in Philip M. Hauser Papers, University of Chicago Archives, Box 25, Folder 5, published in Martin Bulmer, ed., "The Methodology of *The Taxi-Dance Hall*: An Early Account of Chicago Ethnography from the 1920s," *Urban Life* 12 (April 1983):106.

58. Vivien Palmer, *Field Studies in Sociology*, p. 169.

59. Anderson, *The American Hobo*, p. 165.

60. Ibid., p. 166.

61. Anderson, Introduction to *The Hobo*, p. xiii.

62. See Jennifer Platt, "The Development of the 'Participant Observation' Method in

Sociology: Origin, Myth, and History," *Journal of the History of the Behavioral Sciences* 19 (October 1983):379–93.

63. John Landesco, "The Criminal Gang," in "Report to the LCRC, Autumn Quarter 1925," Merriam Papers, Box CXXII, Folder 10.

64. M. H. Haller, Introduction to *Organized Crime in Chicago*, p. xv.

65. Cressey, quoted in Bulmer, "The Methodology of *The Taxi-Dance Hall*," pp. 109–119.

66. A considerable number of these life histories survive in the Burgess Papers, University of Chicago Archives.

67. Burgess, "A Short History of Urban Research," p. 9.

68. Haller, Introduction, p. xvi.

69. E. W. Burgess, "Statistics and Case Studies as Methods of Sociological Research," *Sociology and Social Research* 12 (1927):118. See also E. W. Burgess, "The Family and the Person," in E. W. Burgess, ed., *The Personality and the Social Group* (Chicago: University of Chicago Press, 1929), p. 133.

70. Ernest W. Burgess, Preface, to Clifford R. Shaw, *The Jack-Roller: A Delinquent Boy's Own Story* (Chicago: University of Chicago Press, 1930), p. xi.

71. Shaw, *The Jack-Roller*, p. 17.

72. Ibid., and C. Shaw, *The Natural History of a Delinquent Career* (Chicago: University of Chicago Press, 1931). See also *The Jack-Roller*, and Jon Snodgrass, *The Jack-Roller at Seventy: A Fifty-Year Follow-up* (Lexington, Mass.: D.C. Heath, 1982), particularly the essay by James F. Short, "Life History, Autobiography, and Life Cycle," pp. 135–52. For an insightful discussion of Shaw's work in the context of life-history research, see James Bennett, *Oral History and Delinquency: The Rhetoric of Criminology* (Chicago: University of Chicago Press, 1981), pp. 165–210. For a critical view, see Jon Snodgrass, "Clifford R. Shaw and Henry D. McKay: Chicago Criminologists," *British Journal of Criminology* 16 (1976):1–19, 289–93.

73. Shaw, *The Jack-Roller*, p. 2.

74. Ibid., pp. 21–23 for Shaw's account of the methodology.

75. Ibid., p. 19.

76. Burgess, "Statistics and Case Studies as Methods."

77. Discussion, by Ernest W. Burgess, in *The Jack-Roller*, pp. 184–97.

78. See Kenneth Plummer, *Documents of Life* (London: Allen & Unwin, 1983), and Bennett, *Oral History and Delinquency*.

Chapter 7

1. See Edward Shils, *The Calling of Sociology and Other Essays on the Pursuit of Learning* (Chicago: University of Chicago Press, 1981), pp. 220–24.

2. Howard Odum, *American Sociology: The Story of Sociology in the United States through 1950* (New York: Longmans Green, 1951), pp. 84–85; Seymour Martin Lipset, "The Department of Sociology," in Robert G. Hoxie et al., eds., *A History of the Faculty of Political Science at Columbia University* (New York: Columbia University Press, 1955), pp. 284–303.

3. Faris was born in 1874 and from 1894 to 1904 was a missionary in the Belgian Congo. He studied philosophy and psychology at Chicago under Dewey, Mead, and Angell, obtaining his Ph.D. in psychology in 1914. Robert E. L. Faris, *Chicago Sociology, 1920–1932* (Chicago: University of Chicago Press, 1970), p. 158.

4. The data on changes in personnel of the department are taken from Faris, *Chicago Sociology*, pp. 153–58; Steven J. Diner, "Department and Discipline: The Department of Sociology at the University of Chicago, 1892–1920," *Minerva* 13 (Winter 1975):522–36;

Fred H. Matthews, *Quest for an American Sociology: Robert E. Park and the Chicago School* (Montreal: McGill-Queens University Press, 1977), pp. 85–87; Papers of the Presidents of the University of Chicago, 1925–1945 (cited hereafter as "Presidents' Papers, 1925–45"), University of Chicago Archives, Sociology Department, 1925–30, Budgets and Appointments.

5. "The teachers lived near the university and were in their offices much of the time; the students had ready access to them"; Shils, *The Calling of Sociology*, p. 216.

6. Bedford, born in Iowa in 1876, graduated from Baker University in Baldwin, Kansas, and in the early 1900s was professor of history there and principal of the university's secondary school. From 1908 to 1911 he was a fellow in sociology at Chicago, then was appointed to the staff.

7. A. W. Small to Scott Bedford, 19 February 1924, Presidents' Papers, 1925–45, Sociology and Anthropology, 1925–29, Budget and Appointments, p. 1.

8. Lawrence J. Rhoades, *A History of the American Sociological Association* (Washington D.C.: American Sociological Association, 1981), p. 81.

9. Small to Bedford, 19 February 1924.

10. Bedford taught courses principally in urban sociology, publishing in 1927 a book of readings on the subject, one of the first of its kind. Like Henderson and Zueblin, he was another, slighter, precursor of the urban sociology of Park and Burgess; Diner, "Department and Discipline," p. 531.

11. Professor Bedford resigned on 7 July 1925 and a week later received a year's salary in advance from the university; Presidents' Papers, 1925–45, Sociology Budgets and Appointments, 1925–30. Later correspondence between Bedford and the president of the university and the dean of social science suggests that he was compelled to resign following allegations made by a young woman to senior members of the university; Scott Bedford to Dean Charles Gilbey, 26 December 1939, Harold H. Swift Papers, University of Chicago Archives, Box 134, Folder 14, p. 1. There is a reference to Scott Bedford (though not by name) in Lyn H. Lofland, "Reminiscences of Classic Chicago: The Blumer-Hughes Talk," *Urban Life* 9 (July 1980):256, where Everett Hughes is quoted as saying, "he got arrested in New York putting wooden nickels in the subway. In fact, he used to pay off with five dollars regularly a woman who came around demanding money from him." Social deviants might feature prominently in the object-matter of Chicago sociology, but, as W. I. Thomas learned, deviance among faculty members was not condoned and usually led to a demand for immediate resignation.

12. Ernest D. Burton to Scott Bedford, 14 September 1923, Presidents' Papers 1925–45, Sociology and Anthropology 1925–30, Budgets and Appointments.

13. Department of Sociology, Budget Recommendations for the Year 1921–22, Presidents' Papers, 1889–1925, University of Chicago Archives, Box 18, Folder 5.

14. Albion W. Small to President Judson, 6 May 1921, Presidents' Papers, 1889–1925, Box 18, Folder 5.

15. See especially Matthews, *Quest for an American Sociology*, pp. 105–10, and Winifred Raushenbush, *Robert E. Park: Biography of a Sociologist* (Durham, N.C.: Duke University Press, 1979), pp. 96–106.

16. Matthews, *Quest for an American Sociology*, p. 107.

17. Harold Lasswell to Fred H. Matthews, 9 December 1965, Fred H. Matthews correspondence file, Special Collections Department, Joseph Regenstein Library, University of Chicago, p. 2.

18. Herbert Blumer quoted in Matthews, *Quest for an American Sociology*, p. 108.

19. Letter from Everett Hughes to James Aho, 8 July 1970, published in James A. Aho, *German Realpolitik and American Sociology* (Cranbury, N.J.: Bucknell University Press, 1975), p. 319.

20. See Ralph H. Turner, Introduction to R. H. Turner, ed., *Robert E. Park on Social Control and Collective Behavior* (Chicago: University of Chicago Press, 1967), pp. ix–xlvi.

21. Matthews, *Quest for an American Sociology*, p. 109; Raushenbush, *Robert E. Park*, p. 105.

22. Herbert Blumer to Mrs. Winifred Rorty (Raushenbush), 11 April 1966, Robert E. Park Papers, University of Chicago Archives, Additional MS. II, Box III, folder 1.

23. Faris, *Chicago Sociology*, pp. 33–34; James T. Carey, *Sociology and Public Affairs: The Chicago School* (Beverly Hills: Sage, 1975), pp. 152–59; Nels Anderson, *The American Hobo: An Autobiography* (Leiden: E. J. Brill, 1975), pp. 160–70. See also more generally the James T. Carey interview transcripts in the University of Chicago Archives.

24. Faris, *Chicago Sociology*, p. 34; Lofland, "Reminiscences of Classic Chicago," pp. 269, 281; personal communications from Robert E. L. Faris to the author, 6 July 1980 and 30 September 1980. The surviving records of Zeta Phi, including officer lists and minutes (which I have not had an opportunity to consult) are held by Department of Sociology at the University of Chicago, to whom they were sent in April 1981.

25. Robert E. Park, "Notes on the Origin of the Society for Social Research," *Bulletin of the Society for Social Research*, August 1939, p. 3 (copy in the papers of the Society for Social Research, University of Chicago Archives). This has been reprinted in Lester R. Kurtz, "Robert E. Park's 'Notes on the Origin of the Society for Social Research,' " *Journal of the History of the Behavioral Sciences* 18 (1982):332–40. See also Martin Bulmer, "Chicago Sociology and the Society for Social Research: A Comment," *Journal of the History of the Behavioral Sciences* 19 (October 1983):353–36.

26. Park, "Notes on the Origin of the Society for Social Research," pp. 4–5.

27. This and other statements about their activities are based on the society's records in the University of Chicago Archives.

28. For a fuller discussion of its role, see Martin Bulmer, "The Society for Social Research: An Institutional Underpinning to the Chicago School of Sociology in the 1920s," *Urban Life* 11 (January 1983):421–39.

29. Personal communication from Herbert Blumer to the author, 4 May 1980.

30. Helen M. Hughes, "On Becoming a Sociologist," *Journal of the History of Sociology* 3 (Fall–Winter 1980–81):34. The impact of Child's work on Park's thought is confirmed in Harold Lasswell's letter to Fred Matthews, 9 December 1965; Fred H. Matthews Correspondence, University of Chicago Archives.

31. Blumer to the author, 4 May 1980.

32. For example, Norbert Wiley, "The Rise and Fall of Dominating Theories in American Sociology," in William Snizek, Ellsworth R. Fuhrman, and Michael Miller, eds., *Contemporary Issues in Theory and Research* (Westport, Conn.: Greenwood Press, 1979), pp. 47–79.

33. The earliest summer institute for which records survive in the University of Chicago Archives appears to be the fourth institute in 1926. Details of the second summer institute were located in the Laura Spelman Rockefeller Memorial Papers, Rockefeller Archive Center, Pocantico Hills, Tarrytown, New York, series III, subseries 6, box 70, folder 744.

34. See Bulmer, "The Society for Social Research," pp. 429–32.

35. See Patricia M. Lengermann, "The Founding of the *American Sociological Review*: The Anatomy of a Rebellion," *American Sociological Review* 44 (1979):185–98.

36. In the late 1920s, the *Bulletin* acted as a book club, offering selected books by members (and usually published by the University of Chicago Press) to other members at reduced prices. In the early 1930s, the society itself published two monographs. The first was Park's lecture notes of Simmel's course in Berlin in 1899, Georg Simmel, *Sociologische Vorlesungen gehalten an der Universität Berlin in Wintersemester 1899* (Series 1, number 1; Chicago: Society for Social Research of the University of Chicago, 1931). The second was Everett C. Hughes, *The Growth of an Institution: The Chicago Real Estate Board* (Series 2, monograph 1; Chicago: Society for Social Research of the University of Chicago, 1931), partially reprinted in James F. Short, Jr., ed., *The Social Fabric of the Metropolis* (Chicago: University of Chicago Press, 1971), pp. 33–69. This study is discussed in Lawton R. Burns,

"The Chicago School and the Study of Organization-Environment Relations," *Journal of the History of the Behavioral Sciences* 16 (1980):342–58.

37. See Leonard S. Cottrell, Jr., "Ernest Watson Burgess, 1886–1966: Contributions in the Field of Marriage and the Family," *American Sociologist* 2 (August 1967):148.

38. Herbert Blumer, "Ernest W. Burgess, 1886–1966," *American Sociologist* 2 (May 1967):103.

39. Vivien M. Palmer, "Social Surveys of the Individual Districts of Chicago, B13" in Reports on Sociology Projects under the direction of the Committee on Social Research, Autumn quarter 1924, Ernest W. Burgess Papers, University of Chicago Archives, Box 13, Folder 4.

40. Paul G. Cressey, "Report on Summer's Work with the Juvenile Protection Association of Chicago, 1925," Ernest W. Burgess Papers, Box 149, Folder 5, Outline Diary, p. 1; Preface to Paul G. Cressey, *The Taxi-Dance Hall* (Chicago: University of Chicago Press, 1932).

41. Palmer, "Social Surveys of Individual Districts."

42. Ernest W. Burgess, Preface to Vivien M. Palmer, *Field Studies in Sociology: A Student's Manual* (Chicago: University of Chicago Press, 1928), p. vii.

43. Albert Hunter, *Symbolic Communities: The Persistence and Change of Chicago's Local Communities* (Chicago: University of Chicago Press, 1974), p. 77.

44. Vivien Palmer and Ernest W. Burgess, *Social Backgrounds of Chicago's Local Communities* (Chicago: Local Community Research Committee of the University of Chicago, 1930), p. 3.

45. Ernest W. Burgess, "Basic Social Data" in T. V. Smith and Leonard D. White, ed., *Chicago: An Experiment in Social Science Research* (Chicago: University of Chicago Press, 1939), p. 62.

46. The first was F. Stuart Chapin, *Field Work and Social Research* (New York: Century Co., 1920), though it adopted a rather different view of the nature of field work.

47. Palmer, *Field Studies in Sociology*, p. 19.

48. C. Langlois and C. Seignobos, *The Introduction to the Study of History*, trans. by G. G. Berry. (London: Duckworth, 1898).

49. Palmer, *Field Studies in Sociology*, pp. 30–31.

50. Ibid., p. 107.

51. Ernest R. Mowrer, *Family Disorganization* (Chicago: University of Chicago Press, 1927), pp. 195–215.

52. Edward Shils, *The Present State of American Sociology* (Glencoe, Ill.: Free Press, 1948), p. 10.

53. Ernest Burgess, "Juvenile Delinquency in a Small City," *Journal of Criminal Law and Criminology* 6 (1916):724–28.

54. Jon Snodgrass, "Clifford R. Shaw and Henry D. McKay: Chicago Criminologists," *British Journal of Criminology* 16 (1976):4–5.

55. Reports on Sociology Projects under the direction of the Committee on Social Research, Autumn quarter 1924, Ernest W. Burgess Papers, University of Chicago Archives, Box 13, Folder 4.

56. Report to the Local Community Research Committee, Autumn 1925, Charles E. Merriam Papers, University of Chicago Archives, Box CXXII, Folder 10, p. 11; James Bennett, *Oral History and Delinquency: The Rhetoric of Criminology* (Chicago: University of Chicago Press, 1981), p. 166.

57. Report to the Local Community Research Committee, Autumn 1925.

58. See Snodgrass, "Clifford R. Shaw and Henry D. McKay," pp. 1–19, 289–93; James F. Short, Jr., Introduction to the Revised Edition, in Clifford R. Shaw and Henry D. McKay, *Juvenile Delinquency and Urban Areas* (Chicago: University of Chicago Press, 1969), pp. xxv–liv; James F. Short, Jr., ed., *Delinquency, Crime, and Society* (Chicago:

University of Chicago Press, 1976), esp. pp. 1–88; Bennett, *Oral History and Delinquency*, esp. pp. 165–217.

59. Behavior Research Fund, *The Final Report of the Board of Trustees to the Members of the Behavior Research Fund and Friends of the Institute for Juvenile Research* (Chicago: privately printed, 1948). Copy was kindly supplied by James Bennett.

60. Ibid., pp. 5–27.

61. Snodgrass, "Clifford R. Shaw and Henry D. McKay," p. 5.

62. Clifford R. Shaw, Frederick M. Zorbaugh, Henry D. McKay, and Leonard S. Cottrell, Jr., *Delinquency Areas: A Study of the Geographic Distribution of School Truants, Juvenile Delinquents, and Adult Offenders in Chicago* (Chicago: University of Chicago Press, 1929); Clifford R. Shaw and Henry D. McKay, *Social Factors in Juvenile Delinquency*, vol. 2 of the Report on the Causes of Crime of the National Commission on Law Observance and Enforcement (the Wickersham Commission) (Washington, D.C.: U.S. Government Printing Office, 1931); Clifford R. Shaw and Henry D. McKay, *Juvenile Delinquency and Urban Areas* (Chicago: University of Chicago Press, 1942); Clifford R. Shaw, *The Jack-Roller: A Delinquent Boy's Own Story* (Chicago: University of Chicago Press, 1930); Clifford R. Shaw, *The Natural History of a Delinquent Career* (Chicago: University of Chicago Press, 1931); Clifford R. Shaw, Henry D. McKay, and James F. McDonald, *Brothers in Crime* (Chicago: University of Chicago Press, 1938); see Ernest W. Burgess, "The Work of the Behavior Research Fund," in *Final Report of the Board of Trustees*, pp. 32–64.

63. *Final Report of the Board of Trustees*, pp. 20–24.

64. For accounts of the Chicago Area Project, see Snodgrass, "Clifford R. Shaw and Henry D. McKay"; Short, Introduction to the Revised Edition, pp. xlvi–liv; Anthony Sorrentino, *Organizing against Crime: Redeveloping the Neighborhood* (New York: Human Sciences Press, 1977); Bennett, *Oral History and Delinquency*, pp. 173–78.

65. Ernest W. Burgess and Clark Tibbitts, "Factors Making for Success or Failure of Parole," *Journal of Criminal Law and Criminology* 19 (part 2) (July–August 1928):239–306.

66. Leonard S. Cottrell, Jr., Albert Hunter, and James F. Short, Jr., eds., *Ernest W. Burgess on Community, Family, and Delinquency* (Chicago: University of Chicago Press, 1973), pp. 170–72. The other committee members were Judge Andrew A. Bruce, of Northwestern University Law School, and Dean Albert J. Harno, of the University of Illinois Law School.

67. Mark H. Haller, Introduction to John Landesco, *Organized Crime in Chicago: Part III of the Illinois Crime Survey, 1929* (Chicago: University of Chicago Press, 1968), pp. xvi–xvii.

68. Landesco, *Organized Crime in Chicago* (Chicago: Illinois Association for Criminal Justice, 1929). On the background to this work, see Mark H. Haller, "Urban Crime and Criminal Justice: The Chicago Case," *Journal of American History* 57 (1970):619–35, and Mark H. Haller, "Organized Crime in Urban Society: Chicago in the Twentieth Century," *Journal of Social History* 5 (1972):210–34. See also Mark H. Haller, "Police Reform in Chicago, 1905–1935," *American Behavioral Scientist* 13 (May–August 1970):649–66.

69. Harold D. Lasswell to Fred H. Matthews, 9 December 1965, pp. 1–2.

70. Harold D. Lasswell, *World Politics and Personal Insecurity* (New York: McGraw-Hill, 1935), pp. v–vi.

71. Edward Shils, "Some Academics, Mainly in Chicago," *American Scholar* 50 (Spring 1981):194.

72. See Horace Cayton, *Long Old Road* (Seattle: University of Washington Press, 1970), pp. 184–85. Cayton had a particularly close relation with Park, though not always an easy one. See Shils, "Some Academics," p. 189.

73. "Recollections of Dr. Robert E. Park" by Harold F. Gosnell (circa 1970), Robert E. Park Papers, University of Chicago Archives, Additional ms. II, Box 2, Folder 3. Robert

Park, Introduction to Harold F. Gosnell, *Negro Politicians* (Chicago: University of Chicago Press, 1935), pp. xii–xxv. See also Gosnell's Preface, pp. ix–xii.

74. See George W. Stocking, Jr., *Anthropology at Chicago* (Chicago: Joseph Regenstein Library, University of Chicago, 1979), pp. 16–25.

75. Robert Redfield, *The Little Community* (Chicago: University of Chicago Press, 1960), p. 143. See Robert E. Park, "The Sociological Methods of William Graham Sumner and of William I. Thomas and Florian Znaniecki," in Stuart A. Rice, ed., *Method in Social Science: A Case Book* (Chicago: University of Chicago Press, 1931), pp. 154–75.

76. Shils, "Some Academics," pp. 188–90.

Chapter 8

1. See Dorothy Ross, "The Development of the Social Sciences," in Alexandra Oleson and John Voss, eds., *The Organization of Knowledge in Modern America, 1860–1920* (Baltimore: Johns Hopkins University Press, 1979), pp. 125–30. On parallel developments in the field of law, which involved Robert M. Hutchins and also received the support of the Laura Spelman Rockefeller Memorial, see John Henry Schlegel, "American Legal Realism and Empirical Social Science: From the Yale Experience," *Buffalo Law Review* 28 (Summer 1979):459–586.

2. See Martin Bulmer, "Support for Sociology in the 1920s," *American Sociologist* 17 (1982):185–92.

3. Barry D. Karl, *Charles E. Merriam and the Study of Politics* (Chicago: University of Chicago Press, 1974), pp. 140–43.

4. On political science, see Albert Somit and Joseph Tanenhaus, *The Development of American Political Science: From Burgess to Behavioralism* (Boston: Allyn & Bacon, 1967), and Dwight Waldo, "Political Science: Tradition, Discipline, Profession, Science, Enterprise," in Fred I. Greenstein and Nelson Polsby, eds., *The Handbook of Political Science* (Reading, Mass.: Addison-Wesley, 1975), 1:41 ff.

5. See Paul F. Lazarsfeld, *Qualitative Analysis* (Boston: Allyn & Bacon, 1972), parts 5 and 6; Allen H. Barton, "Paul Lazarsfeld and Applied Social Research," *Social Science History* 3 (October 1979):4–44; and Robert K. Merton, James S. Coleman, and Peter H. Rossi, eds., *Qualitative and Quantitative Social Research: Papers in Honor of Paul F. Lazarsfeld* (New York: Free Press, 1979), part 1.

6. See Peter H. Rossi, "Researchers, Scholars, and Policy-Makers: The Politics of Large-Scale Research," *Daedalus* 93 (Fall 1964):1142–61.

7. Albion W. Small, *The Meaning of Social Science* (Chicago: University of Chicago Press, 1910), pp. 177–78.

8. Karl, *Charles E. Merriam*, chap. 7.

9. Memorandum on a Proposed Institute of Government Research, Charles E. Merriam Papers, University of Chicago Archives, Box CXII, Folder 3, early 1920s.

10. Letter from Leon C. Marshall to President Judson, 13 March 1922, Presidents' Papers, 1889–1925, University of Chicago Archives, Box 61, Folder 10.

11. Leon C. Marshall, "A Plan to Give Our Social Science Group a Position of Leadership (if it deserves it) in the Next Five to Ten Years," Presidents' Papers, 1892–1925, Box 61, Folder 10, attached to letter to President Judson dated 17 March 1922.

12. Letter from Albion Small to President Judson (beginning "My dear Chief"), 3 November 1922, Presidents' Papers 1892–1925, Box 61, Folder 10.

13. Ibid.

14. Small, *The Meaning of Social Science*, pp. 37–38, 51.

15. A. W. Small, "What Should Be the Ideal of Our Own Graduate School of Social Science," paper read 28 February 1923, Charles E. Merriam Papers, University of Chicago Archives, Box CXX, Folder 9.

16. Ibid.

17. Ibid.

18. Charles E. Merriam, "Talk to Instructors in History, Political Economy, Sociology, Philosophy, and Political Science," 1922, Merriam Papers, Box CXX, Folder 5.

19. Circular letter from Charles E. Merriam to social science departments, 19 May 1922, Merriam Papers, Box CXX, Folder 7.

20. Robert E. Park to Charles E. Merriam, 1 June 1922, Merriam Papers, Box CXX, Folder 7.

21. Ernest W. Burgess to Charles E. Merriam, 4 June 1922, Merriam Papers, Box CXX, Folder 7.

22. Karl, *Charles E. Merriam*, p. 121, and reports of the proceedings in the *American Political Science Review* 18 (February 1924):119–66, 19 (February 1925):104–62, 20 (February 1926):124–70.

23. Small to Judson, 3 November 1922, Presidents' Papers, 1889–1925, Box 61, Folder 10, p. 2.

24. Small, "What Should Be the Ideal."

25. See Charles E. Merriam, *New Aspects of Politics* (3d ed.; Chicago: University of Chicago Press, 1970).

26. Karl, *Charles E. Merriam*, pp. 140–44.

27. See James H. Tufts, "Chicago: I Study the City" (autobiographical reminiscences written in 1920s), James H. Tufts Papers, University of Chicago Archives, Box 3, Folder 21.

28. Raymond B. Fosdick, *The Story of the Rockefeller Foundation* (New York: Harper, 1952).

29. See Robert H. Bremner, *American Philanthropy* (Chicago: University of Chicago Press, 1960); Warren Weaver, *U.S. Philanthropic Foundations—Their History, Structure, Management, and Record* (New York: Harper, 1967); Waldemar Nielsen, *The Big Foundations* (New York: Columbia University Press, 1972); and Ben Whitaker, *The Foundations: An Anatomy of Philanthropic Bodies* (Harmondsworth: Penguin, 1979).

30. See Robert E. Kohler, "The Management of Science," *Minerva* 14 (Summer 1976):279–306; Kohler, "A Policy for the Advancement of Science," *Minerva* 16 (Winter 1978):480–515; and Stanley Coben, "Foundation Officials and Fellowships," *Minerva* 14 (Summer 1976):255–40.

31. See Bulmer, "Support for Sociology in the 1920s," pp. 185–92, and Barry D. Karl, "The Citizen and the Scholar: Ships That Crash in the Night," in William H. Kruskal, ed., *The Social Sciences: Their Nature and Uses* (Chicago: University of Chicago Press, 1982), pp. 101–20.

32. Fosdick, *The Story of the Rockefeller Foundation*, p. 193.

33. On Ruml, see Martin Bulmer and Joan Bulmer, "Philanthropy and Social Science in the 1920s: The Case of Beardsley Ruml and the Laura Spelman Rockefeller Memorial, 1922–29," *Minerva* 19 (Autumn 1981):347–407, and the full bibliography therein.

34. This story is outlined in Bulmer and Bulmer, "Philanthropy and Social Science in the 1920s."

35. Extract from Mr. Ruml's Statement of Policy to the Memorial, 1923, Presidents' Papers, 1889–1925, Box 61, Folder 13. The full statement is the General Memorandum by the Director, Laura Spelman Rockefeller Memorial Papers, Rockefeller Archive Center, Series II, Box 2, Folder 31.

36. Ibid.

37. Ibid.

38. Annual Report 1923–24 of the Local Community Research Committee (LCRC) to the President and Board of Trustees of the University of Chicago, 15 January 1924, p. 1. Social Science Research Committee Records, 1923–64, University of Chicago Archives. (Consulted in 1980 when located in the Archives of the Division of Social Sciences, University of Chicago [cited hereafter as "1126 Files"]).

39. For a detailed account, see Martin Bulmer, "The Early Institutional Establishment of Social Science Research: The Local Community Research Committee at the University of Chicago," *Minerva* 18 (Spring 1980):51–110.

40. Annual Report, 1923–24, of the LCRC.

41. Memorial Board of Trustees meeting 26 February 1924, extract from docket, in the Laura Spelman Rockefeller Memorial Policy in the Social Sciences, Merriam Papers, Box CLVII, Folder 11.

42. For a list of projects supported by the LCRC between 1923 and 1930, see Martin Bulmer, "The Rise of Empirical Research: Some Aspects of the Development of the Social Sciences at the University of Chicago," (Ph.D. diss., University of London, 1981), pp. 362–64, 370, 385–90. Full documentation is available in the Social Science Research Committee Records, 1923–64, University of Chicago Archives.

43. Laura Spelman Rockefeller Memorial, *Final Report* (New York: privately printed, 1933); copy in Ruml Papers, University of Chicago Archives, Series I, Box 5, Folder 3.

44. Of this, $1.1 million was given in 1927 for the construction and equipment of the Social Science Research Building, $725,000 for support of the School of Social Service Administration, $625,000 as general endowment (the interest from which would be used to hire additional staff) and $100,000 as a general subvention to the University of Chicago Press, plus other smaller grants. Bulmer and Bulmer, "Philanthropy and Social Science in the 1920s," pp. 389–90; "University of Chicago," Spelman Fund Papers, Rockefeller Archive Center, Series V, Box 6, Folder 860.

45. A detailed breakdown is given in Thomas Vernon Smith and Leonard D. White, eds., *Chicago: An Experiment in Social Science Research* (Chicago: University of Chicago Press, 1929), pp. 36–38.

46. Charles E. Merriam, Informal Memorandum on Social Research: University of Chicago, 2 May 1938, p. 5, in 1126 Files.

47. Fosdick, *The Story of the Rockefeller Foundation*, pp. 200–202; Bulmer and Bulmer, "Philanthropy and Social Science in the 1920s," pp. 378–80.

48. Bulmer, "The Early Institutional Establishment of Social Science Research," p. 92; Bulmer and Bulmer, "Philanthropy and Social Science in the 1920s," pp. 381–82.

49. Bulmer and Bulmer, "Philanthropy and Social Science in the 1920s," pp. 349–50.

50. Fosdick, *The Story of the Rockefeller Foundation*, pp. 207–8; Kohler, "The Management of Science" and "A Policy for the Advancement of Science."

51. Memorandum by Lawrence K. Frank reporting on a visit to Chicago, 9 March 1925, Laura Spelman Rockefeller Memorial Papers, Series III, subseries 6, Box 70, Folder 744.

52. Kohler, "The Management of Science," p. 282.

53. Docket prepared by the director for meeting of trustees, 1 March 1927, Laura Spelman Rockefeller Memorial Papers, Series I, Box 3, Folder 25, p. 6.

54. Charles E. Merriam, Local Community Research Committee Minutes, 9 February 1926, stating the original conception of the university and of Mr. Ruml for the research program; LCRC Three-Year Report, 1924–27, 1126 Files, p. 5.

55. Robert E. Park, quoted in the transcript of the Social Science Research Council Hanover Conference, 26 August–2 September 1926, session on the local research councils, p. 546, Merriam Papers, Box CXXXVI, Folder 2.

56. Not all graduate students in sociology, however, were supported in this way. Important exceptions (they received awards from the department rather than from the LCRC) included Louis Wirth and Herbert Blumer.

57. See Bulmer, "The Early Institutional Establishment of Social Science Research." For one example of the limitations placed by primitive research technology on the Chicago research program, see Robert J. Bursik, Jr., and Jim Webb, "Community Change and Patterns of Delinquency," *American Journal of Sociology* 88 (1982):24–42, esp. pp. 24–28.

58. The titles published in the Studies in Social Science series began in 1924 with *Non-Voting*, followed in 1926 by John P. Goode's *Geographic Background of Chicago* and Carroll Woody's *Chicago Primary of 1926*. In 1927 titles included Gosnell's *Getting Out the*

Vote, Chicago Civic Agencies, 1927, Helen Jeter's *Trends of Population in the Region of Chicago*, Leila Houghteling's *Income and Standard of Living of Unskilled Laborers in Chicago* (done under Edith Abbott's supervision), and Leonard D. White's *City Manager*. Later publications in the committee's series included: Herman C. Beyle's *Governmental Reporting in Chicago*, Claudius O. Johnson's *Carter Henry Harrison I: Political Leader*, and Vivien Palmer's *Field Studies in Sociology* in 1928; in 1929, Earl Beckner's *History of Labor Legislation in Illinois*, L. D. White's *Prestige Value of Public Employment in Chicago*, Edward A. Duddy's *Agriculture in the Chicago Region*, and T. V. Smith and L. D. White's edited collection, *Chicago: An Experiment in Social Science Research*; in 1930, Eugene Staley's *History of the Illinois State Federation of Labor*, L. D. White's *New Social Science* (a selection of addresses given at the opening of the new building), H. F. Gosnell's *Why Europe Votes*, and John Steadman's *Public Health Organization in the Chicago Region*; in 1931, William Brown's *Book and Job Printing in Chicago*, and E. W. Burgess and C. Newcomb's *Census Data of the City of Chicago, 1920* (not in the series). Details from Minutes of the Local Community Research Committee, 1126 Files, and the *University of Chicago Press: Catalogue of Books and Journals, 1891–1965* (Chicago: University of Chicago Press, 1967), p. 256.

59. Up to 1929 the University of Chicago Sociological Series included Robert E. Park and Ernest W. Burgess, *Introduction to the Science of Sociology* (1921); Nels Anderson, *The Hobo* (1923); R. E. Park et al., *The City* (1925); E. W. Burgess, ed., *The Urban Community*, Charles William Margold, *Sex Freedom and Social Control*, and the LCRC's *Social Base Map of Chicago* (all 1926); Lyford Edwards, *The Natural History of Revolution*, Ernest Mowrer, *Family Disorganization*, Frederic Thrasher, *The Gang* and *Map of Chicago's Gangland*, and Harry Emerson Wildes, *Social Currents in Japan* (all 1927); Ruth Shonle Cavan, *Suicide*, Ernest J. Hiller, *The Strike*, Ernest Mowrer, *Domestic Discord*, and Louis Wirth, *The Ghetto* (all 1928); E. W. Burgess, ed., *Personality and the Social Group*, Frances Donovan, *The Saleslady*, and Harvey Zorbaugh, *The Gold Coast and the Slum* (1929). Later titles in the early 1930s included Albert B. Blumenthal, *Small Town Stuff*, Paul G. Cressey, *The Taxi-Dance Hall*, E. Franklin Frazier, *The Negro Family in Chicago*, Pauline V. Young, *The Pilgrims of Russian Town* (all 1932), and Walter Reckless, *Vice in Chicago* (1933).

60. See Spelman Fund, University of Chicago file, Rockefeller Archive Center, Series V, Box 6, Folder 806. The sum of $4,500 per year for three years was paid from 1925 to 1928.

61. Annual Report of the LCRC to the Memorial, 1927–28, Merriam Papers, Box CLVIII, Folder 7.

62. Annual Report of the LCRC to the Memorial 1928–29, Laura Spelman Rockefeller Memorial Papers, Series III, subseries 6, Box 71, Folder 753, pp. 3–5.

63. Presidents' Papers, 1925–45, Budgets and Appointments, Sociology Department, 1925–30, various correspondence 1930.

64. After 1933, Marshall worked for the federal government, as vice-chairman of the National Labor Board and for the National Recovery Administration. Though an important figure at the University of Chicago during the 1920s, Marshall has left little mark on the history of Chicago economics compared to men such as Laughlin, Viner, Knight, Simons, or Henry Schultz.

65. For further details see Bulmer, "The Early Institutional Establishment of Social Science Research," pp. 88–91.

66. See Smith and White, eds., *Chicago*.

67. Raymond M. Hughes, *A Study of the Graduate Schools of America* (Oxford, Ohio: Miami University, 1925).

68. For further discussion, see Bulmer, "The Early Institutional Establishment of Social Science Research," pp. 102–8.

69. William F. Ogburn and Alexander Goldenweiser, eds., *The Social Sciences and Their Interrelationships* (Boston: Houghton Mifflin, 1927), p. 9.

70. See Kohler, "The Management of Science," p. 288.

71. Memorandum by L. K. Frank after visit to Chicago, 9 March 1925, Laura Spelman Rockefeller Memorial Papers, Series III, subseries 6, Box 70, Folder 744, p. 2.

72. Robert E. Park, quoted in the transcript of the Dartmouth conference, Hanover, N.H. of the SSRC, 1926, vol. 2, p. 445, copy in Merriam Papers, Box CXXXVI, Folder 2.

73. Lawrence K. Frank to Charles Merriam, 26 December 1928, Laura Spelman Rockefeller Memorial Papers, Series III, Box 56, Folder 602.

74. See Bulmer and Bulmer, "Philanthropy and Social Science in the 1920s," pp. 397–99.

75. See Barry D. Karl, *Executive Reorganization and Reform in the New Deal* (Cambridge, Mass.: Harvard University Press, 1963), esp. pp. 82, 112–26; C. Herman Pritchett, "1313: An Experiment in Propinquity," manuscript in Merriam Papers, Box CLIX, Folder 3.

76. Robert M. Hutchins, "Address of Dedication (of the Social Science Research Building, 1126 East 59th Street)", in Leonard D. White, ed., *The New Social Science* (Chicago: University of Chicago Press, 1930), p. 1.

77. See Bulmer, "The Early Institutional Establishment of Social Science Research," pp. 104–8.

78. "If cooperative research is possible at all on a large scale. . . . If social research has value. . . . If the type of organization of the social sciences here is useful. . . . If this building does not promote a better understanding of the social sciences, we shall know that there is something wrong"; Hutchins, "Address of Dedication," pp. 1–2.

79. Beardsley Ruml, "Recent Trends in Social Science," in White, *The New Social Science*, pp. 99–111, esp. 103–5.

80. Charles E. Merriam, "A Word in Conclusion: Speech Given at the Conclusion of the Dedication of the University of Chicago Social Science Building in 1929," Merriam Papers, Box CXX, Folder 4.

81. Paul F. Lazarsfeld, "An Episode in the History of Social Research: A Memoir," in Donald Fleming and Bernard Bailyn (eds.), *The Intellectual Migration: Europe and America, 1930–1960* (Cambridge, Mass.: Belknap Press, Harvard University, 1969), pp. 270–337. Allen H. Barton, "Paul Lazarsfeld and the Invention of the University Institute for Applied Social Research," in Burkhart Holzner and Jiri Nehnevajsa, eds., *Organizing for Social Research* (Cambridge, Mass.: Schenkman, 1982), pp. 17–83, is especially illuminating.

82. For a further discussion of the different forms taken by organized research in universities, see Martin Bulmer, "The Social Sciences: Social Science Research in the Modern University," in John W. Chapman, ed., *The Western University on Trial* (Berkeley: University of California Press, 1983), pp. 102–17; Rossi, "Researchers, Scholars and Policy-Makers"; and Peter H. Rossi, "Observations of the Organization of Social Research," in Richard O'Toole, ed., *The Organization, Management, and Tactics of Social Research* (Cambridge, Mass.: Schenkman, 1971), pp. 151–72.

Chapter 9

1. See Barry D. Karl, *Charles E. Merriam and the Study of Politics* (Chicago: University of Chicago Press, 1974), pp. 154 ff.

2. See T. V. Smith and Leonard D. White, eds., *Chicago: An Experiment in Social Science Research* (Chicago: University of Chicago Press, 1929), chap. 2.

3. Karl, *Charles E. Merriam*, pp. 154–55.

4. See Barney G. Glaser and Anselm Strauss, *The Discovery of Grounded Theory* (Chicago: Aldine, 1967), pp. vii, 15, for one representative statement.

5. Henrika Kuklick, "Boundary Maintenance in American Sociology: Limitations to Academic 'Professionalization,' " *Journal of the History of the Behavioral Sciences* 16 (1980):201–19, esp. p. 207.

6. Norbert Wiley, "The Rise and Fall of Dominating Theories in American Sociology," in *Contemporary Issues in Theory and Research*, ed. W. E. Snizek, et al. (Westport, Conn.: Greenwood, 1979), p. 56.

7. Paul Rock, *The Making of Symbolic Interactionism* (London: Macmillan; New York: Rowman & Littlefield, 1979), p. 5.

8. See Rosalie Wax, *Doing Field Work: Warnings and Advice* (Chicago: University of Chicago Press, 1971), pp. 38–41; Evan Thomas, "Herbert Blumer's Critique of *The Polish Peasant*: A Post-Mortem on the Life History Approach in Sociology," *Journal of the History of the Behavioral Sciences* 14 (1978):124–31; and Bernard N. Meltzer, John W. Petras, and Larry T. Reynolds, *Symbolic Interactionism: Genesis, Varieties, and Criticisms* (London: Routledge & Kegan Paul, 1975).

9. I.e., in the generalized images that today's practitioners of the discipline form of its history.

10. Edward A. Tiryakian, "The Significance of Schools in the Development of Sociology," in *Contemporary Issues*, ed. W. E. Snizek et al., p. 227.

11. See J. David Lewis and Richard L. Smith, *American Sociology and Pragmatism: Mead, Chicago Sociology, and Symbolic Interaction* (Chicago: University of Chicago Press, 1980).

12. With a few exceptions: see Otis Dudley Duncan, Jr., ed., *William F. Ogburn on Culture and Social Change* (Chicago: University of Chicago Press, 1964); Robert E. L. Faris, *Chicago Sociology, 1920–1932* (Chicago: University of Chicago Press, 1970), pp. 113–19; James F. Short, Jr., ed., *The Social Fabric of the Metropolis: Contributions of the Chicago School of Urban Sociology* (Chicago: University of Chicago Press, 1971), pp. xv–xviii; Anthony Oberschall, "The Institutionalization of American Sociology," in A. Oberschall, ed., *The Establishment of Empirical Sociology* (New York: Harper, 1972), pp. 238–39.

13. For example, the history of the *modern* social survey in the United States is far from clear, at least prior to the establishment of the Columbia University Bureau for Applied Social Research during World War II.

14. For an important attempt, see Frederick F. Stephan, "History of the Uses of Modern Sampling Procedures," *Journal of the American Statistical Association* 43 (1948):12–39. See also W. F. Maunder, *Sir Arthur Lyon Bowley, 1869–1957* (Exeter, U.K.: University of Exeter, 1972); William Kruskal and Frederick Mosteller, "Representative Sampling IV: The History of the Concept in Statistics, 1895–1939," *International Statistical Review* 48 (1980):169–95; Joseph W. Duncan and William C. Shelton, *Revolution in United States Government Statistics, 1926–1976* (Washington, D.C.: U.S. Government Printing Office, 1976), pp. 32–73.

15. Philip M. Hauser has recalled, in a personal communication, traveling in the early 1930s with Park to a committee meeting outside Chicago. They fell to discussing L. L. Thurstone's remark that he only read journal articles if they contained tables. Park observed that Thurstone reminded him of a little child sitting on a pot reading a picture book upside down.

16. Louis Wirth, "A Bibliography of the Urban Community," in Robert E. Park and Ernest W. Burgess, *The City* (Chicago: University of Chicago Press, 1925), pp. 225–28.

17. Robert E. Park, "The Urban Community as a Spatial Pattern and a Moral Order," in Ernest W. Burgess, ed., *The Urban Community* (Chicago: University of Chicago Press, 1926), p. 4.

18. Helen McGill, "Land Values: An Ecological Factor in the Community of South Chicago" (M.A. thesis, University of Chicago, 1927).

19. Helen McGill Hughes, "On Becoming a Sociologist," *Journal of the History of Sociology* 3 (Fall–Winter 1980–81):34.

20. Emory S. Bogardus to Fred H. Matthews, 12 September 1968, from Matthews Folder, University of Chicago Archives.

21. Ernest W. Burgess, "Research in Urban Society: A Long View," in E. W. Burgess and Donald J. Bogue, eds., *Contributions to Urban Sociology* (Chicago: University of Chicago Press, 1964), pp. 3–4.

22. Ibid., pp. 5–6.

23. University of Chicago Local Community Research Committee, *Social Research Base Map of the City of Chicago* (Chicago: University of Chicago Press, 1926). See also Erle F. Young, "The Social Base Map," *Journal of Applied Sociology (Sociology and Social Research)*, January–February 1925.

24. Vivien Palmer, *Field Studies in Sociology: A Student's Manual* (Chicago: University of Chicago Press, 1928), p. 185.

25. Hughes, "On Becoming a Sociologist," p. 33.

26. All of these monographs were based on graduate work: Walter C. Reckless, "The Natural History of Vice Areas in Chicago" (Ph.D. diss., University of Chicago, 1925); Frederic M. Thrasher, "The Gang: A Study of 1,313 Gangs in Chicago" (Ph.D. diss., University of Chicago, 1926); Ruth Shonle (Cavan), "Suicide: A Study of Personal Disorganization" (Ph.D. diss., University of Chicago, 1926); Ernest R. Mowrer, "Family Disorganization: An Introduction to a Sociological Analysis" (Ph.D. diss., University of Chicago, 1924). See Ernest R. Mowrer interview with James T. Carey, 17 April 1972, Carey interviews, University of Chicago Archives.

27. E. W. Burgess, "Urban Areas," in Smith and White, *Chicago*, p. 137.

28. Ibid., pp. 136–37.

29. Minutes of the Local Community Research Committee, University of Chicago, 30 June 1925, Social Science Research Committee, 1923–64, University of Chicago Archives.

30. Minutes of the LCRC, 29 October 1929.

31. See Milla A. Alihan, *Social Ecology: A Critical Analysis* (New York: Columbia University Press, 1938), and W. S. Robinson, "Ecological Correlation and the Behavior of Individuals," *American Sociological Review* 15 (1950):351–57.

32. Ernest W. Burgess, undated manuscript entitled "Family and Social Data by Local Communities," circa 1928, Ernest W. Burgess Papers, University of Chicago Archives, Box 192, Folder 5, p. 1.

33. See Hyman Alterman, *Counting People: The Census in History* (New York: Harcourt Brace & World, 1969), pp. 238–39; A. Ross Eckler, *The Bureau of the Census* (New York: Praeger, 1972), pp. 56–57.

34. "Census Tracts in American Cities," extract from *Census Tract Manual* (Washington, D.C.: U.S. Bureau of the Census, 1934), Burgess Papers, Box 3, Folder 12.

35. Minutes of the LCRC, 1924–25.

36. Letter from director, U.S. Bureau of the Census to Burgess, 16 June 1924, Burgess Papers, Box 3, Folder 7.

37. E. W. Burgess and Charles Newcomb, *Census Data of the City of Chicago, 1920* (Chicago: University of Chicago Press, 1931).

38. Ibid., p. 3. For an account of the drawing of ward boundaries and the power of ward politicians, see Harold F. Gosnell, *Machine Politics: Chicago Model* (Chicago: University of Chicago Press, 1937), pp. 27–34.

39. Organization Rules, Chicago Census Committee, adopted 14 May 1924, Burgess Papers, Box 3, Folder 12.

40. Minutes of meeting of Chicago Census Committee, 6 June 1924, Burgess Papers, Box 3, Folder 12.

41. Burgess and Newcomb, *Census Data of the City of Chicago, 1920*, p. 3.

42. Ernest W. Burgess and Charles Newcomb, eds., *Census Data of the City of Chicago, 1933* (Chicago: University of Chicago Press, 1933).

43. Burgess, "Research in Urban Society: A Long View," pp. 7–8.

44. Charles Newcomb and Richard Lang, eds., *Census Data of the City of Chicago, 1934* (Chicago: University of Chicago Press, 1934).

45. Louis Wirth and Margaret Furez, eds., Introduction, *Local Community Fact Book* (Chicago: Chicago Recreation Commission, 1938).

46. Louis Wirth and Eleanor H. Bernert, eds., *Local Community Fact Book of Chicago, 1940* (Chicago: University of Chicago Press, 1949); Philip M. Hauser and Evelyn M. Kitagawa, eds., *Local Community Fact Book of Chicago, 1950* (Chicago Community Inventory, University of Chicago, 1953); E. M. Kitagawa and Karl E. Taeuber, eds., *Local Community Fact Book, Chicago Metropolitan Area, 1960* (Chicago Community Inventory, University of Chicago, 1963). No book was produced for the 1970 census, but a Chicago consortium is working on a volume based on 1980 census data. Howard S. Becker has commented on how well provided Chicago is with such data by comparison with other cities such as San Francisco, in his Introduction to Clifford R. Shaw, *The Jack-Roller* (Chicago: University of Chicago Press, 1976), pp. vii–viii.

47. Personal communication from Dr. Frederick G. Bohme, chief of the census history staff, U.S. Bureau of the Census, September 1981.

48. Dedication of Kitagawa and Taeuber, *Local Community Fact Book, Chicago Metropolitan Area, 1960.*

49. Ernest W. Burgess, "The Determination of Gradients in the Growth of the City," *Proceedings of the American Sociological Society* 21 (1927):178–84.

50. Ernest W. Burgess, "Residential Segregation in American Cities," *Annals of the American Academy of Political and Social Science* 140 (1928):105–15.

51. See E. W. Burgess, "Is Prediction Feasible in Social Work? An Inquiry Based on a Sociological Study of Parole Records," *Social Forces* 7 (1929):534.

52. E. W. Burgess and C. Tibbitts, "Factors Making for Success or Failure on Parole," *Journal of Criminal Law and Criminology* 19(2) (July–August 1928):239–306.

53. Clifford R. Shaw, Frederick M. Zorbaugh, Henry D. McKay, Leonard S. Cottrell, *Delinquency Areas: A Study of the Geographic Distribution of School Truants, Juvenile Delinquents, and Adult Offenders in Chicago* (Chicago: University of Chicago Press, 1929).

54. Clifford R. Shaw and Henry D. McKay, *Social Factors in Juvenile Delinquency*, National Commission on Law Observance and Enforcement (Wickersham Committee), *Report on the Causes of Crime* (Washington, D.C.: U.S. Government Printing Office, 1931), vol. 2.

55. See James F. Short, Jr., ed., *Delinquency, Crime, and Society* (Chicago: University of Chicago Press, 1976), pp. 1–19; James F. Short, Jr., Introduction to Clifford R. Shaw and Henry D. McKay, *Juvenile Delinquency and Urban Areas* (1942; rev. ed., Chicago: University of Chicago Press, 1969), pp. xxv–liv.

56. Ernest W. Burgess, "Statistics and Case Studies as Methods of Sociological Research," *Sociology and Social Research* 12 (1927):120.

57. This is confirmed in the Carey interviews with Leonard S. Cottrell, Jr., Walter Reckless, Ruth Shonle Cavan, and Ernest R. Mowrer.

58. *Official Publications of the University of Chicago, 1914* (Chicago: University of Chicago, 1914).

59. Helen F. Hohman, "Biography of James Alfred Field" in James A. Field, *Essays on Population* (Chicago: University of Chicago Press, 1931), pp. xix–xxviii.

60. Dwaine Marvick, Introduction in *Harold D. Lasswell on Political Sociology* (Chicago: University of Chicago Press, 1978), p. 19.

61. *Official Publications of the University of Chicago*, circular of the departments of political economy, political science, history, sociology and anthropology, 1911.

62. *Official Publications*, 1913.

63. *Official Publications*, 1922.

64. Minutes of the LCRC, 15 October 1924.

65. In interviews in 1972 with James T. Carey, Carey interviews.

66. Ernest R. Mowrer interviewed by James T. Carey, 17 April 1972.

67. Personal communication to the author, 26 February 1980.

68. Interview by the author with Harold F. Gosnell, 23 March 1982.

69. See Albert Somit and Joseph Tanenhaus, *The Development of American Political Science: From Burgess to Behavioralism* (Boston: Allyn & Bacon, 1967), pp. 109–33; Dwight Waldo, "Political Science: Tradition, Discipline, Profession, Science, Enterprise," in Fred I. Greenstein and Nelson W. Polsby, eds., *Handbook of Political Science* (Reading, Mass.: Addison-Wesley, 1975) 1:41–7; Heinz Eulau, "Understanding Political Life in America," in Charles M. Bonjean et al., eds., *Social Science in America* (Austin: University of Texas Press, 1976), p. 114.

70. Charles E. Merriam and Harold F. Gosnell, *Non-Voting: Causes and Methods of Control* (Chicago: University of Chicago Press, 1924); Harold F. Gosnell, *Getting Out the Vote: An Experiment in the Stimulation of Voting* (Chicago: University of Chicago Press, 1927).

71. Charles E. Merriam, *New Aspects of Politics* (3d ed.; Chicago: University of Chicago Press, 1970).

72. L. L. Thurstone, "Round Table on Politics and Psychology," Report on the Second National Conference on the Science of Politics, Chicago, 1924, *American Political Science Review* 19 (1925):111 ff.

73. Interview with Harold F. Gosnell, 23 March 1982.

74. Ibid.

75. Published as *Boss Platt and His New York Machine* (Chicago: University of Chicago Press, 1924).

76. Harold F. Gosnell, "Some Practical Applications of Psychology in Government," *American Journal of Sociology* 28 (1921):735–43.

77. Personal communication to the author, 26 February 1980.

78. Harold F. Gosnell, *Machine Politics: Chicago Model* (Chicago: University of Chicago Press, 1937), p. xxii.

79. Merriam and Gosnell, *Non-Voting*.

80. Somit and Tanenhaus, *The Development of American Political Science*, p. 127.

81. Ibid.; Richard A. Brody and Charles N. Brownstein, "Experimentation and Simulation," in Greenstein and Polsby, eds., *Handbook of Political Science*, 7:211–63.

82. Harold F. Gosnell, "Non-Naturalization: A Study in Political Assimilation," *American Journal of Sociology* 33 (1928):930–39, and "Characteristics of the Non-Naturalized," *American Journal of Sociology* 34 (1929):847–55.

83. Gosnell, *Getting Out the Vote*, p. 16.

84. "Instructions for Interviewing Adult Persons in Chicago," and "Explanations to Adult Persons Interviewed," Merriam Papers, Box CXII, Folder 13. The organization of the field research for the nonnaturalization study is discussed further in Martin Bulmer, "The Rise of Empirical Social Research: Some Aspects of the Development of the Social Sciences at the University of Chicago, 1915–1930" (Ph.D. diss., University of London, 1981), pp. 291–96.

85. Letter from Gosnell to Merriam, 13 October 1924, Merriam Papers, Box XXX, Folder 15.

86. Personal communication from Harold Gosnell to the author, 26 February 1980.

87. See Kuklick, "Boundary Maintenance in American Sociology," p. 207.

88. Presidents' Papers, 1925–45, Budgets and Appointments, Sociology and Anthropology, 1925–1930, University of Chicago Archives.

89. Otis Dudley Duncan, Introduction to O. D. Duncan, ed., *William F. Ogburn on Culture and Social Change* (Chicago: University of Chicago Press, 1964), pp. vii–xxii.

90. Ellsworth Faris to William F. Ogburn, 30 June 1926, Ogburn Papers, University of Chicago Archives, Box XXX. Merriam quoted Ogburn's voting studies of 1914 and 1916 favorably in *New Aspects of Politics*, p. 207.

91. William F. Ogburn to Ellsworth Faris, 21 July 1926, Ogburn Papers, Box XXX, p. 2.

92. Ibid., p. 1.

93. Minutes of meeting, 14 October 1926, in the Minutes of the Meetings of the Department of Sociology, 14 October 1926 to 23 August 1939, University of Chicago Archives.

94. Ellsworth Faris to Vice-President Frederick C. Woodward 14 December 1926 (first letter), Presidents' Papers, 1925–45, Budgets and Appointments, Sociology and Anthropology, 1925–1929. Ogburn was receiving a salary of $6,000 at Columbia and Chicago offered him $7,000. At the time, Faris received $5,000 and Park (for two-thirds of the year) $3,333. Even at the height of his fame, Park was never much of a financial burden upon the University of Chicago. The salary differential in Ogburn's favor also showed the seriousness with which the offer was made.

95. "Some four years ago [1922], under the auspices of the American Association of Colleges, the University of Chicago was voted to be the strongest graduate institution in America. Eight departments here were given first place, and one of these eight was our own. . . . The choice for first place came out as follows: Chicago 27, Columbia 12, Harvard 3"; Faris to Woodward, 14 December 1926 (second letter), p. 1, quoting Raymond M. Hughes, *A Study of the Graduate Schools of America* (Oxford, Ohio: Miami University, 1925).

96. Copy in the papers of the Society for Social Research, University of Chicago Archives.

Chapter 10

1. *Official Publications of the University of Chicago* (Chicago: University of Chicago Press, 1927).

2. Ibid.

3. *Official Publications* (1928).

4. Information from Philip M. Hauser Papers, University of Chicago Archives, Box 24, Folder 2, Notes on Sociology courses 401 and 402, circa 1930.

5. See Barbara Laslett, "William Fielding Ogburn and the Institutionalization of a Scientific Sociology" (University of Southern California, 1982), p. 22.

6. Interview with Leonard S. Cottrell, Jr., by James T. Carey, 28 March 1972, Carey Interviews, University of Chicago Archives.

7. Interview with R. E. L. Faris by James T. Carey, 24 May 1972.

8. For example, Clark Tibbitts, "Majority Votes and the Business Cycle," *American Journal of Sociology* 36 (1931):596–606.

9. Copy in Charles E. Merriam Papers, University of Chicago Archives, Box LXXXIX, Folder 15.

10. William H. Sewell, "Thomas C. McCormick, 1892–1954," *American Sociological Review* 20 (1955):237–38.

11. John Henry Mueller and Karl F. Schuessler, *Statistical Reasoning in Sociology* (Boston: Houghton Mifflin, 1961). Alfred R. Lindesmith and Frank R. Westie, "John Henry Mueller, 1895–1965," *American Sociologist* 1 (1966):88–89.

12. Interview with John Dollard by James T. Carey, 14 April 1972.

13. Biographical information from W. Edwards Deming, "Frederick Franklin Stephan, 1903–1971," *American Statistician* 25 (October 1971):47–48.

14. See chap. 9, n. 14. Frederick F. Stephan, "Practical Problems of Sampling Procedure," *American Sociological Review* 1 (1936):569–80.

15. When he died in 1971, an obituary appeared in *The American Statistician* but not in *The American Sociologist*. His Princeton chair was in social statistics.

16. Interview with John Dollard by James T. Carey, 14 April 1972.

17. Personal communications to the author from Philip M. Hauser.

18. Samuel A. Stouffer, Courses Taken by S. A. Stouffer at the University of Chicago, Merriam Papers, Box CVIII, Folder 3.

19. See William F. Ogburn to Ellsworth Faris, 21 July 1926, Ogburn Papers, Box XXX.

20. Barry D. Karl, *Charles E. Merriam and the Study of Politics* (Chicago: University of Chicago Press, 1974), p. 154.

21. President's Research Committee on Social Trends, *Recent Social Trends in the United States*, 2 vols. (New York: McGraw-Hill, 1933). See also B. Karl, "Presidential Planning and Social Science Research: Mr. Hoover's Experts," *Perspectives in American History* 3 (1969):347–409, and Martin Bulmer, "The Methodology of Early Social Indicator Research: William F. Ogburn and *Recent Social Trends*, 1933," *Social Indicators Research* 13 (1983):109–30, which includes a previously unpublished account of the methodology used in *Recent Social Trends*.

22. See Michael Carley, *Social Measurement and Social Indicators* (London: Allen & Unwin, 1981).

23. See the publications listed in Otis Dudley Duncan, *William F. Ogburn on Culture and Social Change* (Chicago: University of Chicago Press, 1964), pp. 354–55, 357.

24. William F. Ogburn and Nell S. Talbot, "A Measurement of the Factors in the Presidential Election of 1928," *Social Forces* 8 (1929):175–83.

25. Mordechai J. B. Ezekiel, *Methods of Correlation Analysis* (New York: John Wiley, 1930).

26. Samuel A. Stouffer, "Problems in the Application of Correlation to Sociology," *Journal of the American Statistical Association* 29 (March 1934), Supplement pp. 52–58, reprinted in S. A. Stouffer, *Social Research to Test Ideas* (Glencoe, Ill.: Free Press, 1962), pp. 264–70.

27. See Allan J. Lichtman, *Prejudice and Old Politics: The Presidential Election of 1928* (Chapel Hill, N.C.: University of North Carolina Press, 1979), pp. 27–34, 40, 94.

28. L. Leon Thurstone, "Autobiographical Statement," in Edward G. Boring et al., eds., *A History of Psychology in Autobiography* (Worcester, Mass.: Clark University Press, 1952), 4:295–321; Dorothy C. Adkins, "L. L. Thurstone," *International Encyclopaedia of the Social Sciences*, ed. David L. Sills (New York: Macmillan and Free Press, 1968), 16:22–25.

29. Annual Report of the Local Community Research Committee, 1927, in Social Science Research Council papers, 1923–1964, University of Chicago Archives.

30. See L. L. Thurstone, "Attitudes Can Be Measured," *American Journal of Sociology* 33 (1928):529–54, reprinted with seven other papers on attitude measurement written between 1928 and 1931 in L. L. Thurstone, *The Measurement of Values* (Chicago: University of Chicago Press, 1959), pp. 215–33. For a contemporary view, see also Harold Gosnell, "The Technique of Measurement," in T. V. Smith and Leonard D. White, eds., *Chicago: An Experiment in Social Science Research* (Chicago: University of Chicago Press, 1929), pp. 107–12.

31. Thurstone, "Autobiographical Statement," pp. 306–7.

32. Thurstone's significance in the context of evolving social science research on attitudes is discussed in Donald Fleming, "Attitude: The History of a Concept," *Perspectives in American History* 1 (1967):287–365.

33. Ibid., p. 342.

34. L. L. Thurstone and E. J. Chave, *The Measurement of Attitude: A Psychophysical Method and Some Experiments with a Scale for Measuring Attitude Toward the Church* (Chicago: University of Chicago Press, 1929).

35. See note 30.

36. Thurstone, "Autobiographical Statement," p. 311.

37. Adkins, "L. L. Thurstone." See also Harry H. Harman, *Modern Factor Analysis* (Chicago: University of Chicago Press, 1969), pp. 3–10.

38. Leonard D. White, *The Prestige Factor in Public Employment* (Chicago: University of Chicago Press, 1929).

39. There is a copy in the Merriam Papers, Box CXII, Folder 13.

40. White, *The Prestige Factor in Public Employment*. See the discussion in H. Gosnell, "The Technique of Measurement," pp. 104–6.

41. Thurstone, "Autobiographical Statement," p. 320.

42. S. A. Stouffer, Courses Taken by S. A. Stouffer at the University of Chicago, Merriam Papers, Box CVIII, Folder 3.

43. *Official Publications* (1929).

44. Samuel A. Stouffer, "An Experimental Comparison of Statistical and Case History Methods of Attitude Research" (Ph.D. diss., University of Chicago, 1930).

45. Carroll Wooddy and S. A. Stouffer, "Local Option and Public Opinion," *American Journal of Sociology* 36 (1930):175–205.

46. Notably "Intervening Opportunities: A Theory Relating Mobility and Distance," *American Sociological Review* 5 (1940):845–67.

47. Herbert H. Hyman, "Samuel Andrew Stouffer, 1900–1960," in John A. Garraty, ed., *Dictionary of American Biography, Supplement 6: 1956–1960* (New York: Scribner's, 1980), p. 605. Other biographical information from M. Brewster Smith, "Samuel A. Stouffer," *International Encyclopaedia of the Social Sciences*, 15:277–80; Donald Young, "S. A. Stouffer," *American Sociological Review* 26 (1960):106–7.

48. See bibliography in Samuel A. Stouffer, *Social Research to Test Ideas* (Glencoe, Ill.: Free Press, 1962), pp. 301–3, esp. for 1933 and 1934.

49. Biographical information from Karl A. Fox, "Henry Schultz," *International Encyclopaedia of the Social Sciences*, 14:65–66, and H. G. Lewis, "Henry Schultz, 1893–1938," *Dictionary of American Biography,* Supplement 2 (New York: Scribner's, 1958), pp. 599–60.

50. *Official Publications* (1927).

51. Theodore O. Yntema, "Henry Schultz: His Contributions to Economics and Statistics," *Journal of Political Economy* 47 (1939):154–55.

52. Anthony Oberschall, "The Institutionalization of American Sociology" in A. Oberschall, ed., *The Establishment of Empirical Sociology* (New York: Harper & Row, 1972), pp. 225–32; Robert E. L. Faris, *Chicago Sociology, 1920–1932* (Chicago: University of Chicago Press, 1970), p. 127.

53. Yntema, "Henry Schultz," pp. 153–62; Harold Hotelling, "The Work of Henry Schultz," *Econometrica* 7 (1939):97–103; Oscar Lange, Francis McIntyre, and Theodore Yntema, eds., *Studies in Mathematical Economics and Econometrics in Memory of Henry Schultz* (Chicago: University of Chicago Press, 1942).

54. Henry Schultz quoted in Yntema, "Henry Schultz," pp. 153–54.

55. George K. K. Link, "Henry Schultz—Friend," in Lange, McIntyre, and Yntema, eds., *Studies in Mathematical Economics*, pp. 3–10. See also Paul H. Douglas, "Henry Schultz as Colleague," *Econometrica* 7 (1939):104–6.

56. Wooddy and Stouffer, "Local Option and Public Opinion."

57. See Harold Lasswell, *Propaganda Technique in the World War* (New York: Alfred A. Knopf, 1927).

58. Interview with Harold F. Gosnell by the author, 23 March 1982. See also Harold Gosnell, "Statisticians and Political Scientists," *American Political Science Review* 27 (1933):392–403.

59. Harold D. Lasswell, "The Cross-Disciplinary Manifold: The Chicago Prototype," in Albert Lepawsky and Edward Buelring, eds., *Search for World Order* (New York: Appleton-Century-Crofts, 1971), p. 421.

60. Thurstone, "Autobiographical Statement," pp. 313–16.

61. See William F. Ogburn, Memorandum on Research in Quantitative Methods, late 1920s, Ogburn Papers, Box XXXVI, Folder 1, pp. 2–3; Thurstone, "Autobiographical Statement," p. 320.

62. Journals of W. F. Ogburn, Ogburn Papers, Box LXI.

63. William F. Ogburn, "Folkways of a Scientific Sociology," in *Studies in Quantitative*

and Cultural Sociology: Papers Presented at the Annual Meeting of the A.S.S., 1929 (Chicago: University of Chicago Press, 1930), p. 2.

64. Ibid., p. 6.

65. Ibid., pp. 10–11.

66. Mark C. Smith, "Robert Lynd and Consumerism in the 1930s," *Journal of the History of Sociology* 2 (Fall–Winter, 1979–80):102–4.

67. Ibid., p. 102.

68. Ogburn, "Folkways of a Scientific Sociology," p. 10.

69. Ibid., p. 6–7.

70. First Report of the Committee on Symbolism for the Social Science Research Building, 12 January 1929, Ogburn Papers, Box XXXI.

71. William Thomson (later Lord Kelvin), "Electrical Units of Measurement," *Popular Lectures and Addresses* (London: Macmillan, 1889), 1:73–74.

72. Karl, *Charles E. Merriam*, p. 155.

73. Floyd N. House, "Statistical Methods and Case Studies," *The Development of Sociology* (New York: McGraw-Hill, 1936), p. 375.

74. See Jennifer Platt, "Whatever Happened to the Case Study?" (University of Sussex, 1981).

75. Charles H. Cooley, "Case Study of Small Institutions as a Method of Research," in Ernest W. Burgess, ed., *Personality and the Social Group* (Chicago: University of Chicago Press, 1929), p. 183–90.

76. Herbert Blumer, "Method in Social Psychology" (Ph.D. diss., University of Chicago, 1928).

77. See William F. Ogburn, "Sociology and Statistics," in W. F. Ogburn and Alexander Goldenweiser, eds., *The Social Sciences and Their Interrelationships* (Boston: Houghton Mifflin, 1927), pp. 378–92.

78. *Bulletin* of the Society for Social Research, 1928–29, in the papers of the Society for Social Research, University of Chicago Archives.

79. In a personal communication to the author.

80. Leonard S. Cottrell, Jr., "Ernest Watson Burgess, 1886–1966: Contributions in the Field of Marriage and the Family," *American Sociologist* 2 (1967):147.

81. Interview with Leonard S. Cottrell, Jr., by James T. Carey, 28 March 1972.

82. Ernest W. Burgess, Notes on the life history record, late 1920s, Ernest W. Burgess Papers, University of Chicago Archives, Box 32, Folder 3, p. 1.

83. See James Bennett, *Oral History and Delinquency: The Rhetoric of Criminology* (Chicago: University of Chicago Press, 1981), esp. pp. 165–210 and 277–82.

84. See Clifford Shaw, *The Jack-Roller* (Chicago: University of Chicago Press, 1930), chap. 1 and the discussion by E. W. Burgess, pp. 185 ff., and Clifford Shaw, *The Natural History of a Delinquent Career* (Chicago: University of Chicago Press, 1930), Editor's Preface and the discussion by E. W. Burgess, pp. 235 ff.

85. Paul G. Cressey, Report to the Local Community Research Committee, autumn quarter 1925, on projects in process in sociology, Merriam Papers, Box CXXII, Folder 10, and Paul G. Cressey, Report on summer's work with Juvenile Protection Association of Chicago, circa 1925, and other documents, Burgess Papers, Box 149, Folder 5.

86. House, "Statistical Methods and Case Studies," p. 372, n. 1.

87. Ernest W. Burgess, "Statistics and Case Studies as Methods of Sociological Research," *Sociology and Social Research* 12 (1927):109.

88. Ibid., p. 120.

89. Stouffer, "An Experimental Comparison of Statistical and Case History Methods of Attitude Research," p. 22.

90. See Ruth Shonle Cavan, Philip M. Hauser, and Samuel A. Stouffer, "Note on the Statistical Treatment of Life History Material," *Social Forces* 9 (1931):200–203; Ruth

Shonle Cavan, "Interviewing for Life History Material," *American Journal of Sociology* 35 (1929):100–115.

91. Samuel A. Stouffer, "Sociology and Sampling," in Luther L. Bernard, ed., *The Fields and Methods of Sociology* (New York: Farrar & Rinehart, 1934), pp. 486–87.

92. Arthur Evans Wood, "Charles Horton Cooley: An Appreciation," *American Journal of Sociology* 35 (1930):710.

93. Interview with John Dollard by James T. Carey, 14 April 1972.

94. Beardsley Ruml to William F. Ogburn, 11 July 1944, Ruml Papers, Series 1, Box 1, Folder 4.

95. John Dollard, "The Changing Functions of the American Family" (Ph.D. diss., University of Chicago, 1931).

96. Interview with John Dollard by James T. Carey, 14 April 1972.

97. John Dollard, *Criteria for the Life History* (New Haven, Conn.: Yale University Press, 1935, and *Caste and Class in a Southern Town* (New Haven, Conn.: Yale University Press, 1937; 3d ed., New York: Anchor Books, 1957), p. 39.

98. The point was made by Burgess in "Statistics and Case Studies as Methods of Sociological Research," pp. 119–20.

99. William G. Ogburn, "Statistics and Art," *Journal of the American Statistical Association* 27 (March 1932):6.

100. Interview with Everett Stonequist by James T. Carey, 15 April 1972.

101. Duncan, Introduction to *William F. Ogburn*, pp. x–xi, xx–xxi.

102. Interview with Antony S. Stephan by James T. Carey, 20 March 1972.

103. W. F. Ogburn to Frank H. Hankins, Smith College, 30 April 1930, Ogburn Papers, Box XXX.

104. Interview with Herbert Blumer by James T. Carey, 22 May 1972.

105. Edward Shils, in a personal communication to the author.

106. For a more elaborate discussion, see Martin Bulmer, "Quantification and Chicago Sociology," *Journal of the History of the Behavioral Sciences* 17 (1981):312–31.

107. Robert Alun Jones and Sidney Kronus, "Professional Sociologists and the History of Sociology: A Survey of Recent Opinion," *Journal of the History of the Behavioral Sciences* 12 (1976):3–13.

Chapter 11

1. The same is true of intellectual history. The history of the social sciences tends to be written in terms of the history of particular disciplines. Such tunnel vision has benefits, but it also has limitations. The influences of disciplines upon one another, and the cross-cutting ties, which link between disciplines as well as within them, tend to be lost sight of. Thus, there is no reference to Park in the index of Barry D. Karl, *Charles E. Merriam and the Study of Politics* (Chicago: University of Chicago Press, 1974), nor to Merriam in the index of Fred H. Matthews, *Quest for an American Sociology: Robert E. Park and the Chicago School* (Montreal: McGill-Queens University Press, 1977).

2. Harold D. Lasswell, "The Cross-Disciplinary Manifold: The Chicago Prototype," in Albert Lepawsky and Edward Buelring, eds., *Search for World Order* (New York: Appleton-Century-Crofts, 1971), pp. 416–28.

3. Everett Hughes, in a personal communication (14 February 1978), writes of Park, Merriam, and their contemporaries "all living in that university neighborhood in Chicago. They had their lunch in the Quadrangle [faculty] Club. They saw and argued with one another in seminars and faculty meetings. Most of them walked to work."

4. Lewis A. Coser, *Masters of Sociological Thought: Ideas in Historical and Social Context* (2d ed.; New York: Harcourt Brace Jovanovich, 1977), pp. 292, 300–301.

5. Ibid., pp. 542–43, 545.

6. Robert E. Park, "The City: Suggestions for the Investigation of Human Behavior in the Urban Environment," in Robert E. Park, Ernest W. Burgess, and Roderick D. McKenzie, *The City* (1925; Chicago: University of Chicago Press, 1967; first published as an article in the *American Journal of Sociology* in 1915), pp. 29–30.

7. Personal communication to the author, 14 February 1978.

8. James T. Carey, *Sociology and Public Affairs: The Chicago School* (Beverly Hills: Sage, 1975), pp. 159–63.

9. Interview with Ernest R. Mowrer by James T. Carey, 17 April 1972, transcripts of the Carey interviews, University of Chicago Archives.

10. Interview with Herbert Blumer by James T. Carey, 22 May 1972, transcripts of the Carey interviews.

11. Lasswell, "The Cross-Disciplinary Manifold," p. 417.

12. George K. K. Link, "Henry Schultz—Friend," in Oscar Lange, Francis McIntyre, and Theodore O. Yntema, eds., *Studies in Mathematical Economics and Econometrics in Memory of Henry Schultz* (Chicago: University of Chicago Press, 1942), pp. 3–10.

13. Edward Shils, "Some Academics, Mainly at Chicago," *American Scholar* 50 (Spring 1981):181.

14. Lasswell, "The Cross-Disciplinary Manifold," pp. 424–25.

15. See Karl, *Charles E. Merriam*, pp. 143–54.

16. See Dwaine Marvick, "Introduction: Context, Problems, and Methods," in D. Marvick, ed., *Harold D. Lasswell on Political Sociology* (Chicago: University of Chicago Press, 1977), pp. 15–35.

17. Interview with Harold E. Gosnell by the author, 23 March 1982. In 1932 Lasswell gave a series of lectures in which he sought to reconcile Marx and Freud by a conceptual analysis of world revolutionary forces. These lectures formed the core of *World Politics and Personal Insecurity* (New York: McGraw-Hill, 1935).

18. *World Politics and Personal Insecurity*, p. 25. Lasswell's main books published while at Chicago, besides *World Politics and Personal Insecurity*, were *Propaganda Technique in the World War* (New York: Alfred A. Knopf, 1927) based on his dissertation; *Psychopathology and Politics* (Chicago: University of Chicago Press, 1930); *World Politics and Personal Insecurity* (New York: McGraw-Hill, 1935); and *Politics: Who Gets What, When, How* (New York: Whittlesey House, McGraw-Hill, 1936).

19. Shils, "Some Academics, Mainly at Chicago," pp. 194–95.

20. Charles E. Merriam to Beardsley Ruml, 6 May 1925, Charles E. Merriam Papers, University of Chicago Archives, Box XXXIX, Folder 10.

21. Made up of $620,000 for building, $65,000 for equipment, and $315,000 to provide for permanent maintenance. Document headed "Advance of Man in a New Age," submission by Local Community Research Committee of the University of Chicago to the Laura Spelman Rockefeller Memorial, 1927, Presidents' Papers, 1925–45, University of Chicago Archives, Box 109, Folder 9, p. 32.

22. Ibid., pp. 30–31. For a full account, see Martin Bulmer, "The Early Institutional Establishment of Social Science Research: The Local Community Research Committee at the University of Chicago, 1923–30," *Minerva* 18 (Spring 1980):94–98.

23. Local Community Research Committee, Minutes, 19 October 1928. Papers of the Social Science Research Committee, University of Chicago Archives (consulted in 1126 Files).

24. The *American Journal of Sociology*, the *Journal of Political Economy*, the *International Journal of Ethics*, the *Social Service Review*, the *Journal of Modern History*, and the *University of Chicago Journal of Business*.

25. Local Community Research Committee, Minutes, 19 October 1928.

26. Karl, *Charles E. Merriam*, pp. 154 ff.

27. William F. Ogburn Papers, Special Collections Department, Joseph Regenstein Library, University of Chicago, Box XXXI.

28. Local Community Research Committee, Minutes, 29 October 1929.

29. Personal communication to the author from Edward Shils.

30. Letter from Fay Cooper Cole to Acting President Frederick Woodward, 26 November 1928, reproduced in George W. Stocking, Jr., *Anthropology at Chicago* (Chicago: Joseph Regenstein Library, University of Chicago, 1979), p. 16.

31. Dorothy Ross, "The Development of the Social Sciences," in Alexandra Oleson and John Voss, eds., *The Organization of Knowledge in Modern America, 1860–1920* (Baltimore: Johns Hopkins University Press, 1979), pp. 125–30.

32. William F. Ogburn and Alexander Goldenweiser, *The Social Sciences and Their Interrelationships* (Boston: Houghton Mifflin, 1927).

33. Ibid., p. 9.

34. "Graduate Study and 'The Chicago School of Politics': Interviews with Gabriel A. Almond and David B. Truman," *News for Teachers of Political Science* 28 (Winter 1981):2.

35. Karl, *Charles E. Merriam*, pp. 286–87.

36. Marvick, "Introduction: Context, Problems, and Methods," pp. 17, 27.

37. Interview with Leonard S. Cottrell, Jr., by James T. Carey, 28 March 1972, transcripts of the Carey interviews.

38. Lasswell, *Psychopathology and Politics*.

39. Interview with John Dollard by James T. Carey, 14 April 1972, transcripts of the Carey interviews.

40. Ibid.

41. Otis Dudley Duncan, Introduction to O. D. Duncan, ed., *William F. Ogburn on Culture and Social Change* (Chicago: University of Chicago Press, 1964), pp. x–xi.

42. William F. Ogburn, "Bias, Psychoanalysis, and the Subjective in Relation to the Social Sciences," *Publications of the American Sociological Society*, vol. 17 (1922), reprinted in Duncan, *William F. Ogburn*, p. 301.

43. Margaret Mead, *Blackberry Winter: My Earlier Years* (London: Angus & Robertson, 1973), p. 111.

44. A. A. Brill, "The Introduction and Development of Freud's Work in the United States," *American Journal of Sociology* 45 (1939):325.

45. In a personal communication to the author, 14 February 1978.

46. Ernest W. Burgess, "The influence of Sigmund Freud upon Sociology in the United States," *American Journal of Sociology* 45 (1939):356–74. See also Robert Alun Jones, "Freud and American Sociology, 1909–49," *Journal of the History of the Behavioral Sciences* 10 (January 1974):21–39.

47. Coser, *Masters of Sociological Thought*, pp. 543–45, and Helen S. Perry, *Psychiatrist of America: The life of Harry Stack Sullivan* (Cambridge, Mass.: Belknap Press, Harvard University, 1982), pp. 232–41.

48. Perry, *Psychiatrist of America*, pp. 251–77 and 441–42, note 9.

49. Ibid., pp. 242–50.

50. David G. Mandelbaum, "Edward Sapir: Contributions to Cultural Anthropology," *International Encyclopaedia of the Social Sciences*, ed. David L. Sills (New York: Macmillan and Free Press, 1968), 14:13.

51. Margaret Mead, ed., *An Anthropologist at Work: Writings of Ruth Benedict* (Boston: Houghton Mifflin, 1959), pp. 90, 209.

52. Perry, *Psychiatrist of America*, p. 358.

53. For a memoir of Max Mason, see Warren Weaver, *Scene of Change: A Lifetime of American Science* (New York: Scribner's, 1970), pp. 28–32, 53–56. For an account of this period in the university's history, see Karl, *Charles E. Merriam*, pp. 156–68.

54. The following account is based on Darnell Rucker, *The Chicago Pragmatists* (Min-

neapolis: University of Minnesota Press, 1969), pp. 25–26; David L. Miller, *George Herbert Mead: Self, Language and the World* (Chicago: University of Chicago Press, 1973), pp. xxxvii–xxxviii; and Mortimer J. Adler, *Philosopher at Large: An Intellectual Autobiography* (New York: Macmillan, 1977), pp. 126–48.

55. Adler, *Philosopher at Large*, pp. 147–48.

56. Rucker, *The Chicago Pragmatists*, p. 26.

57. Adler, *Philosopher at Large*, pp. 135, 173–74.

58. Beardsley Ruml, "Recent Trends in Social Science," in L. D. White, ed., *The New Social Science* (Chicago: University of Chicago Press, 1930), pp. 103–5.

59. Beardsley Ruml, "Each According to the Nature of his Own Experience," paper given before the SSRC, 30 September 1930, Beardsley Ruml Papers, University of Chicago Archives, Series II, Box 1, Folder 11.

60. Adler, *Philosopher at Large*, p. 153, and personal communication from Edward Shils.

61. "Graduate Study and 'The Chicago School of Politics,' " pp. 1–11.

62. Personal communication from Harold F. Gosnell, 23 March 1982.

63. Karl, *Charles E. Merriam*, p. 286.

64. Marvick, *Harold D. Lasswell on Political Sociology*, p. 32.

65. Harold F. Gosnell, *Negro Politicians: The Rise of Negro Politics in Chicago* (Chicago: University of Chicago Press, 1935), and *Machine Politics: Chicago Model* (Chicago: University of Chicago Press, 1937).

66. Stocking, *Anthropology at Chicago*, p. 21.

67. The following discussion draws upon H. Laurence Miller, "On the 'Chicago School of Economics,' " *Journal of Political Economy* 70 (1962):64–69; George J. Stigler, Comment, ibid., pp. 70–71; M. Bronfenbrenner, "Observations on the 'Chicago School(s),' " ibid., pp. 72–75; A. W. Coats, "The Origins of the 'Chicago School(s),' " *Journal of Political Economy* 71 (1963):487–93; Fritz Machlup, Paul A. Samuelson, and William J. Baumol, "In Memoriam: Jacob Viner, 1892–1970," *Journal of Political Economy* 80 (1972):1–15; Paul Samuelson, "Economics in a Golden Age: A Personal Memoir," in Gerald Holton, ed., *The Twentieth Century Sciences: Studies in the Biography of Ideas* (New York: W. W. Norton, 1972), pp. 155–70; Milton Friedman, "Remarks at the 54th Annual Board of Trustees Dinner for the Faculty," *University of Chicago Record* 8, no. 1 (1974):3–7; Don Patinkin, *Essays on the Chicago Tradition* (Durham, N.C.: Duke University Press, 1981), pp. 3–51; Shils, "Some Academics, Mainly at Chicago"; and especially Melvin W. Reder, "Chicago Economics: Permanence and Change," *Journal of Economic Literature* 20 (March 1982):1–38.

68. See Robert M. Hutchins, *The State of the University, 1927–1949: A Report by Robert M. Hutchins Covering Twenty Years of His Administration* (Chicago: University of Chicago, 21 September 1949, privately printed). A more personal and slanted view of the reform of the College and the Great Books program is provided in Adler, *Philosopher at Large*.

69. See Werner J. Cahnmann, "Robert E. Park at Fisk," *Journal of the History of the Behavioral Sciences* 14 (1978):328–36.

70. Edward Shils, *The Calling of Sociology and Other Essays on the Pursuit of Learning* (Chicago: University of Chicago Press, 1980), pp. 217–19.

71. See Gilbert Geis and Colin Goff, Introduction to Edwin H. Sutherland, *White Collar Crime: The Uncut Version* (New Haven, Conn.: Yale University Press, 1983), pp. xxi–xxviii.

72. This last point was suggested in a personal communication by Edward Shils.

73. "Graduate Study and 'The Chicago School of Politics.' "

74. Matthews, *Quest for an American Sociology*, p. 109.

75. Ruth Shonle Cavan, "The Chicago School of Sociology, 1918–1933," *Urban Life* 11 (January 1983):417.

76. See Cf. Patricia M. Lengermann, "The Founding of the *American Sociological Review*: The Anatomy of a Rebellion." *American Sociological Review* 44 (1979):185–98.

77. Both Ogburn and Merriam spent considerable periods of time working on President Hoover's Committee on Recent Social Trends between 1929 and 1933. See Karl, *Charles E. Merriam*, pp. 201–25. During the 1930s, Merriam's interests switched to the national stage almost entirely; see Karl, *Charles E. Merriam*, pp. 226–83, and Barry D. Karl, *Executive Reorganization and Reform in the New Deal* (Cambridge, Mass.: Harvard University Press, 1963). On the tension between local and national orientations at this period more generally, see Barry D. Karl, *The Uneasy State: The United States from 1915 to 1945* (Chicago: University of Chicago Press, 1983).

Chapter 12

1. Philippe Besnard, ed., *The Sociological Domain: The Durkheimians and the Founding of French Sociology* (Cambridge: Cambridge University Press, 1983), esp. pp. 11–89, 139–51; Adam Kuper, *Anthropology and Anthropologists* (London: Routledge & Kegan Paul, 1983), pp. 1–35, 142–55; Richard Brown, "Passages in the Life of a White Anthropologist: Max Gluckman in Northern Rhodesia," *Journal of African History* 20 (1979):525–41.

2. See Edward Shils, *The Calling of Sociology and Other Essays on the Pursuit of Learning* (Chicago: University of Chicago Press, 1980), pp. 217–20.

3. Ibid., pp. 220–24.

4. Samuel E. Morison, ed., *The Development of Harvard University since the Inauguration of President Elliot, 1869–1929* (Cambridge, Mass.: Harvard University Press, 1930).

5. Bernard Barber, ed., *L. J. Henderson on the Social System* (Chicago: University of Chicago Press, 1970), pp. 1–8, 37–53.

6. Seymour Martin Lipset, "The Department of Sociology," in R. G. Hoxie et al., eds., *A History of the Faculty of Political Science at Columbia University* (New York: Columbia University Press, 1955), pp. 284–303, esp. p. 292.

7. Robert M. MacIver, *As A Tale That Is Told* (Chicago: University of Chicago Press, 1968), pp. 98–99.

8. One example is provided by the career of Willard W. Waller, whose scholarly energies were largely dissipated after he moved to Columbia in 1937. See Morris Janowitz, Foreword, to William J. Goode, Frank Furstenberg, Jr., and Larry R. Mitchell, eds., *Willard W. Waller on the Family, Education, and War: Selected Writings* (Chicago: University of Chicago Press, 1970), pp. viii–ix.

9. MacIver, *As a Tale That Is Told*, p. 105.

10. See Albert Somit and Joseph Tanenhaus, *The Development of American Political Science: From Burgess to Behavioralism* (Boston: Allyn & Bacon, 1967), pp. 109–33.

11. E. P. Cheyney, *The History of the University of Pennsylvania, 1740–1940* (Philadelphia: University of Pennsylvania Press, 1940), pp. 410–13. See also "Joseph Henry Willits, 1889–1970," *American Philosophical Society Yearbook, 1980*, pp. 632–35.

12. See Rupert B. Vance, "Howard W. Odum," *International Encyclopaedia of the Social Sciences* (New York: Macmillan and Free Press, 1968), 11:270–72; Rupert B. Vance and Katherine Jocher, "Howard W. Odum," *Social Forces* 33 (1955):203–17.

13. There is a full account of the early history of the institute in Guy B. Johnson and Guion G. Johnson, *Research in Service to Society: The First Fifty Years of the Institute for Research in Social Science at the University of North Carolina* (Chapel Hill: University of North Carolina Press, 1980), pp. 3–55. There is a briefer discussion in Martin Bulmer and Joan Bulmer, "Philanthropy and Social Science in the 1920s: The Case of Beardsley Ruml and the Laura Spelman Rockefeller Memorial, 1922–29," *Minerva* 19 (Autumn 1981):390–92.

14. Friedrich A. Hayek, "The London School of Economics, 1895–1945," *Economica*, n.s., 13 (February 1946):1–31.

15. See José Harris, *William Beveridge: A Biography* (Oxford: Clarendon Press, 1977), pp. 263–310.

16. See Bulmer and Bulmer, "Philanthropy and Social Science in the 1920s," pp. 394–97.

17. See Shils, *The Calling of Sociology*, pp. 182–83; Raymond A. Kent, *A History of British Empirical Sociology* (London: Gower, 1981), pp. 104–7.

18. See James Rowland Angell, "The University and the School of Law," *American Bar Association Journal* 14 (April 1928):1–3.

19. Harry G. Johnson, "Cambridge as an Academic Environment in the Early 1930's," in Elizabeth S. Johnson and Harry G. Johnson, eds., *The Shadow of Keynes: Understanding Keynes, Cambridge, and Keynesian Economics* (Oxford: Blackwell, 1978), pp. 86–87.

20. See James T. Carey, *Sociology and Public Affairs: The Chicago School* (Beverly Hills: Sage, 1975), pp. 153–59.

21. Charles E. Merriam, "A Word in Conclusion: Speech Given at the Conclusion of the Dedication of the University of Chicago Social Science Research Building in 1929," Merriam Papers, University of Chicago Archives, Box CXX, Folder 4.

22. See Frank H. Knight, *Intelligence and Democratic Action* (Cambridge, Mass.: Harvard University Press, 1960), p. 166, note 18. Knight in the 1930s is quoted by Milton Friedman, in "Remarks at the 54th Annual Board of Trustees' Dinner for the Faculty," *University of Chicago Record* 8, no. 1 (1974):4.

23. Quoted by George J. Stigler in a personal communication to the author, 22 March 1983.

24. Edward Shils, in a personal communication to the author.

25. Mortimer Adler, *Philosopher at Large: An Intellectual Autobiography* (New York: Macmillan, 1977), p. 171.

26. Ibid., pp. 136–37.

27. See Steven J. Diner, *A City and Its Universities: Public Policy in Chicago, 1892–1919* (Chapel Hill, N.C.: University of North Carolina Press, 1980); Aarvagh E. Strickland, *A History of the Chicago Urban League* (Urbana: University of Illinois Press, 1966).

28. Friedman, "Remarks at the 54th Annual Board of Trustees Dinner," p. 7.

29. Melvin W. Reder, "Chicago Economics: Permanence and Change," *Journal of Economic Literature* 20 (1982):5–6; George J. Stigler in a personal communication to the author.

30. Reder, "Chicago Economics."

31. Ibid., pp. 8–9.

32. See Anthony Oberschall, "The Institutionalization of American Sociology," in A. Oberschall, ed., *The Establishment of Empirical Sociology* (New York: Harper & Row, 1972), p. 226.

33. See pp. 75–76 above and G. Franklin Edwards, Introduction, *E. Franklin Frazier on Race Relations* (Chicago: University of Chicago Press, 1968), pp. xi–xvi; Everett Hughes is quoted as saying that, in his judgment, "Frazier was Park's most complete student" (p. xvi).

34. Friedman, "Remarks at the 54th Annual Board of Trustees Dinner," pp. 6–7.

35. For the literature on the Chicago school of economics, see chap. 11, note 67.

36. See p. 66 above.

37. Brown, "Passages in the Life of a White Anthropologist," and on its origins, Richard Brown, "Anthropology and Colonial Rule: The Case of Godfrey Wilson and the Rhodes-Livingstone Institute, Northern Rhodesia," in Talal Asad, ed., *Anthropology and the Colonial Encounter* (London: Ithaca Press, 1973), pp. 173–97. A full study of the Manchester school of social anthropology has still to be carried out. For some preliminary comments,

see Ronald Frankenberg, *Custom and Conflict in British Society* (Manchester: Manchester University Press, 1982), pp. 1 ff.

38. Harold Laski, "Foundations, Universities, and Research," *The Dangers of Obedience and Other Essays* (New York: Harper, 1930), pp. 152–53. Laski's attack was first published in *Harper's Magazine* in the summer of 1928. Merriam wrote to Edmund E. Day at the memorial: "I read Laski's article with great interest. It is incomplete, unfair and supercilious, but contains some points that need an hour of thought"; Merriam to Day, 15 August 1928, Laura Spelman Rockefeller Memorial papers, Series III, Box 56, Folder 602.

39. Ibid., pp. 166–67.

40. See Stefan Collini, *Liberalism and Sociology: L. T. Hobhouse and Political Argument in Britain, 1880–1914* (Cambridge: Cambridge University Press, 1979).

41. E. Richard Brown, *Rockefeller Medicine Men: Medicine and Capitalism in America* (Berkeley: University of California Press, 1979), pp. 8–9.

42. Donald Fisher, "American Philanthropy and the Social Sciences in Britain, 1919–39: The Reproduction of a Conservative Ideology," *Sociological Review* 28 (1980):305.

43. Bulmer and Bulmer, "Philanthropy and Social Science in the 1920's," pp. 359–60, 399–403.

44. Robert Kohler, "The Management of Science: The Experience of Warren Weaver and the Rockefeller Foundation Program in Molecular Biology," *Minerva* 14 (1976):280–96.

45. Raymond B. Fosdick, *The Story of the Rockefeller Foundation* (New York: Harper Bros., 1952), p. 201.

46. For further discussion of the role of foundations, see Bulmer and Bulmer, "Philanthropy and Social Science in the 1920's," and Barry D. Karl, "The Citizen and the Scholar: Ships That Crash in the Night," in William H. Kruskal, ed., *The Social Sciences: Their Nature and Uses* (Chicago: University of Chicago Press, 1982), pp. 101–20.

47. For one useful attempt, see Dorothy Ross, "The Development of the Social Sciences," in Alexandra Olesen and John Voss, eds., *The Organization of Knowledge in Modern America* (Baltimore: Johns Hopkins University Press, 1979), pp. 125–30.

48. See Morris Janowitz, "Sociological Theory and Social Control," *American Journal of Sociology* 81 (1975):82–108.

49. See Vernon K. Dibble, *The Legacy of Albion Small* (Chicago: University of Chicago Press, 1975), pp. 53–95.

50. See Lucy Sprague Mitchell, *Two Lives: The Story of Wesley Clair Mitchell and Myself* (New York: Simon & Schuster, 1953), pp. 289–305, 349–62.

51. During 1930 the French sociologist Maurice Halbwachs spent several months as a visitor in the Chicago sociology department, subsequently writing an important though neglected appreciation of the work on urban sociology, "Chicago, expérience ethnique," *Annales d'historie économique et sociale* 4 (1932):11–49. Although impressed by their studies of urban and industrial phenomena, and their efforts to collect data, he criticized the Chicago sociologists' narrow definition of sociology, lack of attention to other disciplines, and the fact that their monographs were books of description rather than of science. More attention should be given to the formulation of hypotheses. Comparing American with German sociology, he observed that "while the German sociologists hardly ever leave theorizing behind, the Americans are perhaps not sufficiently concerned with guiding ideas and perspectives." M. Halbwachs, "La sociologie en Allegmagne et aux Etats-Unis," *Annales d'histoire économique et sociale* 4 (1932):80–1. For a fuller discussion see Besnard, *The Sociological Domain*, pp. 279–283. One German critic, in a general review of American empirical sociology, was more damning in pressing the charge of triviality. Writing at the same period, Karl Mannheim observed: "we must admit a very marked and painful disproportion between the vastness of the scientific machinery employed and the value of ultimate results. The subject and title of most contributions evoke the highest expectations;

yet, after having reached their conclusions, one is tempted to ask disappointedly: 'Is this all?' " (Book review of Rice, *Methods in Social Science, American Journal of Sociology* 38 [1932]:275).

52. Shils, *The Calling of Sociology*, p. 136.

53. Ibid., pp. 199–208.

54. While conducting research in Muncie, Indiana, in 1924 and 1925, Robert and Helen Lynd received advice from L. C. Marshall and Ernest Burgess, and Marshall in particular seems to have played an advisory role of some importance. "Professor Marshall helped decidedly to limit the scope and sharpen the method of the study. His suggestions were incorporated with those already formulated by Mr. Lynd." Memorandum by Galen M. Fisher, executive secretary, Institute of Social and Religious Research, New York City, 16 April 1924, p. 2, in Raymond B. Fosdick Papers, Rockefeller Archive Center, Series IV3AS, Box 2, Folder 15, p. 2.

55. Shils, *The Calling of Sociology*, p. 142.

Index